# Doctor Kane
# of the Arctic Seas

Elisha Kent Kane
Photograph by Matthew B. Brady
1855 or 1856

# George W. Corner

# Doctor Kane of the Arctic Seas

Temple University Press
Philadelphia

Temple University Press, Philadelphia 19122
© 1972 by Temple University
All rights reserved. Published 1972
Printed in the United States of America

*International Standard Book Number: 0-87722-022-0*
*Library of Congress Catalog Card Number: 72-88531*

# Contents

# Illustrations

# Preface

My grandfather Corner, who was about the same age as Elisha Kent Kane, bought the two handsome volumes of *Arctic Explorations: The Second Grinnell Expedition in Search of Sir John Franklin, 1853, '54, '55* as soon as they appeared in the fall of 1856, and kept them to the end of his life on the library shelves of his Baltimore home. My father in his childhood, and I in mine, when time hung heavy on Sunday afternoons in grandfather's devoutly Methodist household, were allowed to leaf over the powerful steel engravings and lively woodcuts of these books. They told of desperate adventures at sea and on the rugged shores of a wonderland of ice and snow, far from our green and sunny Maryland. We marveled at the fortunes of the indomitable doctor (my grandfather, having been a shipowner, always called him Captain Kane) as he pushed his tiny brig farther north than a ship had ever gone, in our hemisphere at least. We saw him clad in furs, a keen little man among his taller and sturdier crew. We watched him drive his team of dogs, meet an unknown tribe of Eskimos, and slay the ferocious polar bear. We shuddered to see his vessel at last hopelessly locked in the ice, and suffered with him and his companions as they made their terrible journey of escape.

All this, to a wondering child, seemed to have happened in the timeless past. Captain Kane took his place among my heroes with Sir Lancelot and Richard Lionheart. It was therefore a surprise, when I grew up, to learn that he had lived in my grandfather's time in the next city to ours, that he had been a member of my own profession, and that my other grandfather had sold him supplies for his expedition. It was then that I turned again to the two volumes and set out to learn more about the man who had written them and sketched the unforgettable pictures.

I found no satisfactory account of Dr. Kane's life and adventures. Contemporary publications obviously did not tell the whole story. There was the quasi-official *Biography of Elisha Kent Kane* by William Elder, written with the approval of Kane's parents immediately after his death, and a slightly more frank potboiler by one Samuel M. Smucker. A strange little book called *The Love-Life of Dr. Kane,* by Margaret Fox, unexpectedly depicted the iron-hearted hero as a romantic and not always wise or consistent young man. Another even odder narrative by one of his Arctic companions, seaman William Godfrey, suggested on the other hand a more truculent character than Kane's own book reveals. Isaac Hayes, medical officer of *Advance,* in his book *An Arctic Boat Journey,* wrote more fully than either Kane or Elder about a serious, if temporary, rift in the expedition not entirely explained during Kane's brief lifetime.

William Elder's discreetly hero-worshiping biography withholds some of the facts. His account of Kane's remarkable early travels is not accurate. Either his prefatory statement that he did not have to suppress a letter or a line of Kane's papers for the sake of his hero's fame is disingenuous, or else he had not read Kane's private journal of the second Grinnell Expedition. He did not mention Margaret Fox at all. Nor was Elder, in 1857, in a position to evaluate critically Kane's scientific and literary achievements.

It appeared to me that the story had never been fully or fairly told, and I began to think that, if no one else undertook it, I might myself some day attempt the task. For two decades this remained only a casual notion, but then the way was partly opened for me by the unexpected privilege of membership in the American Philosophical Society of Philadelphia. There, in historic Philosophical Hall, was Dr. Kane's portrait and also that of his father, Judge John K. Kane, who was secretary and later president of the society. I learned that a nephew and niece of Dr. Kane and several grand-nephews and grandnieces were living in Pennsylvania and that they were understandably jealous of his reputation. Feeling that my connection with the society was a sufficient guarantee of scholarly responsibility, I ventured to call upon the surviving nephew, Francis Fisher Kane, Esq., a Philadelphia lawyer of courtly manners who promptly invited me and my wife to dine at his suburban home. After dinner, in an environment of mahogany and old silver, we sat by his fireside to hear him and his widowed sister, Mrs. Walter Cope, tell us what little they knew of their uncle the explorer, who had died before they were born. They showed us the manuscript of Judge Kane's autobiography and a model of Dr. Kane's brig, *Advance.* Our host and hostess spoke with pride; but when Mr. Kane casually mentioned Margaret Fox (we would never have dared!) and my wife said, "She must have been an attractive girl," Mrs. Cope's downright "*We* never thought so!"

told us that the ladies of the Kane family still felt it necessary to protect their kinsman's memory. We did not pursue that subject any farther.

Some years later, Dr. Kane's grandnephew and namesake, E. Kent Kane, Esq., with equal hospitality received the two of us in his mountain home at Kushequa near Kane, Pennsylvania, where he showed us memorabilia including the silver tea and coffee set presented to Dr. Kane by the British Admiralty. His cousin, Miss Sybil Kent Kane, guided us to relics of the explorer in Kane Manor inn, once the home of the doctor's brother, General Thomas Leiper Kane. Another grandniece, Mrs. E. Paul DuPont of Montchanin, Delaware, likewise entertained us and exhibited memorabilia and manuscripts she has since given to the American Philosophical Society.

In 1967, after writing the first few chapters of this book, I benefited by a windfall such as a biographer might only dream of. The sons and daughters of Mrs. Cope—Mr. Thomas P. Cope, Dr. Oliver Cope, Mrs. Joseph C. Aub, and Mrs. Thomas P. Hazard—made known their possession of a large collection of Kane family papers, including letters, notebooks, travel journals, sketches, and charts. This treasure they have since deposited in the library of the American Philosophical Society. The papers have proved essential to the completion of my narrative. Mr. Thomas P. Cope of Lincoln, Massachusetts, representing the family, has been most encouraging and helpful.

Mrs. A. Waldo Jones of Vinings, Georgia, a descendant of Dr. Kane's maternal grandfather, Thomas Leiper, gave me valuable information about that family line and went to great pains to copy letters from her collection of family papers.

I learned long ago that a Washington lady, Mrs. Fayette B. Dow, née Margaret Elder (not related to the earlier biographer William Elder), was planning to write a life of Dr. Kane. Thinking to relinquish my project if she had such a work well under way, I asked to meet her, but my request was politely evaded. In 1962, Mrs. Dow died, leaving a biography in typescript for which she had not found a publisher. This typescript, and a large collection of source materials and notes, she had bequeathed to Dartmouth College library for its Stefansson Arctic Collection. The librarian of that valuable archive, Mrs. Erika S. Parmi, extended to me on my two visits to Hanover the welcome that Mrs. Dow had gently withheld. The Dow bequest proved to contain many original letters and transcripts and extensive memoranda that added much to my stock of information. The biography could not be made available for some years, but when the death of Mrs. Dow's sister removed all restrictions, I found it not very useful. Mrs. Dow was an enterprising collector of materials but not a talented writer. For her assiduous efforts, however, and for Mrs. Parmi's generous assistance, I am grateful.

At another great archive of Arctic and Antarctic materials, the Scott Polar Research Institute, Cambridge, England, I was very hospitably received and assisted in consulting the diaries and correspondence of Lady Franklin. To Mr. Alan Cooke of its staff, I am particularly indebted. For extensive use of the Kane Papers, the Dreer Collection, and other relevant documents at the Historical Society of Pennsylvania, Philadelphia, I gratefully acknowledge the help of Mr. J. Harcourt Givens, former head of the manuscript collection, and his successor Mr. Conrad Wilson. I have always received a gracious and effective response to my less extensive demands upon the George Peabody Branch, Enoch Pratt Free Library, Baltimore; the Library Company and the Atheneum of Philadelphia; the New York Public Library; the American Geographical Society, New York; the Royal Geographical Society, London; and the Navy section of the U.S. National Archives. Mr. Herman R. Friis, Director of the Center for Polar Archives, U.S. National Archives, thoughtfully sent photocopies of catalog entries relating to Dr. Kane. Mr. Lee S. Martin, New York City, has kindly permitted me to quote from letters in his collection of Leiper family papers.

For help with special problems, I am indebted to many people. Three physicians of great experience in cardiac disease, Dr. John T. King, Jr., of Baltimore, Dr. Robert Louis Levy of New York, and Dr. Francis C. Wood of Philadelphia, read and commented at length on my notes concerning Dr. Kane's repeated illnesses. Professor John A. Wilson, Oriental Institute, the University of Chicago, advised about Kane's travel on the Nile. Dr. Henry Allen Moe of New York and Mr. Edward M. Weyer of Westbrook, Connecticut, helpfully discussed his surveying and charting procedures.

Others who supplied information on special topics were Dr. William B. Bean, University of Iowa; Judge John Biggs, Jr., U.S. District Court for Eastern Pennsylvania; Dr. John B. Blake, National Library of Medicine, Bethesda, Maryland; Miss Carol M. Dean, Troy, New York Public Library; Rear Admiral E. W. Eller, U.S.N. (Ret.) and Captain F. Kent Loomis, U.S.N. (Ret.) of the Bureau of Naval History, Washington, D.C.; Dr. Gilberto de Mello Freyre, Recife, Brazil; Dr. Edward V. Gulick, Wellesley College; Dr. Blair B. Kling, University of Illinois; Miss Eva J. Leech, Brattleboro, Vermont, Public Library; Mr. William R. LeFanu, Librarian, Royal College of Surgeons, London; Rear Admiral Samuel E. Morison, U.S.N.R. (Ret.), Boston, Massachusetts; Mr. Herbert R. Pickett, Registrar, University of Virginia; Dr. S. Dillon Ripley, Secretary of the Smithsonian Institution, and Mr. Samuel S. Suratt, Archivist of the same, Washington D.C.; Dr. E. Carl Sensenig, University of Alabama; Mr. Robert Gray Taylor, Washington, D.C.; The Very Reverend Thomas J. Walsh, Vice-Chancellor,

Roman Catholic Diocese of Philadelphia; Mr. Edwin Wolf, 2d, the Library Company of Philadelphia.

No words can fully express my gratitude to members of the library staff of the American Philosophical Society for their encouragement and unflagging assistance. I mention in particular Dr. Whitfield J. Bell, Jr., Librarian; Mrs. Gertrude D. Hess, Associate Librarian; Mr. Murphy D. Smith, Curator of Manuscripts; Mrs. Hildegard Stephans, Cataloguer; Miss Phyllis L. Croissant, former Reference Librarian; and Mr. Bertram V. Dodelin, Photographer. Mrs. Julianne W. M. Pearson prepared the typescript with alert attention to matters of consistency and accuracy.

Mr. E. Kent Kane, whose interest and encouragement have already been mentioned, read and helpfully criticized the manuscript with knowledge that only a member of his distinguished family could provide.

                              I will drink
Life to the lees: all times have I enjoy'd
Greatly, have suffer'd greatly, both with those
That loved me, and alone; on shore, and when
Thro' scudding drifts the rainy Hyades
Vext the dim sea; I am become a name,
Forever roaming with a hungry heart.
Much have I seen and known; cities of men
And manners, climates, councils, governments,
Myself not least, but honour'd of them all;
And drunk delight of battle with my peers,
Far on the ringing plains of windy Troy.
I am a part of all that I have met;
Yet all experience is an arch wherethro'
Gleams that untravelled world, whose margin fades
Forever and forever when I move.
How dull it is to pause to make an end,
To rust unburnish'd, not to shine in use!
As tho' to breathe were life. Life piled on life
Were all too little, and of one to me
Little remains; but every hour is saved
From that eternal silence, something more,
A bringer of new things.

                              Tennyson, *Ulysses*

# 1

# A Hero's Lineage

On August 6, 1853, the small brig *Advance,* sixty-eight days northbound from New York, flying the Stars and Stripes and commanded by Dr. Elisha Kent Kane, United States Navy, steered her precarious course through pack ice studded with great icebergs, toward the very head of Baffin Bay.

To the young, romantically adventurous explorer who stood upon the brig's quarterdeck, slightly built, even frail-looking beside his burly first officer, the command of a vessel of his own was a new experience. The quest, moreover, that had brought him to these desolate waters was scarcely more than a dream of science blended with humanity. Nevertheless he was already, at the age of thirty-three, a seasoned world traveler. In ten years as a navy surgeon he had seen five continents and had experienced many adventures in the cause of his country and of science, some of them desperate indeed. In the Mexican War he had fought man to man with saber and pistol; he had descended into the crater of a volcano in the Philippine Islands, had nearly died of cholera in China; and once before, in 1850–51, he had shared the perils of the Arctic as medical officer of *Advance* on an earlier and fruitless voyage. Now he faced the greatest and boldest adventure of his life, in a region totally unexplored.

Before him rose the towering headlands of Cape Alexander and Cape Isabella, twin guardians of a bleak waterway opening northward into an unknown region verging upon the Pole. Only once had any vessel passed between these mighty capes, and that ship, under the skilled English seaman Edward Inglefield, had in the previous summer penetrated Smith Sound no more than thirty miles when a fierce gale drove him back into Baffin Bay.

Inglefield, before this forced retreat, had seen navigable water ahead of him for at least another thirty miles, and the icebergs that came drifting southward through the capes had told him that the sound was no mere bay but must somehow communicate with wider waters to the north. If Kane, in *Advance,* now dared to venture farther, and if he met no gale or solid ice, he and his shipmates would within a few days cross the northern limit of the known world and enter a realm of mystery he had long dreamed of, on a quest into which for two years he had invested the full resources of his inquiring mind, his rashly daring spirit, and his romantic heart.

On the way north he had already had trouble enough to daunt a more experienced navigator and a more disciplined crew—alternate calms and stormy weather along the rugged Greenland coast, five days' besetment in the middle ice of Baffin Bay, a head-on collision with an iceberg. Whatever lay before him in Smith Sound and beyond, he and his men were bound to suffer new hazards and still greater hardships.

Two deeply-felt urges had brought Kane to the far north, one a call of human sympathy and international goodwill that he was proud to acknowledge, the other a craving for adventure whose dominant claim upon his spirit he could hardly admit even to himself.

Officially, Dr. Kane and his party of nineteen men constituted the Second United States Grinnell Expedition in search of Sir John Franklin, lost somewhere in the Arctic since 1845 with two ships and 129 men. No less than eleven expeditions, ten British and one American, sent out to find the missing men, had discovered no trace of them beyond an abandoned camp site on Beechey Island in Lancaster Sound, 200 miles west of Baffin Bay. To the continuing British and American search in 1853 Kane was wholly committed. In a farewell letter to his brother at home in Philadelphia, he had solemnly declared that the object of his journey was the search after Sir John Franklin: "Neither science nor the vain glory of attaining an unreached North shall divert me from this one conscientious aim."

He had persuaded himself, however, that the one aim was linked to the other. Disregarding such clues as there were to Franklin's whereabouts, placing him somewhere in the Canadian archipelago, and against all conjectures of other leaders of the search, Kane believed that Franklin and his men, or at worst their corpses and their wrecked ships, were to be found in the unknown north. If this were true, reputation for geographic discovery as well as for self-forgetful humanity awaited the explorer who should find them. For this radical idea about Franklin's whereabouts, improbable as it seems today, Kane had some basis in recent scientific thought. Certain eminent geographers had put forth a hypothesis that about the North Pole there lies, not a frozen waste of pack ice, but a relatively warm body of open water. Kane had tied this idea to the mystery of Franklin's disappearance. What if Sir John's ships, balked of a westward passage, had made their way through the islands north of Lancaster Sound into this open polar sea, where he and his men might be living still, unable to escape but subsisting on the seabirds and fish that must be swarming there? Obsessed by this idea, Kane was convinced that however the English captains might direct their search, he must fight his way northward by ship and sledge through the icy channel that lay immediately before him, the shortest route into the unreached polar ocean.

On August 7, Captain Kane passed the word to his first officer, stout Henry Brooks, to set a course for Cape Alexander. Late that day *Advance* entered Smith Sound and began to work her way along its eastern shore, sometimes pushing through loose floating ice, at times caught helplessly in a dense pack. Kane wanted to get as far north as possible, at almost any cost, in order to gain the best starting-point for the sledge journeys he planned for the next spring. By the 18th of August he had passed beyond the landmarks Inglefield had charted in 1852. *Advance* had at last reached a point farther north than any ship had ever before attained. On the 20th, however, the brig's progress was totally halted by a heavy storm. She was battered and badly nipped by floating ice, her rudder was splintered, and for a time disaster seemed so near that Kane had the men hastily bring up extra clothing and provisions from the hold, in case they had to take to the boats or were cast ashore.

When after the storm *Advance* could make no further headway under sail through the broken ice, Kane had towlines passed to the ice belt along the rocky shore, and all hands, harnessing themselves—"like mules on a canal" said one of the crew—dragged the brig along through wind and snow with the temperature below freezing. Two or three days of this exhausting work began to tell upon the men, depressed by the slow progress they were making and fearful of being trapped by winter in the exposed region where they were vainly toiling. When, finally, one of the deckhands was bold enough to state his opinion that the expedition should turn back, Kane called his officers together in a formal council. Only Henry Brooks, navy boatswain acting as first officer, voted to hold the gain they had made. The rest—John Wall Wilson, master's mate, another navy man; James McGary, second officer, an experienced New London whaler; Isaac Hayes, the expedition's surgeon; August Sonntag, the astronomer; and the two amateur scientists, Bonsall and Goodfellow—all wanted to turn back and lay up the brig for the winter in some safe cove nearer the capes. Carl Petersen, the Eskimo-speaking Greenlander, Kane's interpreter and sledge-master, most frightened of all, bitterly noted that the captain would listen to no advice; "It was his opinion that he must winter farther north than had ever been done by any Englishman, and that the Stars and Stripes ought to wave where no Union Jack had ever fluttered in the polar gale."

Kane stubbornly gave the order to push on, and the men resigned themselves again to the toil of tracking along the ice belt or warping the brig forward with cables attached to the rocks. Finally, in the first week of September she grounded close under the shore ice and was floated with difficulty. After a vain attempt, with some of the men in a small boat, to find a way onward through the broken ice, Kane reluctantly gave up all hope of further progress. Warping *Advance* to the shore, he laid her up for the winter in a sheltered cove from which she never again set sail.

With a rush of homesickness he chose to give this icebound harbor, guarded by naked cliffs, the name of Rensselaer Bay, after his father's well-wooded country place near Philadelphia, where the trees were even now beginning to change color from green to autumn's red and gold, and a mother's prayers were rising daily for his success and safe return.

Elisha Kent Kane came naturally by his enterprise and daring. Few Americans could claim lines of inheritance more representative of the varied life of colonial days and the rising young republic, or ancestors more devoted to their country's service.

The first of the American Kanes, it must be admitted, stubbornly gave his prime allegiance to the old country, though he became a solid citizen of his new homeland and finally reconciled himself to its independence. John Kane (1734–1808), great-grandfather of Elisha Kent Kane, was born in County Antrim, Northern Ireland, and came to New York in 1752 at the age of eighteen. About John Kane's parentage and youth we have to rely on family tradition.[1] His father, Bernard O'Kane (O'Cahan or O'Cahane) is said to have been a man of substance, living on or near the Castle Shane estate of the O'Neills on the northern shore of Loch Neagh. He was somehow associated with Lord O'Neill's affairs and may have been a relative. A staunch Roman Catholic, Bernard Kane maintained, it is said, a private chaplain in spite of the strict Penal Laws. Although, of those Kanes with whom we are concerned in this book, he was the last to have been a Catholic, we shall see that some feeling for the old religion lingered deep in the hearts of his Protestant American descendants.

Bernard O'Kane sent his son John to England for his schooling, we do not know where; but the boy got a classical education, adopted the Anglican faith, dropped the O' from O'Kane, and went to America to make his fortune. At this time there was much religious and political unrest in Ireland. The native Irish Protestants were setting themselves, along with the tempo-

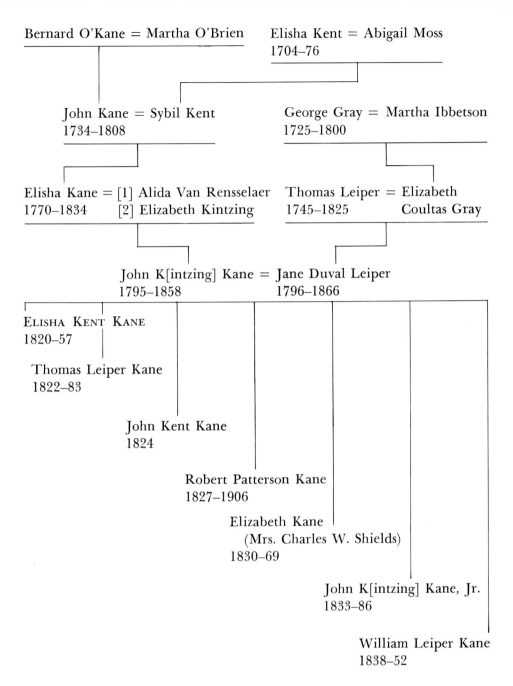

Bernard O'Kane = Martha O'Brien    Elisha Kent = Abigail Moss
                                   1704–76

John Kane = Sybil Kent    George Gray = Martha Ibbetson
1734–1808                 1725–1800

Elisha Kane = [1] Alida Van Rensselaer    Thomas Leiper = Elizabeth
1770–1834     [2] Elizabeth Kintzing      1745–1825       Coultas Gray

John K[intzing] Kane = Jane Duval Leiper
1795–1858              1796–1866

Elisha Kent Kane
1820–57

Thomas Leiper Kane
1822–83

John Kent Kane
1824

Robert Patterson Kane
1827–1906

Elizabeth Kane
   (Mrs. Charles W. Shields)
1830–69

John K[intzing] Kane, Jr.
1833–86

William Leiper Kane
1838–52

Dr. Kane's Ancestors and Siblings

rarily crushed Catholics, against the English rule. In such a climate of feeling County Antrim could have been no comfortable place for the thoroughly Anglicized young man. John Kane was by no means the last of his line to set himself against family traditions, or to interest himself in an alien religion, or to seek fulfillment of his ideals and ambitions far from home.

He prospered in the new country, trading in goods needed by the growing population of the New York and Connecticut countryside. By the time of the American Revolution he possessed large tracts of land in Dutchess County, close to the Connecticut border, and owned a ten-room mansion near the village of Pawling. In 1756, staunch Anglican that he was, an ex-Catholic to boot, John Kane chose his wife from the family of a doubly-dissenting Protestant minister. Sybil Kent was the daughter of the Reverend Elisha Kent, a graduate of Yale in 1729 and a strongly evangelical preacher. As a young man Kent had helped to found a dissident congregation in New Haven, then was pastor of a Congregationalist church in Newton, Connecticut. This pastorate he lost in 1742 because under the influence of the New Light movement, then stirring southern New England, he had become too evangelical for his people. Installed soon after as pastor of a church across the state line in Brewster (in what is now Putnam County, New York), Elisha Kent about 1765 took his flock with him into the Presbyterian fold, holding his pulpit until his death in 1776.[2] Kent was a man of some learning. It is said that his son-in-law John Kane first won his regard by an apt quotation from Horace. Elisha Kent's son Moss Kent was the father of Chancellor James Kent, eminent jurist and the first great commentator on American law.

Sybil Kent Kane bore her husband thirteen children. She remained a Presbyterian and somehow managed to bring them all up in her own and her father's faith, even though her husband clung to his Anglican beliefs. John Kane, said his grandson John K. Kane, "looked down on the Dissenters with sublimated complacency." He refused even to enter his father-in-law's meeting house, which he insisted on calling a "conventicle." In the words of another descendant, he was "undoubtedly ultra-Tory, ultra-churchman, and ultra in his ideas of family discipline."[3]

Such a man could never bow to the civil tempests of his time. At the beginning of the Revolution he showed himself to be a loyalist and was named in the 1779 Act of Attainder. When his property was confiscated, he sent Sybil and the eight or nine children they had by then to live on Long Island behind the British lines while he went to England to plead for compensation for his losses. When the British army evacuated Long Island, Sybil and her children went to Nova Scotia. Long before John Kane dared come back to America, Sybil sent their two eldest sons, John and Charles, to New

York, where they founded the mercantile firm of Kane and Brothers, which established branches in Albany and Buffalo. As the western settlements grew, this became a large business. The fourth son, Elisha (born 1770), grandfather of the explorer, joined the firm and was at first attached to its Albany house, but about 1801 went to Philadelphia to open another branch. By his first wife, Alida Van Rensselaer of the old patroon family of that name and daughter of General Robert Van Rensselaer of Claverack on Hudson, Elisha Kane had two sons and a daughter. Alida Kane died, however, before Elisha moved to Philadelphia, and in that city in 1807 he married Elizabeth Kintzing, daughter of a prominent merchant. She must have been a good stepmother to Alida's young children, for John, the eldest of them, affectionately added her family name to the plain John Kane he was baptized by, and throughout his distinguished career always signed himself John K. Kane. Elisha Kane attained a position of some importance in Philadelphia business circles. He was a charter director of the Philadelphia (now Philadelphia National) Bank. He died in 1834.[4]

One of Elisha Kane's younger brothers, Archibald, went to the West Indies and according to a family legend married one of the two daughters of Soulouque (Faustin I, 1789–1867), grotesque and sanguinary Emperor of Haiti, thereby contracting (if the story is true) a marital alliance stranger even than that which our hero Elisha Kent Kane (Archibald's grandnephew) contemplated a half-century later. Archibald died in Santo Domingo in 1817. His grandniece, Elizabeth D. W. Kane, tells of a "gentlemanly young mulatto" who about 1850 called at the residence in New York of Archibald's sister Sarah Morris Kane, claiming to be Archibald's son. He was coolly received, and disappeared without presenting himself to other members of the family.

We now return to the direct line of Elisha Kent Kane's ancestry. His father, John Kane (Elisha Kane's eldest son) was born in 1795.[5] In spite of the family's Presbyterian affiliations, he was sent to a Roman Catholic school at Mount Airy, then a suburb of Philadelphia, under the charge of Father F. X. Brosius, a highly respected teacher who had many Protestant pupils. At Yale, John K. Kane did not distinguish himself, though he was graduated in 1814, according to his own account "without honor after an idle and rebellious career in college." It appears, however, that privately he read the classics more widely and to better purpose than some of his conformable classmates; he wrote for the college paper, and won the reputation of being the best declaimer in his class. At home again in Philadelphia he studied law with the celebrated lawyer Joseph Hopkinson. Now at last eager to succeed, he increased his command of language and literature by wide reading in Latin and English classics. Admitted to the bar in 1817, he quickly built

John K. Kane
Portrait by Thomas Sully, 1836.
From *Century Magazine* N.S. 34 (1898)

Jane Duval Leiper Kane
Portrait by Thomas Sully, 1824.
From *Century Magazine* N.S. 34 (1898)

up a substantial practice. By supporting Andrew Jackson in the presidential campaign of 1828, he won the President's confidence, and in 1832 was appointed to the commission delegated to settle with France claims made under the Convention of 1831. He also took an active part in Jackson's campaign against the Bank of the United States, writing (it is said) letters and state papers for the President. These political activities were not approved by Kane's Philadelphia associates. His earliest biographer, Henry Simpson, slyly says that he "rejoiced in a social proscription for some time." At the same time he was under fire from another direction; as a high-ranking Freemason he was publicly listed as a political enemy by the Anti-Masonic Party.

John K. Kane for a decade or two was active in local and state as well as national politics. He was leader of the Democrats in the so-called "Buckshot War" of 1838, a political quarrel over a disputed election, so fierce that at Harrisburg the militia was called out to protect the Legislature. In 1845 Kane was appointed Attorney-General of Pennsylvania. In this post he was again caught in the crossfire of political enmity, for he had charge of prosecuting the men arrested during the violent anti-Catholic riots of 1844 in the Kensington district of Philadelphia, and was accused of oppressive efforts to convict them. Thus his combination of personal liberality in religious matters with stubbornness in the cause of justice had brought down upon him the disapproval of the anti-Masons on one hand and of the anti-Catholics on the other.

In 1846 Kane resigned the attorney-generalship to become Judge of the U.S. District Court for Eastern Pennsylvania—reluctantly, it is said, because this eminent post would take him out of politics. On the bench for the rest of his life, he evinced great learning in Roman and European as well as American law. Many of his decisions in admiralty and patent cases have been cited as authoritative.

John K. Kane married, in 1819, Jane Duval Leiper, whose notable ancestry will be detailed below. She is said to have been one of Philadelphia's most beautiful women. Because of her charm as well as beauty, she was chosen, in 1824, when the city entertained the Marquis de Lafayette on his triumphal tour of the United States, to open with him the fancy-dress ball. Family tradition relates that the city's leading artist, Thomas Sully, was so much impressed by Mrs. Kane's appearance in the costume of Mary, Queen of Scots, that he asked to paint her portrait. Seen through Sully's eyes at this time, when she was twenty-eight years old and the mother of two sons, she was a beauty of the Byronic age, with long oval face over a swanlike neck, long straight nose, and dark eyes; but Sully did not conceal the strength of character that he saw behind the lovely features.[6]

John and Jane Kane had seven children, of whom the eldest was Elisha Kent Kane, born February 3, 1820, at the family residence on Walnut Street between Seventh and Eighth streets. Thomas Leiper Kane followed, in 1822; then John, who died in infancy. Robert Patterson Kane was born in 1827; the only daughter, Elizabeth, in 1830; a son named for his father John Kintzing Kane in 1833; and lastly, William in 1838.

The Kanes moved, about 1827, to 100 South Fourth Street. In 1840, separating his home from his office, John K. Kane moved his family residence to Seventh and Locust streets. Not long after he had become a federal judge, he acquired (1848) a large suburban house in North Philadelphia, on Green Lane just east of Old York Road. This place, which the family called "Rensselaer," was their summer home for four years, but after the youngest boy, Willie, died in 1852, Rensselaer had painful memories for a family of strong emotions and great mutual affection. The Kanes therefore gave up the place and for a year or two lived in the city at 36 Girard Street. In 1855, however, Judge Kane purchased land adjacent to Rensselaer, and built to his own design a new house a little farther north, near Chelten Avenue.[7]

Willie was not to be forgotten; the Kanes might dull the edge of grief by leaving the old house, but to keep his memory green they built the new one in a wooded spot the boy had loved, where ferns grew on a rugged boulder known to the other children as "Willie's fern rock." The two eldest brothers were grown men when "Fern Rock" was built—Elisha thirty-three years of age, Thomas thirty-one—and both had experienced many adventures in far-away places, but this site had associations for them older than the house; to Rensselaer and Fern Rock in later years they turned their thoughts of home in hours of loneliness or peril—Elisha when beleaguered by Arctic ice, Thomas from the western mountains and the battlefield. In the autumn of 1853, Elisha Kent Kane gave the name of Rensselaer to the icy harbor where his Arctic expedition made headquarters for two winters, and of Fern Rock to an incongruously bleak islet nearby.

Judge Kane equipped his country house luxuriously. The drawing room was furnished in French style, with pieces the judge's father had bought from the first French minister to the United States. At his mahogany dining table, designed by himself and constructed in England, no less than five presidents of the United States, it is said, were entertained.

Judge Kane, as a man of public spirit and broad general culture, stood high among Philadelphia intellectuals and public men. He was a director of several banks and insurance companies, and an officer or trustee of numerous philanthropic and cultural institutions, including Girard College, of whose first board of trustees he was a member. Elected in 1825 a member of the American Philosophical Society, he was one of its secretaries from 1828 to 1848, vice-president from 1849 to 1857, and president during the last year of his life. Thus prominent as a citizen, a talented speaker and in command of a polished and vigorous English literary style, he was often chosen to deliver ceremonial addresses. Though he published little of his own composition, he assisted several of his friends by editing their works in law and divinity, helped compile a psalmbook, and even (he tells us) revised and practically rewrote a treatise on medicine for a friend in that profession.

The judge, polished as he was, possessed all that firmness of conviction and overwhelming sense of duty for which his grandfather John Kane had been noted. As a trustee of the Second Presbyterian Church he stood with the Old School conservatives when the denomination split in two in 1837, thus aligning himself with the southern wing of the church against the doctrinal and organizational innovations of the New England Presbyterians and also against their abolitionist stand on the slavery question. That issue was to cause him years of stress within his family as well as on the bench. According to a story long current in Philadelphia, the judge showed himself a Spartan father when his second son, Thomas—his pupil in the law and one-time clerk—became an active abolitionist. Thomas, who had been appointed a U.S. commissioner, resigned the office after the passage of the Fugitive Slave Act of 1850, because he could not conscientiously carry out the duty, required of him by the law, of apprehending runaway slaves. As the story goes, Thomas's letter of resignation was so sharp that his father considered it to be in contempt of court and committed the young man to prison—a decision fortunately overruled by the Court of Appeals. Family tradition says that although Judge Kane felt that Thomas had forced this severe decision upon him by an indiscreet letter of resignation, he privately displayed affectionate understanding of his son's principles and attitude.[8] Again, in 1855 Judge Kane roused fierce protest when he committed to prison for contempt a Pennsylvania abolitionist, Passmore Williamson, who failed to produce, as ordered by the court, some runaway slaves whose owner came up from Virginia in pursuit of them. The storm of criticism stirred up by his refusal, in this case, to quash a writ of habeas corpus, is typified by an anonymous letter in the *Morning Chronicle* of Portsmouth, New Hampshire, October 15, 1855. The writer declared that such a man as Judge Kane could surely not be a relative of Dr. Kane, the noble-hearted explorer; "Is he in any way related to that other Cain who killed his brother Abel?" But the judge was so conspicuously honest and public-spirited that his firmness on the bench did not in the long run cost him the regard of his associates in civic and professional life.

The mistress of Fern Rock gave her children a maternal inheritance of ability and enterprise matching that of the Kanes. Her father, Thomas Leiper (1745–1825), had come to Pennsylvania from Scotland in 1765. He began life in America as a tobacconist and later owned large stone quarries in Delaware County, Pennsylvania. During the Revolutionary War, Thomas Leiper not only contributed his personal resources to the cause of independence, but also helped to organize the First Troop of Philadelphia City Cavalry; he fought at Trenton, Princeton, the Brandywine, and Germantown, and as treasurer of his troop carried (it is said) the last subsidies of the French to the American army at Yorktown. In times of peace Leiper took part in many practical undertakings including the construction of canals and a railroad; he was a director of the Bank of Pennsylvania and the Bank of the United States, and of the Franklin Institute. As a personal friend and strong supporter of Thomas Jefferson, Leiper was active in the Democratic party, and was a member and for a time president of the Common Council of Philadelphia.[9]

Thomas Leiper's wife, Elizabeth Coultas Gray, was a daughter of George Gray, whose name is still attached to Gray's Ferry Road in southwest Philadelphia. Born a Quaker, Gray was no pacifist. In the troubled 1770s he was a member of the Council of Safety, and as speaker of the Pennsylvania Assembly he stood for resistance to the British Crown. Gray's wife, Martha Ibbetson Gray (Elizabeth Gray Leiper's mother and therefore great-grand-mother of our hero Elisha Kent Kane), was London-born and by religion a Moravian. Before leaving England, it is said, she qualified herself for colonial life by studying with a surgeon-apothecary. During the British occupation of Philadelphia Mrs. Gray put her apothecary's training to noble use by caring for the sick and wounded Americans in the Walnut Street Prison. She acted as surgeon as well as nurse, supplied food and medicines at her own expense, and wore down the nagging opposition of the commander of the prison. Her daughter Elizabeth, the future Mrs. Thomas Leiper, was her chief assistant at the prison. For this service Martha Gray was given in 1778 a testimonial of gratitude signed by officers of the Pennsylvania, Maryland, and Virginia militia.[10]

Jane Leiper Kane of Fern Rock, coming from two generations of brave and public-spirited Americans, added Quaker and Moravian ancestry to the Catholic, Anglican, and Presbyterian strains of her husband's famiily. Like her forebears she was no pacifist. During the "Buckshot War," feeling was high in Philadelphia and still higher in Harrisburg, the state capital, where John K. Kane was leading the Democrats in a legislative battle that threatened to end in gunfire, and a brother of hers was also in the fray. She wrote to her husband, "They tell me that our house is threatened, that you are upturning society, and are not far from treason. I thank God, I have a husband and a brother whose patriotism does not startle at words."[11] Her son-in-law (Bessie Kane's husband, Charles W. Shields) wrote of her that she was "one of a family distinguished for its women, and [was] herself distinguished for the energy, nerve, elasticity, and warmheartedness which became famous in her son."[12] William Elder, Elisha Kent Kane's official biographer, also remarks on the resemblance of the explorer's traits to those of his mother—"Elisha was, emphatically, her son."

Thus Elisha Kent Kane had among his American ancestors three Revolutionary patriots and a Tory loyalist; by religion, Presbyterians, Congregationalists, Dutch Reformed, Methodists, a one-time Quaker, a Moravian, a Roman Catholic turned Anglican; by national origins, people of Irish, English, Scottish, and Dutch birth; by occupation, merchants, a tobacconist and quarry-owner, a minister, a lawyer, a New Amsterdam patroon. Among these forebears an extraordinary proportion are on record as men and women of strong will and enterprise, eager and able to make a mark in the world, but determined to go their own way in matters of opinion, and willing to stake their lives and fortunes for causes dear to their hearts.

These characteristics have run true in many of John K. Kane's descendants and notably molded the lives of his two eldest sons. Before proceeding to set forth, in the rest of this book, the character and lifework of Elisha Kent Kane, something must be said about the careers of Thomas Leiper Kane and Elisha's other siblings, all of whom will reappear briefly in our narrative. Their lives will show what kind of family it was whose social world of Philadelphia, Rensselaer, and Fern Rock, Elisha Kent Kane renounced for worldwide travels, prodigious adventures, early fame, and premature death.

The second son, Thomas Leiper Kane, shared his elder brother's zest for venturesome service far from home. As a young man, he studied law with his father. Admitted to the Philadelphia bar in 1846, he became clerk of his father's court and a U.S. commissioner. In that year a Mormon elder, Jesse Little, came to Philadelphia bringing an appeal to the influential Judge Kane to help secure governmental protection for the Mormons, who were about to leave their settlement at Nauvoo, Illinois, because of the persecution which had already led to the murder of their prophet Joseph Smith. Moved by this tragic situation, Thomas L. Kane immediately started west to give his personal support. Reaching Nauvoo after the exodus, he visited the refugees then temporarily settled on the Mississippi near Council Bluffs. Gaining the warm friendship of Brigham Young, Kane became a recognized advocate of justice for the Mormons.

During this visit to the Mormon camp Thomas Kane was prostrated by an illness thought at first to be the "bilious fever" (malaria) characteristic of the river valley, but followed by a lingering intermittent fever. This was probably a flare-up of pulmonary tuberculosis, which was to recur throughout his life. At Albany, New York, after his return to the East in the fall of 1846, he was again ill and his death was expected. More than once in later years he was again seriously ill with pneumonia, pleurisy, or pulmonary hemorrhages, and with fever. Yet he fought his chronic ill health with tenacity. Following the example of his elder brother Elisha—victim of rheumatic fever—Thomas Kane repeatedly rose from a sickbed to fulfill with incredible exertion some call of duty, in peace or in war.

Back in Philadelphia, in 1847 Thomas Kane took up another dangerous cause, that of the Negro slaves. He became an abolitionist and thereby plunged into the contention with his father, the judge, which has already been mentioned. Kane wrote antislavery articles for the press and—it was rumored—conducted at Fern Rock a station on the Underground Railroad. From 1848 to 1850 he was chairman of the Free Soil Central Committee of Pennsylvania. In 1857, when trouble with the Mormons in Utah threatened to culminate in fighting between the settlers and federal troops, Kane's sympathy with the Latter Day Saints led him to volunteer to go to Salt Lake City to intercede with Brigham Young. This he did, with the cordial approval of President Buchanan, but against the strong opposition of his father, who thought the venture quixotic. Traveling by sea to Panama, across the Isthmus by land, thence to San Pedro, California, by sea, he finally made the long hard overland journey to Utah. Although he was desperately weary and ill when he reached Salt Lake City, he was successful in his mission. The Mormon leaders abandoned their resistance, averting bloodshed, and the U.S. army and a new federal governor, Alfred Cumming, exercised sufficient restraint to bring the affair to a peaceful conclusion. With his family's characteristic tolerance for other people's religion, Thomas Kane admired the Mormons' piety and respected their religious beliefs. He was not baptized a Mormon, as rumor had it, but he won a firm place in their regard as a sympathetic friend and advocate at Washington, their "Sentinel in the East." His statue in bronze now stands in the rotunda of the Utah state capitol at Salt Lake City.

Thomas Kane was too ardent a fighter for social causes to be content with a lawyer's career in Philadelphia. He emigrated to the mountains of northwestern Pennsylvania, where he founded the town of Kane in McKean County. When the Civil War broke out he organized a regiment of hunters and lumbermen known as the "Bucktails." He was severely wounded in an early campaign, and later was taken prisoner at Harrisonburg in the Valley of Virginia. Having been exchanged, he was given the brevet rank of brigadier general for gallantry at Chancellorsville. On the eve of Gettysburg he was ill with pneumonia in a Baltimore hospital, but before he regained full strength he rejoined his brigade on the second day of the great battle. "A little coal of hell-fire, he was," said one of his orderlies; and a fellow officer who saw him in battle described him as a small, slender figure with enormous flashing black eyes, running along a low earthwork in a rain of bullets, waving his sword and in self-forgetful fury shouting to his men, "Lie down, you damned fools, do you want your heads shot off?" One of the men had to pull him down into shelter.

Worn out by exposure and wounds, General Kane resigned his commission in November 1863 and returned to Kane, Pennsylvania. He had fought, it is said, in thirty-five battles and was five times wounded. Before the war he had married a second cousin; they founded a family with two lines of Kane ancestry, known to their Philadelphia kin as the "mountain Kanes." The general presided almost like a feudal baron over his thousands of acres of mountainous forest land and over his town of Kane, until he died of pneumonia in 1883.[13]

Robert Patterson Kane, the third brother, was head of his class at a Philadelphia high school. Admitted to the bar in 1849, he proved himself a skillful lawyer, dealing chiefly with patent and admiralty cases. In 1861 he enlisted with the First Troop, Philadelphia City Cavalry, which his grandfather, Thomas Leiper, had helped to organize, and served with it during the war. His only son, Francis Fisher Kane, is remembered by older Philadelphians of today as a courtly gentleman and able lawyer who did not hesitate to stand up for unpopular liberal causes. Once after World War I Francis Fisher Kane coolly presided under fire of brickbats at a meeting in Independence Square on behalf of federally-imprisoned conscientious objectors.

Elizabeth Kane, the only daughter of John K. and Jane Leiper Kane, like many a girl of good family in her day, sang and composed music, taught a Sunday school class, and remained at home with her sorely tried parents during the years when Elisha was in the far north. After her father's death in 1858 she married, at the age of twenty-nine, Charles Woodruff Shields, a graduate of Princeton University and Princeton Theological Seminary, who became a leading Presbyterian divine. He was professor of the harmony of science and revealed religion at the seminary, and later also of modern history.

John K. Kane the second became, like his eldest brother Elisha, a physician. He studied at Jefferson Medical College, taking the M.D. degree in 1855, just in time to join the navy medical corps and get assigned as surgeon to the relief expedition sent north that year to rescue Elisha Kent Kane's party from the Arctic. He settled in Wilmington, Delaware, and became a prominent and well-loved physician and surgeon. He was for two terms, 1879–80, president of the Medical Society of Delaware.

William, the baby of the family, a precociously bright and sweet-tempered boy, died at fourteen of some long-drawn-out and painful disease, in which he was cared for at the last by his eldest brother, Elisha, then at home between the two Arctic voyages.[14]

Judge Kane and his family, with all their great gifts, did not quite attain the full poetic blessings of "household happiness, gracious children, debtless competence, golden mean." With Willie's death grief had entered the house; two at least of the sons were at times more headstrong than gracious —for them the golden mean was not enough—but the family possessed the assurance conferred by professional success and social position; they had the love of learning, ambition and a proud sense of duty, and warm brotherly affection. All five children who lived to adult age led, in their various ways, successful lives, two of them with conspicuous valor; the others, if less venturesome, with talent and devotion.

# 2

# Education for Adventure

ELISHA KENT KANE grew to manhood in the two decades 1820–40. We know little about his boyhood and early schooling. Almost the only source of information for this period of his life is the biography by William Elder, written at the family's request and with their assistance.[1] Only one of Elisha's schoolteachers is mentioned by name, and what we learn about him is rather surprising; John K. Kane, leading Presbyterian layman as he was, and a Mason, had his elder sons tutored by a Roman Catholic schoolmaster. This fact may have stirred up no gossip at the time, for in the 1820s and early 1830s the political cry of "no popery" had not yet been loudly raised; but Elder, writing in 1858, when the Know-Nothing party was nationally active, discreetly saw fit to omit mention of Elisha's Catholic teacher. A less inhibited biographer of the same year, Samuel M. Smucker, in his *Life of Dr. Kane*[2]—a potboiler but occasionally revealing—tells us that "The first place of instruction which Dr. Kane attended was that conducted by Mr. Waldron in Eighth Street near Walnut, in his native city. This gentleman, who has since become a priest of the Roman Catholic Church, was a man of superior education, and fully competent to perfect his pupils in all the elementary branches of learning." There is a bit of mystery here. One Edmond Q. S. Waldron was, in fact, ordained to the priesthood in Philadelphia in 1847, for service in the diocese of Baltimore, where he disappears from our ken.[3] Mr. Kane may well have employed him as a teacher, before his ordination—as mentioned earlier, Kane had himself attended a Catholic school—but Waldron can hardly have been keeping a school of his own. His name was never listed in the Philadelphia directories. The story of a Catholic tutor is, however, confirmed and perhaps fully explained by a casual remark of the late Francis Fisher Kane, who recalled having heard that his grandfather so greatly respected the traditions of the Church that he employed a priest to tutor his sons in Latin.[4] The story is important only for its evidence of the independence and religious tolerance of John K. Kane, who was in other matters not always tolerant, and also because it points once more to the persistence in the Kane family line of something deeper than mere respect for the religion of their remote Irish ancestors. This feeling, we shall see, reappeared in the thinking of Elisha K. Kane at a time of great emotional stress, when he advised Margaret Fox to become a Roman Catholic.[5]

Let us hope, in respect for the cloth, that Waldron was not really the first teacher of the Kane boys, as Smucker has it, for Elder tells a story of their earliest school days that is creditable to Elisha, but not to the teacher. The latter, says Elder, was about to cane little Thomas for some petty offence, when Elisha, himself not yet nine years old, stood up and cried "Don't whip him, he's such a little fellow; whip me." The master, taking this for mutiny, replied "I'll whip you too, sir." The set-to ended with Elisha aching not only from his caning but also from a heartfelt sense of injustice.

Evidently Elisha with his independence and high spirits was in his preadolescent days a trial to his teachers and to his parents as well. In the posthumous *Biography of Dr. Kane*, Elder, wishing no doubt to please Elisha's mourning father and mother but seeing that there was a good deal to apologize for, devotes ten pages to a heavy-footed account of reckless adventures in treetops and over city roofs, and a midnight climb to the top of the kitchen chimney, with only little Tom holding the slack of his brother's lifeline. Among other boys Elisha's short stature and slender frame did not reduce his belligerency. Like every true-hearted American boy in storybooks of the Romantic period, the little hero of Elder's narrative had his victories over neighborhood toughs "big enough to break every bone in his body"—once when he gallantly undertook to protect some little girls from bullying, more often in defense of his own person. Rebellion in the schoolroom, we are given to think, was an everyday affair. But Elder, with a biographer's hindsight, sentimentally concludes that

> It was not the monkey mirthfulness nor the unprincipled recklessness of childhood that he was chargeable with but something more of purpose and tenacity in exacting deference and enforcing equity than is usually allowed to boyhood. To arbitrary authority he was a regular little rebel. . . . So Elisha earned the character of bad boy, while he was in fact exercising and cultivating the spirit of a brave one. . . . It might be only the impulse which lifts the lark into the clouds to sing her morning hymn, and leads the chamois to the dizziest heights

of the Alps . . . or it might be a habitude providentially induced and adjusted for the after work of his adventurous life.

The boy, Elder admits, was an unpromising scholar from his eighth to his thirteenth year. He simply would not study his lessons in the classical text-books. Once when he was threatened with expulsion from school, his mother put him on his honor to study for her sake. He stuck to his books for a week with success, but suddenly gave up the effort because he said he had to keep a promise he had made to himself, not to conform to the teacher's demands.

Whatever family tensions may have been created by the boy's headstrong disposition were not revealed to outsiders. John K. Kane, profound lawyer and perfectionist litterateur, at times despaired of his son's future, but Elisha seems always to have respected his father and he certainly loved his mother. These parents, however tried and puzzled, protected and guided him as best they could in his conflicts with the schoolmasters. "His schools and teachers were frequently changed," says Dr. Elder, but he "was not sacrificed to the authorities."

We may reasonably doubt that the situation was as bad as it was depicted by the biographer making literary capital out of the contrast between Kane's youthful recklessness and his responsible, even heroic, manhood. Outside the detested schoolroom young Elisha reveled in such hobbies as a bright boy finds for himself. He made a collection of minerals, and set up a laboratory in an outhouse where he tried experiments in chemistry. "There was riding at breakneck speed to be done; there were trees and rocks to climb . . . chemistry, geology, and geography to explore" and there were books of his own choosing. His stolen reading at this time was *Robinson Crusoe* and *Pilgrim's Progress*, and chemistry textbooks.

It would be good to know what he read a couple of years later, at fifteen and sixteen. For a boy with a love of books and his eyes opening to the world about him, this was an exciting time. In England and America the Romantic movement was at full tide. In novels and poetry, painting and music the high themes were heroic adventure, courtly love, and the quest for personal experience in a world of wonder. Sir Walter Scott's first great romance, *Ivanhoe*, appeared in 1820, the year of Elisha's birth. Three years later James Fenimore Cooper launched the earliest of his *Leatherstocking Tales* about the buckskin knights errant of the American forest.

In the world of reality as well as of fiction there were pioneers and adventurers whose true tales fired the imagination of American boys. Daniel Boone had died in 1820, but Kit Carson would soon take Boone's place as legendary hunter and scout. The schoolboy of 1835 had only to look at the maps in his geography book to see what exciting journeys were open to men of daring in the unmapped areas of our own continent. The achievement of Lewis and Clark in opening a route through the Rockies and down the Columbia River to the Pacific was fresh in everyone's mind. Following them, trappers and woodsmen were exploring the southern passes from the plains to California. When Kane was sixteen, Washington Irving gave serious literary form to the romance of far western America in *Astoria*, a brilliant narrative of exploration, fur trading, and settlement in the northwest. A few years later Kane must have heard much talk in his father's circle about the first great maritime exploration fostered by the United States, the expedition of 1838–42, under Lieutenant Charles Wilkes, to the Antarctic Ocean, the Pacific islands, and the American northwest coast. The American Philosophical Society, of which John Kane was secretary, supported the Wilkes Expedition and took an active part in planning it. His eldest son, while a medical student, no doubt saw and read with excitement a letter Mr. Kane received from Titian Peale, artist-naturalist on U.S.S. *Vincennes* of Wilkes's flotilla, written from New Zealand, April 5, 1840, informing the society of the expedition's discovery of the Antarctic continent.[6]

The Arctic regions of North America also were being explored, largely by English seamen bent on their own romantic quest for the Northwest Passage, a hoped-for navigable route from the Atlantic to the Pacific through icy waters north of Canada. In 1818–19 John Ross and William Parry had forced their ships westward from Baffin Bay, Parry getting as far as Melville Island, where the ice blocked further advance. Their narratives of exploration were widely read in America. Well known also were the travels of another seaman, Captain John Franklin, of the Royal Navy, who had made his way by land through Canadian wilds to the Coppermine River and thence to the Arctic coast of northern Canada. Finding open water there in summer, Franklin had set his heart upon the prospect of himself breaking through to that region by ship from Baffin Bay and on westward to the Pacific. On the very day of Kane's birth in February 1820, John Franklin and his companions George Back and Robert Hood were in the snowy Canadian woods near Lake Athabasca, traveling by dog sledge toward the headwaters of the Coppermine.[7]

For Elisha Kent Kane—whether or not he read of these Arctic explorations or knew anything about Franklin, whose fate was so strangely to determine his own—it was the love of adventure and curiosity about distant lands, not the classics of a past age, that drew him back at last to his neglected schooling. Rebellious youth sometimes unwittingly and unexpectedly heads in the right direction. Ironically, it was Elisha's unruly and erratic career in school that saved him from an academic regime that might have suffocated him, and finally sent him instead to the fresh and stimulating atmosphere of a new university, strong in the natural sciences. There he found himself intellectually and scholastically.

For a time he had continued to rebel against his schooling, though with diminishing resistance. From his fourteenth to his sixteenth year he resigned himself, none too effectively, to preparation for college. At this period, for the first time in his life, his health was poor. What was wrong with him is not recorded. His biographer Elder, a physician by training, would no doubt have been more explicit if he had been informed about this early illness. A physician today is inclined to guess that this was a first attack, in relatively mild form, of rheumatic fever, which within a few years was to recur far more seriously, accompanied by endocarditis, and would influence the whole course of his life. Ailing, and subjected, we may be sure, to heavy pressure from his parents to get on with his studies, he found it hard to work consistently, but somehow made progress enough in languages, mathematics, and drawing to encourage the hope that he could carry on in college. With his love of outdoor life, and a bent for mathematics, he thought of becoming a civil engineer.

John K. Kane, a loyal Yale man in spite of his own indifferent undergraduate record, wanted his eldest son to follow him there. The two of them, in fact, went to New Haven to see about entering Elisha as a freshman. But the boy was deficient "in certain studies which the ritual of Yale required"—presumably Latin and Greek—and on the other hand was so much in advance of Yale's requirements in the natural sciences that he would have lost a year in adjusting his studies to the regular curriculum. To complicate the problem, during the stay at New Haven Elisha developed physical symptoms clearly pointing to the heart as the seat of his illness. It began to look as if a full course of college studies might be too much for him.

At this juncture John K. Kane thought of the University of Virginia, opened only a decade before, which offered a very liberal curriculum with much freedom of election of studies. He knew the university well. In 1828 his brother-in-law and closest friend, Robert Maskell Patterson, had been offered its chair of natural science. To help him make up his mind about the post, Patterson asked Mr. Kane to accompany him on a visit to Charlottesville. Both men were deeply impressed by the university, then in operation only three years, and Patterson accepted the professorship. On this visit the future judge first met Virginia's scholarly professor of medicine, Robley Dunglison, who had been selected by an emissary of Thomas Jefferson to occupy the university's medical chair.[8] In 1836 Dunglison moved to Philadelphia to join the faculty of the Jefferson Medical College. His friendship with the Kanes deepened, and he was close to the family when the question of Elisha's college education was being discussed. John K. Kane also heard much about the University of Virginia through the Rogers brothers, talented scientists with Philadelphia connections. The eldest of them, the geologist Henry Darwin Rogers, came back to Philadelphia, his native city, in 1835, as a professor in the University of Pennsylvania, just at the time when his brother William Barton Rogers, also a geologist, had taken the chair of natural philosophy at Charlottesville, and was therefore at hand to inform Mr. Kane as to the state of affairs at the University. Furthermore, Elisha's cousin Robert Patterson (son of Robert Maskell Patterson) was there as a student, having matriculated in 1836. Thus a chain of friendships between Philadelphia and Charlottesville had been forged, by which the anxious parents of Elisha Kent Kane were assured that the young man, if sent to the University of Virginia, would be under the eyes of friends and moreover would become a pupil in physics, geology, and civil engineering, of William Barton Rogers, already at thirty-one years of age a scientist marked for high distinction.

The time at which Elisha enrolled at the University of Virginia is not certain.[9] It is probable that he began as a special student in the fall of 1837 (i.e., in his eighteenth year) but did not matriculate until the next year. The catalogue for 1838 lists him as a student in his first term, taking courses in mathematics and civil engineering. In a copy of the catalogue, now in the library of the American Philosophical Society, which Elisha sent to his father, he has added the initials N.P. (for Natural Philosophy or physics) to the "M." and "C.E." following his name, and in a note to his father on the pamphlet says "They [the listings] are not very exact as you find Bob [Robert Patterson] has two extra tickets and I one too little."

The little faculty of nine professors included several men of distinction whose classes Kane attended. Gessner Harrison, chairman of the faculty and professor of classical languages, perhaps appealed to this particular student chiefly by his interest in geography, having written a book on the geography of the classical lands. Charles Bonnycastle was the author of popular mathematical textbooks. William Barton Rogers, destined to become the first president of the Massachusetts Institute of Technology, taught single-handed several subjects in which Kane, intending to be an engineer, was directly interested—physics, geology, mineralogy, and civil engineering. Rogers was also State Geologist, heading a team of field workers in a geological survey of Virginia. With Rogers on the survey staff at the time when Kane was at the university was his brother James Blythe Rogers, M.D., also a competent scientist.

All we know about Kane's studies at the University of Virginia is that at last he could devote himself largely to subjects in which he was really interested. He stood very high in chemistry and geology, and did good work also in mathematics and even in Latin and Greek.

William Barton Rogers was at that time engaged in mapping the geological formations of the Blue Ridge Mountains. Young Kane was permitted to join some of the field trips and also, we may assume, to study the mineral specimens and fossils which the field parties brought back to the laboratory. Somewhere in the course of his education he had learned to write excellent English, primarily no doubt in his cultivated family circle and especially by association with his father, who wrote and spoke extremely well. Elisha made further progress in English, according to Elder, at the university, largely by conscious reflection of the language of the lecturers and his textbooks. In short, the once reckless, rebellious lad was growing to intellectual manhood, and was beginning to put his special talents to effective use. Had not disaster struck him in the form of severe illness, he might well have entered upon a career of civil engineering or, even more likely, might have become an able research geologist and professor.

By the autumn of 1838 some physician at Philadelphia or perhaps the college physician at Charlottesville had definitely diagnosed the boy's recurrent illness as rheumatic fever. The minutes of the college faculty for November 1, 1838, record that

> Mr. Elisha K. Kane made application through the chairman for leave to occupy a vacant room in the old library above stairs, viz. the S.E. room. He stated as the ground of his application, that he was subject to a rheumatic affection of the heart and that his dormitory smoking badly, he was obliged to keep his window partly open, and was consequently exposed to currents of cold air, seriously endangering a recurrence of his malady that he had already suffered from this cause. Dr. Griffith, who had been consulted by Mr. Kane, confirmed this statement, and expressed the opinion that it was very important to Mr. Kane's health that he should have a room more comfortable and with less exposure.

The request was granted, and Elisha's cousin and roommate, Robert Patterson, was allowed to room with him in his new quarters.[10]

Excerpts from letters of Robert Patterson to his mother and sister give us glimpses of Elisha's college years of alternating illness and earnest study.

> November 13, 1838
> ... I do not think Elisha continues as well as he was. His frequent complaints of his heart sometimes lead me to fear that his old complaints will pay him another visit this winter. However, rheumatism has not yet given him any of its twinges. He is a hard student—I think most too much so. I frequently tell him that he was sent here for his health and not for his mind; and I am thinking that he does not exercise as he ought; but he says that he always feels worse after exercise. We are go-

ing to commence exercising before breakfast, and begin tomorrow morning. . . .

April 18, 1839

. . . Elisha has got back to torment me with his everlasting cleaning; yet the room does look so nice, that I put up with the means for the sake of the end. . . .

June 6, 1839

Elisha is well and studying hard. I discover that he stands among the best, in all his classes, and should be a little astonished if he does not distinguish himself at the end of the session. He is with Mr. Rogers in his laboratory every evening. A kind gentleman is the same, and a tolerable lecturer, but he can't hold a candle to Father. . . .[11]

It must have been quite soon after this last hopeful letter was written that Elisha suffered a very severe attack of rheumatic fever. His father, summoned to Charlottesville, had to take the young man home to Philadelphia, wrapped in a blanket and traveling by easy stages because of the pain in his inflamed joints. After he reached home, symptoms of endocarditis (inflammation of the lining and valves of the heart), a frequent complication of rheumatic fever, set in. Elisha was dangerously ill for a long time. The family despaired of his life, and got little hope from the doctors. One of them saw fit to warn him, after a severe paroxysm of pain and suffocation, that another such attack might at any time end his life—a cruel thing to say, possibly justified by the need to keep the patient physically at rest. It is no wonder that the tense, sensitive youth, ill and in pain, his career apparently wrecked, fell into a mood of depression that lasted long after the acute illness subsided. Finally his father, believing that the trouble was no longer organic, applied a desperate remedy. "Elisha," he said, "if you must die, die in the harness." The lad accepted this stern advice. Facing probable disability and possible early death, he determined to go on with his lifework, come what might. While at the University of Virginia, with a boy's enthusiasm he had told his cousin Robert Patterson that he meant to make his mark in the world. This aim was now intensified to a burning desire to make his mark while his strength held out. Yet the depressive effects of this illness never fully wore off. "There is the best authority," says Dr. Elder, "for the opinion that his ailments had always in them a preponderant character of neuropathic disturbance."[12] This we shall see to be clearly evident in Kane's later illnesses. Some of his self-diagnoses will seem bizarrely improbable and must be interpreted as exaggerated or neurotic. But there is no doubt that all his many illnesses were superimposed upon recurrent rheumatic fever. The marvel is not that under this handicap he became something of a hypo-chondriac, but rather that in the eighteen years he still had before him he endured, by his own choice, journeys more arduous and physical hardships more severe than most men could have withstood in perfect health.

Medical friends of the Kane family, among whom two of the closest were Robley Dunglison and Robert Maskell Patterson, felt that civil engineering was no career for a young man convalescing from an attack of rheumatic heart disease. He would be better off, they thought, in the medical profession. Not only would he be spared strenuous outdoor activity, but as a doctor he could understand and manage his own physical disabilities. This latter was not necessarily good advice; the injunction "Physician, heal thyself" does not work well in its literal application to medical men, for self-diagnosis and self-treatment are more likely to deepen a doctor's apprehensions than to relieve them. At any rate, young Kane decided to study medicine, and in the fall of 1839, according to the custom of the time, he entered the office of a Philadelphia physician as an apprentice. His preceptor was Dr. William Harris, graduate of the University of Pennsylvania's Medical Department in 1812, whose office at Twelfth and Walnut streets was not far from the Kane residence, then at 100 South Fourth Street.

At the same time, presumably, Kane enrolled in the University of Pennsyl-vania as a medical student. At that period, to obtain a medical degree the student was required to apply himself to the study of medicine for three years, and to attend two full courses of medical lectures. During the three years he was expected to be the private pupil, for at least two years, of a respectable practitioner of medicine. The apprenticeship system was, how-ever, already beginning to break down, and that particular requirement was no longer strictly applied by the university.[13] Dr. Harris's tutelage was probably nominal. He was, no doubt, a competent practitioner, but there is nothing to show that he was outstanding as a private teacher. Kane may have read medical books in Harris's office, perhaps compounded his pre-scriptions and visited patients with him.

During the school term of less than six months, from October to March, the formal curriculum consisted solely of lectures by the seven professors, with clinical demonstrations and ward rounds at the Pennsylvania Hospital and at Blockley (now the Philadelphia General Hospital). The school was the oldest and most distinguished in the country. Its professors all stood at the head of their respective branches of the profession. Two of them, the chemist Robert Hare and the anatomist William E. Horner, were outstand-ing scientific investigators. Their teaching could not fail to interest young men who like Kane had a natural inclination toward science, but no laboratory work was done by the students themselves. After Kane's association with Rogers at Charlottesville, where he had been admitted to the professor's laboratory, it must have been dull indeed to sit on hard benches five hours a day listening to lectures and merely watching experimental demonstrations and dissections. Students might, if they wished, arrange with the professor of anatomy, or with an extramural teacher, to dissect the cadaver. Whether Kane did so is not recorded.

In his second year of medical study, however, Kane had all the practical work he could handle, for he secured an appointment as "resident physician" at Blockley. With only one term of lectures behind him and only such practical experience as he may have picked up in Dr. Harris's office, he possessed of course no such competence as today's interns, already M.D.s; a more accurate designation of his post would be "resident student." Kane's duties presumably included keeping records of the patients, dressing wounds, cupping and bleeding, administering first aid, and assisting in operations. Some of his notes on his cases survive and show great care in recording medical details.[14]

As a medical student Kane was well liked by hospital patients and nurses. Sixteen years later, when all Philadelphia was mourning his death, young Dr. John K. Kane, Jr. asked some of the older employees of the Philadelphia General Hospital if they remembered his brother. Their recollections, even allowing for the favorable bias caused by grief and sympathy, picture a kind, friendly and exceptionally dutiful doctor. One of the male nurses of the lunatic asylum said that Dr. Kane was universally popular. He was attentive to his patients, sober and quiet, not like other young men. A woman ward attendant, said John Kane, "cried when I saw her and begged me to come in and tell her all about him. . . . He was the handsomest young man she ever saw. Such a beautiful complexion and slender figure. . . . He was very kind in his manner and had a very soft voice when he spoke and was always familiar and ready to come in and sit down in a friendly way, not proud and haughty like some." Belle Burns, who had been a housemaid in the residents' dormitory when Elisha Kent Kane lived there, wept too and spoke of the little doctor from the depths of her warm Irish heart: "She would never see his like again—so pretty, with his sweet young face and lovely complexion like a girl's and his curly hair. There was never so fine a gentleman came to Blockley with his pretty gentle manners. . . . 'I used to tell him that he would kill himself with his hard work all day and sitting up of nights studying but he only laughed at that.'" There were even the embarrassingly grateful patients (every good intern has them) who insisted on crediting their cure to the youngest doctor, the one they saw most often in the ward, rather than to the visiting physicians. One of the Blockley patients vowed that Kane had saved his life in an acute illness by insisting on the application of leeches to his head, against the advice of an older doctor.[15]

During his residency, Kane was himself far from well, according to his immediate superior in the hospital staff. This was William Marcellus McPheeters, a North Carolinian who afterward became a professor of medicine in St. Louis. Graduated in 1840 from the University of Pennsylvania Medical School, McPheeters was a senior resident physician at Blockley for a year thereafter. Kane and he for six months lived in the same room and became cordial friends. McPheeters later told Dr. William Elder that Kane

> was labouring under a serious organic affection of the heart—dilatation with valvular disease, which gave rise to a very loud *bruit de soufflet* (bellows sound), accompanied by the most tumultuous action of the heart from any violent exertion. He was unable to sleep in a horizontal position, but was under the necessity of having his head and shoulders elevated, almost to a right angle with his body. He was fully aware of the gravity of his disease, as he often remarked to me that he never closed his eyes at night in sleep without feeling conscious that he might die before morning; yet this consciousness did not seem to affect his spirits, or to check his enthusiasm. . . . I have always thought that the uncertain state of his health had a good deal to do with his subsequent course of life, and the almost reckless exposure of himself to danger.[16]

More than a century later medical science is able to explain this paradox of a young man with seeming heart failure, yet able to carry on his daily tasks. The eminent cardiologists mentioned in the Preface, who acted as consultants to the author on Kane's medical history, suggest that his alarming symptoms were caused by paroxysmal atrial fibrillation, a transient irregularity of the heart beat often associated with stenosis (narrowing) of the mitral valve. No doubt the severe attack of rheumatic fever with endocarditis a year before had damaged Kane's heart valves and had affected the atrial musculature to some extent, but as yet not enough to limit his restless activity. The heart was still a good pump.[17]

In the spring of 1841, McPheeters left the hospital to enter private practice. Kane, still a year short of his M.D. degree, succeeded him as one of the senior resident physicians. About this promotion, Samuel Smucker delicately—and no doubt justly—wrote, "Although some of this success may be ascribed to the patronage of friends, much of it should be attributed to his own personal merits." The duties of an intern (for that was the nature of his post) were as heavy then as now, but Kane, in spite of his physical disabilities, and a full schedule of medical lectures during almost half the year, managed to carry on his hospital work. He also found time for a research project on a topic then of great interest in obstetrics, which he proposed to report in the graduating thesis then required of every candidate for the degree of M.D.

Most graduating theses were unoriginal essays, put together from textbooks and the professors' lectures. A graduate of 1854, for example, submitted a thesis on gunshot wounds, in which he remarked that he had no personal experience with such injuries; all that he knew about them he had gathered from Professor Gibson's lectures. Once in a while a student of some original- ity produced a thesis based on wider reading than that required by routine class work, or even upon clinical observations, or the examination of botani- cal specimens, or a few chemical experiments. Very few had serious research to report, as did Kane.

The topic of his dissertation was suggested by Robley Dunglison, the eminent professor of the Institutes of Medicine at Jefferson Medical College. Dunglison, well acquanted with the Kane children through his close friend- ship with John K. Kane, no doubt perceived that Elisha had never yet worked hard enough at any routine task to make a success of it. He might, however, respond with enthusiasm to the challenge of a novel and even sensational problem, especially one so important that success could win him the fame he had already begun to crave.

The subject is now quite obsolete, but how Kane worked on it is for us a fair measure of his intelligence and judgment. Fortunately we can discuss it in somewhat greater detail and more frankly than did Kane's biographers of the 1850s, anxious not to offend lay susceptibilities in a prudish age. In 1831 Jacques-Louis Nauche, a French physician of considerable experience and reputation, announced to the Paris Society of Practical Medicine his discovery of a new test for early pregnancy, based upon a peculiar condi- tion of the urine after the first month of gestation.[18] He had found, he declared, that to tell whether a woman is pregnant, one has only to let a specimen of her urine stand undisturbed in a tall glass in a moderately warm place. At any stage of gestation after the first month, within a day or two there will form, on the surface of the fluid, certain specks and filaments which soon unite with each other to create a thin scum. Portions of this scum will sink to the bottom of the glass, forming a milky deposit. The rest remains on the surface and becomes a crust or pellicle firm enough to be lifted off. These appearances are more or less clearly distinguishable from other kinds of cloudiness, deposits, and scums forming in urine. Nauche believed that they resulted from the presence in pregnancy urine of a hypothetical substance which he called *kiesteine* (also spelled kyesteine; pronounced ki-ĕs-tĕ-ēn) from the Greek word *kyesis,* a conception.

Nauche's account was quite promptly confirmed by several medical men in France, Germany, and England. Professor Robley Dunglison was sufficiently impressed by these reports to suggest that Kane should look into the matter.[19] Kane began his study with the conviction, not unusual in young scientists when they take up a research problem, that he could handle it better than his predecessors. The foreign physicians who published on the subject had reported, between them, a total of sixty cases. For reliable results, Kane thought a larger number of cases should be examined and judged with caution. "A candid spirit," he says, "not too much biased in favor of theory to admit the existence of observed exceptions . . . is not less important to the formation of correct opinions than the most careful and varied scrutiny of facts." The gentlemen who had treated on the subject, he politely remarks, were no doubt aware of the necessary precautions, but they had observed isolated instances rather than systematically assembled groups of cases, and had failed to detect any exceptions to their general conclusions. The young investigator's insistence upon the accumulation and comparison of a considerable number of cases reflected a new outlook in medical science recently opened up by Pierre C.-A. Louis of Paris, who was teaching the profession to improve the classification of diseases and the art of diagnosis by statistical analysis of the phenomena of disease. One of the American pupils of this distinguished innovator, William Wood Gerhard, returned to Philadelphia in 1833 and was a lecturer at the Philadelphia General Hospital while Kane was resident there. Through his teaching Kane must have seen that the statistical method was as clearly applicable to the kiesteine problem as to the clinical questions which interested Gerhard. He therefore, in spite of his many other occupations as medical student and intern, undertook to collect a sufficiently large series of observations on kiesteine to permit statistical analysis.

During the year or less in which Kane studied the test, he examined 85 cases of undoubted pregnancy, of which 68 showed a true kiesteine pellicle. Eleven were doubtful, and six negative, but two of the latter were complicated by serious illnesses, leaving only four "absolute exceptions": that is, failure of the kiesteine reaction. As controls he collected 28 cases in which there was no pregnancy, including 16 women long past the possibility of child-bearing, from 60 to 100 years of age, as well as a few males. No typical kiesteine pellicle formed on the urine of any of these nonpregnant persons. An interesting section of the report deals with cases in which the subjects of the tests attempted to deceive the investigator, either by substituting specimens from other women on the ward or by giving false histories. For a very young medical student this must have been a new kind of education in the ways of the world. Kane also ran a number of tests for other hospital doctors who presented him with puzzling cases. Doing these "blindly," that is without being told in advance whether the patient was thought to be pregnant, he arrived at a correct diagnosis, he says, in a gratifying number of cases and thus won respect for his studies among the hospital staff and students.

Kane concluded that although kiesteine was not an unerring sign of pregnancy, the true pellicle not always being distinguishable from other scums and deposits, still it was among the best available indications of early pregnancy. "Where pregnancy is possible, the exhibition of a clearly defined kiesteine pellicle is one of the least equivocal proofs of that condition." This conclusion, like the observations upon which it was founded, was for that time quite sound.

When we consider that this study was conducted by a medical student in his earliest twenties, in a period when very little experimental medical research was being done in the United States, Kane's achievement is truly remarkable. The clear, readable style of his dissertation reflects a natural aptitude for writing, disciplined by the literate environment of his home and good college training. Its scientific balance and its insistence on correct procedure stem from his training under William Barton Rogers and also, no doubt, the example of Pierre Louis received through William Wood Gerhard. The dissertation made such an impression upon Kane's professors that the faculty officially requested him to publish it. Appearing in the *American Journal of the Medical Sciences* in 1842,[20] it attracted a good deal of attention in Europe as well as America, and was cited by several subsequent investigators. In 1861, however, a leading English obstetrician, Braxton Hicks, voiced a dissenting opinion. He had seen kiesteine pellicles on specimens from virgins and from sterile married women, and emphasized this disconcerting fact so strongly that the work of Nauche, Kane, and the dozen other proponents of kiesteine went into the discard. Yet the test probably rested, ·if shakily, upon solid biological foundations. We now know that during pregnancy the urine contains several hormonal substances which might stimulate the growth of microorganisms responsible for the kiesteine pellicles.

Elisha Kent Kane was graduated in medicine at the University of Pennsylvania's commencement in March 1842. One of his professors, Samuel Jackson, speaking at another commencement in 1857, a few weeks after Kane's death, recalled the day, fifteen years earlier, when Kane had stood upon the same platform to receive his doctor's diploma. "However sanguine his anticipations of professional success and reputation," said Jackson, "(and it is a fair presumption that such were entertained by him), he was fully justified in that expectancy. He was the foremost student of the class; the thesis he presented to the Faculty had been honored by a vote of approbation and a request for its publication." And Jackson added that no one had as yet either contradicted the kiesteine test or added anything significant to what Kane had written about it. Rarely does a graduating dissertation win its young author such a position of authority, to be kept for twenty years. Elisha Kent Kane had begun to make his mark in the world.

# 3

# Navy Doctor at Large

JOHN K. KANE, like other masterful fathers, was slow to realize that his sons were growing up. Even after Elisha had reached his majority and was about to become a doctor of medicine, lawyer Kane's concern for his highstrung eldest son, so intense, so restless, so prone to overstrain his damaged heart, led to parental intervention that must have greatly irked the younger man. Apparently Mr. Kane feared that the exertions of a private medical practice would be too much for Elisha. A salaried post in government service would relieve him from much of the stress of making a living in an overworked profession. The Medical Corps of the navy, for example, offered a healthy, largely outdoor life on long voyages, with regular occupation and opportunity for scientific observations, and from time to time navy yard assignments close to home—in short, a career that ought to suit Elisha's tastes and physical limitations. Accordingly, without telling his son what he was doing, Mr. Kane wrote a letter early in 1842 to Abel Upshur, Secretary of the Navy, asking that the young man be granted a warrant of examination for appointment as a naval surgeon. Mr. Kane's letter, no doubt, was a personal one. It is not to be found in the navy archives, although it brought a prompt reply. Secretary Upshur, a former Virginia judge, was not disinclined to favor the personal plea of a fellow lawyer who happened to be very influential in Pennsylvania Democratic circles.

Elisha Kent Kane was surprised and disconcerted when just before commencement in March 1842 he found in his mail a letter from the Secretary of the Navy, directing him to report to the Philadelphia Navy Yard to be examined for a commission.[1] His own plan had been to set up a medical practice and continue research in civil life. But whether convinced by his father's arguments or bound by filial duty, he accepted the situation and presented himself to the examining board. When told at the end of the examination that he had been passed for navy service, he informed the board, according to Elder, that he suffered with chronic rheumatism and cardiac disturbance, but—says Elder—"The metal in the man outweighed his physical infirmities in their estimation and they refused to re-examine him." Evidently he had as yet sustained no very serious damage to his heart muscle or heart valves from the rheumatic fever with which he had suffered five years before.

The daguerrotype portraits made of Dr. Kane about this time, one in civilian garb, one in navy uniform, show a small, slightly-built young man of trim figure, with youthful features and a calm visage.[2] One, at the age of twenty-three, gives a hint of illness, the other, twenty-seven, of gravity and repression. Many people who met Kane have mentioned his quiet manner and reserve, broken only when eager advocacy of a cause or the enthusiasm of a traveler's tale loosened his tongue and brightened his features. But no such ardor was likely to show in a daguerrotype or ambrotype of the 1840s, considering the long exposure with the subject's head clamped in a hidden support.

The small United States Navy of 1842 had no vacancy for an assistant surgeon. Kane was not commissioned until the next year. How he filled his time between graduation and his first service assignment is not recorded. Apparently he attended lectures at the Jefferson Medical College, Philadelphia, for he registered there in November 1842. He seems, however, not to have been well that winter; in January 1843 he wrote to Secretary Upshur that while awaiting orders he proposed to recruit his health by a voyage in a merchant vessel, and requested that if he was out of the country when his name came up for appointment, his absence would not vitiate his commission.[3] He did not, in fact, make such a voyage, but found something far better, offering him everything he craved in the way of travel, medical and scientific observation, and a part in an undertaking of national and indeed international importance. An American embassy was going to the Far East. Following upon British action in China—the "Opium War" of 1837–42—Hongkong had been ceded to the British and five other maritime cities were designated as "treaty ports" open to British ships. Other governments were anxious to benefit by the concessions. On behalf of the United States, President Tyler and Secretary of State Daniel Webster were sending an expedition which they hoped would make a still wider breach in China's isolation by negotiating a commercial treaty, not at a seaport but in the forbidden capitol, Peking.

Secretary Webster had planned the diplomatic approach to the Chinese authorities and it was at first assumed that he would himself head the delegation. To impress the Chinese authorities, the party was to travel in a fleet of four vessels, mounting in all more than 200 guns—the new steam frigate *Missouri*, the frigate *Brandywine*, the sloop of war *St. Louis*, and the brig *Perry*. Although naval vessels carried surgeons, the party would be accompanied by a physician of its own.

Here was a chance for Elisha to see the world, for his father could pull enough wires to get him attached to the mission. John K. Kane's friend, Nathaniel Chapman, professor of medicine at the University of Pennsylvania, willingly recommended his brilliant pupil of the class of 1842 to Mr. Webster, who was no less willing to gratify the wishes of so good a Democrat as John K. Kane. The appointment was honorary; that is to say, unsalaried, carrying no naval rank. Elisha had next to apply to Commodore Foxhall A. Parker, who was to command the fleet on the long voyage to China, for acceptance as a "passenger" on the frigate *Brandywine*, and finally he had to get permission from Secretary Upshur to travel in that capacity.

Daniel Webster did not, after all, head the mission. When he unexpectedly resigned his cabinet post early in 1843, the treaty negotiations were entrusted to the Massachusetts statesman Caleb Cushing, whose term in Congress had just expired. Cushing, formerly a Whig, had fallen out with Henry Clay, but for some time had been voting for Democratic measures in Congress. He was happy to confirm Webster's appointment of Dr. Kane as medical officer to the China delegation. Kane was therefore aboard the *Brandywine* when on May 24, 1843, she sailed from Norfolk for China. Commissioner Cushing himself was not aboard the frigate. He sailed later on the *Missouri*, on July 31, 1843, and made port at Gibraltar on August 25. Cushing was ashore there the next day when the *Missouri* accidentally took fire and burned to the water's edge. The rest of the fleet having gone southward by a more direct route, Cushing followed by way of Malta and Cairo to Bombay.

About the time of the *Missouri's* departure from America, John K. Kane wrote to the then Acting Secretary of the Navy, A. Thomas Smith, requesting that Elisha's naval commission be expedited,[4] and that after receiving it he might retain his connection with the legation. Dr. Kane was in fact commissioned as Assistant Surgeon, U.S.N., on July 1, 1843 and, as he hoped, his assignment to regular naval duty was postponed until his return from the Orient.[5] Meanwhile he was not put on the navy's payroll.

From the day he sailed for China in May 1843 until he returned to Philadelphia on April 6, 1845, Kane's life was filled with travels so wide and adventures so incredible that a biographer may well hesitate to recount them without documentary evidence of a kind that is now, alas, largely missing.

Most of what we know about Kane during these two years comes from the official *Biography* of 1858 by William Elder, who was himself frustrated by lack of detailed information. Elder's sources were a few letters to the family and friends, not all of which are now to be found in public or family archives.[6] We can of course trace Kane's voyage to China and some of its events from the record of Caleb Cushing's expedition, but after Kane left the Cushing commission in mid-1844 there are only fragmentary memoranda and a couple of recorded conversations with men to whom Kane talked in after years about his fantastic travels. The narrative which follows necessarily rests upon Elder's account except when it is possible to add a date or a significant fact ascertained from other sources. To what extent the reports of Kane's itinerary and his fortunes and misfortunes in the navy are colored by his own exuberance or that of his official biographer, the reader must judge for himself. There will certainly be occasion, as we follow the journey, to note discrepancies and overstatements in Elder's narrative, but Kane's presence at places named in this chapter, at the times here stated, may be taken as factual.

From Norfolk *Brandywine* crossed the Atlantic to Madeira, and after touching there recrossed southwestward to Rio. Such an apparently indirect course was often followed by sailing vessels in order to take advantage of prevailing winds. She must have made port at Rio sometime in August. There, says Elder somewhat inaccurately, the party arrived "just in time to witness the coronation of the Empress of Brazil and the officers of the legation took part in the ceremonial." The Emperor, Dom Pedro II, had been crowned two years before, at the age of fifteen. The ceremonies attended by Kane and his companions must have been those celebrating Pedro's marriage to Princess Theresa Christina of Bourbon.[7] The bride having already been wedded to Pedro by proxy in Naples in May 1843, the ceremony was repeated with the bridegroom present, in the Imperial Chapel at Rio on September 4, after which the royal couple received the populace in the Municipal Palace. Doubtless Kane attended the reception and witnessed some of the public festivities which followed with all the gaiety of the Brazilian people.

While the ship was in port at Rio, Kane began his career as a scientific explorer in foreign parts by visiting the "Eastern Andes of Brazil," presumably the Organ Mountains, whose wildly jagged profile is visible from Rio. Elder says that Kane examined with some care the geological character of the region, so different in its relatively recent orographic features from the age-worn Blue Ridge where in his college days at Charlottesville he first studied mountain geology. It would be interesting, incidentally, from the medical standpoint, to know how much mountain climbing he attempted on this trip.

From Rio *Brandywine* proceeded to Bombay by way of the Cape of Good Hope. While at sea, Kane had leisure to study geometry, algebra, navigation, and European languages, and to read the Bible and Shakespeare. After arrival at Bombay on October 25 there was a long wait, for Commissioner Cushing, on his way by sea from Suez, did not arrive until November 28.[8] Kane had time to visit several places of artistic and scientific interest near Bombay—the Western Ghats for mountain scenery at Khandala, the famous sculptured caves at Elephanta, and lesser-known ones at Karli. He even traveled by palanquin to the caves of Ellora, almost two hundred miles inland at Hyderabad. Still at leisure before sailing for China, he crossed to Ceylon, and with officers of the British garrison joined an elephant hunt near Kandy.

The *Brandywine*, with Caleb Cushing aboard, called at Columbo, Ceylon, December 9, and reached Macao Roads in the Bay of Canton February 27, 1844. During the long voyage Kane had the privilege of association with Cushing, one of the most learned, studious, and capable diplomats who ever served the United States. He developed a warm friendship, moreover, with Fletcher Webster, Daniel Webster's eldest son, who accompanied Cushing as secretary to the legation. Kane was again busy with his books, now and then pushing them aside to wander and climb about the ship—"for hours in the stateroom buried in mathematics," wrote Fletcher Webster, "and then next seen at the masthead or over the ship's side."

At Macao the legation was joined by the two leading American missionaries of Canton, the Reverend Peter Parker, M.D., and the Reverend Elijah C. Bridgman, who were to serve as interpreters, with the title of Joint Chinese Secretaries. Parker, as competent a diplomat as physician and surgeon, proved invaluable to the United States commission. The story of their long and tedious negotiations with the emperor's plenipotentiary Ki-Ying is well told by Claude M. Fuess in his biography of Cushing.[9] The Chinese officials kept the commissioner waiting for months, and stalled his every effort to proceed to Peking. The American diplomats in fact never officially set foot on Chinese territory. All the conferences took place in a temple in the Portuguese colony of Macao, and there at last the treaty, very favorable to American and British trade, was signed in August 1844. Cushing sailed for the United States on August 24.

Kane might have borne the long wait with some degree of patience if it had promised a visit to Peking, but under the circumstances his restless nature made him long to get away from Macao, where he was not really needed. His services as physician to the American party were nominal. Peter Parker, a medical man of far greater experience, was constantly at hand, and Portuguese doctors were also available. In the spring of 1844 Cushing readily granted Kane leave to extend his travels to the Philippine Islands, then a Spanish colony whose geology and natural history were little known to Western science. Foreseeing that the negotiations with the Chinese diplomats would be long-drawn-out, the navy ordered *Brandywine*, after the American delegation was ashore, to proceed to Manila to survey marine stores and supplies left there by the U.S. East India Squadron. Crossing the China Sea, she arrived at Manila March 17, 1844. Kane had provided himself, before leaving America, with letters from the Roman Catholic Archbishop Eccleston of Baltimore and Bishop Kenrick of Philadelphia, and with similar credentials from American Protestant mission boards. With these to introduce him the young doctor seems to have been accepted at Manila as a scientific personage, and quickly found companions for his explorations.

Awaiting him at Manila were letters from home, among them one in particular to which, let us hope, he dedicated at least an hour or two and perhaps a few sighs before he took to his travels again. Like many another young man bent on seeing the world, he had left a loving girl behind him at the home port. Mary Leiper, daughter of his maternal uncle George Gray Leiper, was then sixteen years old. Her parents lived close to Philadelphia at their estate, Lapidea, near Chester, and during the year when Kane, no longer busy with his studies, was waiting orders from the navy, they saw much of each other. She completely lost her heart to the brilliant cousin who had distinguished himself in medical school and now, in spite of his frail health, was going to sail away, heaven knew whither, in all the glory of a naval officer's uniform. To Kane, as they danced together at a Philadelphia party, or walked in the country at Lapidea, this was nothing more than a cousinly flirtation. Not so to Mary; hardly able to bear his absence, she poured her feelings into a breathless three-page letter addressed to him at Manila. A few excerpts will serve to show how deeply she cared for him.

> How much I still miss you, more than ever since my return home, for the last time I was here, previous to my last visit to your mother or *rather* to her *son*, we were together and walked up the creek over the falls, little dreaming it would be the last time—but why is it that I always look upon your absence in the light of Death? Are we not both young and is not the climate going to do wonders for your heart? . . . I looked anxiously for it [a farewell letter] until after the ship had sailed and could scarcely believe that Elisha Kane who prides himself on keeping his promises, could have raised the hopes and have broken his word to one who would *die* rather than do so. . . . Now Elish' must I say *farewell,* every time I write it a pang shoots through my heart. . . .[10]

Mary did not soon get over her love for Elish'. Through almost a decade to come he was to receive her epistles, for a few years as warm as this first love letter to Manila, later more calm as she saw him losing his heart to others and knew she could never claim him for her own.

When William Elder wrote his biography he could find only meager records of Kane's travel in the Philippines. Fletcher Webster told him, he writes, that Kane had "proceded all the way across the island of Luzon and saw all its greatest curiosities." The anonymous author of a sketch of Kane's career in Simpson's *Lives of Eminent Philadelphians* (1859)—probably Kane's brother Thomas—tells with tantalizing brevity of still longer journeys. Dr. Kane, he says, widely explored the islands,

> much of which travel, including Camarinas and Mindoro, was made on foot. ... His charts are still preserved, but we believe have not been published. ... He devoted much attention to the volcanic region of Albay, expecting to connect his observations with subsequent travels in Sombava. His sojourn among the Negritos and Araturas was one of romantic interest. ... His associate during a part of this exploration, the lamented young Baron Loë, sank under the effects of the hardship and exposure which attended it and died in Java.[11]

Albay, in Camarinas Province of southeastern Luzon, most distant from Manila of the places Kane is said to have visited in the Islands, is more than 200 miles from the capital. How much Kane saw of the island of Mindoro cannot be even guessed.

But the exploit of which Kane was most proud took place only forty miles from Manila. Elder's version of his descent into the crater of Taal makes it seem a risky venture indeed. The story no doubt came from Kane himself through a letter, or a verbal account recalled by the family.[12] Kane was accompanied by a young German he had met, a Baron Loë, who was (says Elder) a relative of Prince Metternich. The two explorers were escorted by natives provided by the clergy of a neighboring religious establishment. The volcano is situated on a small island in Taal Lake. Its crater, two miles in circumference, rises about one thousand feet above water level. Its basin is filled with hot water, except where four or five sulphur-covered cones project above the watery floor. The volcano has a long record of destructive eruptions, three at least in the eighteenth century and one in 1808, thirty-six years before Kane's visit. His chief aim (besides the adventure) was to secure specimens of volcanic minerals from the crater and a sample of the water, which he supposed would contain sulphuric acid. Arriving at the top of the rim, Kane and Baron Loë found themselves on the edge of an almost vertical cliff more than a hundred feet high, from whose base a sloping layer of volcanic ashes descended gradually to the steaming water.

Apparently Kane's companions were seriously alarmed by his intention to descend into this veritable cauldron, for he took the time to prepare a penciled note absolving them from responsibility.

Dr. Kane in the Crater of Taal Volcano
From (anon.) *Kane, der Nordpolforscher* (Leipzig, 1869)

Being about to descend into the Crater for the first time since its great alteration, I would exempt my friends from all participation in my attempt, and I beg that this may be forwarded to my friends at home, should I not return.

> E. K. Kane
> April 14, Manila Time
> Crater of Taal
> Batangas

To: J. K. Kane, Esq.
Philadelphia

The two men began to descend the cliff, Kane carrying his water bottle, but they soon came to a projecting ridge over which they dared not pass. Further progress was impossible without ropes. Loë clambered back to the rim, but Kane would not heed the shouted advice of his party to give up the descent. Under Loë's supervision the guides fashioned a rope from bamboo gathered in the nearby jungle, which they let down to Kane, who looped its end around his body and was lowered to the ashy slope. There he slowly picked his way over the hot ashes and secured his sample of sulphur water. Returning to the base of the cliff, the ground giving way under his tread, he stumbled and fell. The hot ashes had charred his boots, but he reached the base of the cliff and was hauled up exhausted and almost senseless. Baron Loë revived him with the aid of restoratives from the monastery. As the party returned over Taal Island, a mob of pygmy natives gathered to protest its profanation of the god of the volcano. The explorers had to take shelter in a thicket and fire their revolvers as a sign to the friars to come to the rescue.

Elder tells us no more of Baron Loë. Shortly after the Taal episode Loë went to Java and there died, while Kane, in spite of his damaged heart, withstood all the stresses of his journey in the Islands and returned to Macao in fine fettle.

Kane rejoined the American legation at Macao sometime before June 1844. Elder reprints large portions of a letter to his parents in which, in the florid style of a young man proudly recounting his part in exotic affairs of state, he gaily describes ceremonial dinners and luncheons with the Chinese dignitaries.[13] But once the negotiations were ended, and Cushing's party began to prepare for their departure, Kane resigned his volunteer post with the commission. He sat through one more official dinner on June 25 and then, as he wrote later to his parents, two hours afterward was in a chartered boat, armed to the teeth, and threading the ladrone dangers of the Canton River. "I was a freed man."

He had taken the extraordinary resolution to settle for a time at Whampoa

Reach, a busy harbor up-river from Macao and Canton, where he meant to practice medicine and thus refill his purse, depleted by his travels, in order to go exploring again. He formed a partnership with a young English surgeon, Michael O'Sullivan, who conducted a hospital boat in Whampoa harbor, serving the crews of foreign ships. A notice that ran for several weeks, July to September, 1844, in an English-language newspaper published at Hongkong, *The Friend of China and Hongkong Gazette*,[14] read as follows:

### Whampoa Hospital
For the greater convenience of Vessels lying in the Whampoa and Blenheim reaches, the Hospital vessel is moored off the Bombay Creek.

M. O'Sullivan, Member of the Royal College of Surgeons,
London
E. K. Kane, M.D., Graduate of the University of Pennsylvania,
Philadelphia

The venture lasted about six months and was financially successful, netting Kane three thousand dollars, but ended in a severe illness that forced him to abandon medical practice in China. One episode alone stands out vividly. The famous medical missionary Peter Parker, who so skillfully served both his own country and China as interpreter and adviser to Caleb Cushing, had resumed his medical work at Canton. Kane was in his company in the autumn of 1844, and was invited to assist him in a difficult operation in the Ophthalmic Hospital. Kane's propensity for out-of-the-way adventures in out-of-the-way places had won him a part in a surgical feat of record-breaking magnitude.

The case was that of a Chinese beggar who had been afflicted for ten years with a tumor of the face of a kind called by pathologists "mixed tumor of the parotid gland," constantly growing and now actually larger than the man's head. Only a surgeon as bold as Peter Parker would have undertaken to remove it, and perhaps only a fatalistic Oriental already inured to suffering would have consented to an operation so formidable. Foreseeing grave difficulties, Dr. Parker arranged for two assistants, one of them Kane and the other an English medical missionary resident at Canton named Samuel Marjoribanks.

This operation took place just two years before the first use of ether anesthesia in major surgery at the Massachusetts General Hospital in October 1846. In pre-anesthetic days, speed was necessary as well as great manual dexterity, if the patient was not to be tortured beyond all endurance. Opium could only dull the pain. Parker's incision over the cheek and neck had to be eighteen inches long, in order to free the tumor, which after removal measured two feet six inches in circumference, and weighed 8¾ pounds.

Parker kept his two assistants tensely at work passing instruments, threading needles, and mopping up the field of operation. A bystander with watch in hand, as was the custom, reported completion of the operation in twenty-one minutes from the first incision. The patient bore his ordeal courageously and made a complete recovery. He was so grateful that Dr. Parker installed him as porter of the Ophthalmic Hospital, where he welcomed incoming patients and—best of propaganda for Western surgery—reassured them by retelling his own story.[15]

The record of this operation is buried in one of Peter Parker's medical reports. It is not mentioned in any published account of Kane's life, not even in that of William Elder, who as a physician himself would have been interested in a performance so extraordinary. No doubt Kane thought the tale too gory for family correspondence, and any memorandum he may have kept in his private journal must have been lost in the Nile, the next year, with other records of his travels in the Far East.

Near the end of 1844 Kane was severely ill at Whampoa with a disease designated as "rice fever," presumably cholera. He was cared for in the home of a Mr. Ritchie, a merchant with Philadelphia connections. While convalescent, he decided to return to America. A surviving page of a diary written on the eve of his journey poignantly reveals the mental turmoil of a lonely young man far from home, whose career has once more been broken by illness.

> Tomorrow I leave Macao, and with feelings perhaps the most unenviable that I have ever experienced.
>
> China had been my first field of action and responsibility. It was here that casting off the dependence of a child I assumed the self-sustaining duties of a man and here after repeated efforts and hope deferred—away from friends, away from influence—deeply in debt and depressed in everything—youth's great capital, a healthy frame and self-relying hope, at last brought its inevitable return.
>
> Endeared by the associations connected with surmounted difficulties, rectitude of purpose and increasing success soon conquered the disgusts of my Whampoa residence. I felt myself improving in my profession and advancing in experience. My present success redeemed all my previous failures—it exceeded all my expectations. My debts had been paid, my position established and, in a little heaven of self satisfaction, I was looking forward with almost childlike delight to what? To day dreams.
>
> To publications which would advance my reputation and gladden dear father's heart. To collections which would secure me consideration at home. To a little fortune which if not a competence would at least show my capacity to *acquire* and by enabling me to practice my profession at home, prove how much I valued the quiet pleasure of affection, than the success of selfish

absence. This then was China. The only drawback to my prospective success was the climate, and that with the "all men think all men mortal" feeling I voted a bugbear. The sickly season which so few resist was nearly over and my health miraculously throve. The postponed pleasure was now before me, I at last felt that I could gladden those I loved by an account of my success, and a hurried letter gave vent to my hopes.

Three days after its completion and one before its departure, I was delirious —for three weeks my life was despaired of, and when at last I awoke from the stupefaction of a frightful fever it was to feel, not that disease had crushed my energies, nor sickness broken down the pride of manhood, but that both were useless.—Nature's frail instrument the carcass had broken down.

My well-founded hopes were thus rendered completely visionary. Worm-like I had wrought my slime into a palace; I could not writhe myself within its walls.

In justice to myself I attempted that which might have destroyed me. I rose from the sick-bed—arrived again at Whampoa—saved myself from robbery— and urged on by returning strength, succeeded in settling my affairs and collecting the wreck of that which might have been a competence—and that done relapsed. . . . [Following page missing.][16]

Kane had sold his share in the hospital ship to one George Cone Lunn, Member of the Royal College of Surgeons of London,[17] and on January 25, 1845, he sailed for Singapore in company with a Mr. Dent, son of a British official at Madras, who was himself returning to his home because of ill health.

Little is known about this stage of Kane's long and adventurous journey home. William Elder conjectures that the ship touched at Borneo and Sumatra, where he assumes Kane must surely have gone ashore to see as much of the islands as he could while the ship was in port. The sole evidence for this is that six years later when Kane, returning from a year in the Arctic, reached Upernavik in Greenland, his first taste of a fresh vegetable—a radish—recalled the choicer fruits of his earlier travels, "the mango of Luzon and the mangosteen of Borneo, the cherimoya of Peru, the pine of Sumatra, and the seckel-pear of Schuylkill Meadows."[18] Dubious evidence this, for though Kane had indeed been in the Schuylkill Valley and in Luzon, he was certainly never in Peru. He could have eaten cherimoyas in Mexico, mangosteens at Singapore, and pineapples in Luzon. But a couple of islands, more or less, scarcely affect the record of this champion wanderer, who must have been the most widely traveled American of his time.

Among the surviving Kane papers there is a worn page bearing an incomplete and sparsely dated schedule of the latter part of the journey.[19] The ship apparently reached Galle, Ceylon, on February 19. Whether or not Kane got as far as Calcutta is not clear. Elder implies that it was there that he was introduced to a wealthy nobleman, Dwarkanath Tagore (grandfather of the poet Rabindranath Tagore), who was setting out for England to visit Queen Victoria's court. Prince Tagore (for so he was styled by courtesy) took Kane into his entourage, Elder tells us, while Dent went on alone to Madras. Elder says that "several months were spent in a tour of exploration through the interior of India, including the ascent of the Himalaya Mountains," but this statement can only be a gross exaggeration. Although we do not know just when Kane reached India, nor when he left it (his memorandum referred to above is not clear on these points), the whole trip from Ceylon to Suez was made between February 19 and April 3, 1845. Kane can have been ashore in India only two or three weeks at most. He says nothing about the Himalayas in his published writings, although he liked to recall his travels and was by no means reticent about them (in his Arctic books, for example, he several times mentions his observations of glaciers in the Alps). Nor is there any reference to the Himalayas in reports of conversations about his Eastern travels published by two men he met in the Arctic, William Parker Snow and J. R. Bellot. How he made the next stage of his homeward journey is almost equally unclear. Elder's account is self-contradictory, stating on one hand that Kane was invited to travel with Dwarkanath Tagore by sea, and on the other hand, most improbably, that he visited Persia and Syria, which implies an overland journey. Did he really travel with the merchant prince Tagore in a comfortable steamer, or did he find some more romantic and far more adventurous route through the Near East? Elder's story is so vague, and so much at variance with the very slight evidence from other sources, that the whole question had better be relegated to our Notes.[20]

We can at least be sure that by April 1845 he was in Cairo. There he presented to the aged Pasha Mahommed Ali a letter of introduction given him by Tagore, and obtained a safe-conduct for travel in Egypt. The Egyptian Society of Cairo, a kind of learned academy, elected him to membership, also on Tagore's recommendation. Hiring a boat and pilot on April 15, he proceeded up the Nile.[21] The river trip was not without its risks and misfortunes. Stopping at Dendera to inspect the ruins, Kane and his guide drew their boat up the sloping shore, with some of his baggage, and bivouacked for the night. When he awoke in the morning the boat was gone, with his trunks containing part of his collections and papers. His valuable watch had also disappeared. He had with him on the river bank, fortunately, his money, a traveling desk, a clock, and a carpet bag containing three shirts and a pair of slippers. The boat was found downstream, stranded and half full of water. A few days later Kane spied his watch in possession of his interpreter and got it back after a tussle with the man, who escaped in possession, no doubt, of other plunder from the swamped boat.

Heartsick at his loss, he doggedly pushed on. On May 2 he was writing home from Thebes:

> I have been for some days wandering about in a state of amazement . . . there is something so vast in the dimensions of these colossal ruins that I cannot embrace details; and, indeed, I almost fear that I shall leave Thebes without a definite impression of anything but magnitude.
>
> My paper is resting upon the enormous foot of one of the Osiride columns in the Memnonium; my breakfast, yet awaiting me, is on the other. Forty-eight columns are behind me, grouped around my bed; and the roof which they support throws its shadow upon this respectable epistle. I have taken lodgings in the temple of Sesostris.[22]

He learned that Richard Lepsius, a young Egyptologist destined to win a great reputation, had arrived at Thebes on April 16 on his return journey from the Blue Nile, and was lodged in the great temple at nearby Karnak.[23] Kane, wearing native dress, and with a beard so long, he said, that he had to tuck it in, crossed the river to meet the German traveler, whom he found sipping coffee while he copied hieroglyphics. Kane's family name was sufficient to introduce him, for (as it happened) earlier that year Lepsius had been informed of his election to foreign membership in the American Philosophical Society by a letter signed by John K. Kane, who at that time was secretary of the society. The two young men—Lepsius was thirty-four years old, Kane twenty-four—talked long about the German's travels, which Kane reported at length in a letter to his father.

Kane seems at this time to have been in very good health. In spite of the heat he walked—so he told his father—an average of twenty-six miles a day. The figure is hard to believe, but his diary shows at least long visits on foot to the ruins at Luxor, Karnak, and the Valley of the Kings. At some time during this stay, according to Elder, he was attacked by thieving Bedouins and in the fight with them sustained a wound in one leg which troubled him for a fortnight. This did not, however, prevent him from getting about. Before he left the region he went, of course, to see the two statues of Amenophis III, and there he recklessly undertook to climb the more northerly of these colossi, long famous as the "Vocal Memnon." For this adventure, as for every exploit of his adventurous career, he had a scientific excuse. The seated Pharoah, about seventy feet high, holds between his stony knees, about thirty-three feet above the ground, a tablet ten inches thick which, Kane thought, might bear hieroglyphics on its underside. Its upper surface can readily be seen by an observer who climbs to the statue's head by an easy route up the back, but the underside cannot be viewed in that way. Against the advice of his native attendants, as at Taal volcano the year before, Kane took the risk. He worked his way upward between the Pharoah's legs—a stiff exercise for a man with a damaged heart and a wounded leg—but after a tedious effort found himself braced under the projecting stone tablet, unable either to climb higher or to descend. While he hung cramped under the tablet, his boatman went to fetch a guide, who climbed the statue by the rear, to the top of the lapstone whence he let down his sash to Kane, whose fortunately light weight permitted the rescuer to haul him up over the tablet's edge.

Kane's diary of his Egyptian adventures explicitly states that after his thorough visitation of the Theban region he returned downriver to Cairo. He did not, as his biographer Elder would have us believe,[24] go farther up the Nile Valley; but this high-strung young traveler did not begin his trip in the relative comfort of his boat. Instead, he sent the boat to await him at Girga, about 125 miles downstream. He hired a couple of dromedaries and with his guide took the desert route to Abydos to visit the temples there and the reputed tomb of Osiris—a none-too-comfortable trip of about seventy miles, apparently requiring three days and two nights. Rejoining his boat he continued downstream, stopping at Saqquara for the Step Pyramid and Serapeum, and at Masara for the ancient quarries.

From Cairo he went on to Alexandria. There he sought the help of a surgeon to treat his leg, and immediately afterward suffered an illness which Elder in his biography calls the plague, no doubt accepting Kane's own self-diagnosis set down in one of those now missing letters home, and says that it nearly cost Kane his life. During this illness, Kane's collections of natural history and antiques which he had sent down the river ahead of him were dissipated and lost. We need neither take literally the diagnosis of bubonic plague, nor dismiss the illness lightly. It is no wonder that the weary traveler, discouraged by the loss of his papers and most of his wardrobe, probably undernourished and feverish from an infected wound, thought himself near death. We shall see more than once that Kane when ill generally gave to his symptoms the name of some deadly disease he had read about. This kind of anxiety—it would not be fair to call it hypochondria—is not uncommon in young medical men.

Scarcely recovered from the fever, whatever it was, and not really well enough to travel, Kane set out for Greece in the company of a lieutenant in the British army. This must have been early in June; a dated letter quoted by Elder shows that he was in Athens on June 10, 1845. Touring Greece on foot, very slowly because of his recent illness and injury, he visted Eleusis, the Attic city of Thebes, and Livadia. Apparently recovering his strength, he climbed, we are told, to the 5,000-feet summit of Mount Helicon, and on the brink of the Hippocrene Fount cut a walking stick for his father. From there he went by way of Thermopylae and Parnassus to the Gulf of Corinth. Finally he "traversed the Morea [Peloponessus] thoroughly" and took a steamer from Patras to Trieste. Thence the route led through northern Italy and Switzerland to Paris. How thoroughly Kane studied what he saw on the way we cannot know, but many references in his later writings, comparing Arctic vegetation, geology, and glaciation with what he had seen in the Alps, suggest careful observation in his traverse of Switzerland.

Kane reached Paris by mid-July. From there he wrote to his parents a long and evidently intensely emotional letter, now known only from a paraphrase by William Elder, who found its substance and its tone too deeply personal for publication in 1858 while Judge Kane and Jane Leiper Kane were still living and grief for the dead explorer was fresh in American hearts. Among the missing documents which a biographer of Elisha Kent Kane longs to see, this must have been one of the most revealing. Elder says that any one of its pages would justify all the admiration of his heroism, his feeling, and his skill in writing that his public record subsequently won him. The letter shows that in mid-1845 Kane was—incredibly—planning to return to the Philippine Islands and set up a surgical practice at Manila. If he did as well financially as at Whampoa in the previous year, he could accumulate, he thought, enough money to finance a proper tour of the world! Against any such plan he felt the full force of his parents' wish that he would return and settle down at home, but still he claimed the right to follow the career of travel and exploration upon which he had resolved. At his request the U.S. Minister to Spain, Washington Irving, successfully applied to the Spanish Council of Public Education for permission for Kane to take the examination for a license to practice in the Philippine Islands at Manila, rather than (as usual) at Madrid.[25] However, Kane did not carry out this project. Traveling from Paris through France and Italy he went to England and thence to America. He arrived at Philadelphia some time in the late summer of 1845.

In a little more than two years Dr. Kane had voyaged on the North and South Atlantic and Pacific Oceans, the Indian Ocean, the Mediterranean and Adriatic Seas; he had set foot on all five major continents and had made extensive journeys on three of them. The total extent of his travels, conservatively estimated, was almost forty thousand miles. If Kane had settled down in Philadelphia and had not lost his notes and sketchbooks, he might have written a travel book as fascinating to American readers as the two narratives of Arctic exploration that he produced a few years later. He already commanded a lively style, judging from his letters, even if he had not yet acquired the disciplined elegance of his second Arctic book; he could sketch landscapes and objects of scientific interest more than adequately to furnish materials for professional draftsmen and engravers; and he had gentle humor and a keen eye for the picturesque and for scenes of grandeur.

He could talk well enough about his journeys to impress even another world traveler whose wanderings had been as extensive as his own. The restless adventurer William Parker Snow, who met Kane in 1850 when the American Arctic ship *Advance* and the British *Prince Albert* were icebound together in Lancaster Sound, recalled later that Dr. Kane, the surgeon and naturalist of the American expedition, was of an exceedingly slim and apparently fragile form, with features to all appearance far better suited to a genial clime than to the roughness and hardship of an Arctic voyage.

> I found that he had been in many parts of the world that I myself had visited, and in many others that I could only long to visit. . . . Ever smiling Italy . . . sturdy Switzerland, the Alps, the Apennines, France, Germany, India, Southern Africa. Then came Spain, Portugal and my own England: next appeared Egypt, Syria, and the Desert. With all these he was personally familiar, in all these he had been a traveller. Rich in anecdote and full of pleasing talk, time flew rapidly as I conversed with him.[26]

Yet his travels, extensive as they were thus far, had been merely the wanderings of an enterprising tourist and dilettante scientist, not of a seasoned explorer. His apprenticeship was not yet finished.

# 4

# Coast Fever and War Fever

WEARIED BY HIS LONG TRAVELS, and warmly received at home by family and friends, Dr. Kane, it seems, was for a while in a mood to settle down in Philadelphia at the age of twenty-five and begin the private practice of medicine. He was certainly ready to abandon the naval career into which his father's intervention had plunged him two years before. The navy had never called him to active service in his rank of assistant surgeon, or even put him on the payroll. He had always been seasick in heavy weather, and moreover (as Elder asserts) he was too democratic to tolerate the rigid distinctions of rank and the often harsh discipline of the old-time navy.[1] His parents longed to have him permanently ashore. Although Judge Kane had gotten him into the navy for the good of his health, it was all too clear that the doctor's sea voyages were for him merely a way to reach distant lands where he could indulge his taste for adventures far too risky for a man with a damaged heart.

After a restful stay with the family, Kane took a house on Walnut Street and fitted up a doctor's office there; just where we do not know, because he left Philadelphia again so soon that the publishers of the city directory never caught up with him. His name does not appear in the directories for 1845 and 1846.

Unfortunately for his parents' hopes of keeping him at home, just at this time he discovered an exciting new chance of adventure. War with Mexico was in prospect, with virtual certainty of active service for a junior surgeon. Kane put aside all thought of resigning his commission, and this time welcomed his father's intervention to make sure he would stay in the navy on favorable terms. Judge Kane therefore in March 1846 wrote to the Secretary

*49*

of the Navy, George Bancroft, hoping that Elisha's services on U.S.S. *Brandy-wine* with the Cushing legation could be counted toward the two-year period required before an assistant surgeon could be examined for promotion. The Secretary apparently said it could not be counted, and suggested that the doctor had better have another tour of sea duty. He offered Dr. Kane an assignment to the old frigate *United States,* flagship of a squadron then about to sail for a cruise on the West African coast. Judge Kane replied that his son would be glad to join the ship and would write an official letter to that effect.[2] For Dr. Kane this acquiescence was merely making the best of a bad bargain. Duty with the African Squadron would take him directly away from the scene of war and subject him to the dull routine of an unrewarding voyage.

In May 1846, *United States* was refitting for her long cruise at Charlestown, Massachusetts, where Dr. Kane was ordered to join her. Three years before, when he sailed for China, he had left a love-struck girl behind. This time he left two of them, both—like himself—in a sadly agitated state. Mary Leiper was of course one; the other was another cousin, Helen Patterson, daughter of Kane's distinguished uncle by marriage, Robert Maskell Patterson and sister of his college roommate. From Boston Kane wrote to Helen a strangely unhappy, distraught letter.[3]

>                    Tremont House, 7th May
> Dearest Helen, It is very late, and after a toilsome day I might well seek
> quietude in slumber did not the words which commence this letter
> renew my wakefulness by awakening my heart.—Very dearly and truly
> do I love you darling Nelly.—A love looking to any thing but its own
> gratification; and after what has passed why should I doubt but that you
> love me. I do *not* doubt, you must love; it would lower and degrade
> you not to.
>    My affection can do you no harm, it interferes not with your prospects
> nor your pleasure, it resigns all obligation, demanding nothing, and
> thinks not of itself.—Love me then, dear darling Nell, for you have seen
> your last of poor Elish—and the love will cost you nothing.— I cannot
> revisit Philadelphia.
>    It is very hard to be thus for weeks within a day from one's second self
> but I must endure it. Write often, as yet I have received no letters.
> Mary Leiper has written me a cruel letter. My reply will heap coals of
> fire upon her head.—I feel that it is the kind affectionate letter of a *gen-tleman* but as, in truth dear Helen to you, that language is *too warm,*
> I could not bear to send it without letting you know that such words
> had passed between me and another and that other not yourself. Read

it, seal it, and forward it to its destination, and that done, assure yourself of my confidence and my love. . . .

J—— the pure and J—— the impure have both written since my depar-
ture. Strange that from such I should receive letters before yourself,—
One speaks of my not having bid good bye, and the other (Oh dear
Nelly!) in humility—only blessed me. Do write to me.

Now for a request. Tell Pat that you wish to send your Daguerreotype
to Virginia, make him escort you to Langenheim's, have it taken and
send it to me. I some how or other feel that you will do this. for I know
that you love me, and loving me you have promised to regard all
reasonable wishes.—Do it quickly. . . .

Did you receive my picture I gave it to Solomon for you. Every evening
when you go to bed open it, lay it upon the sheet beside you and try
and think of the poor wanderer who but for you might have occupied its
place—Dear Nelly; I have much to thank you for, but do you not think,
in recalling dear old times, that while you have yielded much, you
have withheld more. Answer me candidly and truly. Do you not, when
you think of me, absent and alone, on the eve of a perilous voyage, and
perhaps to see you never again—: —reproach yourself sometimes in your
heart of hearts for not having enjoyed less sparingly the bountiful cup
of whose pleasures we barely sipped? Answer me for this is my last
allusion to that portion of our past dream—Let it be forgotten *forever*.

Farewell, darling Nelly, appreciate as it deserves a love which would
elevate you, were I even a brute; for such love as mine cometh but
rarely to woman.—Remember me then, and remember me kindly, as one
who has once been your lover but is now your friend.

This is sufficient evidence that Kane had loved Helen Patterson, and
still did. But what had gone wrong? Was it only that finding himself entangled with two young women at once he had rejected one and been rejected
by the other? Or had the cousins, carried away by romantic affection, first
forgotten and then bitterly remembered a strong antipathy of the Leiper
family to the marriage of cousins?[4] Had Kane himself perhaps declared an
end to their hopes of marriage, in a revulsion based on his chronic ill-health
and his dedication to a career of dangerous adventure?

Two other letters among Kane's surviving papers may in some way be
connected with this drama of parting and heartbreak. In some way, let us
repeat, for they deepen the mystery rather than explain it, and indeed cannot be read, even after 125 years, without a sense of bewilderment. On February 4, 1846, when Kane, then in Philadelphia, had been at home from his
Far Eastern travels about five months, John Taylor, Jr., husband of Kane's

cousin Mary (Helen Patterson's elder sister) wrote to him from "Hazle-wood" near Port Royal, Virginia, a letter with scandalous implications. He wrote, he said, in reply to Kane's request to find a temporary home for a young woman, J——, who was pregnant. He knew of a good country family near Fredericksburg who would take such a lodger, and he would see to the arrangements. He went on to banter Kane with hearty vulgarity, on his prowess as a lover and the lack of guile that had got him in trouble.[5] Nearly four months later, on May 27, 1846, Dr. C. C. Van Wyck, a Philadelphia physician, wrote in a more serious tone, also discussing financial arrangements for boarding the girl. Now nearing the time of childbirth, she was in Philadelphia under Van Wyck's care. The friendly doctor told Kane not to trouble himself unduly, for he had done "as much and more than could be asked of any individual in a like fix," and was under no further moral or other obligation toward the girl than he had endeavored to fulfill.

Are we to take these letters at their face value, to mean that Kane when he sailed for Africa, like many a sailor in every age, left a seduced girl and a bastard child behind him? The girl was presumably "J—— the impure" of Kane's letter to Helen Patterson. Like "J—— the pure" she cannot now be identified. Nothing further about the girl appears in surviving correspondence, nor does anything in Kane's later history suggest the existence of an illegitimate child. With every allowance for the ways of ardent and reckless young men, the implication does not fit what we know of Kane's character. Letters from Kane's parents to him at this time give no hint of such strain as a scandal of that sort would surely have produced in the judge's household. Neither do the frequent letters of Thomas Leiper Kane, most intimate and confiding of brothers, written to the doctor on the eve of his departure for Africa, suggest knowledge of such an affair.

He joined his ship on May 5, 1846. Before the end of the month she was on the way to her first African port at Praia, Cape Verde Islands. According to the logbook of *United States*,[6] while Kane was aboard her she made two cruises from Praia to Principe Island in the Gulf of Guinea, on one of these cruises, or both, calling at Freetown (Sierra Leone), Monrovia, Accra, and Ouidah. No doubt Dr. Kane found most of his superior officers congenial; Commodore George C. Parker was a Philadelphian, and the fleet surgeon, Thomas Dillard, was like Kane a medical graduate of the University of Pennsylvania. Nevertheless the cruise was uninteresting and uncomfortable. Another American naval surgeon on the African patrol a decade later unhappily wrote home of "a Station everywhere warm, and in most places hot . . . dull monotony and general uninterestingness, rarely except in a few places tempting a visit to the shore, whether for recreation or for curiosity, and dooming us to a shipboard life during nearly the whole cruise."[7] And Kane himself, writing to the eminent Philadelphia physician Robley Dunglison about some interesting medical cases, said that "of all the miserable blanks in one's existence the most miserable is an African cruise."[8] He did his best to fill up the blank by leaving the ship whenever he could, to enjoy the strange sights and exotic landscapes of West Africa. A passage from a letter to his mother, July 13, 1846, from Praia devotes seven pages to a description of that town and its surroundings in a vivid style which he was later to refine and purge of whimsicality, into the distinguished prose of his books on the Arctic:

> Take Porto Praya by moonight, or in early sunshine or late sunset, or any other charitable season when its imperfections are shrouded and its best traits improved. At such periods of kind obscurity, every ripple of its dark bay becomes a crescent spangle and its shoreline is haloed with the white glories of the surf. Its scanty palm trees cut against the sky, and whether they be palm trees or pitchforks, perform their only object in a black foreground which enables you to slur over the town to the soft shadows of the mountains which lie beyond it. One of these is more than 6000 ft. high, rising on one side by a series of easy planes and then, as if ashamed of its regularity, tumbling down in a frightful precipice. This is the Pico de San Antonio, one of those biblico hobgoblin mountains known to every child on the island.[9]

The most exciting thing to study ashore in West Africa was the slave trade. According to Elder, always inclined to a generous estimate of Kane's travels, he "visited the slave factories from Cape Mount to the River Bonny in the Gulf of Guinea"—a coastline of more than 1,200 miles with four or five seaports. This stretch included the coast of Dahomey and the adjacent shore known as the "Slave Coast."

Kane's interest in the problem of Negro slavery was very natural in a Philadelphian of his time. The morality of slavery was already a burning issue in America, and nowhere more actively debated than in Pennsylvania. When Kane was a schoolboy of thirteen, the arch-agitator William Lloyd Garrison had come from Boston to join the Pennsylvania abolitionists in founding the American Anti-Slavery Society. The elder Kane boys, Elisha and Thomas, must have heard much talk, pro and con, in their father's circle about the slavery question. Thomas Kane, when he grew up, ardently took part in the movement as it shifted from propaganda to political action through the Free Soil Party. Admitted to the bar in 1846, while his elder brother was away on the African coast, Thomas two years later became secretary of the Free Soil Central Committee of Pennsylvania. His stand must have been very distasteful to his father; John K. Kane, now a federal judge, having been associated in politics with the southern Democrats and in religious affairs with the conservative southern Presbyterians, did not approve the militancy of the New England abolitionists and their Pennsylvania allies.

Judge Kane's sons respected their able father, and Elisha, at least, gave ample evidence of more than respect—a lifelong affection that withstood all the tensions between the dominant parent and his independent sons. As for Thomas, his temperament and his training in the law gave him deep concern for social justice. Contention with his father over the slavery question in later years came perilously near an open break, if the story is true that Judge Kane committed his son to prison for contempt of court because of the young man's strong letter refusing to serve as U.S. commissioner after passage of the Fugitive Slave Act.[10] The two brothers were very close to each other in affection and sentiment. Elisha's interest in the operations of the slave trade on the African coast no doubt reflected brotherly sympathy, whether or not he agreed with Thomas's extreme views, and consciously or unconsciously expressed their mutual need to be independent of their father.

When in Brazil with the Cushing legation in 1843, Dr. Kane had met Francisco Felix de Sousa, a famous Brazilian slave trader who made his headquarters in Dahomey, at the coastal town of Ouidah.[11] When *United States* was in port there, Kane and a couple of other officers were entertained for two days by de Sousa's sons in the family's luxurious residential compound and were given a tour of their slave factory. Diplomatically avoiding any show of distaste, Kane won their confidence and heard how their seamen eluded the American and British naval vessels patrolling the coast. Fascinated, he wrote down in his notebook a detailed record of his visit together with a long account of horrible conditions and shockingly high mortality aboard a slaveship that was overhauled by the Americans.[12]

De Sousa was about to send a caravan to Abomey, capital of the country, bearing tribute to the imperious and warlike King Gezo. Securing leave to join the caravan, Kane made the sixty-mile journey and was formally presented to the monarch at court. Elder's sketchy account of this visit is based on one of Kane's youthfully enthusiastic letters, not now available in full. If Dr. Kane saw half the savage pomp and murderous cruelty reported by English travelers of the time—among them Sir Richard Burton[13]—it is no wonder that he came away feeling that African tribesmen who were shipped to American plantations were better off than many who escaped the slavers only to suffer at home.

Thomas Kane was not happy at the continued separation from his elder brother during the cruise. In November 1846 he wrote to Elisha: "Good Lord, when I think of the ungodly, uncomfortable, wearing soul and body life of a navy surgeon it makes me only deeply sorrowful to think that circumstances would have forced you to live in the damned berth a day."[14]

With extraordinary generosity Thomas went on to offer Elisha an advance of $1,800 from the $2,000 salary of a law clerkship Judge Kane had at his disposal and would award to Thomas. With this money Elisha, if he would come home, could set himself up in practice. Whether or not he was tempted by this proposal, we do not know. For the time being, he was bound by his assignment to duty on *United States*.

Young officers cooped up aboard ship in all the tedium of an offshore patrol, in a hot, humid climate, with little recreation ashore, sometimes found each other intolerably irritating. For some reason we cannot now guess, Kane developed a particular dislike for one of the line officers, Lieutenant George A. Prentiss. Evidently his dislike was reciprocated. The two quarreled more than once, and finally, at sea one morning in January 1847, there was another flare-up in which Prentiss took offence at something Kane said or did, and Kane in turn interpreted Prentiss's angry words as insulting not only to himself but to the entire Kane family. For the second time, it seems, in their running quarrel, the little doctor challenged Prentiss to a duel. He got a more or less temperate reply:

> Frigate, The States
> At Sea, Jan. 5 1847
>
> Sir
> I disclaim altogether any allusion to, or reflection upon your family, in my remarks this morning. Those addressed to yourself were deserved, by your indelicate, and insulting interference in my affairs.
> I tell you plainly, as I once before told you, I cannot give you the meeting you seem to desire, while our official relations remain as they are. You well know the consequences would be disastrous to *me* whatever the event, while *you* would go unscathed. Should however any of your friends of my rank, or who are unconnected with the Navy, think I have treated you unjustly, it will leave me no excuse for declining a meeting.[15]

A duel between Prentiss and Kane never took place, for shortly after this affair Kane was no longer in condition to fight. The West African coast was not only depressing, it was very unhealthy. After the squadron's first stop at Cape Verde, six of the frigate's crew fell ill with a tropical fever, and Kane, as assistant surgeon, had been busy for two months before the set-to with Prentiss, caring for the sick men. A month after the quarrel, on February 1, 1847, he himself came down with a very severe case of what Fleet-Surgeon Dillard called "coast fever" and was acutely ill for ten days. The fever lasted three weeks in all, and left him prostrated. Dr. Dillard feared for his life if he stayed in "this baleful climate" and sent him home by a merchant ship from Praia. "I part with him with regret," he wrote, "and shall miss him much. I lost not only a useful and necessary assistant, but a valued and esteemed young friend."[16]

It is not now possible to know just what this illness was. "Coast fever" was not a clinical entity recognized in the medical literature of the day, but a popular term covering vaguely any fever that could not be readily identified by outspoken signs such as the jaundice and black vomit of yellow fever or the regular paroxysms of malaria. The febrile diseases to which white men were especially liable on the west coast of Africa included, besides these readily recognizable diseases, dysentery and (no doubt) typhoid fever.[17] According to an American doctor who was on the coast a few years after Kane, "Those fevers generally known as African fever, Guinea fever, Bulaw fever, or coast fever, are doubtless malarious in their origin."[18] But continuous prostration for three weeks does not suggest malaria, and Dillard would surely have recognized yellow fever, dysentery, or a recurrence of the rheumatic fever from which Kane had suffered nine years before. Perhaps this was typhoid fever, as suggested by the duration of the febrile stage and the great debility it caused, and also by the occurrence of an abscess of a salivary gland, mentioned in the letter about to be quoted.

Kane arrived at a home port early in 1847, his slight frame still emaciated and weak. From Baltimore, en route to Philadelphia, he wrote to his father:

> About thirteen days from the beautiful Island of Principe, our Guinea cruise over, and glad thoughts of Madeira ahead;—I was "taken down" with African Fever—the letter of my dear and excellent friend Dillard will give you its course—for its results, behold me at Barnum's [*Hotel*], awaiting some one of the home trio, yourself, Tom, or Pat.
>
> Now I wish you to understand that I do not *need* your escorts, for I can walk about passably, and even enjoy the Ale and Quinine which medical command had inflicted (all of which explain to dear Mother) but then my fever delighted in manifold novelties, Abscess of the Salivaries by way of an entremet and Oedema of the Scalp by way of [*missing word:* dessert?]—Hence, dear people, renovation is tardy, the legs are earthquaky, and the brain weak,—Added to these—thanks to the Salivaries: I have a Robinson Crusoe beard, and—thanks to causes which I leave you to guess at—a Shaven Scalp.—I feared then, being nervously inclined, to thrust upon you my shorn and unshorn visage.
>
> I shall at once return with you by the day or night conveyance. Only announce your advent by magnetic telegraph and tell no one out of the

immediate home, of your departure, Show Dillard's letter, the more the better, but let me have no one save the little circle to meet me. No kin's folk greetings—no Fuss. These things do not chime in with broken prospects and broken health.[19]

Kane's mental depression wore off too quickly, perhaps, for his physical good. Before he had regained full strength he went to Washington to petition for transfer to the army and assignment to the forces in Mexico. All he got from this trip was another severe illness that kept him in Washington for weeks, with a further period of convalescence at home, lasting all summer. In August, as if giving up all hopes of going to the war or even getting another naval assignment, he applied for the post of physician to Girard College, in Philadelphia.[20] It is hard to imagine how he would have borne so unadventurous a task as looking after the health of a pack of schoolboys, within a couple of miles of his home. Fortunately someone else got the post. Meanwhile Kane's chance for military glory was running out. General Winfield Scott's brilliant campaign and bloody victories led to the capitulation of Mexico City on September 13, 1847, and brought the fighting almost to a close.

However, Scott's communications through the mountainous country between the Gulf Coast at Vera Cruz and Mexico City were still subject to harassment by the enemy and in fact United States troops were under siege at Puebla, directly on the route from the Gulf to the capital. Adventure was still waiting for Kane if he could only get to Mexico before the war was all over. For this he had to go once more to Washington. To escape the family's solicitude, on October 23 he took advantage of a "Wistar Party," an evening of dignified sociability conducted by a select group of members of the American Philosophical Society. Attending, no doubt, as his father's guest, he left the party inconspicuously and took the night train to Washington.

Elder hints that Kane carried his plea directly to the White House. There is nothing in President Polk's diary, however, to show that Judge Kane's son called upon him at once.[21] More likely it was Secretary of State Buchanan to whom Kane first appealed. Buchanan, a Pennsylvanian and a lawyer, of course knew Judge Kane well and had in fact been elected to the American Philosophical Society while he was its secretary. Buchanan was, moreover, a close friend of George Leiper of Lapidea, Dr. Kane's uncle by marriage. At any rate, Dr. Kane got another of his lucky breaks, if it can be called good luck to risk a valuable life merely for adventure. The President and his Secretary of State at that very moment urgently needed a trustworthy messenger to carry an important secret message to General Scott. Kane, having turned up at the opportune moment, was offered and accepted the assignment. The Navy Department at once put him on special orders. A few days later he received a further directive from the Navy Bureau of Medicine and Surgery and from the acting surgeon general of the army to visit the general hospitals and field hospitals in Mexico, in order to study and report on their surgical cases and statistics. This inspection duty, for which he was not especially qualified, was perhaps a screen for his real task of getting the President's message through to General Scott.

What the message was, Kane's earlier biographers either did not know or could not tell, but its nature is now clear. The capable President and the victorious commander of the armies in Mexico, General Scott, were seriously at odds. Political jealousy of Scott was running high in Washington, even in the White House, and conflicting policies for making peace with Mexico brought the trouble to a head. Nicholas V. Trist, Chief Clerk of the State Department, sent to Mexico to negotiate a truce, with Scott's approval had offered the Mexicans concessions unacceptable to the administration. The President had written to Scott, ordering Trist's recall and a postponement of negotiations until the military victory was complete. For weeks he had waited in vain for a reply to these orders, which General Scott did not receive (or perhaps chose not to acknowledge). Meanwhile the President learned that Trist was still continuing his negotiations against orders, and believed that Scott was abetting the envoy's insubordination.[22]

On Saturday, October 23, the cabinet discussed the situation with deep concern. The President, tired and angry, directed Secretary Buchanan to prepare a new dispatch confirming Trist's recall and insisting upon delay of the negotiations. Scott was ordered, furthermore, to forward duplicates of all dispatches he had sent to Washington since early June. Buchanan's dispatch almost certainly was the message Kane was to deliver to General Scott by word of mouth, if and when he reached Mexico City through enemy-infested territory. President Polk's diary for Monday, October 25, reads, without mentioning Kane by name, that "a special messenger left this morning as bearer of dispatches to General Scott and Mr. Trist. The dispatches were those which I ordered to be prepared in the Cabinet meeting on the 23d instant." Actually, Kane did not receive his final orders from the Navy and War departments until November 5. He left for Mexico via New Orleans on November 6.

The little navy doctor must have felt a great sense of importance and personal freedom when he set out on his long journey bearing a confidential message from the President to the commander-in-chief in the field, and responsible to no superior officer until he reached General Scott. There is no detailed record of his route, but since he wrote to his parents from Cincinnati and Louisville we know that he traveled by way of the Ohio and Mississippi rivers to New Orleans.[23] Apparently he reached the Ohio River by way of Pittsburgh—a long journey by rail, canal, and stage coach, for the Pennsylvania Railroad had not yet reached the Ohio Valley. Hard as the trip must have been, it did not satisfy Kane's zest for adventure, and on the way to Pittsburgh he enlivened it by a dangerous diversion—a ride on the cow catcher of the locomotive. He wrote to a friend in Philadelphia a jocular account of this performance: "Never had I such a twenty miles of one excluding absorbing topic, how to hold on! . . . I tore the heel from my boot, and smashed my thumb on the drag chain;—but I held on; and after it was all over, sneaked on to the cars, much relieved—a wiser and a better man."[24]

A steamboat of the Cincinnati-Pittsburgh Packet Line no doubt took Kane to Cincinnati, whence he wrote to his mother on November 11. From Cincinnati another river boat took him to Louisville, where he could take a through steamer to New Orleans. At Louisville, in preparation for the overland journey from Vera Cruz to Scott's headquarters at Mexico City, he bought a horse, a full-blooded gray gelding, the finest steed, an army officer said later, that he had ever seen in Mexico. The two, man and beast, were to be constant companions for the next three months, and almost to die together, at the climax of their hectic journey. But the trip down the lower Ohio and the Mississippi was uneventful, and they disembarked on the levee at New Orleans on November 21. From Louisville, on November 12, Kane had at last written to his father, explaining and defending his unannounced departure from Philadelphia eighteen days before.

> My sudden departure will, I fear, tell against me in your own estimation, although I cannot help hoping that, with the Mrs. Grundies at large it may be widely different. I cannot help remembering our conversations in which fickleness and instability were the attributed motives, and your fears that the community would think likewise. But in sober truth, Father mine, never did a man leave a comfortable and happy home urged by more direct and impulsive instigations of propriety. . . . Content yourself therefore with the fact that the Philadelphia Kane family is represented in the war.

Kane sailed for Vera Cruz on the U.S. ship *Fashion,* on November 23, 1847, with a mixed company of soldiers and civilians, and a cargo of military supplies, including a deckload of cavalry horses. It must have been a slow voyage if the dates we are given are correct. The ship encountered a severe storm and was so near to foundering that the horses had to be backed overboard. Kane was about to jettison his own prized mount but some army officers restrained him. The ship drove on before the gale with stove-in bulwarks. Her pumps were choked, and all hands worked desperately below decks, baling the water out with camp kettles. Miraculously, the ship was blown between the reefs of Vera Cruz harbor and made port without loss of human life. She docked on or about January 1, 1848. Next day Kane rode out of the city with a party of army officers going to overtake their regiments on the route to the interior. With them he reached the Castle of Perote, a stronghold firmly in possession of the United States Army.

Since no escort beyond Perote was immediately available, Kane stayed with an army surgeon there for a day or two, and then took the risk of continuing his journey with a scouting party officially known as the "spy company," consisting of 120 mounted men armed as lancers, most of them Mexican renegades—"skinners, bandits, and traitors." The company was commanded by one Dominguez, himself a disaffected former Mexican soldier and, like many of his men, having a police record.[25] In spite of its dubious makeup the spy company served General Scott's army faithfully, though after the fashion of guerillas rather than of regulars, as Kane was soon to discover by bitter experience.

On January 6 the spy company, with Kane near its head, was nearing Nopaluca, twenty-five miles from Puebla. Going over a rise in the road, they encountered a company of Mexican lancers with whom were several distinguished officers, notably Major General Torrejon, who had fought the Americans gallantly at Buena Vista ten months before, and Brigadier General Antonio Gaona, former Governor of Puebla, who was accompanied by his son, Major Gaona. A furious fight began at once. The spy company had the advantage of being on slightly higher ground. Kane, riding into the thick of it, came into hand-to-hand combat with young Major Gaona and his orderly. The latter struck Kane with his lance, causing a slight flesh wound, but Kane at the same moment slashed his saber across the major's chest, severing one of his intercostal arteries. All around them the men of the spy company were fighting the lancers with desperate courage. If taken prisoners they would be hanged as traitors. Several of the Mexican party were killed and others took flight, leaving their officers and their wounded as prisoners. The guerilla chieftain, Dominguez, unfortunately recognized old General Gaona, who had once ordered him publicly whipped for thievery. Regardless of the rules of war, Dominguez did not call off his men when they murderously attacked the high-ranking prisoners. Major Gaona, bleeding on the ground, in desperation called out to Kane to save his father. The doctor, attacked at this moment by some of the spy company, parried four saber cuts from these erstwhile allies, but he received a lance wound in the lower abdomen, and his horse, deeply penetrated by a lance below its shoulder, fell to the ground with its rider. Rising, Kane drew his pistol, frightened off his attackers, and saved the Mexican officers.

Major Gaona was still on the ground and growing weak from loss of blood. Kane, no longer a warrior but a surgeon, in spite of his own wound took his late enemy as a patient and with no other instruments than a table fork and a piece of packthread tied off the major's severed artery. The party then prepared to resume its march toward Puebla, which was held by the United States forces. The wounded were put on a Mexican cart. Kane, lifted into the saddle of his fallen horse, succeeded in getting it up and rode it a few miles until the exhausted beast fell once more. Kane himself, transferred to another horse, found that he could no longer ride and was helped into the cart with the other wounded men. His servant got the horse up again and forced it to struggle on. While trying to quench its thirst in a wayside pool, the poor creature slipped into the water and died. Kane, passing in the cart, had the grief of seeeing it there.

On reaching Puebla Kane was housed in army quarters, while the captured Mexican officers were held in the Governor's Palace, now U.S. headquarters. Kane had assumed that the two generals and the junior officers were his personal prisoners, but the U.S. Governor, Colonel Thomas Childs, made General Gaona's plight even more painful by ruling that they had been captured by Dominguez. To a U.S. officer, Albert G. Brackett, the general said, in tears, "I respect the Americans. They are a brave and magnanimous people, but I have been captured by that man, who is a thief and a robber. My honor is gone."[26] In 1848 soldiers could still afford to be chivalrous. General Gaona's prison in his home town was only a short distance from his luxurious mansion. Colonel Childs sent Major Gaona there to recuperate from his wound, and shortly thereafter paroled the general and sent him home as well.

The gratitude of the Mexican officers and their families to Kane was boundless. Someone at Puebla wrote home to the *Philadelphian* newspaper that the Gaonas, father and son, publicly declared to Colonel Childs that they owed their lives to Dr. Kane.[27] The general offered Kane the choice of his own stables to replace the dead horse. A *fiesta* in Kane's honor was being prepared, when he fell deathly ill, and a day or two later the Gaonas took him to their estate, where he lay in a coma for twelve days. "At the General's princely mansion," said the *Philadelphian*'s correspondent, "Dr. Kane was given the benefit of every comfort and luxury. The General and his distinguished lady and refined and accomplished daughters took upon themselves all the offices of menials, suffering the nursing and tending him to be shared only by the physicians, four of whom they had in waiting night and day." The Mexican doctors and an American army surgeon who saw Kane daily

Dr. Kane Wounded in Fight with Mexican Cavalry
From (anon.) *Kane, der Nordpolforscher* (Leipzig, 1869)

all diagnosed this illness as "congestive typhus fever."[28] Another American officer, W. W. H. Davis, who visited Kane during his convalescence, never forgot the idyllic scene he witnessed in the sickroom:

General Cushing, on whose staff I was serving & who had been appointed a member of the Military Commission to enquire into the Charges and Counter Charges of Generals Scott, Worth and Pillow, was ordered to proceed to Pueblo to meet the other members of the Commission. We left Mexico under the escort of a squadron of dragoons arriving there the third day. On learning the misfortune that had befallen Doctor Kane on his way up from Vera Cruz, the General invited me to accompany him to call on the Doctor. We were ushered into the drawing room and there was presented as beautiful a picture as I ever witnessed in war time. Dr. Kane was lying on a cot; on one side sat Senora Gaona, an elegant-looking matron of 40: on the other her daughter, a beautiful girl of 18, watching over the sick man, with the same tenderness and care they would have given a son and brother. General Gaona, a distinguished-looking man, joined his wife and daughter in expressions of gratitude for the timely interposition of the invalid, at the risk of his own life that saved the life of husband and father. There never was seen a more striking example wherein "Grim-visaged war hath smoothed its wrinkled front." After spending half an hour there we withdrew and returned to our quarters.[29]

Leaving Kane at Puebla, the spy company went on to Mexico City, 160 miles to the west. General Scott thus learned of the fight at Nopaluca, and heard that someone bearing a message for him was delayed at Puebla. It seems, however, that he did not know the identity of the messenger nor why he had not yet come to headquarters. Not unnaturally, Scott was anxious for news from Washington. In spite of his total military success he knew that his position as commander-in-chief was precarious. The administration's jealousy had been exacerbated by the disaffection of some of his senior officers, especially General Gideon J. Pillow, friend of President Polk, who had brought charges of maladministration against him. In a report to the War Department, January 12, 1848 (six days after the fight), Scott wrote

I have not had a line from any public office at Washington of a date later than October 26. The spy company has returned from Vera Cruz; but it seems that dispatches for me had been intrusted to a special messenger (I suppose from Washington) who, after a delay of many days at Perote, came up with the company to Puebla, where he again stopped and retained my letters. . . . The spy company had a very successful affair with a large party of the enemy, and captured some forty prisoners, including three generals.[30]

Kane was not well enough to travel to the capital until February 13, when he set out, traveling in a cart, in company with a military force of 2,000 men.

Meanwhile another messenger, Conrad F. Jackson, had left Washington January 13, bearing orders relieving Scott of his command and appointing General William O. Butler to succeed him. Jackson may have traveled from Puebla to Mexico City with the same detachment as Kane. At any rate he arrived at headquarters and delivered his dispatches to Scott on February 18. Kane's message to Scott was thus superseded, and if (as we must suppose) he arrived at the same time as Jackson or a day or two later, and if he carried out his orders to deliver it in person, it now meant nothing to Scott, who does not mention it in his *Memoirs*.

The army surgeons at headquarters promptly declared Kane unfit for further service. They ordered him to the United States for treatment of his unhealed lance wound, and sent him down to Vera Cruz in a four-horse ambulance guarded by thirty dragoons. Before taking ship he wrote to someone at home (probably his father) in the disheartened, self-conscious mood that so often followed his adventures when they ended in serious illness, that he was

> a broken-down man. My hair would be gray, but that I have no hair. My hopes would be small, but that I have no hopes. Expect never to see me again, and my luck may prevent you from being disappointed. . . . Perhaps the fact of having saved six lives may make me a more important person in your eyes. It was a dear bargain, but I do not regret it.[31]

It had indeed been a dear bargain. Kane's mission to General Scott had failed of its purpose. His pride in his brief career under arms was mingled with remorse, for the only enemies against whom he had drawn his sword had heaped coals of fire upon his head. He was left with a tired mind and a body still further weakened by fatigue and illness. But at last he had won what he had long craved and risked his life for, many times over—fame and public honors. The city of his birth was about to place a hero's laurels upon his weary head.

By the end of March, glowing accounts of Kane's exploit at Nopaluca and the report of his subsequent illness reached Philadelphia through letters from the front printed in the *Philadelphia Inquirer* and the *Pennsylvanian*.[32] The editor of the *Pennsylvanian*, deeply impressed, declared that "the remarkable adventure of our young friend Doctor Kane surpasses the wildest dreams of romance." Seventy citizens of Philadelphia ("the properly accredited representatives and exponents of its thoughts and feelings," says Elder) subscribed to the gift of a magnificent gold-sheathed ceremonial sword. Their letter of presentation was signed by Thomas Dunlap, a leading lawyer; by John M. Read, attorney-general of Pennsylvania; and (surely to Kane's special pleasure) by his teacher Dr. Nathaniel Chapman, professor of medi-

cine in the University of Pennsylvania and first president of the American Medical Association. "The eloquent gratitude of your prisoners," they wrote, "and the honorable approval of your superior, will be found in the archives of your country; and those who surround your own home in your native city claim to record their sense of your courage, conduct, and humanity in the memorial now offered."[33]

Not all Kane's fellow-citizens were ready, however, to appraise so highly the story of his adventures in Mexico. It sounded too much like grand opera—the exotic setting; the two noble-hearted young men, Kane and Gaona, once enemies, now united in friendship; the courtly old general and his gentle wife; even a high-born señorita ministering to the wounded hero. Kane should have brought her home a bride, to be the darling of Rensselaer. But even without a wedding march in the last act, could so romantic a drama really have been acted out in real life? Who, in fact, had seen it played? Contemporary newspaper accounts, written with war-time fervor, came solely at second hand from letters written by people who had not taken part in the fight at Nopaluca, and obviously reached the press through acquaintances of the Kane family. The only reports by any participant ever to be published were those of Kane himself in letters to Scott's successor, General William O. Butler, and to the Secretary of War, which were not written until later and were not made public at the time.[34] When Dr. William Elder, writing his biography of Kane ten years later, came to this episode, he was afraid that it would still be doubted. Anxious to prove its authenticity by official records, he relied chiefly on documents of the most unromantic kind, relating to Kane's claim for reimbursement for the loss of his valuable Kentucky horse. The letters that Elder thus gathered in the biography, together with the reports presented here, of other people who (unknown to Elder) met Kane and the Gaonas at Puebla, leave no doubt as to the general course of events at Nopaluca. That Kane behaved with chivalric courage is sufficiently attested by the gratitude of the Gaona family, freely expressed to several United States officers and recorded also in a courteous exchange of letters between the General and Colonel Childs, printed by Elder.

In return, Kane's parents were deeply grateful to the Gaonas, as shown by a letter written about March 4, 1848.[35]

Much honored Sir,
    The letters of our son Doctor Kane have apprised us how deeply we are indebted to you and to your admirable household. They have told us in glowing language that you met him an enemy on the battlefield,

and that your generous sympathy with a wounded stranger carried him to your house, watched at his bedside with parental assiduity, and saved his life. Your family has vied with you in these Christian offices.

You are yourself a father, Sir, and can understand that fullness of heart, which seeks in vain to express its gratitude in words for obligations like these. Possibly at some future time, when this unnatural war shall have ceased, and our two republics are restored to those relations of kindness which ought never to have been interrupted, some member of your family or some one of its friends, visiting Philadelphia, may enable us and all whose blood mingles with ours, to testify how constantly and fervently we bear upon our hearts the name of Gaona.

We are, Sir, most respectfully

the father and mother of your guest and friend

JKK

JDLK

After a summer of slow convalescence at home, Doctor Kane was once more ready for at least light navy service, and applied for a post at the Philadelphia Navy Yard, which however was denied him because he was still only an assistant surgeon. Next he thought of joining an expedition to the Pacific coast. President Polk entered in his diary for December 27, 1848, that

> Judge John K. Kane of Philadelphia called and spent half an hour. His object was to have his son, who is a surgeon in the Navy, ordered to accompany the Joint Commission of officers of the Army and Navy who are about to proceed to the coast of California and Oregon with a view to select suitable points for naval stations and for military defense.[36]

Nothing came of this proposal, and Kane, tired of waiting, finally applied for assignment to the store ship *Supply,* which was under orders to sail for Lisbon, Mediterranean ports, and Rio de Janeiro.[37] His departure was delayed and he had time to write several times from Norfolk, Virginia. A letter to his mother in February, 1849, reveals with surprising frankness a rift in the domestic affairs of the family at home. The younger Kanes seem to have been badly upset by what they considered their father's unfair allotment of their pocket money. With the superiority of an elder brother who has outgrown such annoyances, Kane sides with his brothers and sister. He writes of the "Kane driblet system" and even of the "detestable moral atmosphere" it created. Yet a few months later he could write gaily enough to his father, humorously complaining of navy life and like any discontented subaltern gibing at the "old fool commodore," John Drake Sloat, commandant of the Norfolk Navy Yard and by other accounts an excellent officer.[38]

*Supply* sailed on March 5, 1849. By the pilot boat, off Cape Henry, on March 8 Kane wrote to his father "somewhat heavy hearted and not sick save at the idea of this renewal of my objectless life-expending pilgrimage. Good bye all."[39] The ship had not been long at sea when Kane, as usual, began to suffer severely from seasickness. He must have reached a serious state of physical and mental depression when one night in April he was suddenly stricken with what he thought was tetanus.

> Suddenly, a sense of tightness, as if every flesh-fibre of my being was a fiddle-string and some hosts of devils were tuning me up, came over me. This lasted a fraction of a minute and was gone. Of these foretastes of Tophet I had four during the night . . . an utter, unqualified conviction of inevitable death. I penned a "god Bless You"—which as a specimen of calligraphy during a tetanic spasm, I enclose. . . . That done, I a second time bled myself and fainted, and according to the shore-doctors who saw me next morning, saved my life. I lost forty ounces of blood and took twenty-two grains of laudanum.[40]

There is no good reason to think this was genuine tetanus. It may have been tetany induced by loss of calcium following excessive vomiting during seasickness. In the following weeks he twice mentioned, in his correspondence, drinking milk as if it satisfied a special craving.

*Supply's* cruise was, as Kane expected, no more exciting than a trampship voyage.[41] She called at Gibraltar April 3, Spezzia (Greece) April 15, Port Mahon (Minorca) May 5, Rio de Janeiro July 1, at each place unloading or loading stores for U.S. naval vessels based on those ports. The only unusual events were that one day at sea the purser fell overboard and was picked up, and another day a Halifax schooner hailed *Supply* requesting medical assistance for her ailing captain. Kane boarded the vessel, took off the man, performed some sort of operation, and kept him aboard ship for postoperative care. The record of daily life on *Supply,* if generally dull, provides, however, a background for understanding Kane's later treatment of unruly sailors. Elder says that he detested the cruel discipline of the navy; on the other hand critics of his book *Arctic Explorations* accused him of harsh treatment of two members of his own expedition. What he saw aboard *Supply* was far worse. She was not a happy ship and her crew was a sorry lot. Each and every one of her eighteen seamen and three of her six petty officers were at one time or another during the seven months' cruise punished with the cat o' nine tails: tied to a stanchion and given six or twelve lashes across the bare buttocks, for various offenses—drunkenness, skulking, fighting, smuggling liquor aboard, insubordinate and mutinous behavior, or desertion (which we would call nowadays absence without leave). Three of them got "the cat" after each shore leave, four times during the cruise. One man was whipped three times and on another occasion (for trying to strike the captain and later threatening him on shore) was put in irons for three days until Kane for medical reasons advised his release. Navy regulations required the surgeon to attend these degrading and often bloody whippings. Aboard *United States* Kane had seen a man given fifty lashes after a court-martial. Rough as his own discipline was at times on his Arctic expedition, at least he had no cat o' nine tails aboard his ship.

By the time the *Supply* reached Rio, on July 1, Kane was feeling much better. Early in September the cruise ended at Norfolk, and he was soon recuperating once more at home. His next assignment was to the surveying steamer *Walker,* bound to Mobile Bay on coastguard service. On her way she must have stopped at Charleston, South Carolina, for Kane, evidently exasperated by the dullness of life aboard a small vessel on a routine cruise, wrote on January 16, 1850 from the Charleston Hotel a letter to his mother in which he poured out with humorous exaggeration his yearning for desperate adventure:

> My dearest Mother,
> Never before have little things formed so equilibrium-disturbing an aggregate, never have trifles so taxed a man used to the greater vicissitudes of life.
> Could the Charleston Hotel burst out into a comforting conflagration and I descend from the fifth story with sixteen small children bundled into an entry carpet, or could even the Cape Fear Steamboat boiler have burst opposite the Lighthouse so as to have enabled me pleasantly to float ashore on a tea box—with fat Mrs. Colonel Huger tied to my neckcloth in a state of strangulation—there would have been something to relieve the littleness and undo the miserable tediousness of small adventures under which most hopelessly and without comfort I groan.[42]

Was this nonsense a warning to his mother of new adventures to come? He was in fact already dreaming of new journeys far beyond anything he had already experienced, in lonelier seas, on more desolate shores, amid unpredictable dangers, in a quest so romantic and so bold that it promised only death or worldwide fame. All the world knew that Sir John Franklin, a gallant English naval officer, was lost in Arctic waters, somewhere north and west of Baffin Land, with two ships manned by 129 officers and men. They had not been heard from since August 1845. Several British vessels had gone in search of him without result. Other expeditions were planned. There was

Elisha Kent Kane at Twenty-Seven
From a daguerreotype, *Century Magazine* N.S. 34 (1898):482

talk in 1849 of an American party. Kane himself must have told friends that he would like to join such a cruise, for in December, 1849, he received a letter from a Baltimore acquaintance offering to go with him. When he wrote to his mother so gleefully on January 16, 1850, about his craving for wild adventures, he must have read in newspapers picked up at Charleston that, on January 4, President Zachary Taylor had recommended to Congress that the United States government should send an expedition to Arctic waters to search for Sir John Franklin and his companions. The American squadron would need surgeons on its two ships. Whether or not Kane made up his mind at once to volunteer, he had time to think about it while at sea after leaving Charleston. *Walker* arrived at Southwest Pass, Louisiana, on February 24, 1850, then turned eastward again. On March 20 Kane posted a letter to the Secretary of the Navy, offering himself for the Arctic expedition, which was still awaiting authorization by Congress. Apparently he did not at once tell his parents about this commitment. From somewhere on the shore of Mobile Bay he wrote home on May 1 an almost maudlin rhapsody on the peaceful charms of southern life; one would think that he had happily resigned himself to semitropical indolence.[43] Actually he was impatiently awaiting word from Washington. On May 12 a telegram arrived, detaching him from the Coast Survey and ordering him to proceed at once to New York for duty with the Arctic Expedition.

Before we follow this reckless young physician upon the last and greatest adventures of his life, let us review his character and qualifications. Thirty years of age, small of stature, lithe and muscular but handicapped by a recurrent disease, rheumatic fever, that had several times incapacitated him for weeks at a stretch. Eldest son of a well-placed family; well educated, fond of literature, able to write clear and vigorous, even poetic, English; a lover of nature and natural beauty, a gifted scientific observer, a skilled draftsman, a good shot. At times almost a prig, inclined to patronize and gravely counsel juniors of his own family and class on manners; quick-tempered, critical of discourtesy and disloyalty wherever, whenever evinced. Devoted to his mother; ambivalent toward a dominant father whom he admired and at heart loved. Schooled in the formal courtesies of his age; gracious to faithful underlings, friendly with his equals, at ease with statesmen and men of affairs. Except for a few intervals between cruises, his social life had been that of a man among men. Avoiding any commitment to the two women who loved him, he had declared to friends that his precarious health forbade him to offer himself in marriage. Yet even in full manhood he was boyishly romantic, craving heroic adventure in defiance of recurring illness, aiming at greatness to be won in a lifetime he expected to be brief. We see a little farther into his hopes and dreams when we recall that his favorite poet was his contemporary, Alfred Tennyson—young Tennyson of *The Lady of Shalott,* whose chosen knight rode past her bower with no thought but the quest of noble deeds; Tennyson whose arch-adventurer Ulysses resolved at last to sail beyond the sunset till he die.

# 5

# The Search for Sir John Franklin

DOCTOR KANE was now about to begin his own adventurous part in an international drama of Arctic exploration, fraught with mystery, heroism, and tragedy. This was a turning point in his life. Heretofore his travels had been those of an eager, restless, scientifically curious young man. Henceforth he was to follow with mature devotion what he took to be a dual call of humanity and science. To understand how he was first gripped by Sir John Franklin's disappearance and then by the geographical problems it raised, we must see the whole pattern of these mysteries as they presented themselves to Kane when he volunteered for Arctic service and during his first northern voyage in 1850–51, against its background of Arctic history and geographical research, international rivalry, national politics, private philanthropy, a wife's undying hope, and the selfless courage of a thousand seamen.

Sir John Franklin was sent out by the British Admiralty to seek a northwest passage to the Pacific Ocean. His two vessels—his flagship H.M.S. *Erebus*, Captain James Fitzjames, R.N., and her companion H.M.S. *Terror*, Captain Francis R. M. Crozier, R.N.—sailed from London May 26, 1845. They were last seen by an English whaler on July 22 of that year, moored to an iceberg in Baffin Bay in longitude 75°10′ W., latitude 66°13′ N., awaiting an opening in the floes through which they might reach the western side of the bay.

Franklin's quest was an old one, renewed in the Romantic spirit of the early Victorian age. The dream of a northern sea route from Europe to India began almost as soon as Columbus and his sixteenth-century successors established the existence of an American continent barring the way in temperate latitudes. William Baffin, seeking such a route in 1616 for the Muscovy

71

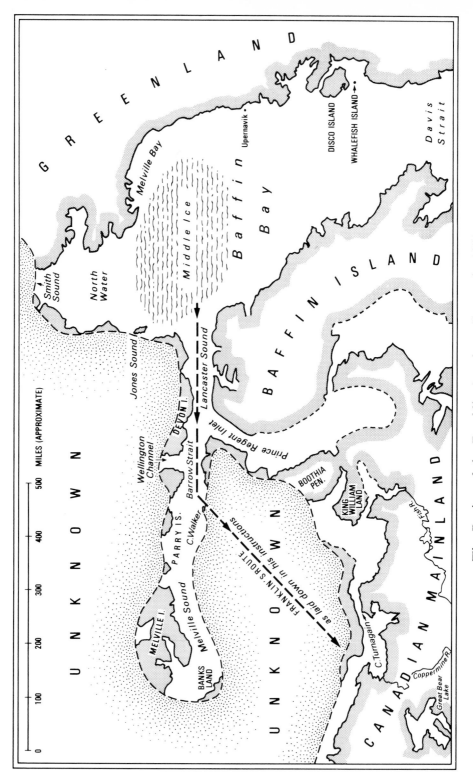

The Region of the Franklin Search, as Known in 1850

Modified from R. J. Cyriax, *Sir John Franklin's Last Arctic Expedition* (London: Methuen, 1939)

Company, pointed the way by discovering the great bay that now bears his name. Obviously the route from Europe must lead past southern Greenland through Baffin Bay and thence by some exit from its waters to the west. Baffin in fact found two apparent westward openings, which he named Lancaster Sound and Jones Sound, and still another, Smith Sound, leading northward at the head of the bay. But he could not work his ship far into these ice-bound channels, and for two hundred years they remained unexplored. In 1818, however, Sir John Ross, resuming the search for a northwest passage, entered Lancaster Sound but soon found it blocked, as he thought, by a range of mountains. The following year his lieutenant, William Edward Parry, who did not believe in the mountains, returned under orders to try to get through Lancaster Sound and if possible to reach Bering Strait. It was achievement enough that he did make his way through the corridor formed by Lancaster Sound and Barrow Strait into Viscount Melville Sound. Parry discovered and named the land masses which form the northern side of the corridor beyond North Devon—Cornwallis, Bathurst, and Melville Islands— saw Banks Island to the southwest of Melville, and noted the straits opening to the north between the islands, one of which, Wellington Channel between Devon and Cornwallis islands, was later to be the scene of discoveries and calamities in which Dr. Kane was deeply involved.

While Parry was in Arctic waters, another British naval officer, John Franklin, was in 1819 appointed to lead an overland expedition to explore the coast of the North American mainland. At that time the only known points on the coast were the mouth of the Coppermine River, northwest of Hudson Bay, and the mouth of the Mackenzie River, far to the west. On this expedition, in spite of terrible hardships, Franklin and his surgeon-naturalist John Richardson in 1820–21 reached and descended the Coppermine and by boat traced the shoreline eastward for 555 miles. On another journey in 1826 Franklin worked westward from the Mackenzie River to the north coast of Alaska, while Richardson went eastward as far as the Coppermine. Thus the only unexplored gap in the passage from Atlantic to Pacific waters was that of 400 or 500 miles between Parry's farthest west and the farthest eastern point reached by Franklin and Richardson. Between these two points was an unknown area presumably filled with barren islands and ice-clogged channels.

From 1827 to 1834 Franklin was employed in less rugged duties, as commander of a frigate on the Mediterranean station, and as Governor of Tasmania. In 1845, however, he sailed again for the Arctic. The remarkable voyage of Sir James Ross (nephew of Sir John Ross) to the Antarctic in 1839–43 in H.M.S *Erebus* and H.M.S. *Terror* had rekindled interest in Polar travel and revived the dream of a northwest passage. Meanwhile Franklin's

Sir John Franklin and His Captains
From *Illustrated London News,* September 13, 1851
(Crozier, *Terror,* left; Fitzjames, *Erebus,* right)

former companion George Back and other explorers had mapped almost the whole northern coastline of America eastward of Franklin's Point Turnagain. A naval expedition was planned, to find a way southward from Parry's islands to the known waters off the Canadian shore. Franklin, though nearing sixty years of age, claimed the command as the senior British officer with Arctic experience then in England. Next under him was Francis R.M. Crozier, who had been with Parry on three Arctic voyages, and with James Ross to Baffin Bay and to the Antarctic. Other officers and the crews were the pick of the Royal Navy.[1]

The two now famous ships *Erebus* and *Terror*[2] were overhauled, further strengthened, lavishly equipped, and provisioned for three years. So confident were the officers that some of them took their personal silver plate along for use in the officers' mess. H.M.S. *Terror* had a library of 1,200 volumes. The voyage at first proceeded smoothly. Officers and crew, in their last letters sent back from Greenland, told of a safe and pleasant crossing of the Atlantic and high expectations for the passage across Baffin Bay to Lancaster Sound.

Franklin proceeded under definite instructions from the Admiralty which were in complete accord with his own ideas. He was to enter Lancaster Sound, continue into Barrow Strait and if possible push to the westward without loss of time, not stopping to examine any openings to the northward, until he reached the longitude of Cape Walker. Thence he was to attempt to penetrate to the south and west, and then to pursue as direct a course for Bering Strait as circumstances permitted. If this route were blocked by ice or land masses he might try to pass directly westward from Barrow Strait by way of Melville Island. If this failed he was to turn back and in his second summer enter Wellington Channel and attempt a passage around Cornwallis Island.

Franklin of course would have no way to inform the Admiralty which of these three routes he actually took, unless he got far enough south to make contact with men of the Hudson's Bay Company or chanced to meet Eskimos who would get word to some outpost of civilization. Following the usual custom of Arctic explorers, he was to build cairns on conspicuous headlands and leave in them written records of his progress.

No word of any kind came back from the expedition. When more than two years had passed by, the search began in all three regions to which Franklin, according to his instructions, might have penetrated. In case he had reached the Beaufort Sea west of Melville Island, the Admiralty early in 1848 hopefully ordered two vessels, then in the northern Pacific Ocean, to pass through Bering Strait and look for *Erebus* and *Terror* along the northern coast of Alaska and the Canadian mainland. Late in March, Sir John Richardson and John Rae of the Hudson's Bay Company left London for New York and Montreal to begin a journey through the Canadian wilds with instructions to search the coast from the Mackenzie River to the Coppermine. Third—and this is the only aspect of the search with which we are to be concerned in connection with Dr. Kane's voyages—the experienced explorer Sir James Ross, recently knighted for his Antarctic achievement, with two ships, *Enterprise* and *Investigator,* followed Franklin's outbound route in hope of finding clues to the course he had pursued toward Cape Walker and beyond. After successfully crossing Baffin Bay and entering Lancaster Sound, in the autumn of 1848 Ross's vessels were caught in the ice of the sound, and he had to winter there, losing seven men from malignant scurvy. His sledging parties, however, covered hundreds of miles of the rocky coast without finding any trace of Franklin's men. During the next summer drifting ice floes fortunately carried both ships back into Baffin Bay, whence they made their way home to England.

The return of Sir James Ross in 1849 after this unsuccessful effort and the lack of news from other quarters deeply stirred the English people and awoke their determination to renew the search. By January 1850, enormous efforts were under way. *Enterprise* and *Investigator* were sent out again, this time on the long voyage to Bering Strait with orders to meet there two vessels already in Pacific waters and try to reach if possible the mouth of the Mackenzie River. On the Atlantic side no less than four British expeditions took up the search by way of Lancaster Sound, two of them sent out by the Navy and two by private sponsors. For the Admiralty William Penny, an experienced whaling captain, sailed in April in the *Lady Franklin*, with a tender, *Sophia*. The Admiralty also fitted out a squadron of four vessels commanded by Captain Horatio Austin in *Resolute,* accompanied by *Assistance* (Captain E. Ommanney), *Intrepid* (Lieutenant Sherard Osborn), and *Pioneer* (Lieutenant J.B. Cator). These vessels left England in May.

The two private expeditions sprang, one from manly affection for the lost commander, the other from wifely devotion. Sir John Ross, the veteran Arctic traveler, at the age of seventy-three insisted upon going to seek his old friend Franklin. Collecting funds with some difficulty, partly from friends, partly from his private purse, Sir John organized a flotilla of three vessels, the yacht *Felix,* its tender *Mary,* and *North Star.* He too sailed in May. Lady Franklin, née Jane Griffith, a woman of great persistence and considerable private means, not only used the full force of public sympathy in her distress to persuade the British government and public to contribute to the search for her husband, but she also put her own money and that of a group of friends into equipping a vessel, *Prince Albert,* in which Captain Charles C. Forsyth set sail for Baffin Bay in June 1850.

Lady Franklin also began a compaign for American aid. On April 4, 1850, she wrote directly to President Zachary Taylor, asking for the sympathy of our people and such aid as the government could give, particularly by alerting American whalers to look for traces of Sir John's ships. The President sent her letter at once to his Secretary of State, John M. Clayton, who replied before the month was out. Although he made only a general promise that the administration would do what it could, the tone of his letter was so warmly sympathetic that when, early the next year, the correspondence finally reached the Senate, Clayton was accused of forcing the hand of Congress by implicitly promising an American expedition.[3]

Neither the White House nor the State Department took immediate action, beyond releasing the news of Lady Franklin's appeal so that the Baffin Bay whaling fleet might be alerted. As for an expedition, the President was advised that the United States Navy had no vessels suitable for heavy work in the ice. Moreover, there was not time to get an appropriation from Congress before late spring, when the search vessels must set out. Even if he requested it, there would be opposition to the expenditure of public money to search for men of a wealthy foreign country who anyway must have been dead for two or three years. On the other hand, appeals for government action were coming in; for example Silas Burrows, a New York ship owner and merchant, wrote to Secretary Clayton in June, 1849, urging an expedition to find Franklin.[4] After thinking the problem over for eight months, President Taylor on January 4, 1850, sent to Congress the correspondence with Lady Franklin, with a presidential message asking an appropriation for fitting out an American expedition.[5] It was the news of this step, printed in a Charleston newspaper, that told Dr. Elisha Kent Kane in his safe and dull berth with the coast guard, that more adventure might be afoot for him.

Pending action by Congress, which was bound to take weeks and maybe months, an influential private citizen, Henry Grinnell of New York, took the matter vigorously in hand. This high-minded and wealthy merchant felt deep concern for the lost explorer and his men. As a ship owner and as the son of a New Bedford sea captain he knew the perils of the sea. Entering into direct correspondence with Lady Franklin, Grinnell offered to buy at his own expense two ships and fit them out for the search if the navy would provide officers and crews, and supply the necessary provisions and scientific equipment. Urged on by Lady Franklin he had a petition to Congress printed and circulated, beginning in February 1850. This was presented to the Senate by Senator Henry Clay on April 5, and was followed by another petition from merchants and other citizens of Philadelphia. Both were referred to the Senate Committee on Naval Affairs.[6]

Meanwhile Grinnell was quietly conferring with navy people, particularly, we must assume, with Lieutenant Matthew Fontaine Maury, of the Naval Observatory and Hydrographic Office, later to be known as the founder of American oceanography. Maury's pioneering studies of the physical geography of the sea made him eagerly interested in Arctic exploration. He evidently helped to find a leader for the proposed expedition, for the first officer to whom the command was offered, Lieutenant C.R.P. Rodgers, had been attached to the Coast Survey, with which Maury's hydrographic work was closely associated; and the man who finally accepted the dangerous assignment, Lieutenant Edwin J. De Haven, was a member of Maury's staff at the time.

Combining a reputation for bold seamanship with some knowledge of oceanography, De Haven was thirty-four years old in 1850. After varied assignments at sea, he was with the Wilkes Expedition to the far southern seas, 1838–43. As acting master (i.e., junior lieutenant and navigation officer) of Wilkes's flagship *Vincennes,* he gained experience in handling a vessel under Antarctic conditions, when the ship was off the great ice barrier in January, 1840, in considerable difficulties with floating pack ice and icebergs.

Without waiting for Congress to authorize the Franklin search expedition, De Haven began at once to plan with Grinnell about procuring ships and with Maury about technical equipment. On March 14, in New York, he met Grinnell for the first time. Visiting shipyards together, they chose a stout new schooner of 91 tons and gave her over to ships' carpenters to strengthen her for buffeting against Arctic seas and ice. This was to be the smaller vessel of the squadron; rerigged as a hermaphrodite brig (brigantine) she became the *Rescue.* A larger brig of 144 tons, *Advance,* was purchased somewhat later. De Haven began also to work out lists of equipment and provisions, and all the details of fitting the two vessels for a year and possibly more. Grinnell wrote to Lady Franklin that he hoped the expedition would sail about the first of May.[7]

This was a bit optimistic. A joint resolution initiated in the House of Representatives did not reach the Senate until April 29.[8] It provided for accepting Grinnell's offer of the two vessels and directed the Secretary of the Navy to man them, to provision them for three years, and to lend such necessary nautical and scientific instruments as the navy could spare. On May 1 there was a long and sharp debate between some of the most famous of the Senate's leaders. Strange as it may seem today, the speakers divided along party lines, Whigs for and Democrats against the proposed expedition. Senator Henry Clay led for the resolution; Jefferson Davis was the principal opponent. Clay and his Whig followers, notably William H. Seward and Lewis Cass, argued their case on the obvious grounds of humanity, our friendship with Great Britain, and the acclaim to be won for our nation by American seamen if they should find Franklin's men alive or solve the manner of their disappearance. Against it the Democrats raised a variety of objections, partly prudential, partly intended to embarrass the Whig President and his Secretary of State. Some of the speeches were tinged with the spirit of "America first"; Senator Jefferson Davis thought that the expenditure of public money for a purpose "not national" might be unconstitutional. Senator King of New York and others felt that to accept ships from a private citizen would discredit our navy. Senator Foote of Michigan even suspected Henry Grinnell of trying to advertise his mercantile business. Foote and other Democratic senators asserted that President Taylor and his cabinet advisers had injudiciously committed themselves to the project and then left Congress to bear the responsibility for its adoption or rejection. After an eloquent discussion lasting much of the day, the Senate adopted the joint resolution by a vote of twenty-eight to sixteen.

De Haven was now assured of his command, although he still had to await official orders. On May 6 he sent to William Ballard Preston, Secretary of the Navy, his estimate of officers and men and a list of rations somewhat more ample, more varied, and more expensive than the regular navy rations, for which the daily allowance was twenty cents per man. He asked permission to buy special clothing for the men in place of "slop clothing" of navy issue. Above all he begged for prompt dispatch of formal instructions for the voyage. As yet, he told the Secretary, he was not even known officially as the commander. Maury, however, promptly began addressing De Haven by the courtesy title of "Commodore" and on May 15 sent him lists of instruments, both those that the Naval Observatory and Hydrographic Office could supply and others that De Haven, busy as he was, would have to purchase in New York. Maury wrote again the same day and the next, listing the scientific observations De Haven was to make—water and air temperatures, specimens of sea water and water from hailstones, bottom mud, fossils, etc. "Pack them well," he insisted to the harassed commodore.[9]

Official instructions for the conduct of De Haven's voyage were dated May 15, 1850, seven days before he sailed. Signed by the Secretary of the Navy, they were drawn up in close consultation with Maury.[10] It must be admitted that they reflected Maury's zeal for scientific investigation as much as the stated purpose of finding the lost men of Franklin's expedition. That the larger of De Haven's vessels was named *Advance,* the smaller one *Rescue,* was only a coincidence, of course, but a suggestive one. Plans for the search, however, were logically based on what was known and what could be conjectured about Franklin's movements after his ships were last seen in Baffin Bay almost five years before. Franklin, the reader will recall, was to cruise westward through the corridor of Lancaster Sound and Barrow Strait and thence if possible to proceed southward toward the Canadian mainland. If balked by ice from following that course and also from going directly westward, he was to go northward up Wellington Channel. De Haven was instructed to follow the same route as far as the entrance to Wellington Channel on the north and Cape Walker on the south side of Barrow Strait. Once in that region, De Haven was to use his own judgment, except that he was not to turn toward the Canadian mainland, for (as the instructions read) "Nearly the entire front of the continent has been scoured without finding any trace of the missing ships." If De Haven could not get into Barrow Strait he was to return to Baffin Bay and try the two more northerly openings (or supposed openings), namely Jones Sound and Smith Sound.

Thus far there was nothing peculiar about the navy's plan for the voyage. Similar considerations were guiding British parties that were heading for the same region that summer. But there was a special reason for the instruction to search only northward from Barrow Strait, a reason frankly based on a fantastic conjecture about the North Polar region, that beyond the icy barriers along the northern shores of Europe, America, and Asia there lies around the North Pole an open sea of relatively warm water free from ice. This hypothesis was not new.[11] It goes back to the sixteenth century when an English merchant, Robert Thorne, first suggested that a navigable route from Europe to the Pacific might lie across the North Pole. William Barents and Henry Hudson both believed in an Open Polar Sea, but the idea was contradicted by the experience of later seventeenth- and eighteenth-century whalers and explorers who found inpenetrable ice barriers in the latitude of 80°. In the nineteenth century, however, the hypothesis was revived when

Russian explorers found large areas of open water (called in their tongue *polynyas*) to the north of the icy margins of Spitzbergen. These were thought to be parts of an open sea. One of the first geographers to support the idea was Maury, in the back of whose mind it had been stirring for some years before the extensive explorations of the Franklin Search brought it to the front. The proposed Grinnell Expedition gave him a hope of seeing it tested by American explorers guided by his thinking. The arguments for this hypothesis—so difficult for us to appreciate now that the once unknown Arctic Ocean has been traversed by dog sledge, balloon, airplane and submarine—seemed reasonable. Not only Maury but also European oceanographers had deduced from studies of northern oceanic currents that somewhere to the far north there must be a region where the subsurface northward current comes to the surface and turns southward through Baffin Bay and the Greenland Sea. This could not happen in a region of solid ice. Beasts and fowls, moreover, had been observed migrating northward from Canada over the ice floes, presumably on an instinctive journey toward a more genial climate. Maury also adduced the fact that whales had been caught in North Pacific waters, in whose bodies were imbedded harpoons marked with the names of Baffin Bay whaling ships—a fact which seemed to prove the existence of ocean waters sufficiently ice-free to allow these air-breathing mammals to surface freely. Finally, extrapolation to the unknown circumpolar area of isothermal lines based on thermometer readings taken in sub-polar localities, suggested that the region of greatest cold is not at the Pole, but farther south, on the parallel of 80° north latitude.

Maury's hypothesis of the Open Polar Sea, first clearly set forth, perhaps, in the navy's instructions to De Haven, was not publicly stated until the appearance in 1855 of Maury's widely acclaimed book, *The Physical Geography of the Sea*,[12] in which he devoted a chapter to it. His ideas were, however, soon known by other oceanographers, of whom the most prominent was the German scientist, August Petermann, then in London, who based upon this concept his advice to later participants in the Franklin Search.

De Haven's official instructions thus reflected not only a reasonable deduction as to Franklin's whereabouts, but also an important conjecture of the leading American expert on oceanography. De Haven was a matter-of-fact seaman, to whom orders were orders, not a man to be enthused by a scientific hypothesis. But to Kane, the young navy doctor, who had volunteered to join the American expedition, the Open Polar Sea was to become a dream, a hope, a goal for years to come.

On Sunday, May 12, 1850, Dr. Kane was bathing in the warm waters of Mobile Bay, Alabama, when he was called to receive the telegram he had long been hoping for from the Navy Department, detaching him from the Coast Survey and ordering him to proceed immediately to the Brooklyn, N.Y., Navy Yard for duty with the Arctic expedition. Seven and a half days later he was in New York and in forty hours more was at sea on the *Advance*. To have made such a journey of thirteen hundred miles in a week was at that time a feat in itself, fatiguing enough to daunt a traveler much more robust than Kane. He must have left Mobile by the first available stagecoach on Sunday afternoon or Monday morning, on the thirty-six-hour journey over the high road to Montgomery. From that city to Cheraw, Alabama, terminus at the time of the railroad being pushed eastward to Atlanta, Georgia, he had a rail trip of thirty-five miles, taking three hours. From Cheraw to Atlanta was twenty-four hours, again by stagecoach; from Atlanta to Augusta, twelve hours by railroad connecting with another railroad for the three-hour trip to Charleston, South Carolina. Thence a steamboat took him to Wilmington, North Carolina, in sixteen hours. From Wilmington he traveled by train to Richmond, Virginia, in twenty-four hours; by another train from Richmond to Baltimore, Maryland, in ten and a half hours; and still another from Baltimore to Philadelphia in six more hours. Spending most of a day with his parents, first resting and then gathering equipment for the Arctic, he took a night train for the five-hour journey to New York City. The time thus spent in actual travel totaled 144 hours, a little more than six days. Allowing for the stopover in Philadelphia and the inevitable loss of time changing from stagecoach to railway to steamboat, Kane cannot have slept in a bed between May 12 or 13 and the early morning of May 19, except on the steamboat from Charleston to Wilmington. That he withstood this tedious, exhausting journey and joined his ship ready for duty speaks well for the state of his health at the time.[13]

Just when Dr. Kane had broken the news to his family that he had volunteered for the Arctic expedition is not clear, but at any rate he telegraphed Judge Kane, from somewhere along the way, to expect him in Philadelphia shortly. The judge was not happy about his son's new venture. Writing to his daughter Bessie, who was visiting friends in New York, he gave vent to his feelings like a good Democrat as well as an anxious parent:

> I cannot rejoice that he is going on this expedition; his motive is praiseworthy, but I think the project a wild one, and I fear inadequacy in the outfit. I wish most sincerely that Sir John Franklin was at home with his wife again, leading dog's lives together as they used to do,—or that Mr. Clayton had not been silly enough to write Lady F. his pretty letters of promises,—or that General Taylor had not been such a sneak as to avoid the responsibility of carrying them out or urging Congress to do so. But it is as it is and we must make the best of it:—

Oh! this Glory! when the cost is fully counted up, it is no such great specu-
lation after all.[14]

Elisha's arrival at Philadelphia in the small hours of Monday morning,
May 20, necessitated a hasty nocturnal migration of the Kane household from
suburban Rensselaer to the city house of Mrs. Kane's sister, Mrs. Robert M.
Patterson. A letter from Mrs. Kane to Bessie reveals a mother's feelings
about having an Arctic explorer in the family.

> I feel as if I had not yet waked from a hideous dream, and have been trying
> to shake off thought by house keeping bustle, but still a heavy weight oppresses
> me, and I feel as if Elisha had parted with us for an interminable period, per-
> haps forever.
>
> On Sunday night I went off to prepare for bed, leaving your father and Tom
> chatting in the office:— Just as I stepped into bed they came over to my room
> to consult the State House clock, finding it was considerably after ten they
> concluded to retire themselves, when the dogs commenced such an uproar that
> Tom raised the window, to find—Mr. Field was on the piazza, "Come down I
> have a telegram from Elisha." We were summoned to town, dear Aunt Patter-
> son had made arrangements to receive us. Elisha would be in by the 3 o'clock
> train from Baltimore and probably start for New York at 9.
>
> By this time Godfrey [coachman] was roused; it was near two before we were
> deposited at your Aunt's. By half-past Elisha was with us, and by 4 o'clock the
> beds and sofas received our wearied bodies. At six your Aunt and myself were
> ready to collect the various adjuncts to the heavy or rather hurried work before
> us. Before seven Elisha was called by previous arrangement, and was refreshing
> himself in a bath—and by seven we were all at the breakfast table—and Disco
> and Anthony engaged in the library overhauling E's trunk—throwing aside
> useless garments, replacing others and raising a pile of soiled clothes absolutely
> startling. Your Aunt, however, is never conquered by difficulties, her women
> were ordered to come to a pause in the family wash, and concentrate their ener-
> gies on E's apparel and they were ready in due time.
>
> Your father, Patterson, John & Willie started off on missions after polar
> articles, and Godfrey came with the carriage and I rode with Elisha (to be in
> his company) whilst he was on duty that required personal attendance. At noon
> Tom and a cab relieved Godfrey of the carriage, and by two Aunt's diningroom
> received our entire family and Cousin Mary.
>
> Your father and the boys saw him fairly off; and I am anxiously thinking of
> all belonging to this annoying business; wondering if Elisha found the provi-
> sions for the voyage full and complete, whether he was able with Tom's assist-
> ance to supply his own deficiencies in New York and a crowd of other equally
> disagreeable and saddening reflections fill my mind.[15]

Late in the day Elisha and his brother Tom boarded the train for New
York, where Elisha's last day ashore was as hectic as that in Philadelphia.

Around the expedition's rendezvous at the Astor House (provided rent-free by the management) there was great bustle of enthusiastic volunteer helpers. Dr. Kane was introduced to a group of ladies who were putting up fruit cakes in sealed tins, to enhance the expedition's rations. Kane's own last-minute preparations, made with Grinnell's personal assistance, were scarcely less amateurish. His brother Thomas had given him a magnificent robe of Utah wolfskins, a present from the Mormons for Thomas's services in 1846.[16] To this he added a stock of coarse woolen clothing. Professor Elias Loomis of New York University, mathematician and physicist, helped him choose a set of practical instruments for measuring temperature and geomagnetic force, but unfortunately these did not reach the Navy Yard in time to be put aboard the brig.

His shopping completed, Kane crossed the East River and reported for duty. The two little vessels of De Haven's squadron were lying at the dock, so small that only their masts showed above the overhanging edge of the wharf. Kane was startled to see how insignificant they looked in comparison with the line-of-battle ships and other large naval vessels close by. *Advance*, of 144 tons, was smaller than a present-day harbor tugboat; *Rescue*, 91 gross tons, looked scarcely big enough to accommodate her complement of seventeen men. The two brigs, their decks strewn with as yet unstowed supplies, had no look of naval trimness. "They seemed to me," Kane later wrote, "more like a couple of coasting schooners than a national squadron bound for a distant and perilous sea." But soon enough he learned that their small size, coupled with strong and heavy build, adapted them better for combating the ice than any vessels previously fitted out for the Arctic. Grinnell and De Haven had chosen them because they were specially built for hard duty. *Advance* had been used for transporting machinery. Grinnell had ordered her to be doubly sheathed with two-and-a-half-inch oak planking; her bows were shielded with sheet-iron strips, and the first seven feet of her hull from keelson up to the deck was solidly filled with timber. Within her hold extra beams, oaken knees, and shoring timbers were inserted wherever possible. Her rudder could in an emergency be easily unshipped and taken aboard. The decks were double-planked, with tarred felt between the two layers of wood, and the whole interior was lined with cork. The deck gear—winch, capstan, and windlass—was of the latest construction. *Rescue* had been similarly strengthened and equipped.

For these far-sighted precautions Grinnell and De Haven were responsible. As to general stores, living comforts, and such necessities as firearms, the vessels were ill provided. There was food enough for two years and more, but it was not sufficiently varied to ward off scurvy, the bane of all long sea voyages at that time; stoves for heating the men's quarters were antiquated and almost inaccessibly stowed; the ball-loading government-issue muskets were unsuited for hunting Arctic game. For these and other deficiencies the Navy Department was to blame, although it had ample excuse in the delays at the White House and in Congress that forced the navy to work in great haste. Judge Kane had been right when he feared that the expedition would not be adequately equipped.

About one o'clock on the afternoon of May 22, 1850, the two brigs cast off from the Navy Yard wharf and were towed to sea by a steam tugboat. A few privileged friends were on board as far as Sandy Hook. Henry Grinnell and his sons accompanied the squadron in his beautiful yacht, the *Washington,* built with the lines of a pilot boat. On the wharves of Manhattan crowds of people cheered the departing seamen, and below the Battery steamships and ferry boats blew final salutes. Off Sandy Hook, in a rough sea, *Advance* put her landsmen guests aboard an accompanying craft, and in the black windy night she and her consort were on their way to northern waters. Only *Washington,* somewhere near in the dark, would still be with them in the morning and for two days more to the New England coast, as a convoy of friendship and encouragement.

# 6

# The First U.S. Grinnell Expedition

KANE FOUND his fellow-officers competent and friendly. De Haven, commodore of the squadron and captain of *Advance*, was like Kane a Philadelphian, but the two had never met until Kane reported for duty aboard *Advance*. At first sight, De Haven (as he recalled later) doubted the little doctor's fitness for an Arctic voyage.[1] But Kane soon won his commander's confidence and a friendship sprang up between them that was never to be broken.

The other officers, all young men, like their commodore were to bear responsibilities far above those of their actual rank, had they been serving in a frigate or other large fighting ship. William H. Murdaugh, a passed midshipman, was first officer of *Advance* with the rank of acting master (equivalent to lieutenant, junior grade, today). Kane and he were already acquainted, for Murdaugh had been aboard the flagship *Brandywine* on her voyage to China with Commissioner Cushing's diplomatic mission. Midshipman William I. Lovell, second officer of *Advance*, seems to have been a quietly companionable man. Midshipman Samuel P. Griffin, serving as captain of *Rescue*, was to prove himself extremely able and efficient during the darkest hours of the cruise. Midshipman Robert P. Carter, his first officer, with the rank of acting master, was a Virginia aristocrat, one of the Carters of Shirley. Almost to the day of sailing he had expected to have the command of *Rescue*. He bore his disappointment silently and served loyally under Griffin, but throughout the voyage poured his feelings into a diary, in which he appears almost continually discontented and unhappy.[2] Benjamin Vreeland, surgeon of *Rescue*, took his M.D. at the College of Physicians and Surgeons of Columbia University in 1845, and was thus by three years Kane's junior in the medical profession.

The crews of the two vessels had been assembled, like the ship's stores, at the last moment. Not a man of them had been in far northern waters, and some hardly knew the ordinary duties of sea life. *Rescue* had a so-called steward who spoke only French but did not know how to cook; the bo'sun had to teach him what to do with his pots and pans. Some of the men were not physically fit. Kane informed the chief of the navy Bureau of Medicine and Surgery, Dr. Thomas Harris, by letter from the first Greenland port, that among the thirteen seamen aboard *Advance* one had tertiary syphilis, one was afflicted with recurrent epileptic attacks, another had a marked "strumous diathesis" (presumably tubercular adenitis), a fourth from some other cause was so unfit that he had to be sent home.[3] On *Rescue* one seaman was under Dr. Vreeland's care, too ill for duty at the time of Kane's report.

On the two tiny brigs not even the captains had cabins of their own. De Haven roomed with the two mates and the doctor in a cabin so small that there was barely room for the four bunks, four camp stools, four lockers and a folding table. "The officers lived in a truly republican manner," said an Englishman whose ship they met in Lancaster Sound three months later.[4] For the three line officers to be thus cooped up with the doctor, who was seasick most of the way to Greenland, must have been a severe test of their comradeship. Besides being seasick, Kane was miserably cold. His first entries in his diary, he tells us, were little else than a self-centered record of personal discomfort. The cabin and the crew's quarters were unheated, though the temperature was falling daily as the vessels made their northing. The stoves on which the men would have to depend for winter warmth were stowed so deeply in the holds that they could not be brought out and put to use. Aboard *Rescue* life in the officers' quarters was if anything even less comfortable. She was slower than *Advance* and rolled heavily. Her deck leaked into the cabin. Poor Midshipman Carter, damp, seasick, and unhappy, scrawled in his diary: "Oh what an ass I am for joining this business."

Nevertheless the two brigs had a good passage to Greenland. On June 7 Kane saw his first iceberg, off Cape Race, Newfoundland—"a great mass of whiteness floating in the sunshine . . . about twice as large as Girard College." On the night of the 9th, *Advance* struck a shelving iceberg, carrying away her jib-boom and martingale, but thanks to her solid bow she slid off smoothly into open water. On June 20 the Greenland coast loomed up, Sukkertoppen's peak rising above a foggy sea. On board *Advance,* Kane, who had evidently been thinking deeply about Franklin's disappearance, wrote a long letter to his father outlining his opinion that the lost explorers might still be alive. They could have escaped starvation, he thought; Franklin's ships, *Erebus* and *Terror,* were amply stocked with food, and, moreover, the animal life of the Arctic is so rich that the men should be able to support themselves by hunting, as indeed Sir John himself in his early travels, Dr. John Rae, and others had very nearly done. In this Kane was an early proponent of radical ideas rigorously tested in action seventy years later by Vilhjalmur Stefansson.[5] Judge Kane was pleased with the doctor's letter; by now he had reconciled himself to his son's joining the Grinnell Expedition. When in September the letter (brought from Greenland by a returning merchant ship) reached Philadelphia, the judge proudly read it at a meeting of the American Philosophical Society.[6]

On the night of June 24 the sun did not drop below the horizon. Next day *Advance* made harbor at the Whalefish Islands, just missing Horatio Austin's squadron, *Resolute* and *Assistance,* which had left only a day earlier for the region of search. Kane had been so badly run down by seasickness that De Haven feared he might not withstand further travel under the increasingly severe conditions they would soon face. He offered to send the doctor home, along with the sailor Kane had ordered to return, by a whaler that happened to be leaving for a United States port. But the doctor would not take his own medicine; he balked at his commanding officer's proposal, and De Haven gave in.[7] On shore Kane had opportunity for a bit of geologizing, botanizing, and anthropological study, when at De Haven's order he and Lovell went to Lively (Godhavn) on the neighboring island of Disco, to report to the Danish colonial official and to negotiate with the Eskimos for a stock of furs. *Rescue* having caught up with her speedier consort on the 27th, the two brigs sailed northward June 29 "through a crowd of noble icebergs" and on July 1 encountered field ice for the first time.

De Haven now faced the great problem of every skipper who took a ship into Baffin Bay: how to work his way past the "middle ice." In summer the middle part of the Bay is almost filled with a vast pack of floating ice interspersed with bergs, brought down by currents running southward from Smith, Jones, and Lancaster sounds. This pack is driven against the western shore of the bay, presumably by forces resulting in part from the earth's rotation. Thus a lane of relatively open water is left along the Greenland shore, through which ships may cruise northward into the great bight of Melville Bay and thence westward across Baffin Bay through a comparatively iceless region known as the North Water. To cross south of the middle ice, as the whalers sometimes did, would not give ready access to Lancaster Sound. Passage through the middle ice was dangerous when not impossible. Parry made it in 1819 but failed in 1824 after two months of waiting and effort. The North Water was, therefore, the preferred route, even though Melville

Bay offered by no means an easy passage into open water. The whalers, in fact, called part of it "the Devil's nip."

Skirting the Greenland coast, De Haven's squadron on July 7 met the great barrier of the middle pack. As it happened, he espied a large open passage leading westward as far as the eye could reach. Bold seaman that he was, he determined to chance it. What his two mates thought of this we do not know, but Kane opposed the venture, although as surgeon he was scarcely entitled to advise his commanding officer.[8] Evidently De Haven and Kane were by that time on brotherly terms. With a four-knot breeze the brigs sailed on through open water amid loose ice, *Advance* towing *Rescue* to avoid separation, until 5 P.M., when the ice began to close around them and they were caught fast. De Haven did his best to move them on by sending the men onto the ice with crowbars, boat hooks, ice anchors, and warping line, but after half the night's work at the winches the ice was solidly packed around both vessels. The position was latitude 74° 08′, longitude 59° 01′. Thus trapped well out in Baffin Bay they lost twenty-one valuable summer days. Occasional desperate efforts to warp the brigs forward never gained more than a few yards at a time. Climbing to the foretop Kane could see nothing but snow-covered ice with a few distant bergs, and fifty miles away a tall peak, the "Devil's Thumb," rising above the dark hills of western Greenland. On July 17 the crews held a sports meeting on the ice. Some of the officers, Kane among them, walked out in search of game. Kane busied himself also recording the birds and fishes he observed, and sketching icebergs.

To his diary Kane gave much time, for De Haven, no penman, had already turned over to him the role of historian of the voyage. Often he wrote at night behind the curtains of his bunk, while his fellow officers, exhausted with the hard work of warping the ship, were heavily asleep. In these lonely night hours his thoughts were much with his family at home. Although he was consciously assembling notes for a book, the readers he foresaw most clearly were his brothers, especially his beloved Tom. For them he dramatized his experiences and observations, often in familiar terms—*Advance*'s living quarters "about the same area as Father's library"; "an open water as wide as the Schuylkill at Gray's Ferry." When the book appeared, three years later, many of these homely comparisons had found their way into it, among Kane's vivid descriptions of icy seas in turmoil and his carefully-wrought notes on Arctic geology and wildlife, and the strange ways of the Greenland Eskimos.

The three weeks' imprisonment of *Advance* and *Rescue* in the ice of Baffin Bay ended suddenly on July 28. On the afternoon of that day the barometer fell sharply, the wind shifted and stiffened almost to a gale, and the floes broke apart brusquely, releasing the brigs from their floating prison. Setting their mainsails, they made their way eastward through the loosened pack for the inshore circuit of Melville Bay.

On August 7 *Rescue*'s men killed a polar bear and distributed fresh bear's meat steaks to both crews. Kane, ready as usual for an experiment, ate freely of the bear's liver, though he had read that the Eskimos and the whalers would not touch it for fear of poisoning. Several explorers had recorded serious illness and even death following a meal of bear's liver. Kane, however, suffered no ill effects whatever, and recommended it to his companions as a tasty dish. During the rest of the cruise they often ate it without harm. They were lucky; polar bears' livers are now known to concentrate exceedingly large amounts of vitamin A and are therefore often highly toxic.[9] Perhaps the bears of Baffin Bay in 1850–51 were starved for fresh, vitamin-containing diet as were the human wanderers in that barren waste.

De Haven's squadron worked its way safely northward beyond the middle ice and then westward across the North Water. On August 19 they were nearing the opening of Lancaster Sound, when two vessels overtook them—*Lady Franklin* and her small tender, *Sophia*, of William Penny's command. Exchanging news with the British officers, De Haven learned that Austin with two of his four vessels had gone to the northern end of Baffin Bay. Sir John Ross's supply ship *North Star* was somewhere in Lancaster Sound. On the 21st, *Advance* overtook the topsail schooner *Felix*, Sir John's own vessel. One of her officers shouted across the waves to De Haven, "You and I are ahead of them all." Sir John himself came on deck, a square-built old man, to Kane's medical eyes looking quite fit. Next afternoon Lady Franklin's *Prince Albert* came up, and her captain, Charles Forsyth, with his civilian aide William Parker Snow went aboard *Advance* for some hours. Kane made friends at once with the exuberant Snow, like himself a world traveler. We owe to Snow, in his book on *Prince Albert*'s voyage, an impression of Kane at this time:

> Of an exceedingly slim and apparently fragile form and make, and with features to all appearances far more suited to a genial clime, and to the comforts of a pleasant home, than to the roughness and hardships of an Arctic voyage, he was yet a very old traveller by sea and land. . . . A congeniality of sentiment and feeling brought us deep into personal conversation.

*Prince Albert*, a schooner no bigger than *Rescue*, followed the Americans westward into Barrow Strait. Snow, watching the Americans working *Advance* through streaming ice floes, greatly admired their bold seamanship:

> An officer was standing at the heel of the bowsprit, conning the ship and issuing his orders to the men at the wheel in that short, decisive, yet clear manner

which the helmsman at once understood and promptly obeyed. There was not a rag of canvas taken in, nor a moment's hesitation. The way was before them; the stream of ice had to be either gone through boldly or a long detour made; and despite the heaviness of the stream, they pushed the vessel through in her proper course. Two or three shocks, as she came in contact with some large pieces, were unheeded; and the moment the last block was past the bow, the officer sang out "Steady as she goes in her course"; and came aft as if nothing more than ordinary sailing had been going on.

Late on August 19 the two ships entered Lancaster Sound. *Rescue,* for once making faster progress than her consort, disappeared somewhere ahead, leaving *Advance* and *Prince Albert* to follow together. On August 25, passing Cape Riley, near the entrance of Wellington Channel into Barrow Strait, men of both the American and the British vessels noted two cairns on the cape. Landing, they found a canister containing a record left ten days before by Captain Ommanney, commanding *Assistance* and *Intrepid* of Austin's squadron. Ommanney's party had found traces of encampments on Cape Riley and also on Beechey Island (actually a peninsula) on the east side of

*Advance, Prince Albert,* and *Rescue* near the Devil's Thumb, Melville Bay
From P. L. Simmonds, *The Arctic Regions* (Auburn, N.Y., 1854)

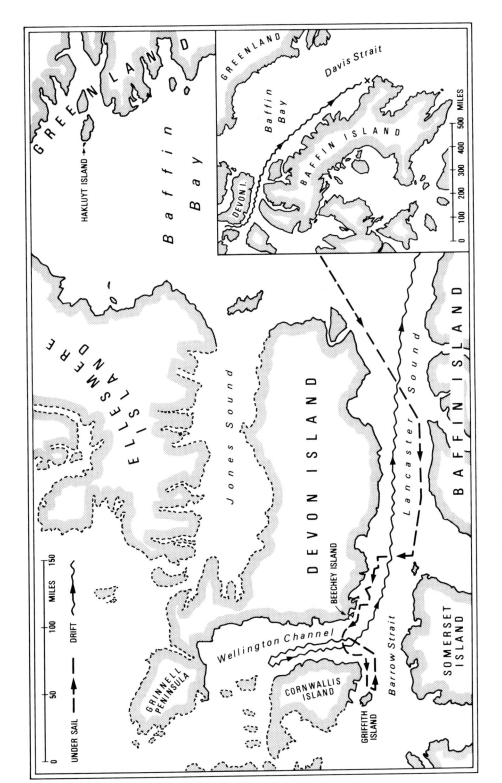

Route of First U. S. Grinnell Expedition, 1850–51

Map labels:

GREENLAND

HAKLUYT ISLAND

ELLESMERE

Baffin

Bay

Jones Sound

DEVON ISLAND

BEECHEY ISLAND

Wellington Channel

Lancaster Sound

Barrow Strait

BAFFIN ISLAND

SOMERSET ISLAND

GRINNELL PENINSULA

CORNWALLIS ISLAND

GRIFFITH ISLAND

UNDER SAIL

DRIFT

MILES

0    50    100    150

Inset map labels:

GREENLAND

Davis Strait

Baffin Bay

BAFFIN ISLAND

DEVON I.

MILES

0    100    200    300    400    500

Wellington Channel at its junction with Barrow Strait. Later De Haven learned that Griffin in *Rescue* had come upon Ommanney's vessels and had shared with him this discovery of definite signs of Franklin's presence five years before. This was the first clue to Franklin's movements after he was last seen by the whalers in Baffin Bay in 1845. Kane, going ashore with a party from *Advance,* inspected the deserted tent sites, discarded meat-tins, animal bones, and broken pieces of a boat that marked the temporary habitation of a detachment undoubtedly from one of Franklin's ships.

On August 27, 1850, the meeting of four expeditions in seven vessels set up a kind of explorer's club at the mouth of Wellington Channel. Ross and Penny had tried to pass westward through Barrow Strait but were stopped by dense ice and returned to shelter at Beechy Island, where they found De Haven's vessels moored. Ommanney with *Intrepid* and *Assistance* was caught fast in the pack, only fifteen miles to the west.

On this fateful day De Haven and Kane went ashore to see what Penny had found on Beechey Island. While they were talking with Penny, one of his men came running with the cry, "Graves, Captain Penny, graves! Franklin's winter quarters!" In great excitement De Haven, Penny, Commander Phillips of *Lady Franklin,* and a party from *Rescue* followed the messenger to the crest of the isthmus and there gazed upon three headboards marking the burial place of men from Franklin's ships, one of whom had died January 1, 1846; one April 3 of the same year; and a third on a date not indicated. Nearby were heaped stones indicating the sites of huts, an armorer's forge, and a carpenter's shop, and what appeared to have been an observatory. Innumerable fragments of canvas, wood, iron, and brass were scattered about the site, and more than six hundred empty meat tins had been carefully filled with pebbles, as if for use as ballast in small boats. Sledge tracks in the snow around the camp site gave evidence of reconnoitering parties. The place had evidently been deserted in a great hurry; one of the officers had left behind him a pair of cashmere gloves laid on a rock to dry and weighted down by stones. To the immense disappointment of the searchers, no trace of any written record could be found, nor anything else to tell them in what direction Sir John Franklin and his men had gone when, presumably in the spring of 1846, they had left their winter quarters for a destination that remained unknown.

In this state of uncertainty William Penny, practical man of action, outlined a program to which Sir John Ross, the senior officer present, and the other captains readily agreed. Penny would undertake the western search to Cape Walker and beyond; Ross would go to Prince Regent Inlet to recall the little *Prince Albert* from the exploration, now unnecessary, of that perilous region; and De Haven would turn northward through Wellington Channel.

Nothing could have pleased Kane better. Northward lay the way to Maury's open polar sea if such a sea existed; northward was in any case the way to unknown regions close to the Pole; and it might well be the way to Franklin. Kane, like every officer in the international flotilla at Beechey Island, had his own hypothesis as to Franklin's course. He believed that Franklin had left his winter quarters of 1845–46 in haste to take advantage of a sudden opening of the ice and had pressed to the north up Wellington Channel. We know now from records found later that this was not the case. Franklin had indeed gone up Wellington Channel, but before, not after, wintering at Beechey Island. In his first summer, 1845, he had attempted to pass westward beyond Cape Walker but was blocked by dense ice. Taking advantage of his alternative option to try Wellington Channel, he had managed to circumnavigate Cornwallis Island, returned to Barrow Strait, and settled down at Beechey Island for the winter. In the next summer, 1846, he sailed across the strait and down Peel Sound, only to become icebound off King William Island. Without knowledge of these facts, Kane's hypothesis was as good as any. It was to rule his thinking for five years to come, and to determine his route when in 1853 he led his own expedition toward the Pole, a thousand miles from the region where Franklin had died and his men had gone on to their dreadful end.

On the morning after the graves were found, Austin's flagship *Resolute* was pushed by drift ice into the same cove in which the other ships were moored. His steam tender *Pioneer* was also in sight, grounded off the point of Beechey Island. Thus seven of the search vessels were now within hailing distance, with Ommanney's squadron, *Assistance* and *Intrepid,* not far off to the westward. Commodore Austin aptly named the little harbor "Union Bay." Kane called on Sir John Ross aboard *Felix* and enjoyed a long talk with that veteran of three Arctic voyages. Sir John thought that Franklin had probably gotten through to the west. Next visiting *Resolute,* Kane was struck with admiration of the British vessels—their perfect organization and above all their efficient stoves and warm clothing. "In comparison with them," he wrote in his journal, "we have nothing, absolutely nothing."

*Advance* and *Rescue* now began to work across Wellington Channel to the eastern shore of Cornwallis Island, which they reached on September 5. On the way, Kane shot his first polar bear with a flintlock rifle, the best that *Advance* could offer. He took an oar in the boat that went off to pick up the carcass—hard work, rowing through broken ice. Evidently he was in far better health than he had been ten weeks before when De Haven would have sent him home. Next morning he skinned the bear, a heavy task because the creature was eight feet eight inches from tip to tip, and weighed about 1,600 pounds. When Kane returned to Philadelphia, he gave the skin to the Academy of Natural Sciences.

While De Haven's squadron was temporarily delayed by pack ice off Cornwallis Island, Austin's and Penny's vessels passed him going westward, but on September 10 *Resolute, Intrepid, Pioneer, Lady Franklin, Sophia, Advance,* and *Rescue* were all together once more, moored to land-fast ice near Griffith's Island at the southwest corner of Cornwallis Island.[10] A violent storm on the 12th periled all the ships. *Rescue* parted her cable and was carried out to sea. The thermometer dropped to 8° Fahrenheit. *Advance's* shivering men enviously watched the smoke curling from cabin stoves on the English vessels, but their own ship was still without heat. That night the ice broke up, freeing the ships, but De Haven, still quite properly concerned about the danger of being frozen in, decided to start for home. First, however, he had to find his consort, missing overnight. On the 13th, *Rescue* was discovered lying safely under the lee of Griffith's Island, but with her rudder post badly split. De Haven asked Griffin's opinion, as commander of *Rescue,* whether a return to the United States was advisable, and received in writing a strong recommendation to return.[11] Taking *Rescue* in tow, *Advance* struggled eastward. Two days later the ice again closed around the two brigs and they were helplessly locked in. A strong current running northward carried them, unwilling and alarmed, along the western shore of Wellington Channel into unknown northern reaches. In his journal, Kane graphically described

> the wild, but scarcely varied incidents of our continued drift through Wellington Channel . . . the ice-tables, now broken up into tumbling masses, and piling themselves in angry confusion against our sides, now fixed in chaotic disarray by the fields of new ice that imbedded them in a single night—again, perhaps, opening in treacherous pools, only to close round us with a force that threatened to grind our brigs to powder.

There were no more signs of animal life, and the temperature steadily fell. At Kane's urging De Haven had the hold opened and got out a lard lamp which brought the thermometer in the officers' cabin up to 44°. The northward drift carried *Advance* onward past unknown headlands for seventeen days.

Taking the discoverer's privilege, De Haven gave the names of his patrons and his officers to various features of the landscape—Maury Channel, Griffin Inlet, Murdaugh's Island. In turn the officers placed De Haven's name on a cape on Cornwallis Island. On September 22, 1850, from latitude 75° 24′ 21″, a new land of great extent and considerable altitude was seen stretching across the northern end of Wellington Channel from northwest to north-

northeast. This land, the most important discovery of the American expedition, De Haven named after Henry Grinnell.

With a dozen search vessels in the region that summer and the next, new islands, headlands, bays, sounds, and channels were being named right and left. Unfortunately sometimes two explorers, ignorant of each other's routes, gave different names to the same geographical feature. This happened in the case of De Haven's Grinnell Land. Late in 1851, after Penny and Ommanney had returned to England, a map published there on the basis of Admiralty reports called the new land "Albert Land," erroneously stating that it had been seen by Ommanney on August 26, 1850, the birthday of Queen Victoria's consort, thirty-four days before De Haven saw it. A perfectly correct additional statement that one of Penny's officers actually landed on that previously unknown shore in May 1851, of course did not affect De Haven's priority. Because the American expedition had little more to report, in the way of geographical discovery, than this new land, the English claim irritated American geographers.[12] Kane devoted more than seven pages of his published narrative to defense of De Haven's priority, closing, however, with a warm tribute to the noble character of his British friends of the Arctic, and to the honorable gentlemen of the British Admiralty, whom he did not blame for the error or officiousness of a cartographer. In fact, the Admiralty later handsomely acknowledged the American discovery. British as well as American maps have ever since kept the name of "Grinnell Peninsula" for this land, since found to be a northwesterly extension of Devon Island. But the episode rankled in Kane's mind until he himself could without any question of priority attach Grinnell's name to a still greater discovery of his own.

At the end of September 1850, both brigs, still trapped in Wellington Channel, were barely moving through tumbling masses of ice, which at times heaved them bodily from the water and held them half-careened on a mound of tilted blocks. In near-zero weather there was still no heating of the always damp cabins except by the lard lamps. Stoves were still so deeply stowed in the hold that they could only have been found by putting other stowage on the shore, which could not be reached, or on the still treacherous ice. On the first day of October, however, the brigs appeared to be finally caught in firm ice, and the crews began to "break hold" in preparation for wintering. The men took down the sails from the spars and stacked them under cover on deck, put the boats and five tons of coal on the ice, and sent a party ashore to establish a cache of provisions. After all this labor, that very afternoon the ice suddenly broke up with terrifying speed, and the exhausted men had to undo their work. All hands of both brigs, including the two surgeons and even the members of the land party, returning cold and hungry, had to turn to in this grave emergency. Everything was gotten back aboard the vessels except a ton or two of coal.

Following this break-up, unexpected so late in the season, northward movement of the ice gave way to a southward drift. The temperature fell still further. The stoves, fortunately, had been freed when the stores were moved, and on the 19th they were set up in both brigs, to the great satisfaction of the thoroughly chilled crews. By mid-October the brigs had drifted almost down to the mouth of Wellington Channel, and were surrounded by dense ice. Kane, in better health than some of the other officers, and not so much needed in nautical emergencies, volunteered to lead a party ashore to Beechey Island, where Sir John Ross's twelve-ton tender *Mary* was wintering as an emergency base. Tumbling ice made the trip impossible. Facing a winter in the ice, out of communication with the other search parties, De Haven had a tentlike housing built over *Advance*'s deck. The officers' cabin and the men's quarters were thrown together by removing a bulkhead, and all hands lived together in this almost airtight, damp, smelly space. For recreation the officers walked and hunted on the ice whenever the pack was solid enough; aboard ship they read or played chess. Kane, said Robert Carter in his diary, was the best chess player aboard. He entertained himself, and no doubt edified the men, by giving evening lectures on scientific topics—the atmosphere, the workings of the barometer, etc. On Sundays the captain regularly held divine service and read the naval *Rules and Regulations* as if *Advance* were a ship of the line on routine sea duty.

On November 9 the sun did not appear above the horizon. Later that month the two brigs, close together in a great drifting floe, were clearly moving eastward down Barrow Strait toward Baffin Bay. The first weeks of December were hazardous in the extreme. Kane wrote in his journal that "the Grinnell Expedition is as likely to be searched for hereafter as to search." *Rescue* was so badly crippled by the ice that De Haven had to take her men aboard *Advance*, packing thirty-two human bodies into the already crowded and dank living space. *Rescue*'s captain, Griffin, acting as executive officer of both brigs, began to drill the crews for a possible abandonment of the vessels; food and stores were packed for a march over the ice, and a party of officers and men tested these preparations by spending the night in tents on the floe at −27° Fahrenheit.

As Christmas approached, Dr. Kane noted signs of deteriorating health in the men. Their faces were bleached to a waxlike pallor, and their eyes were sunken. Some of them complained of shortness of breath. Some developed cravings for strange foods such as frozen ham fat and sauerkraut swimming in olive oil. At night they dreamed of luscious fresh foods and awoke to face another day on salt pork and stale potatoes. Tempers were getting short.

By December 21 Kane began to see definite signs of scurvy among the men. Eight of them had sore, swollen gums. One man came down with pneumonia, but fortunately recovered. The two crews observed Christmas Eve with a special dinner, at which Canot the steward produced such delicacies as he could command and a glass of wine for each man. There was speechmaking with labored efforts at gaiety and a play staged at a temperature, indoors, of 4° above zero. Next morning all hands joined in a footrace on the ice, in midwinter darkness, but all the officers except Griffin were exhausted by the exertion. Lovell, the strongest man among them, collapsed in a faint. More signs of scurvy appeared. "Strong men pant for breath upon climbing a ladder," wrote Kane in his journal, "and an indolence akin to apathy seems to be creeping over us."

On the 28th the drifting vessels were carried out of Lancaster Sound into Baffin Bay, moving at the rate of five miles a day. There was another effort to be jolly on New Year's Day, 1851—a plum pudding and a bottle of wine— "but there was no joy in our merriment; we were weary of the night." Yet twilight was returning, and every day at meridian hour land could be dimly discerned along the distant shore. Perils continued. On the night of January 13 widespread cracks in the ice endangered both vessels; all hands were on deck from one A.M. until half-past six, with shoulder harness and bedding strapped on their shoulders, sledges, and their one rubber boat ready for abandoning the ship in case she was crushed by the ice.

De Haven had succumbed to scurvy, and was so ill that Dr. Kane and Dr. Vreeland feared he might die. Griffin, admirably calm and clear-headed, was temporarily in command, supervising the emergency measures, though he, like every man aboard, was complaining of sore gums, joint pains, loss of appetite and general debility. Kane, though relatively well, found himself so weak that merely to carry his carbine was a burden, and he almost gave way to the depression characteristic of this miserable disease. When the sun at last came above the horizon at midday, the men gathered to greet its blessed light, sailor fashion, with three cheers. The doctor had no heart to join them; he wandered away from the ship to a solitary spot where he could watch the rising day-star in moody recollection of a sunnier land at home.

With more and more of the men falling ill, Kane took firm command of the medical situation. He made his fellow officers get out on the floe for exercise in temperatures which at the lowest reached −53° Fahrenheit. Even though the effort caused joint pains, at times almost unendurable, he had the men kicking a football, or sliding like schoolboys on the ice, or tramping with a gun in hope of getting a seal or a fox. He advised De Haven to order increased rations of meat, potatoes, sauerkraut, and stewed apples; had the men air their bedding and let fresh air into the stinking cabin; and began to dose them with quinine and salts of iron. Nevertheless, at the end of February, all but five of the twenty-four crewmen had ulcerated gums and blotched limbs. All eight officers also were affected in various degrees. "Old pains were renewed, old wounds opened. . . . Our commander, certainly the best constitution among us, was assailed like the rest. . . . Purpuric extravasations appeared on his legs, and a dysentery enfeebled him to an extent far from safe."

In an amusing passage in his narrative of the cruise—amusing, that is, if we forget that the men's very lives were at stake—Kane tells of his ingenious ruses to get the uneducated sailors to take his antiscorbutic medicines, foods, and exercise:

> James Stewart, with purpuric blotches and a stiff knee, had to wag his leg half an hour by the dial, opposite a formidable magnet. . . . Stewart had faith; the muscular action, which I had enjoined so often ineffectually, was brought about by a bit of steel and a smearing of red sealing-wax. They cured him.

Another man who would not take the doctor's prescribed sponge baths was cajoled into sponging himself with an allegedly medicinal fluid consisting of water made brown with coffee and acidified with vinegar. "He never would have washed with *aqua fontana*," said Kane. Some of the men would not eat vegetable food, obstinately preferring only salt junk, hard tack, and tinned beef. For these patients Kane compounded a mixture of olive oil and lime juice, followed by raw potato and sauerkraut, "pounded with molasses into a damnable electuary. They ate nobly, and got well."

Kane himself, potentially the poorest risk of all, with his latent rheumatic fever, showed milder signs of scurvy than any of his fellow officers, and not only kept on his feet in spite of heavy work caring for the sick, but remained physically and mentally active throughout the voyage. His heart, as yet but slightly damaged, was still equal to the strains of hard work and malnutrition. Moreover, the frigid environment, harsh as it was, protected him from the repeated infection with viruses of the common cold that in his home climate would have reactivated the lurking streptococci of rheumatic fever.

Early in March, when the drift had dragged the two brigs south to latitude 72°, De Haven and Griffin decided to repair *Rescue*'s damaged bow and stern. Ingeniously, they sunk a pit in the ice about her hull, eight feet deep and large enough for four men to work in. Only the keel was left imbedded in the ice. In this novel dry dock the hull was carefully inspected, a new bowsprit installed, and the broken stern-post replaced. De Haven, fearing the possibility of disaster for one or the other of his vessels in the icy turmoil that was likely to occur when the pack finally broke up, was greatly relieved to have both vessels again in navigable condition. The air temperature rose above freezing for the first time on March 7, and with returning warmth Kane's scurvy patients began to improve. A southwesterly gale on the 20th opened large cracks in the ice, but Kane with his usual recklessness continued his walks on the floes. Once he was caught in a sudden sleet storm some distance from the ship, and lost his way until Griffin, alarmed, went in search of him. On their way back (Kane calmly wrote when the danger was past), "We were blown over a few times, and tumbled over, no matter how often."

April 19 brought daylight all day. On the 22d, *Rescue*'s men moved back to their own ship. Spring housecleaning began; the decks were cleaned up, the forepeak restored. The officers' cabin was again walled off from the dismal half-deck, and their bunks were made up for comfortable sleeping. Some of the men were still badly off with scurvy. They were getting some fresh game but not enough. "I hardly think," wrote Kane, "that any organized expedition in these regions was ever so completely deprived of anti-scorbutic diet as we are at this time." Captain Griffin fainted from overexertion, and several of the crew also had spells of faintness. To make matters worse, the unaccustomed sunlight brought a new malady, snow blindness. De Haven was the most seriously affected. Kane for two weeks at the end of May could not see well enough to write up his journal and had to dictate to the mates. On May 11, however, he was well enough, or imprudent enough (he himself admits), to undertake a seal hunt. He did not get a seal and fell on the ice, immersing one arm and his gun in the cold water.

On May 19 land was visible for the first time in ninety-nine days. The brigs, still firmly held in floating ice, had drifted almost to the narrows of Davis Strait. On the 19th, *Rescue*'s men shot a very large bear—"what a glorious feast for our scurvy-ridden ships." On the 31st, Kane mapped the ice floe in which the brigs were imbedded, finding it 5½ miles long by 3½ miles across. Five days later, June 5, the floe suddenly broke up with violent cracking and overriding of the ice pans, "as if our ice were a carpet shaken by Titans." *Advance*, however, was not yet set altogether free; she was still locked fast by the stern in a mass of ice as long as herself. On the 8th this persistent fragment of the pack broke away and dropped the brig at last down into the water.

This blessed release occurred near the western shore of Davis Strait, almost at the Arctic Circle. The nearest place at which De Haven could hope to find rest and food for his weary and ailing men was at the Whalefish Islands. Setting sail eastward through a field of scattered ice pans and immense bergs, *Advance* and *Rescue* made port June 17 at Lively (Godhavn) on Disco Island. There, said Kane, they "ate inordinately of eider and codfish, and seal, . . . drank largely of the smallest of small beer, and danced with the natives, teaching them the polka." The health of the men daily improved. But De Haven was impatient to rejoin the Franklin search. After five days at Lievely, the squadron sailed on June 22, anchored for a day at Pröven, and set off northward again on July 1, hoping to get across to Lancaster Sound in time for another season of exploration.

De Haven, from hard experience of the past year, had become expert in handling his vessel in the ice—"the best ice-master afloat," said Kane,—but the elements were against him in this second attempt to reach the North Water. On June 26 both brigs were badly caught in a young ice field, in a strong shoreward current between a group of immense icebergs and the rocky coast. *Rescue* made fast to a crag, and *Advance* to the ice, but *Advance's* ice anchors slipped and she drifted within a rifle shot of the rocks. On the verge of disaster, she struck a grounded block of ice and was for once saved by the enemy that had so often nearly wrecked her. The captains of two whaling ships that De Haven's flotilla met a few days later thought *Advance's* escape miraculous. From them the expedition obtained fresh beef, eggs, turnips, and potatoes, "enough to eat out every taint of scurvy." Making port briefly at Upernavik, the Americans found there some newspapers, and on June 9 another whaler met them with mail. Kane sat up all through the sunlit night, reading his letters from home and the news of the world.

Reaching the solid pack of the middle ice on July 10, the brigs were again brought to a standstill, and on the 12th they were overtaken by Lady Franklin's schooner *Prince Albert,* fresh from Britain on her second Arctic cruise, this time under Captain William Kennedy, a Canadian of Orkney ancestry and a devout Presbyterian. Kane was better prepared to understand Kennedy's evangelical ways than was his Roman Catholic first officer, Ensign Joseph-Louis Bellot of the French navy, "an accomplished and gallant officer" (says Kane), who had volunteered for the cruise. Bellot had ample opportunity to cultivate acquaintance with the Americans, for the three vessels, trying in vain to work their way through heavy ice, remained close together for almost a month, and their officers visited back and forth. Bellot and Kane went hunting seals together. Bellot, delighted with this companionship, wrote in his diary that "Dr. Kane and I get better and better acquainted, and there is no subject of our conversation on which I do not receive useful information from him." Bellot, like William Parker Snow the preceding summer, noted that the Americans in their sturdy little ships were bold and resolute, though badly equipped. But life aboard *Advance* was not all hardship. Once, when Bellot was invited to dine with De Haven and his officers, he was enchanted to find that *Advance's* and *Rescue's* cooks were both Frenchmen, able to prepare grilled seal and roast reindeer to his Gallic taste. "Ces artistes," he said, "me font trouver délicieuses les grillades de phoque et le rôti de renne." They had evidently learned a great deal during the voyage![13]

One day in August Kennedy and Bellot again came walking over the ice to visit *Advance*. When almost at her side, Bellot slipped into a crack in the ice and might have drowned had not Kane, leaping to his assistance, joined Kennedy in pulling him out. Two years later, almost to the day, Bellot, promoted to Lieutenant de Vaisseau and back in the Arctic with Inglefield in *Phoenix*, went to his death in much the same way. Slipping on the ice in a heavy wind, he was blown into a crevasse and was not seen again.

When August was almost half over neither De Haven nor Kennedy had escaped from their bafflement at the southern face of the middle ice. Both commanders began to lose hope of reaching the region of search that summer. On August 13 Kennedy dipped his flag to *Advance* and *Rescue,* and turned southward. De Haven and Griffin obstinately battled with the ice for a few days more but on the 19th they too gave up and started southward. "The game had been played out fairly," wrote Kane; "Lancaster Sound was out of the question, and for our scurvy-ridden crew, a nine months' winter in the ice of North Baffin would have been disastrous." Stopping for refreshment at Upernavik and Holsteinsborg, the two brigs continued their homeward voyage through heavy weather off Newfoundland. After a run of twenty-five days, *Advance* docked at New York September 30, 1851. *Rescue* made port safely on October 7. De Haven and Griffin had brought their little ships through countless perils without losing a man. The commodore, ranking again as a mere lieutenant, and *Rescue*'s captain, once more a midshipman, resumed everyday life in the navy, and Kane began moving heaven and earth to get back to the Arctic.

# 7

# Lobbying, Lectures, and Courtship

LIEUTENANT DE HAVEN, whose sense of duty as a naval officer equaled his courage and seamanship, lost no time in preparing his official report of the voyage of *Advance* and *Rescue*. Three days after he had docked his brig at Brooklyn Navy Yard, he sent the report off to the Secretary of the Navy at Washington.[1] This duty done, De Haven quietly ended his career as an Arctic explorer. Not so Kane, who for a few months enjoyed the robust health and vigor he had regained in the germ-free atmosphere of the far north. As De Haven and he had long since agreed, Kane's urgent and immediate duty was to write an account of the expedition for the general public. At home in Philadelphia he began work at once, but made slow progress, for somehow he had caught the public eye far more than his commander. Invitations to lecture about the expedition's adventures and discoveries began to come in almost before he could settle down with his notes and charts. Such calls could not be denied, for Kane was already dreaming of getting back to the Arctic and the Franklin Search, at the head of an expedition of his own. Money would be needed, and lecture fees must be garnered while public interest was keen.

Kane began his career as a public lecturer on no less a platform than that of the Smithsonian Institution at Washington—only four years old as a center of scientific research but already the pride of the nation. Invited by its first Secretary, the distinguished physicist Joseph Henry, to give one of its regular lecture series, Kane made his first appearance there on December 29, 1851. In spite of dreadful weather and almost impassable streets—the eastern seaboard was having one of the worst winters on record—Dr. Kane drew capacity audiences. To make sure that everyone in the Smithsonian hall could see the little doctor, Joseph Henry had the stage raised, and also (as he wrote in his diary) "had the speaker elevated," doubtless on a podium.² George Gray Leiper, Kane's maternal uncle, who happened to be in Washington at the time and heard the lectures, wrote to his daughter Martha that "when he mounts the rostrum he looks more like a boy of seventeen than one who travelled on the sands of the desert, the African seas, been pent for months in the ice and when released to be floating in company with stupendous icebergs which made the bravest tremble for their personal safety."³

Kane began modestly.

> The legitimate object of your excellent institution is to impart knowledge and diffuse information. Feeling this I ought perhaps to apologize for coming before you. I am not a lecturer but traveller only and my object in describing a portion of the globe remote and rarely visited is less to advance new facts than to engage or perhaps mature your sympathies for a gallant band of our fellow men who are buried in its recesses.⁴

"Lectures well written, voice rather feeble," wrote Henry. In spite of this cool comment, the doctor won and held his audience. According to the *National Intelligencer,* leading Washington newspaper, the first lecture was heard with profound attention. This was a narrative of the Grinnell Expedition, concluding with Kane's conjecture—by this time a conviction—that Sir John Franklin and his ships had passed northward through Wellington Channel in the summer of 1846, to unknown regions near the Pole.

On the night of Kane's second lecture, December 31, 1851, according to the *National Intelligencer* the weather was so cold and stormy that the Smithsonian authorities decided at first not to light up the lecture hall, but so many people came that Secretary Henry had to let them in. This lecture Kane devoted to the supposed position of Franklin's ships in (as Kane imagined) an open or at least comparatively iceless sea, where the crews of *Erebus* and *Terror,* "unable to leave their hunting ground and cross the frozen Sahara which intervened between them and the world from which they are shut out," were subsisting upon the supposedly plentiful animal life of the great polynya.

In his third and last Smithsonian lecture, attended by an overflow audience, Kane described the perils of the Arctic and also its strange meteorological phenomena—the auroras, mirages, and apparent distortions of sun and moon as seen in parhelia and paraselenae. He ended with eulogies of De Haven and his men, a warm tribute to Henry Grinnell and an eloquent appeal for renewal of the Franklin Search by a second American expedition. "One of the most interesting courses ever to be delivered at the Institution," said the *National Intelligencer.*⁵

On January 19, 1852 Kane spoke in Philadelphia at the Musical Fund Hall; on January 24 he was in New York, apparently also for a lecture; on January 28 and 30 he spoke at the Maryland Institute in Baltimore to two audiences each of more than two thousand people, and on the intervening night at York, Pennsylvania.[6] At the time, the cold was so intense that the Susquehanna ferry on the Philadelphia, Baltimore, and Washington (now Penn Central) Railroad was at times blocked by ice, and at the peak of the cold wave, passengers got through only by crossing the wide, icebound river on foot from Perryville to Havre de Grace. This stage of Dr. Kane's lecture tour could have been little more comfortable than his Arctic travels of the winter before.

Kane had been elected a member of the American Philosophical Society while still in the Arctic, May 17, 1851, on the nomination of five distinguished Philadelphians. He addressed the society for the first time in Philosophical Hall on May 7, 1852, exhibiting specimens of vegetable matter found on the shores of the Arctic Sea "during the long ice-drift of the late Grinnell Expedition."[7] On the same day he wrote to Henry Grinnell that he had received letters from Lady Franklin asking whether he would take part again in the Franklin Search. He had replied to her that he would indeed resume the search, serving under William Penny or leading a party of his own.[8] Lady Franklin had been led by some of her advisers to think that Sir John, of whose route after the spring of 1846 nothing still was known, might have broken through to the west of Melville Island and, living or dead, was to be found somewhere west of the Canadian archipelago. She wanted Kane to take *Advance* to the region north and east of Bering Strait in company with her own little steamer *Isabel*. Kane said he would fall in with this plan though his own judgment was averse to it. To take *Advance* around Cape Horn to Alaska would have given him adventure enough, but he did not believe that Franklin was to be found in western Arctic waters.

In fact, Kane at this time must have been sadly asking himself whether he would ever go north again. Intense work on his book and the lecture trips in foul weather had combined to light up his old illness, and threw him into a deep mental depression. Attempting his own cure, he administered to himself a severely "reducing" treatment, but only made himself worse. At last a medical friend, shocked at his condition, persuaded him to give up the self-prescribed drugs and resume a sensible diet. A weighty factor in Kane's gloom at this time was the illness of his youngest brother, the lovable fourteen-year-old Willie, who in the spring of 1852 had developed some sort of slow fever (tubercular meningitis?) and went steadily downhill. Dr. Kane, after he had pulled himself together, insisted upon acting as physician-nurse to the boy, and sat long hours at his bedside until he died on August 25.

On September 17 Kane spoke again at the American Philosophical Society, on the ice drift in Baffin Bay.[9] His choice of that topic suggests that he was planning to go directly to the head of the bay on his next voyage. He had staved off Lady Franklin's scheme for sending *Advance* and *Isabel* to Bering Strait, as well as another invitation from her to join a search party to be based on Nova Zembla. Nor had he any thought of returning to Lancaster Sound and Wellington Channel, to be baffled again as De Haven and the British commanders had been baffled in 1850–51. That seemingly impossible route he willingly left to Sir Edward Belcher, who with four fine ships was already, in 1852, on his way to another and far worse entanglement. Kane had determined that if he could get together an expedition of his own, he would bypass the western exits of Baffin Bay—Lancaster Sound and Jones Sound—and push northward all the way to Smith Sound at its head and try to reach the utterly unknown regions beyond. There, he believed, he would find open water leading to the hypothetical Open Polar Sea. Wishfully he cherished his conjecture of 1850–51, that in 1846 *Erebus* and *Terror,* favored by a summer warmer than usual, had passed beyond the head of Wellington Channel. In that case Franklin and his men might be found somewhere on the shores of the circumpolar ocean, locked within its icy rim but, as he had hopefully told his Smithsonian audience, subsisting upon the rich animal life that Maury and other students of the Arctic supposed to exist there.

If such a haven existed, Smith Sound offered a more direct entry into it than the western exits of Baffin Bay along a route hitherto unexplored. Whether or not such a route might lead to Franklin's ships, in any case it offered a sure opportunity for geographical discovery, possibly even access to the North Pole. In fact, a European geographer of great authority had already proposed Smith Sound as a route to the Pole. In April, 1846, Vice-Admiral Baron Friedrich Petrovitch Wrangel of the Russian navy addressed the Royal Geographical Society of London on "The Best Means of Reaching the Pole."[10] Two decades before, Wrangel had directed a polar expedition by ship and dog sledge, based on the coast of eastern Siberia. Speaking from experience gained on that journey, he proposed that a well-equipped vessel should proceed through Baffin Bay to the west coast of Greenland at about 77° north latitude, above Melville Bay, find a harbor there, and, as soon as the sea froze over in the autumn, send a large party of men with dog sledges into Smith Sound to about 79° N. Thence a smaller party would travel on, along the west coast of Greenland, toward the Pole. Wrangel's paper was discussed by Sir John Barrow, who, having had his own bitter experience in the Arctic, expressed a cautious hope that Wrangel's plan might succeed. Sir John knew nothing, he said, about sledges, dogs, and drivers (British expeditions before the Franklin Search had made no use of dogs for travel over the ice), but he would accept Baron Wrangel's views on that subject. He pointed out, however, that the baron seemed unaware that nothing at all was known about Smith Sound. Baffin, who put it on the map, actually never entered it. He merely saw, from a distance of fifty miles, a break in the mountainous shore at the head of the bay. Parry, who confirmed the existence of an opening in that region, got no farther than Baffin. Sir John Barrow agreed that if there is indeed a passage leading northward, its exploration by sledge would be eminently worthwhile. But as for himself, the sturdy old seaman declared, he would prefer "a couple of strong, roomy, well-built sailing vessels, well stored with provisions, so that all concerned, during the most inclement weather may have substantial houses over their heads."[11]

Kane, so far as we know, had done no serious reading about Arctic travel before his hasty assignment to De Haven's squadron in 1851. He must have learned of Wrangel's ideas from the British officers—Sir John Ross and the others—with whom he had long talks during the rendezvous at Beechey Island in 1850, or from Kennedy and Bellot, who would have been even more up-to-date on the whole question of access to the farthest north. Whether or not Dr. Kane learned of Wrangel's paper in this way while in the Arctic, certainly he would have found it after his return to Philadelphia, in the library of the American Philosophical Society, in volume 18 of the *Journal of the Royal Geographical Society* for 1848. Once having heard, or read, of Smith Sound as a route to the north, he never put aside the hope of trying it. That the very existence of such a passage between the headlands so distantly seen long years ago by Baffin and by Parry was merely a conjecture, gave only greater zest to this ardent and romantic young man who a year before had seen the way north through Wellington Channel shut in his face by ice and storm. He could not rest until he met the challenge, however uncertain and dangerous the route.

Kane, it must be remembered, was still an officer of the United States Navy. The Navy Department, in order that he might get to work on his narrative of the Grinnell Expedition, had not recalled him to active duty, but could do so at any time. To keep himself free while he matured plans for a second voyage, he would have to get the Secretary of the Navy to put him on special orders. Fortunately for his hopes, President Fillmore had in July appointed a new Secretary who by his own romantic temperament and scientific interest was equipped to appreciate Kane's bold and imaginative ideas. John Pendleton Kennedy of Baltimore, successful lawyer, man of letters, and politician, had put himself in the front rank of Southern literary men by his three novels of early American life, *Swallow Barn, Horseshoe Robinson,* and *Rob of the Bowl.* A patron of literature and science, Kennedy had generously helped Edgar Allen Poe get his first editorial job. While in Congress he had shown his understanding of scientific values by sponsoring the appropriation that enabled Samuel F. B. Morse to build the telegraph line from Baltimore to Washington.[12] When Kane went to Kennedy in the fall of 1852 to explain his hopes, the Secretary received him so warmly that the two men developed a friendship that lasted throughout the rest of Kane's life.

Kane's first recorded meeting with Kennedy was in mid-November, 1852. Before that time he had submitted his plan for a direct approach to polar waters to Professor Alexander Dallas Bache, Superintendent of the U.S. Coast Survey, and had won Bache's full agreement. Yet, he frankly admitted, he was entering upon the search with no overwrought opinion of its success.

> The chances of finding Sir John Franklin are very few, and it may be that we are not permitted to reach the open water which forms the just field of our efforts . . . but it stands out so prominently among the few expedients which remain unattempted that I conceive it to be a duty to give it a trial.[13]

Kennedy's private journal for December 5, 1852 records that

> about the middle of the month I had a pleasant little party at dinner with Dr. Kane of the Arctic Expedition and Lt. Gillis of the Astronomical Department [of the navy] and Mr. Etheridge, my chief clerk. Kane had brought his drawings—a rich portfolio of polar scenes—to show us. I have given him permission to go again, at the request of Lady Franklin, on the new Expedition recently set on foot by Mr. Henry Grinnell and Mr. Peabody.[14]

Returning to Philadelphia, Kane on the 22d had encouraging news from England which he hastened to pass on to Secretary Kennedy. Lady Franklin, to whom he had communicated his plan, had written urging him to go ahead with it. Meanwhile, Henry Grinnell—who would again lend *Advance* for the cruise—had obtained a contribution of $10,000 from George Peabody, the American-born London banker, and was writing to other rich friends asking for financial help. Secretary Kennedy followed up his verbal approval by issuing an order placing Passed Assistant Surgeon Kane on special duty to prepare for the expedition.

Another piece of news from England deeply excited Kane and aroused his envy. An English seaman had beaten him to Smith Sound. A few months earlier, Lady Franklin, having found no one to take her steamer *Isabel* to Bering Strait, offered to give the vessel to anyone who would carry on the search in any direction. Lieutenant Edward Augustus Inglefield of the Royal Navy took up the challenge and on July 6, 1852, with seventeen men, left London in *Isabel*. He steamed to the head of Baffin Bay and in late August entered Smith Sound, reaching north latitude 78° 28′ 21″, about 80 miles farther north than any previous navigator in the region of Baffin

Bay. Still more exciting to Kane, from his most northerly point Inglefield had seen to the northward open water stretching through seven points of the compass. Beyond the northern horizon, beyond the range of Inglefield's spy-glass there might be—who could say?—the Open Sea of Maury's hypothesis and Kane's dreams. Inglefield himself was inclined to believe this, but before he could steam farther to the north a gale arose to drive him back and out into Baffin Bay. Proceeding southwestward to Jones Sound he mapped its previously unknown shores; thence to Lancaster Sound to exchange mail with Sir Edward Belcher's station ship *North Star* at Beechey Island, and to leave supplies there for Belcher's squadron, now out of touch to the north and west. Continuing his voyage with unvarying skill and freedom from mishaps, Inglefield reached London early in November.[15] "Considering expenditure of time, money, and effort," writes Augustus W. Greely, "this is one of the most successful of modern Arctic voyages. Inglefield laid down 600 miles of uncharted coast, rectified many errors, outlined Smith Sound, and penetrated far into Jones Sound."[16] Kane's admiration of Inglefield's performance was mixed with jealous fear that next summer the brave and competent Englishman might return to the Arctic ahead of the Americans and actually reach that Open Polar Sea whose existence both Inglefield and Kane now accepted with strengthened confidence.

On December 14, 1852, Dr. Kane publicly announced his plans in a lecture before the American Geographical Society of New York. Rightly expecting a large attendance, the society held the lecture in the chapel of Columbia University, which (according to report) "was well filled by a most intelligent audience."[17] George Bancroft, celebrated historian and president of the society, was in the chair. To Kane's special delight, Henry Grinnell, then one of the society's vice-presidents, was present. Kane's lecture on this occasion is the only one of his public addresses of which we have the full text.[18] In a clear, direct, even elegant style he gave first a brief description of Baffin Bay, its geography, winds, currents, and movements of the ice. Thus having led his hearers to the Arctic ice barrier, he traced its outlines along the coasts of Europe, Asia, and America—a circumpolar ring 6,000 miles long, 2,000 miles in diameter. Confidently he set forth the reasons for supposing—nay, believing—that beyond that barrier lies an open sea teeming with birds and fishes under milder skies and warmer air than are to be found on its icy margins. Into this great polynya Sir John Franklin must have penetrated. Recalling once more the evidence gathered by Penny and De Haven at Beechey Island in 1850 that Franklin had in 1845–46 wintered at the southern mouth of Wellington Channel, Kane, misinterpreting what he called "the complete proofs since offered that Franklin did not proceed to the east or west," declared that he must have passed up Wellington Channel to the north:

> Here we have lost him; and save the lonely records upon the tombstones of his dead, for seven years he has been lost to the world. To assign his exact position is impossible; we only know that he has travelled up this land-locked channel, seeking the objects of his enterprise to the north and west. That some of his party are yet in existence, this is not the place to argue. Let the question rest upon the opinions of those who, having visited this region, are at least better qualified to judge of its resources than those who have formed their opinions by the fireside.

The British Admiralty, he said, had shown its own acceptance of some such hypothesis about Franklin's whereabouts by sending Sir Edward Belcher's squadron of four ships to Wellington Channel, but these vessels, Kane thought, could never pass into the Open Polar Sea.

In conclusion Kane explained his own plans. Grinnell would lend once more the well-tried brig *Advance*. The navy would provide a crew and provisions. The Naval Observatory, the Smithsonian Institution, and the American Philosophical Society and other learned organizations would provide him with scientific instruments. Improving upon Baron Wrangel's proposal, he would push his ship as far as possible into Smith Sound. During the first summer, fall, and winter he would set up advance depots by small boats and later by dog sledge on the unknown shores ahead of him, and in the second summer he would point his sledges toward the Open Sea. "Once there, if such a reward awaits us, we launch our little boats, and bidding God speed us, embark upon its waters."

This brilliant performance on the lecture platform, compounded of Kane's personal charm and his lucid style warmed by romantic emotion, left his audience with no doubts as to the soundness of the project. At its conclusion the American Geographical and Statistical Society voted to thank the Secretary of the Navy for the liberality with which he had lent the aid of his department to the expedition destined for the Arctic seas, and directed its president, George Bancroft, to appoint a committee of five to devise measures for promoting the scientific organization of Dr. Kane's expedition, to be discussed with the Secretary of the Navy, the Coast Survey, and the Smithsonian Institution.

Kane's parents and intimate friends had learned to expect him always to do rash and improbable things—to descend into a seething volcano, to risk his neck climbing the Vocal Memnon, to start for the Arctic on one week's notice—but they were still scarcely prepared for the suddenness and the reck-

The Fox Sisters
From lithograph by N. Currier, 1852
(Margaret, left; Katharine, center; Leah, right)

lessness with which at the age of thirty-two he fell in love with the most conspicuous, most talked-of, most enigmatic young woman in America. Margaret Fox, sensational spiritualistic medium, heroine of the "Rochester Rappings," was nineteen years of age when Elisha Kent Kane first saw her in Philadelphia, sometime in November 1852.

The story of Margaret Fox and her scarcely less ill-starred younger sister Katherine has been told many times[19]—how as children, one thirteen, one twelve years of age, in their parents' farmhouse in Hydesville near Rochester, New York, they began to receive messages from the spirit world through mysterious knockings in the night; how they claimed to have solved the murder of a man last seen in that house years before; how their shrewd elder sister Leah, Mrs. Fish, transferred them to her home in Rochester to display their mysterious gift, and finally took them on tour, chaperoned by their unobtrusive mother. Soon they were a national sensation, in New York, Philadelphia, Washington, and Boston, drawing throngs of important people to their séances. At a private sitting in New York the circle around the table included George Bancroft, James Fenimore Cooper, William Cullen Bryant, and Nathaniel Parker Willis,[20] none of them perhaps believers but all impressed by the seemingly innocent charm of the two dark-eyed young girls. Such children, said Horace Greeley, could never have been guilty of sordid deception, nor could they have known how to mislead the numerous committees of physicians and scientists to whose tests they had submitted. When Greeley's wife was beside herself over the death of their only child, he took Katie Fox into his home for weeks. Half-skeptical himself, he had no explanation of the spirit rappings, but welcomed the consolation his wife received from Katie's mediation of the dead boy's messages.[21] Even outspoken skeptics thought both the Fox sisters very bright and very quick to penetrate the minds of those who sought to know, through their ministrations, how the departed were doing in the other world. Nathaniel Parker Willis described the physical appearance of the Fox spiritualist party as he saw it in 1850, when Margaret was seventeen years of age:

A stout lady, of the ordinary small-town type of maternity, led the way, followed by three young ladies considerably prettier than the average. The two Misses Fox, as well as their married sister, have nerves so plumply clad in health and tranquility, that it is difficult to reconcile their appearance with the fact that they have been worked upon for two years by the phenomena of unexplained visitations; and indeed through the evening we were struck with their combined good-humor and simplicity, and the ease and unpretentiousness with which they let their visitors (from both worlds) have their own way. They evidently won the respect and liking of all present, as the evening went on.[22]

At any rate, to Kane's eyes, Margaret Fox, when he first met her during the sisters' engagement in Philadelphia, for all her nationwide notoriety was a vision of demure innocence. One morning late in November 1852, out of sheer curiosity about the spiritualistic manifestations, he called at the Foxes' quarters in the "bridal suite" of the Union Hotel. Seeing a very young lady sitting by the window with a book in her hand, he thought at first he had knocked at the wrong door; but Mrs. Fox came at once to receive him for a sitting. When the famous medium, Miss Fox, was summoned, she turned out to be the same quiet girl who had just now been doing her lessons by the window. According to Margaret's ghost-written book, Dr. Kane afterward told her that at this first interview he determined to make her his wife.

> Little as she suspected his feelings, he loved her at first sight. . . . The winning grace of her modest demeanor and the naive refinement apparent in every look and movement were evidence of a nature enriched with all the qualities that dignify and adorn womanhood. . . . Perhaps no young girl ever lived more free from the least idea of coquetry or conquest. . . . She never appeared in public without some older lady, and in the sittings was invariably accompanied by her mother. Young as she was, and thus secluded from familiar approach, it is not likely that she had ever thought of beaux, of the admiration of the other sex.[23]

Dr. Kane's impetuous admiration of Margaret did not extend to the spirits and their messages to her patrons. On his second visit, the next day after the first, he told her that he considered her spirits a fraud, her life a deception. "This is no life for you, my child; you ought to go to school." Henceforth a frequent caller at the Union Hotel, he began his courtship circumspectly. On December 7 he left a note for Margaret's mother: "Dr. Kane will call at three o'clock P.M. for the purpose of accompanying Mrs. and Miss Fox for an afternoon drive."

During December 1852 and January 1853, Kane wrote to Margaret or called at the hotel every few days, or on a sunny winter day took her, with a chaperon, for a drive about the city and suburbs. On one of these drives, a cousin of the doctor by marriage, Mrs. H. J. Patterson, came in her own carriage to accompany them. Young Margaret must have responded favorably to Kane's cautious though assiduous advances, for, one day toward the end of January (as she recollected some years later), after attending a séance, Kane lingered in the parlor of the Fox suite and engaged her in a long conversation about her future and his. She was fitted for better things, he said, than for the life she was leading, of charlatanism and deceit. She must quit it forever and prepare herself for something better. If she would leave her family, go to school, and thus forget the past, he would be proud to make her his wife. But, he said, "You must not engage yourself to be my wife unless you can give me all your love—your whole heart, unless you can sacrifice for me all other anticipations and prospects."[24]

To this lordly proposal of marriage he added (if we are to believe Margaret) the downright fib that he had never been in love before. True, he said, he had to some extent committed himself to a lady of means whom his father wished him to marry; but this had been dictated by filial respect, and he would release himself from all obligation to the lady and make himself free to pledge himself to Margaret alone. Carried away by his eloquence, Margaret "accepted the vows of this impetuous lover to whom she looked up with admiration and respect, and with growing regard . . . but as yet none of the impassioned fervor that marked his attachment to her. She was still a child at heart."

It must be said, before we go farther with the story of this troubled

Margaret Fox
From *The Love-Life of Dr. Kane* (New York, 1866)

romance, that all that has been generally known about it comes from a biased source, Margaret herself. When the affair was over—Kane dead, and Margaret on the downward slope of her career—impelled by penury and pique she published Kane's letters to her in a strange little book, *The Love-Life of Dr. Kane*, which his family tried in vain to suppress. Outside of this book there is no documentary evidence that Kane ever proposed marriage to Margaret or seriously intended to make her his wife. The nearest approach to valid evidence appears in an undated letter published in facsimile in the *Love-Life*, presumably written on the eve of his departure for the Arctic in May, 1853.

> . . . Then live, dear Maggie, until God brings me back to you—and then meeting my eye with the proud consciousness of virtue—we will resign ourselves to a passion sanctioned by love and marriage. Golden fields shall spread before us their summer harvest, silver lakes mirror your very breath. Let us live for each other—Farewell![25]

This letter is in Kane's handwriting and its style, too, is his. To what extent other letters printed in the book were altered or expunged by Margaret's ghost editor cannot now be known. They are certainly introduced by a deliberate lie about Margaret's age, making her a child of thirteen when she first met Kane, although actually she was nineteen years of age.[26] Doubtless her letters to Kane, or at least the earlier ones, were polished by her editor. A few surviving original letters of 1853, in her handwriting, among the E. K. Kane papers at the American Philosophical Society's library are not so maturely expressed as those of the same period printed in the *Love-Life*.

The letters are, however, correct about such matters as Dr. Kane's whereabouts at different times between 1852 and 1857, his lecture engagements and his illnesses. The tone of affectionate banter, condescension, and moralizing with which he often accompanied his declarations of love, matches that of the letters he wrote to his mother, brothers, and sister. The book's general picture of the affair accords fairly well with what can be gleaned from a few contemporary newspaper references and letters of gossipy Philadelphians. Margaret was a scantily educated and socially inexperienced village girl, suddenly plunged into notoriety under the thumb of her calculating elder sister Leah and the chaperonage of her strict but vacillating mother. The courtship was evidently conducted much as the *Love-Life* tells, with Victorian circumspection, the proper degree of reserve on Margaret's part, and Tennysonian fervor on Kane's. On one occasion the two lovers went with a party to Laurel Hill Cemetery. Leading Margaret to the family vault of the Kanes, Elisha recited a gloomy stanza from Longfellow's *Psalm of Life* (thinking no doubt of his own damaged heart):

> Art is long and time is fleeting
> And our hearts, though stout and brave
> Still like muffled drums are beating
> Funeral marches to the grave.

and added with Gothic sentimentality, "Here, Margaret, will be *your* last resting place." The memory of this episode she cherished long afterward as evidence of Dr. Kane's confidence that their courting was to end in marriage.[27]

And so the courtship went on, with alternate hours of romantic exuberance and sorrowful reflections, and lovers' misunderstandings tenderly resolved, with preachments by Kane and protestations by Margaret; and, behind it all, forebodings about the distaste of Kane's parents for the upstart Margaret; anxiety too about the reluctance of Mrs. Fox and the dominant Leah, who dreaded losing Margaret or rather the dollars she gathered at the séance table. The Foxes were never sure of Kane's intentions; if honorable, marriage would take Margaret from the troupe; if otherwise, a scandal would cost them the following of God-fearing people who made up their patronage. Kane's courtship had to be carried on in large part by letter, for at frequent intervals he was off on a lecture tour or in New York and Washington seeking advice and assistance for his expedition, begging the navy and the Smithsonian Institution for the loan of instruments and apparatus, or negotiating for stores of food and ships' supplies with which to stock the hold of Grinnell's brig *Advance*.

The Foxes too were on the move. At mid-January 1853, they transferred their séances to New York, and about the middle of February they were in Washington for the same business. Dr. Kane, wherever he was, wrote or telegraphed to Margaret every few days, amidst his heavy correspondence about the expedition. To Lady Franklin, according to her niece and secretary Sophia Cracroft, at the end of 1852 he was writing twice a week, and she—persistent lady—to him by every mail.[28] To the Secretary of the Navy, to Henry Grinnell, to the scientists Spencer F. Baird, Alexander Dallas Bache, and Matthew Fontaine Maury he wrote many times. He spent hours in Washington with Maury planning oceanographic research in Arctic waters. Maury's daughter, who saw Kane on one of his visits to her father, recalled him as "an interesting looking but silent little man with dark hair and keen black eyes."[29]

Kane corresponded with the world-famous savant Alexander von Humboldt in Berlin, hoping to get a German naturalist for the Arctic cruise. From England he received letters of advice and encouragement from the experienced Arctic travelers Sir William Parry, Sir John Richardson, Sir James Ross, and Colonel (later Sir) Edward Sabine. For the Navy Department he had to prepare a detailed statement substantiating De Haven's discovery of the land at the head of Wellington Channel which the Americans had named for Henry Grinnell. To numerous people of all sorts who wanted to join his expedition or whom he wanted to go with him as seamen or scientists, he was endlessly writing in his always clear hand and polished style. In addition to this immense correspondence, he was putting every available hour into drafting his book of the first Grinnell Expedition, which must be ready for press before he was to sail north again in the spring.

In spite of all this correspondence and writing, Margaret had at least twenty letters or telegrams from him between mid-January and mid-March 1853, besides occasional presents by mail or express. They met, of course, when he happened to be in the same city with her. On Sunday night, January 23, 1853, he wrote from Philadelphia:

> Maggie Darling:—Why do you not write to me? Have you forgotten your friend? Or does your new life drive from you the recollection of old times?
>
> I go to Baltimore on Tuesday, and then to Washington to see the President. Oh, dear Maggie, when I think of you in your humble calling, and of myself with my toiling vanities and cares, I only feel that I am about to leave you; and feeling this, how very, very much I love you.
>
> I am a fool for this, yet I know that you have some good reason for not writing. Send me a lock of your hair; for unless it comes I will not come on to see you.
>
> Kiss Katy for me, and tell her I am *your* friend, and therefore her own. If ever trouble presses his cold hand—colder, Maggie, than the spirits, come to your one friend, for he alone has no coldness. Remember his warm hands, his glowing kisses, and his steadfast, trusting heart; and then you cannot forget him.[30]

A few days later he sent her from Washington (dutifully addressing it to her mother) a copy of *Undine* by De La Motte, a now almost forgotten classic of the Romantic period about a water nymph who loved a wandering knight and through marriage to him acquired an immortal soul.

On January 25 Kane lectured at the Maryland Institute in Baltimore, repeating his success of the past year, with an audience of three thousand. "The gallant speaker," said the *Baltimore Sun*, "was often interrupted by loud applause." Next day he was in Washington, "to meet the great men," he told Margaret—a joint meeting of the Senate Committee on Naval Affairs and Navy Department heads, with Secretary Kennedy in the chair, at which he explained his plans in the hope of a congressional grant that never materialized. On the 30th he gave a public lecture at the Smithsonian Institution, where he was proud to notice among the audience a famous traveler and writer after his own heart, Washington Irving. From February 12 to 17 Kane was in New England. He was a dinner guest of the mayor of Boston on the 13th, lectured at New Bedford on the 15th and at Boston on the 16th in the New Music Hall. From this trip he collected about $1,400 toward the expedition, a good take considering the competitive entertainment Boston was offering at the same time—Blitz, a conjurer; Alboni, a popular Italian contralto; and Ralph Waldo Emerson on the lecture platform.

Before he got through this crowded week Kane was ill and despondent. On a cold, rainy day he wrote Margaret a long letter. A few excerpts will suffice to show his low state of mind.

> Maggie, I am sick—sick at the hotel—sick with hard work, and with nobody to nurse or care for me. You saw how wretchedly I looked when in New York; I am far worse now, and without any chance of resting. Is it any wonder, then, that I long to be with you, to have again the lazy days and sit by your side talking nonsense? . . . To you I am nothing but a cute, cunning dissembler, a sort of smart gentleman hypocrite, never really sincere, and merely amusing himself with a pretty face. . . . Until you look upon me with trust and brotherly confidence you can never love me. . . . Some day or other I will say to myself, "Am I not injuring my dignity by thus throwing away upon a person in a walk of life different from my own, feelings which she can never understand and of which she is not worthy?" . . . If I did not so love that dark-eyed little Maggie of mine, I would not write to her thus. . . . I am very sick, Maggie, but I hope not cross. Don't be hurt at what I say, but write to me every mail. . . . God bless you.[31]

Kane's troubles followed him home to Philadelphia. His illness, whatever it was, persisted, and his despondency was deepened by a letter from Lady Franklin which he received on February 26, enclosing a message he was asked to pass on to Secretary Kennedy, expressing gratitude for his official interest in the Franklin Search. To Kennedy, Kane himself wrote

> The same mail to my great mortification brings me the news that the British Admiralty have adopted my scheme of search and are about to prosecute it with the aid of steam. Nothing is left to me but a competition with the odds against me, and for this, even, I must hasten the preparations for my departure. I will be in Washington without the delay of an hour, and shall do myself the honour of reporting to you. [32]

This word from England could only mean that Inglefield was to take a steam vessel once more to Baffin Bay and make another attempt to traverse

Smith Sound—Inglefield, the keenest rival Kane could have, with the experience of his last summer's voyage to guide him, and a steamer to outrace Kane's brig. The "news" was, as it turned out, an unfounded rumor, but it was enough to strain Kane's nerves to the limit. According to Elder, Kane was at the time too ill to write, and had to dictate the foregoing note to Kennedy. He did not get off to Washington at once, or indeed until April. He must have been still unable to travel when another blow fell. On March 4 President Fillmore's term of office expired. His cabinet, including Kane's friend John P. Kennedy, left office with him, and the new President, Franklin Pierce, appointed as his Secretary of the Navy James C. Dobbin, an unknown quantity as far as Kane's part in the Franklin Search was concerned.

Dr. Kane's early plans for his expedition had been quite ambitious. In an undated draft intended for someone in authority or with financial means, perhaps Kennedy or Grinnell,[33] Kane proposed a squadron of two sailing ships with a steamer to tow them, manned by fifty officers and men, and provisioned for a three years' cruise. To pay for all this he hoped for a congressional appropriation of $160,000. Henry Grinnell drafted a memorial to Congress. Secretary Kennedy did his best to promote it, backed by leading government scientists. Joseph Henry, Secretary of the Smithsonian Institution; Alexander Dallas Bache, Superintendent of the Coast Survey; and Matthew Fontaine Maury, Superintendent of the Naval Observatory, joined in a formal application to the Secretary for the assistance of the Navy Department. Joseph Henry, as already mentioned, hastily arranged for Kane to give a special lecture on January 26, 1853, before the Senate Committee on Naval Affairs, Secretary Kennedy, and the heads of Navy Department divisions, at which Kane explained his plans and requirements.

But in spite of such high-level support, no enthusiasm for the project developed on Capitol Hill. Even more now than in 1850, Congressmen were disposed to regard the Franklin Search as useless. Seven years had gone by since *Erebus* and *Terror* were last heard from. Let the British, if they must, continue the hopeless search for their own lost seamen.

Early in April, Kane went to Washington once more to talk with some of the senators, and on April 10 he had a long talk with President Pierce at the White House. But neither there nor at the Navy Department, where James C. Dobbin was now Secretary, did Kane find anything more than good wishes for his voyage. Mr. Dobbin was willing to make good his predecessor Kennedy's promises to assign navy volunteers to the crew and to provide certain supplies, but said that he could legally do no more.

The expedition would therefore have to be a private enterprise. By the time of Kane's address to the American Geographical and Statistical Society in December, 1852, he was talking of only one vessel, the *Advance*. For financial resources he would have to depend largely on what he could raise himself. He wrote to his commander of 1850–51, De Haven,

> . . . To my great gratification the Secretary gave me special duty orders so as not to reduce my pay. Stimulated by this I got together my friends and raised quite a sum of money, Mr. Peabody alone giving $10,000. Mr. Grinnell gave me the *Advance,* and by my own exertions, and hard work it was, I found myself the holder of the money, the vessel, and the contract.[34]

By the beginning of March 1853, Mr. Grinnell had put *Advance* in dry dock in New York, to be overhauled for the voyage, and Kane was getting together his crew and supplies. He had gratefully accepted the navy's assignment of a few seamen and petty officers, but he would not ask for commissioned officers, who might outrank him. He could have had William Murdaugh, capable sailing master of *Advance* on the first Grinnell expedition, but did not invite him. He did invite his friend of 1850–51, Lieutenant Bellot of the French navy, but that gallant officer was trying to persuade his government to put him in charge of an expedition of his own, and therefore declined Kane's invitation as well as a call from Lady Franklin to join an English ship she was hoping to send out in 1853. Captain Penny, lately Bellot's commander in *Prince Albert,* wrote to Lady Franklin volunteering to serve under Kane—an extraordinary compliment from a seasoned sea captain, considering Kane's lack of experience in nautical command; but nothing came of that. Also very complimentary was the volunteering of some of his shipmates of 1850–51. Henry Brooks, late boatswain and second officer of *Advance* under De Haven, wrote

> I understand that you are agoing out again in search of Sir John Franklin I don't know any man that I would rather serve under. As I was with you on the First Expedition I would like to be with you on the last.[35]

Kane thought so well of Brooks that he appointed him first officer for the new cruise, but he nearly lost him after all. Though steady and trustworthy at sea, Brooks was a heavy drinker on shore. While awaiting the voyage he went on a spree so prodigious that he was summarily dismissed from the navy. To save him for the Arctic cruise Kane had to appeal to Secretary Kennedy to restore Brooks to duty. Mr. Kennedy exacted a pledge to stay away from drink, which Brooks dutifully signed and deposited with Mr. Grinnell. To Kane's relief the man was reinstated. Kane was not so optimistic about another alcoholic, a younger brother of one of the members of *Advance's* 1850–51 crew. The boy had no experience at sea and Kane turned him down.

William Morton, a young Irish-born navy man, who also had been one of

*Advance*'s crew on the first Grinnell voyage, volunteered for the new cruise. He reported to Kane in the spring of 1853 and at once made himself indispensable as a sort of valet-companion and messenger and, when Kane fell ill, as nurse. Among the civilian volunteers were Amos Bonsall, a Pennsylvania farmer, Henry Goodfellow, an intelligent and literate friend of Judge Kane's family, and Jefferson Baker, a country boy, in earlier years an occasional hunting companion of Dr. Kane.

By dint of many letters and interviews Kane was also getting together his professional staff. As surgeon he chose Isaac Israel Hayes, twenty-one years old and not yet out of medical school at the University of Pennsylvania when he volunteered for the expedition. Hayes took his M.D. degree a few weeks before departure for the Arctic. To appoint a man so inexperienced would have been rash indeed if Kane had not himself been a physician and surgeon with Arctic experience. Hayes knew something of natural history and thus to a certain extent made up for the failure to obtain a German-trained naturalist through Alexander von Humboldt. Henry Goodfellow was also to serve as natural history observer. Kane himself would take care of geology and geography, for which he was qualified by his training, years before, in Virginia with William Barton Rogers, by his wide travels in South America, Asia, and Europe, and by his experience on the first Grinnell Expedition.

For astronomical observations he fortunately did not have to depend upon amateurs. A young German named August Sonntag volunteered for the expedition. Little is known about Sonntag's origin and education, except that before coming to America he had been on the junior staff of the observatory at Altona near Hamburg. At Kane's request Secretary Kennedy gave him an appointment at the U.S. Naval Observatory, but the salary was so small that Kane, through the American Philosophical Society, raised $400 in $25 contributions to add to Sonntag's compensation.[36] The Smithsonian Institution voted $500 for physical instruments, and the coast guard lent apparatus for the study of terrestrial magnetism. The Naval Observatory provided accurate thermometers and navigation instruments including chronometers and compasses. A novel item of equipment was a photographic camera, chosen by Kane after much correspondence with Maury.[37] Amos Bonsall was taught to operate this apparatus, which, however, failed to work in the Arctic.

The Philadelphia Academy of Natural Sciences offered to help plan biological equipment, but its advice was so overwhelmingly elaborate that Kane had to get Spencer F. Baird of the Smithsonian Institution to cut down the academy's list. As Baird wrote to George P. Marsh, scientist and diplomat,

Dr. Kane's second Grinnell Expedition starts for Greenland the middle of April. He will have about 250 dollars worth of traps, which I am now getting in train. The Dr. was applied to by a committee from the Phila. Academy of Natural Sciences in regard to making collections; they suggested various articles of apparatus, the aggregate somewhat bulkier than his little vessel; many of them more complex than Babbage's calculating machine. In despair he came to me, and I soon made out a list of available articles which the Secretary [of the Smithsonian Institution] approved.[38]

Kane's medical training gave him special concern about the food on which he and his men were to depend for two or three years. He busied himself all spring securing special foodstuffs to supplement his navy stores. Through Mr. Grinnell he arranged to have the pioneer food packer Gail Borden—later of condensed milk fame—prepare in Texas two thousand pounds of pemmican and a large quantity of Borden's meat biscuits. From another experimentally-minded packer in Baltimore, Henry Evans, he secured several barrels of specially pickled cabbage hopefully intended to protect the crew from scurvy. For the same purpose he carried a few barrels of malt extract and a compact apparatus for brewing beer. For journeys to be made by sea, by land, and over the ice *Advance* carried a number of rubber and canvas tents, five boats (one of them a novel metallic lifeboat), and five or six sledges. Some of these latter he designed himself; others were copied from a model supplied by the British Admiralty. And, as Dr. Kane recorded with pride, *Advance* carried a well-stocked library.

In mid-April Kane moved to New York to supervise the assembling of *Advance*'s crew and cargo, but he had only a week of this exciting final work on shore when a near-calamity struck. He came down with another attack of rheumatic fever, one of the worst he ever had. Henry Grinnell and his wife rescued him from the hotel where he lay helpless and in severe pain, and had him cared for in their own home. Their son Cornelius acted as messenger and correspondent for Kane, and William Morton of *Advance*'s crew took on the duties of sick nurse. Grinnell senior saw to the enrollment of *Advance*'s crewmen as they reported for duty, and kept his eye on the work of fitting out the brig. Judge Kane in Philadelphia relieved his ailing son of another heavy burden, that of finishing his book on the first Grinnell Expedition. So successfully did the judge carry out this task that the chapters he completed show no trace of separate authorship. Dr. Kane was far into the north when Harper and Brothers brought out the book. He was not to see a copy of it for two years.[39]

By May 17 the attack of rheumatic fever was wearing off. Kane, now able to write, told his friend Kennedy that "after a cruel attack of inflammatory rheumatism and three weeks of helplessness on my beam ends" he found himself ready to start northward. "We leave next week," he wrote.[40] But this was overoptimistic. He began to visit the brig daily, but his inflamed joints were still so stiff and sore that in the mornings, before he could get out of bed and be driven to the dock, Morton had to massage his limbs for a full hour. It would be two weeks before he and his brig were either of them ready to sail. Indeed, to sail at all so soon after his severe illness was as desperately rash as anything else he ever did in a consistently rash career. His only consolation in this bitterly depressing time was word received from Lady Franklin that Captain Inglefield, his supposed rival, had not yet left England for Baffin Bay.

During these last weeks of intense work followed by physical suffering, Dr. Kane had not forgotten Margaret Fox. Indeed, she was more than ever on his mind and heart. In March his persistent pleading to get her away from her family and the séances had begun to sway the perplexed girl and her equally puzzled mother. Kane and Margaret were both in New York at the time, and the decision was made by letters from the Foxes' seat of action on 26th Street and Kane's temporary residence at a hotel. Some of the messages were carried by Cornelius Grinnell, who was becoming Kane's fast friend. "A very interesting girl," he reported to Kane, but added that he had almost no opportunity to talk with her because her relatives watched so closely. Troubled as both were, the girl by family pressures, Kane by urgent affairs and illness, neither was in a mood for florid love letters. Their correspondence at the time reads more like that of a brother and sister. With doubtful veracity Margaret told him that her mother had been perfectly willing, all the while, to let her go to school.

> Now I will leave it with you. If you think we had better drop it here for ever, I am willing. If you still think I had better go to school, I will do so. I did not let mother see your note. But asked her if she was perfectly willing to let me give up the "knockings" and go to school. She said she was. . . . Now do, dear Ly, tell me what I had better do. Now can I see you in the morning. Will you not come here. I can never let you go away without seeing you. Do come here. You need not even see Leah.[41]

Kane immediately replied, March 19, in his most admonitory style:

> Your life is worse than tedious, it is sinful, and that you have so long resisted its temptations shows me that you were born for better things than to entertain strangers at a dollar a head. Do, dear Maggie, stick to your good intentions. I will not depart one jot from my promises. I will talk with Mr. Grinnell and Dr. Hawks and get them to advise with me. If they can recommend a school the money will be forthcoming. All I ask is to see you a good and virtuous girl growing up to be a blessing to others instead of a curse. Do avoid your wretched sister as much as possible. [42]

Mrs. Fox still held out against Kane's urgings. In March, under pressure from Leah and others of her kin, she had written him a sharp note[43] forbidding him ever to see Margaret again, because he was not fit, she said, to associate with an innocent girl—but she signed it "Yours respectfully." Some time that month or the next, however, she gave Kane written permission to place Margaret in school at his expense. She refused to accept Kane's money herself, nor would she choose the school. That, she wrote, she must leave to him.[44]

Here the affair stood, when Kane's illness of April 1853 delayed his efforts to find for Margaret a suitable home and school. Dr. Hawks suggested the Misses Edwards' school in New Haven, Connecticut, and recommended a family in that city who would take Margaret into their home.[45] In mid-May Mrs. Fox, Margaret, and Kane went to New Haven to look into this proposal but thought the proffered living quarters unsuitable.[46]

Kane's aunt, Mrs. Elizabeth Leiper of Lapidea near Chester, Pennsylvania, now came to his aid. A friend of hers, a Mrs. Turner, wife of the manager of a cotton mill near Lapidea, in a rural hamlet called Crookville, about eighteen miles west of Philadelphia, would receive Margaret and see to her schooling. "Family unexceptionable, mother and daughters well informed, tastes cultivated, cheerful dispositions and religious," wrote Mrs. Leiper to Elisha.[47]

Kane wanted a portrait of his beloved to take with him on his voyage. He commissioned a celebrated Italian painter then in America, Joseph Fagnani, to paint it. Margaret gave the artist his final sitting on the afternoon of May 26, her last day in New York before leaving for Crookville. Kane, busy as he was and weakened by illness, insisted on accompanying Margaret and her mother to Margaret's new home. Late on the 26th he sent Morton to the Foxes' New York lodging to accompany the two ladies to the railway station, where Kane joined them. At Philadelphia Mrs. Fox and Margaret stopped at the Girard House. Next morning, "after a melancholy breakfast," wrote Margaret, the three took a carriage to Crookville—a drive of four hours. The village, now totally obliterated—not even its name is to be found on current maps—was about four miles north of Chester, on Ridley Creek, just above the bridge by which Providence Road crosses the stream.[48] Its only buildings were William T. Crook's cotton mill, a few houses of his workpeople, and a church. The Turners lived on a farm on the outskirts of the village. To this retreat Kane consigned poor Margaret, who for six years had lived in the best city hotels and high-class boarding houses, amid a constant stream of people to whom she was a figure of wonder and admiration. Taken from her family's companionship and given into the care of strangers, bereft of her lover who would soon be beyond the reach of all communication, and bound over to dull lessons and the homely quiet of a rural home, she bade farewell to Kane with tears and watched him drive away, with fear in her heart that she might never see him again. But she had not taken account of his reckless devotion. Mrs. Fox, who returned to New York by a late train, told him of Margaret's distress, and next morning he impetuously dashed back to Philadelphia and Crookville for—this time—a final parting.

Three days later, May 31, 1853, he sailed from New York in *Advance* with his crew of seventeen officers and men, bound for St. John's, Newfoundland, and thence to the unknown reaches of Smith Sound. Cornelius Grinnell wrote to Margaret Fox,

> The day was beautiful and every man was in town at the appointed hour. As the vessel passed along the wharves of the North River, she was saluted with cheers from the crowds assembled, and by guns from the shipping. Two steamers accompanied us to sea, filled with people. The Doctor was in good spirits, and was quite well, having entirely recovered from his rheumatic attack.[49]

Judge Kane and his three younger sons, Thomas, Pat, and John, had come over from Philadelphia to see *Advance* sail and were aboard one of the vessels that accompanied her to Sandy Hook and beyond.

Once at sea, Dr. Kane had leisure to reflect on the fearful task he had undertaken. To his brother Thomas he wrote a farewell letter to be returned to Philadelphia by any ship he might meet upon his way northward:

> Now that the thing—the dream—has concentrated itself into a grim, practical reality, it is not egotism, but duty to talk of myself and my plans. I represent other lives than my own. . . .
>
> The object of my journey is the search after Sir John Franklin: neither science nor the vain glory of attaining an unreached North shall divert me from this one conscientious aim. . . . God bless you, my own dear brother. Do justice to my motives, and believe neither in unmixed good or unmixed evil in this world of medley.[50]

# 8

# To the Unknown North

IN SPITE of rough weather, *Advance* arrived off St. John's, Newfoundland, eighteen days after her departure from New York. Doctor, now Captain, Kane as always on his voyages had suffered from seasickness. He had, moreover, by no means fully recovered from his recent attack of rheumatic fever. According to his shipmate, Henry Goodfellow,

> Instead of the former restlessness and intense vitality, he had the subdued look of a broken-down invalid. In the interval between this period and that of his departure he had recovered in a great degree the tone of his bearing; but he was far from being either well or vigorous. . . . His debility did not prevent his frequent presence and activity on deck. He superintended the work upon the sledge apparatus and equipment; and interested himself in the course and speed of the brig.
>
> He was fond, on fine afternoons when the sun shone out, of reclining on a large tarpaulin-covered box on the quarterdeck, where wrapped in a buffalo-robe, he would write his journal or watch the working of the ship and seem to forget his exhausted frame. . . .
>
> As we advanced along the coast of Greenland, he seemed stronger, and underwent the exposure belonging to boating among the settlements with the alacrity of a well man.[1]

While the brig was beating her way past New England and Nova Scotia, Kane had begun to take stock of the officers and men he and Henry Grinnell had so hastily assembled. At this stage of the voyage, there were seventeen men aboard the brig, beside himself. His roll read as follows:

John Wall Wilson, Sailing Master    Henry Brooks, First Officer

James McGary, Second Officer

William Morton, Steward

Christian Ohlsen, Carpenter

Henry Goodfellow

George Riley

Jefferson Baker

Isaac I. Hayes, M.D., Surgeon

August Sonntag, Astronomer

Amos Bonsall

George Stephenson

George Whipple

William Godfrey

John Blake

Peter Schubert, Cook

Thomas Hickey

To those he added later, in Greenland, Hans Christian Hendrik, huntsman, and Carl Petersen, master sledge driver and Eskimo-speaking interpreter, making a party, all told, of twenty men.

Brooks, navy boatswain acting as first officer of *Advance*, biggest and physically strongest man in the party, proved to be Kane's main reliance in manifold difficulties and dangers. Wilson, another of the navy volunteers, as sailing master or "master's mate" outranked Brooks, but Kane discovered before they reached Greenland that he lacked experience and had no control over the men. After a frank talk with him, Kane installed Brooks as executive officer, leaving Wilson on an uncertain footing that further reduced his authority. In the roster of the party printed in *Arctic Explorations, 1853, '54, '55*, Kane gave Wilson no title at all, though he listed him next after Brooks and Dr. Hayes. Wilson never got over this and other slights he felt he received from Kane.[2] McGary, a New London whaling man, was second officer. Christian Ohlsen, ship's carpenter, of Danish birth, had been on whaling vessels as far north as Davis Strait. Sonntag had special status as astronomer, serving under Kane's direct command, but Dr. Hayes and the quasi scientists Amos Bonsall and Henry Goodfellow, were assigned to watches under the respective deck officers. Morton, nominally steward, seems to have reported directly to Kane as a general aide to the commander. Peter (or Pierre) Schubert was the ship's cook. He had been employed, it is said, in the kitchen at Delmonico's famous New York restaurant, but whether as cook or scullion is not stated. Because the navy's volunteer detachment did not provide a full quota of ordinary seamen, Henry Grinnell, acting for Kane during his illness of May, had filled out the crew with what he could pick up on the New York waterfront. Two of these last-minute recruits, William Godfrey, a harbor boatman, and John Blake, a sailor from Baltimore—both of them of unknown and probably discreditable antecedents—were to make serious trouble aboard the brig, even before she reached Arctic waters. We shall hear much of Godfrey's deeds and misdeeds. As for Blake, the fact that in the records of the cruise he turns up under an alias, as "William Hussey" or "Huzza," about as often as "John Blake," hints at a past as dubious as Godfrey's. Irish-born Thomas Hickey was the cabin boy.

Dr. Kane with Officers and Morton
Engraved by J. McGoffin from drawing by C. Schuessele
(Left to right: Bonsall, Brooks, Kane, Hayes, Morton)

While convalescing, Kane was also shakily playing a new role—captain of his own ship and commander of a raw, largely inexperienced crew. Self-consciously acting out his part, he put on a show of authority that concealed inner uncertainties revealed only in letters to his family and then between the lines. Writing from the brig, at sea, June 8, he told his sister first of his seasickness, so bad that one day his routine noon observation with the sextant had almost been spoiled by a spell of vomiting—an embarrassing situation, to say the least, for a commanding officer. Then, as to his unaccustomed problems of leadership and discipline,

You will ask how I get along on the more difficult part of command—the management of the little family of officers and men now under my control. I can only answer—Well for the days that have passed, and hopingly for the days to come. . . . Soon—disgustingly soon for our better natures—we learn to take to ourselves the perquisites of accident—and this trade of authority sits so easily upon me that I feel as if to be toadied was a natural and inevitable province of my peculiar self. The best piece at table—the best places on deck—the smile at a bad joke—the affected comprehension of a good one—the deference to an absurd idea—the jump at a request or suggestion—all these—which would kill dear Tom—I take as naturally as the filling of a Burgomaster's pipe —smoking, puffing, pausing, and casting away, just as it suits or does not suit *I myself.*

But in truth I am a better man than you think me. A better man indeed, than I thought myself—for I fight against this "Big Injin" feeling and try to keep myself from lowering by lifting up those around me. I find something rebelling against the exercise of an artificial power—a digust at even the necessary despotisms of authority—and while a conviction of their necessity comes over me as a sort of sober puzzle I try by every means in my power to diminish and soften down their exercise.

On deck I am as curt and unbearable as my worst enemy could desire—but if I do see a man or men in a state of reasonable sunshininess I strive hard not to cloud him, and with every one—when I can enjoy the luxury of finding one off duty, I am as free and easy as if on shore. Shame to me that I should make a merit of such a confession. So we wear into harness and so *the harness wears into us.*

To this he added a postscript intended to comfort Mrs. Kane, who evidently had written, motherlike, to remind her wandering son of his religious duties. She must at the same time have poured out her anxieties for his physical safety and said something bitter about difficulties of family life at Fern Rock, from which she wished she could get away. With a characteristic mixture of humor for himself and almost impertinent sermonizing for her, he wrote

We have prayed every morning with washed hands, and a grace at meals, all standing around the table in a manner most reverent and hopeful. Even Henry Goodfellow no longer smiles disrespectfully at my devotions and I really don't see why as far as the formula goes I am not a good and pious man.

Rheumatism-like Bob Acres courage has "oozed out at my fingers' ends" and every hour shows me that the path ahead is full of promise and reward. Now my mother—my Christian Mother—why repine? Do you think that I will work the more happily with the consciousness of leaving behind me a mother fretting away life's blessings—denying to her God the just gift of gratitude, a serene spirit—urging her frail system of flesh beyond its apportioned powers and perhaps depositing it before I return in that cheering family Sepulchre-Egyptian establishment at Laurel Hill.[3]

Mother Kane, this won't do—I speak selfishly—It will never do for you, dear, gentle, loving, growling, root-scraping provident she-bear as you are, to leave your cubs.—Hibernate, my Mother—gather smiles and fat in the bright summer time. Look God's Sun in the face, and when damp, musty winter comes hibernate—suck your paw. Thus you will live to bless us all—to cheer that Father, and watch [over] the still living predecessors of little Willie. Do, my own dear Mother, do all this.

Hans Hendrik
Woodcut from sketch by Dr. Kane,
*Arctic Explorations, 1853, '54, '55*
(Philadelphia, 1856) 2:74

William Godfrey
From Godfrey's *Narrative of the
Last Grinnell Exploring Expedition*
(Philadelphia, 1857)

A single month at Mrs. Wickham's, the converse of a single congenial Christian woman aided by change of scene and hot bread would do it all—So much for our material natures!![4]

When the brig came to anchor outside the rocky narrows of St. John's harbor on June 16, Kane went ashore to call upon the governor, who received him warmly and made him a present of six valuable Newfoundland dogs and as many barrels of seal flippers on which to feed them. While ashore, Kane bought a couple of sledges. On the 18th the brig was towed into the harbor. The governor came aboard for a ceremonial call, accompanied by his suite with their ladies and by officers from the British garrison. In recognition of the expedition's humane purpose of searching for Sir John Franklin, the Newfoundland government remitted all port charges. A crowd of citizens appeared on shore to cheer the American party. The local Masonic Lodge held a special meeting and reception for Dr. Kane, having learned somehow that he had joined the order just before leaving New York. "Marked excitement," wrote Kane in his private journal.

He sailed from St. John's on the 19th, and after another slow passage caused by heavy winds entered the harbor of Fiskernaes in southern Greenland on the 30th, amid the clamor of the whole village. Here Kane added another man to his crew, Hans Christian Hendrik, an Eskimo youth of nineteen years, recommended by the local superintendent of the Danish trading post as an expert in paddling a kayak and a skilled hunter with the javelin. At first sight of this fat, good-natured, and stolid boy, Kane was not impressed, but when Hans proved his skill by spearing a bird on the wing, the doctor engaged him at once. As hunter to the party Hans was to draw a small wage plus the bonus of a rifle and a new kayak, and also a gift to his mother of two barrels of bread and fifty-two pounds of salt pork. Many times during the next two years his marksmanship with spear and rifle saved his companions from hunger.

*Advance* put out to sea again on July 1. On the 4th her crew enjoyed a special dinner, drinking toasts to Independence in porter and whisky, and topping off with plum pudding. All hands were granted an extra period of rest after their long struggle against head winds and heavy seas. Next day, however, serious trouble broke out. Whether from a 5th of July hangover or the effects of sheer discomfort and hard labor in the little wave-battered brig, William Godfrey, the tough harbor boatman from New York's East Side, and his equally tough ally John Blake took offense at an order from First Officer Brooks and assailed him (says the journal) with "insubordinate and disrespectful language."

Kane, inexperienced in the command of seamen, had expected to control his men by the firm but friendly treatment he had outlined in his letter of June 8 to his family and more officially, months earlier, to Spencer F. Baird: "They say, among our naval friends, that subordination can only be preserved by distance and reserve. This idea is repugnant to the kindly feelings of one's nature. 'Non semper arcum tendit,' and I intend to try to be exacting on duty and bearable when off of it."[5] Kane's treatment of the two insubordinate deck hands was certainly firm. He had them tied hand and foot, covered them up with warm buffalo robes, and put them (with loosened bonds, let us hope) in a dark space between decks. He gave them a supply of bread and water, and to make their confinement secure, ordered Ohlsen the carpenter to nail down the booby hatch over their heads. There he left them, Godfrey for one day and Blake for two. After this cooling-off period in darkness and semistarvation the men asked to be released and "promised to be good boys," as Kane wrote to Cornelius Grinnell (incidentally stating the period of confinement as four days rather than the shorter time he entered in his journal.) "Since then," he wrote, "they have been two of our best men." This incident did not alarm him; his corps of officers was so strong, he felt, that he had no fears as to good discipline and a happy ship.[6] Whether Godfrey and Blake-Hussey were incarcerated for one day or four, the punishment seems, today, severe. But Henry Goodfellow, long afterward, reminded Kane's sister that it was mild compared with the practice of the U.S. Navy, at that time, in similar cases of insubordination.[7]

There was no further trouble for a few days, but on July 11 Godfrey erupted again. The crew came aft to report that he was making a disturbance in the seamen's mess. Kane deputed Ohlsen and McGary to see what was up. They confirmed the report from the forecastle and recommended getting rid of the offender by putting him aboard an English whaler bound homeward. The men volunteered to carry on Godfrey's duties, but Kane, reluctant to lose a strong, active seaman, had a man-to-man talk with the culprit and gave him a fortnight to turn over a new leaf. Apparently Godfrey promised to behave; at any rate he remained aboard the brig and kept the peace for several weeks. Dr. Kane chose not to mention these episodes in his account of the northward voyage in *Arctic Explorations, 1853, '54, '55,* saying only in a later part of his narrative that he had "a couple of men on board whose former history I would give something to know—bad fellows both of them, but daring, energetic, and strong. They gave me trouble before we reached the coast of Greenland." His biographer of 1858, Elder, who had access to Kane's journal, suppressed the story completely. Nor did Godfrey care to reveal his outbreaks in a self-exculpatory narrative he published shortly after Kane's death. He merely says that although he became a general factotum aboard the brig, he never had the good fortune to be a favorite with the officers.[8] But distrust and resentment between Kane and Godfrey lingered on until the last days of the expedition, when all animosity was set aside amid desperate peril.

On July 17, *Advance* put in at Proven, where Kane found old friends from his stay there with De Haven in 1851. Inglefield, they told him, had made port at Proven twelve days before. His steamer *Isabel,* like *Advance,* had fought bad weather on the way north. She would have to conserve her coal, and Kane no longer feared that Inglefield would beat him to Smith Sound and whatever lay beyond. Not till later did he learn that the brilliant English officer was not heading for Smith Sound at all, but for Beechey Island in Wellington Channel to communicate with Belcher's squadron. At Proven, Kane completed his stock of furs for the sledge trips. Leaving port in light winds, the brig half sailing, half drifting, Kane put Brooks in temporary command and set off in the whaleboat to visit native settlements among the islands, where he bought dogs. Meanwhile the pack already aboard broke into a barrel of seal flippers and gorged themselves so heartily that four of them died. Nevertheless Kane still had twenty-two superior sledge dogs plus those given him by the governor of Newfoundland, and a few others not so good, numbering thirty-two in all; and some of the bitches were pregnant. Returning to the brig, on the 20th he reached Upernavik, where also he was entertained by the Danish superintendent, Governor Fleischer.

In his address to the American Geographical Society, December 14, 1852,[9] Kane had mentioned his intention to make a stop at this last outpost of civilization to buy sledge dogs and hire two or three men to drive them. One would expect that this final contact with civilized human beings would have evoked, from a man of his sentimental temperament, an emotional passage in his record of the voyage. In fact, Kane's journal barely mentions the three-day stay at Upernavik, and there is scarcely a word about it in his book, *Arctic Explorations, 1853, '54, '55.* Yet he must have recalled the visit with mixed feelings because it was here that Carl Christian Petersen joined the expedition.

Petersen, born at Copenhagen about 1815, was in his youth apprenticed to a cooper, but left Denmark for Iceland and then went to Disko in Greenland to work at his trade. He was promoted to the post of "vice-governor" or assistant manager of the trading colony at Upernavik, where he was living when the Franklin Search got under way. He mastered the difficult language of the Eskimos and learned their art of driving dog teams. He also learned to speak English. Because of these skills Captain William Penny, when his vessel *Lady Franklin* had stopped at Upernavik in 1850, had taken Petersen with him as Eskimo-speaking interpreter and chief sledge driver. Shortly after Petersen's return from that voyage, Inglefield, bound in 1852 for the northern tip of Baffin Bay and Smith Sound, in *Isabel,* asked him to go along, but the Dane declined. Isaac Hayes, who later went through many adventures with him, said that Petersen was a cautious man, "with somewhat of the persistence of a frontiersman's recollection of wrongs done to him."[10] He was also, evidently, opinionated, and likely to be overcritical of his shipmates and his commander; but in 1850–51 he had served Penny well and had proved himself an expert and resourceful dog driver.

Kane had high hopes of Petersen. To Cornelius Grinnell he wrote from Upernavik:

> It was quite a regular piece of diplomacy to obtain him as he had refused Inglefield, and settled himself down to a quiet winter with his wife. But he is now fast, and upon terms which considering his great Arctic experience, I consider moderate. . . . I give Petersen thirty dollars a month, with a small advance in pork; part of the above sum being paid to his wife by the Governor of Upernavik.[11]

Evidently Dr. Kane expected Petersen to become leader of the sledge parties if he himself were to be disabled, for he continued, with a touch of personal feeling not often displayed in his journal at this stage of the voyage:

This step I regard as the most fortunate for the success of the Expedition that could have happened. By the blessing of Providence, whatever may be my own strength or weakness, health or disease, I now feel as if some results were certain. Your Father's hopes and my reputation cannot now be entirely obscured. I have never, my dear friend, doubted my own will or energy; but it was my duty to guard against contingencies, independent of these; and to secure that which would place me beyond the drawbacks of the body. Petersen is accompanied by his own sledge and dog-team, completing my full complement for travel.

But Carl Petersen, once aboard the brig, was far less confident of the expedition's success than was his commander. He found the vessel strongly built but poorly provisioned, the crew inadequate in numbers, experience, and discipline. Among them only his fellow countryman Ohlsen appeared to know his business. The ship, moreover, was not well commanded; Dr. Kane, he said, was rash and stubborn, and no seaman. "A presentiment whispered to me" (he wrote a few years later) "that this ship would never return and my experience, perhaps, would prove useful to these daring but unskilled Americans."[12]

*Advance* sailed from Upernavik July 23, 1853, her personnel augmented by Petersen and about twenty more dogs. In alternating periods of perfect calm and offshore breezes from south and east, she found herself in four days off Wilcox Point, at the southern headland of Melville Bay, the great indentation in Greenland's west coast, shallow in depth but 150 miles wide from cape to cape. On the waters of Baffin Bay, southwest and west of Melville Bay, lay the great floes of the middle ice, made up of heavy ice pans interspersed with bergs. Whalers who penetrated the upper part of Baffin Bay had long since found out that when in summer the middle ice drifts westward from Greenland, it leaves open water along the coast, bordered by a firm shelf of more or less smooth land ice ("ice belt") anchored to the shore. Through this temporary channel the whalers were accustomed to make their way north at the beginning of summer, sailing when they could, but when the winds dropped or were unfavorable they used the ice belt to "track" their vessels, that is, to tow them by the manpower of their crews, as canal boats are drawn by mules along a towpath.

Explorers in the Franklin Search had generally followed the same route. Those captains who attempted instead to cross the middle ice westward or northward bound had usually been balked by the pack, as De Haven was in 1850. But if they attempted the shore route later in the summer, they found

Icebergs near Kosoak
Engraved by J. McGoffin from drawing by J. Hamilton after
Dr. Kane's sketch, *Arctic Explorations, 1853, '54, '55,* 2:57

the land ice was breaking up and was no longer safe for tracking; and the once-open water lane was clogged with floe ice. Thus in 1849 the British vessel, *North Star,* was hopelessly entangled in the pack and carried northward, and in 1851 De Haven, in his second summer's attempt to work his way northward, was balked and had to turn back, whereas *Prince Albert,* leaving him, worked a successful passage to the west. Before *Advance* reached the southern front of the middle ice on July 29, Kane had observed that the ice belt was already so broken and decayed that the inshore track would be very difficult. The ice pack in the open bay was, on the other hand, fairly loose and with its icebergs was drifting favorably to the north. He resolved, therefore, to stand to the westward and bypass Melville Bay by an outside passage. This gamble nearly failed; for the next few days after he entered the pack, *Advance* was almost constantly in great danger. Alternately ramming his way through loose ice or mooring the brig to an iceberg, Kane kept his crew at work long hours at a stretch, laboriously taking in or setting sail, hacking away at obstructing tongues of ice with the ice saw and ice axes, or getting into the boats to carry mooring lines to neighboring icebergs which might temporarily protect the brig from the grinding pack. On Sunday, July 30, *Advance* collided head-on with a large berg. The situation must have been critical, though in his narrative of the voyage Kane tells us only that "we drove into a couple of icebergs, carried away our jib-boom, and destroyed one of our quarter boats." In his journal he did not even mention the collision, the relevant entry being merely "Sunday. No divine service, crew exhausted."

Petersen, who was greatly alarmed by this accident, asserts that the doctor rashly let the brig hold her course until it was too late to avoid a collision. Just before the crash, he says, First Officer Brooks asked him to take the helm, though why Brooks should do any such thing Petersen does not explain. According to his story it was he who with great presence of mind called out to Sonntag to slack off the mainsail and thus let the vessel move away from the iceberg. Kane and Brooks, he says, fell to accusing each other of carelessness, and meanwhile Ohlsen temporarily assumed charge of the wheel and got the brig out of her perilous position.[13]

On the next day Kane espied a berg of gigantic proportions drifting steadily northward while the loose ice slipped by either side. After four hours' labor a boat crew made fast to this great mass of ice and thus the brig was carried along until ten o'clock at night, when the lookouts spied an open lead in which the vessel was got under sail again. On the way, wrote Dr. Kane, he and his men

> were favored with a gorgeous spectacle which hardly any excitement of peril could have made us overlook. The midnight sun came out over the northern crest of the great berg, our late "fast friend," kindling variously-colored fires on every part of its surface, and making the ice around us one great resplendency of gem work, blazing carbuncles, and rubies and molten gold.

The next few days were spent in a loose pack, with a helpful offshore breeze. Here, Kane noted, everything depended upon practical experience of the ice. Not willing to trust anyone else to select open-water leads for his course, he spent the whole day with McGary in the crow's nest as the little vessel pitched and rolled amid floating ice—surely the most miserably uncomfortable post in the world for a man with aching joints and a tendency to seasickness. By midnight of August 3 *Advance* was safely in the North Water, quite free of the pack, and scudding toward Cape York under full sail on a northwest wind. Kane's venturesome choice of his route through the middle ice—whether a rash gamble, or the fruit of good judgment based on his scientific observation of the ice in 1850–51—had brought him through those immense floes in seven days since he abandoned the inside track of the whalers. On August 6 the headlands of Cape Alexander and Cape Isabella, marking the entrance to Smith Sound, were in sight. These mountainous capes, twin Gibraltars of the north, fifteen hundred feet high, and faced with precipices eight hundred feet from top to bottom, impressed even the dull-

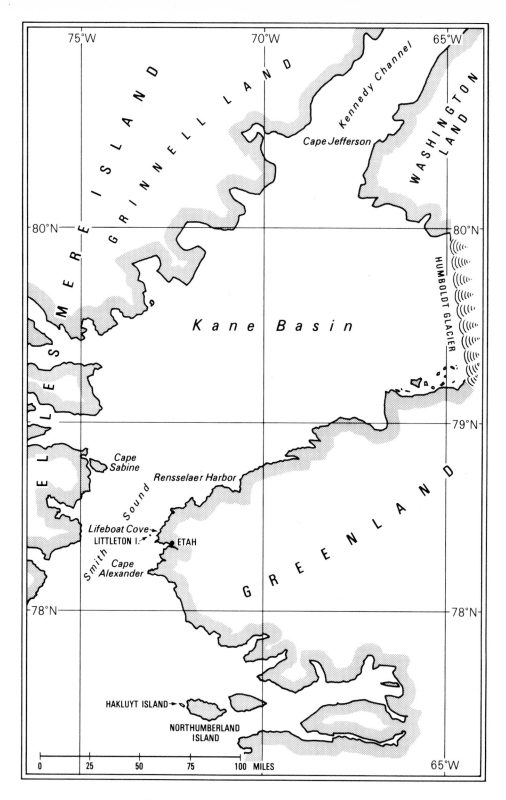

The Region Explored by Kane, 1853–55

est seamen with their somber magnificence. On the morning of the 7th, Kane, now well into Smith Sound, could see ahead of him Littleton Island and beyond it Cape Hatherton, farthest north of the landmarks charted and named by Inglefield the year before. Littleton Island, conspicuous and accessible at latitude 78° 24′ north, was obviously a good landmark near which to leave a record of the expedition and a supply of stores in case of need on his return. Kane therefore took to the Greenland shore his little metallic life boat loaded with a small cache of food and blankets. In a cove about two miles from the island he buried the boat and its cargo under a pile of stones over which the men poured water to freeze and consolidate the mound. They wedged a flagpole into its crevices and unfurled a United States flag. With three cheers for Lifeboat Cove, the landing party returned to the brig.

During the next few days the vessel had to work through loose ice, at times packed firmly enough to drag her helplessly along, fortunately still to the northward. Finally, after a hard struggle by the crew, she was free again. But Kane's troubles were never finished. In a poignant entry in his narrative he tells of his problem of feeding the dogs—at this time fifty-seven of them in the space of a modern harbor tugboat. Two bears shot at the head of Baffin Bay lasted them only eight days, and now, in Smith Sound, the hungry beasts were again howling for food and rushing across the deck in a wild pack when anything resembling food was brought aboard. They tried to break into the deckhouse where the pemmican was stored. One of them, says Dr. Kane, devoured two large birds' nests he had collected from the rocks— a full peck at least of feathers, filth, pebbles, and moss. Kane spotted a walrus and tried in vain to shoot it, but during the hunt luckily found a recently dead fourteen-foot narwhal, six hundred pounds of meat not too fetid for the dogs.

Another of his plagues recurred on August 11 when the irrepressible Godfrey abused and assaulted Mr. Wilson. Bonsall, Ohlsen, and McGary, assigned to investigate the row, blamed it on Godfrey, and Kane again put him under the booby hatch with an allowance of bread and water, but on the 13th let him have a full ration of meat, and on the 14th released him temporarily. A gale had suddenly come up from the south and the ice was closing in. To have kept the man below decks under a nailed-down hatch in dangerous weather would have added inhuman mental torture to his punishment, and moreover Kane might at any moment need every able-bodied man on deck. On the 15th the sea was quieter and Godfrey was again put down the hatch, for how long the journal does not say.

During the brief interlude of good weather that followed, Kane calculated his position and found it could not be matched with the Admiralty charts, hastily based on Inglefield's reports, which had been furnished to him; nor could he identify any of the landmarks described by Inglefield. He was at last farther north in Smith Sound than his predecessor had been and was well into the wide basin into which Smith Sound opens northward, and to which geographers afterward gave the name "Kane Basin." There was heavy weather again on the 20th. Trying to hold at anchor Kane lost his best bower and 500 fathoms of hawser. With battered bulwarks and a splintered rudder, the brig was near disaster. Kane's description of this time of dire anxiety lasting thirty-six hours is one of the most tensely exciting in his story of constant alarms and adventures.

On August 22, at flood tide, he had the towlines passed to the ice belt along the shore, and all hands dragged the brig three miles along the coast. As they struggled ahead in snowy, freezing weather, Kane collected twenty-two species of flowering plants. Yet winter was evidently closing in. So much new ice was already surrounding *Advance* as to cause alarm about the possibility of escape the next summer, and yet Kane was not as far to the north as he wanted to be for the spring journeys by sledge. His men were weary of warping and tracking the brig, and depressed by the slow progress of the past week. One of the deckhands—Kane does not name him—was bold enough to state his opinion that the expedition should turn back. Kane called his officers together at once in a formal council. All but Henry Brooks were convinced that further progress to the north was impossible. To turn back meant, of course, delaying the search. Kane decided to make at least a temporary halt in the small bay—"Rensselaer Harbor"—in which she now lay, while he reconnoitered the region to the north, in hope of further progress. Though some of the men thought Kane merely stubborn, and Carl Petersen privately accused him of mistaken zeal to outdo his British rivals,[14] the men took the decision loyally. A boat's crew ferried the lines again and again to a rocky islet or grounded iceberg and then resigned themselves with the rest of the men to the endless roundabout at the capstan, Kane taking his place among them. Deeper in the bay the ice was less dense, and they again moved to the ice-belt for another spell of towing by manpower. Towing was easier work than warping.

On August 26 the vessel went aground close under the land ice, and could not be moved at the next high tide. The men put ashore everything they could carry, put out the boats, loaded the heaviest anchor into one of them, and carried hawsers to the rocks to secure the vessel if she should suddenly be floated off the bottom. In the night, on a falling tide, she keeled over so far that the cabin stove, full of glowing coals, was thrown down and set fire to the deck. Kane, sacrificing August Sonntag's pilot-cloth coat, choked the fire until the men could dip sea water from the "firehole" cut in the ice for

Crossing the Ice Belt
Engraving by R. Hinshelwood from drawing by J. Hamilton based on sketch
by Dr. Kane, *Arctic Explorations, 1853, '54, '55,* 1:92

such an emergency and pass it down to the cabin. A close shave, Kane said, for his store of gunpowder was close to the scene of the fire.

After several days of such dangers and discomforts, Kane began to consider how much he was likely to gain by any more such desperate labor. But open water along shore was temptingly visible for miles ahead. He resolved to take a boat and crew along this difficult pathway, far enough to see what lay ahead and hopefully to find a good place to lay up the brig for the winter. For this venture he took his best and lightest whaleboat, dubbed "Forlorn Hope," on which he stowed a light sledge together with food and surveying instruments, including his heavy theodolite. To go with him he picked several of his best men—Brooks, Bonsall, McGary, Sonntag, Riley, Morton, and—physically if not temperamentally one of the best—John Blake. Ohlsen was to stay behind in command of *Advance,* and Hayes was charged with keeping the logbook—a double slight to the nominal master's mate, Wilson.

Tracking the "Forlorn Hope" by manpower along the narrow and often obstructed water lane between the ice belt and the floes, the party made about seven miles on each of the first two days. At night, bedded down in the boat, with a meal of pemmican and hot tea, they forgot their troubles and slept well. But on the third day out they found their waterway hopelessly blocked by a ten-foot wall of shore ice under limestone cliffs a thousand feet high.

Hauling the boat up on the icy ledge, they unshipped the sledge and began to drag it over the broken surface of the shore ice. Rounding a point into another bay, they had to cross a small glacier and large river. On September 7, Kane, leaving four of his party to rest, went on with three volunteers and a reduced load of food, camping gear, and light surveying instruments. They crossed the pack ice of the new bay to an 1,100-foot headland, which Kane named Cape John W. Francis.[15] Here, well beyond 78° 50' north, he climbed the headland and from this lookout saw a great stretch of the basin, filled from shore to shore with solid ice to beyond 80° N. With his telescope he thought he descried traversable areas, but at last reluctantly put away his glass, convinced that there was no hope of working his ship further north. He had seen no place offering as much shelter against winter gales, and yet as likely to favor liberation of the brig in the spring, as the bay where he had left her a few days before. There, he had made up his mind, he would spend the winter.

Returning southward over the same rugged route, the party of eight reached *Advance* safely after ten days' absence. His comrades gathered anxiously among them, he tells us, waiting for news of his decision.

> I told them in a few words of the results of my journey, and why I had determined upon remaining, and gave at once the order to warp in between the islands. We found seven-foot soundings and a perfect shelter from the outside ice; and thus laid our little brig in the harbour, which we were fated never to leave together—a long resting place to her indeed, for the same ice is around her still.[16]

To this cove he gave the name Rensselaer Harbor, after his father's country place near Philadelphia, and described it in almost lyrical terms: "It was secure against the moving ice," he wrote, "lofty headlands walled it in beautifully to seaward . . . yet it was open to the meridian sunlight, and guarded from winds, eddies, and drifts."

By September 10 the thermometer had fallen to 14° Fahrenheit and the pack around the brig was so strongly cemented by young ice that the men could walk and sledge upon it. One iceberg had been frozen in, only sixty paces from the vessel. Brooks and a party were busily transferring the contents of *Advance*'s hold to a hastily built storehouse on a small island nearby; McGary and Bonsall were listing and arranging the stores, Ohlsen and Petersen were putting up a wooden housing over the brig's deck, from planks brought along for the purpose. On Sunday, September 11 Kane wrote in his journal:

> Today came to us the first quiet Sunday of harbour life. We changed our log registration to the familiar home series [of hours] that begins at midnight

August Sonntag in the Magnetic Observatory at Rensselaer Harbor
Woodcut from sketch by Dr. Kane, *Arctic Explorations, 1853, '54, '55*, 1:166

[instead of the 8-bell ship's time]. It is not only that the season has given us a regular habitation, but there is something in the return of varying day and night that makes it grateful to reinstate this domestic observance. The long staring day, which has clung to us for more than two months, to the exclusion of the stars, has begun to intermit its brightness. Even Aldebaran, the red eye of the Bull, flared out into familiar recollection as early as ten o'clock; and the heavens, though still somewhat reddened by the gaudy tints of midnight, give us Capella and Arcturus, and even the light of home memories, the Polar Star. Stretching my neck uncomfortably at the indication of our extreme northernness, it was hard to realize that he was not directly overhead, and it made me sigh, as I measured the few degrees of distance that separated our zenith from the Pole over which he hung.

We had our accustomed morning and evening prayers, and the days went by, full of sober thought, and, I trust, wise resolve.

With Sonntag's advice, Kane chose a site for what he called the observatory, a shack on an islet rising a hundred yards from the brig, where he would keep his thermometers, barometers, and magnetic instruments. His tide register was mounted on the brig. The islet he called "Fern Rock" after the little knoll on the Rensselaer estate that his dead brother Willie had loved—"a little spot that I long to see again."

Arrangements now had to be made for the sledging parties that were to lay depots of provisions along the route northward toward the supposed Open Polar Sea which, if Maury's conjectures were correct, Kane expected to find not too far beyond the expedition's wintering place. For the advance party he chose the thirteen-foot sledge given him by the British Admiralty, named "Faith." This would be drawn by seven to nine men.

Petersen, who had charge of the dogs, began to retrain them, after the long confinement on the brig, for their work with the lighter sledges to be used on short journeys. Meanwhile Kane sent Wilson, Dr. Hayes, and Eskimo Hans on a journey into the interior to see what the region was like and whether it offered a prospect of fresh game. They returned after a few days, having climbed to the ice cap that stretched inland beyond the scope of their vision. They espied a few reindeer and numerous hares, but merely to see them gave little promise of a food supply, for travel on the ice cap was very difficult.

On September 20 the depot party, led by McGary, with Bonsall and five men—Baker, Riley, Whipple, Godfrey, and Hickey—left for the north. Dr. Kane accompanied them for sixteen miles, driving the light sledge "Little Willie," drawn by his dog team. Returning, he continued to set up the observatory and to settle down in the winter quarters provided by the brig, now housed in by the shedlike superstructure the carpenters had built over her deck. On the 30th a series of accidents nearly brought the expedition to a sudden end. *Advance,* like other wooden ships, had her quota of rats, which had become a constant annoyance. The two medical men, Kane and Hayes, putting together their knowledge of chemistry, tried to kill the pests with what Kane called the vilest imaginable mixture of vapor, brimstone, burnt leather, and arsenic. While the hold and cabins were filled with this stifling gaseous concoction, all hands spent the night in a chilly bivouac on deck. They were, it appears, less comfortable than the rats, who also survived their part of the ordeal. The doctors then determined to dose the rats with carbonic acid gas. After shutting down the hatches and stuffing every crack in the cabin bulkheads, they lit three stoves full of charcoal in the confined area. All went well until the cook, Schubert, ventured below without Kane's knowledge, out of professional zeal, says Kane, to season a soup. William Morton saw him staggering in the dark and went to drag him into the open air, but fell as he reached Schubert. The others hauled them up, the cook unconscious and Morton's strength almost gone.

The next phase of the disaster, says Kane, was of a graver kind. One of the stoves in the cabin set fire to the deck. Kane, who himself first smelled burning wood, went down to trace its origin and at the foot of the ladder became unconscious from inhaling the fumes. Brooks, ever at hand in emergencies, dragged him out. Coming to himself at once, he gathered the nearest members of the crew, who quickly extinguished the fire with water drawn up through the "fire-hole" in the ice alongside. Next day the men found twenty-eight dead rats in the hold. Both the cook and the captain were still affected by their partial asphyxiation—Kane up and about but suffering with palpitations and vertigo, Schubert groggy but enjoying a day off in his bunk, where Kane heard him merrily singing the folksongs of his native France.

By October 10 Kane was beginning to worry about the depot party under McGary, now out twenty days. If they had carried out his instructions to leave every pound they could spare at the depots, their own supplies must be running low. He decided to go out to look for them, taking with him only one man. He had not hands enough for a sledge party and the ice was in any case not solid enough for a large team and several men. As companion he took with him John Blake, who had evidently regained his commander's confidence since his incarceration under the booby hatch seven weeks before. Taking the lightest sledge and four of the best Newfoundland dogs, the two men set out with the temperature 4° Fahrenheit above zero. For five days they averaged twenty miles a day over very difficult terrain. Once when the men had been trotting all day alongside the sledge, they came upon ice so badly crevassed that the hinder pair of dogs slipped into the water three times in twenty-four hours, and finally all four dogs and the sledge went in together. The sledge stayed afloat and the men hauled it out. To avoid freezing, the men and dogs all started at a run for the solid ice and there, after sixteen hours of travel and exertion, they camped near the shore. "The dogs slept in the tent with us," wrote Kane, "giving us warmth as well as fragrance. What perfumes of Nature are lost at home upon our ungrateful senses! How we relished the companionship."

On the 15th they sighted ahead of them the returning depot party, all seven of them in good condition except that some had severely frost-bitten fingers and toes. Their food was almost gone. McGary reported that they had reached latitude 79° 50′ (probably an overestimate), and had seen an enormous glacier, discharging into the sea as far as their vision reached. This glacier Kane later named after Alexander von Humboldt; it is the largest in the known world. McGary's attempt to make his way around it to seaward proved utterly risky. Returning to the last shore point his party reached, McGary cached the third and northermost depot, 670 pounds of pemmican, 40 pounds of Gail Borden's meat biscuits, and some articles of general diet.

Kane returned to winter quarters ahead of the rest, taking with him on his light sledge Amos Bonsall, whose frost-bitten feet had lamed him. The brig was proving fairly comfortable. When the outside temperature at the end of October had fallen to 25° below zero, the cabin thermometer read 65° above, and even the housed-over deck was above freezing.

Winter, however, was setting in. The last of the walrus had left for the south. The sky daily grew darker. The surrounding hills could be seen only at midday and aboard ship the lanterns were always lit. No white men had ever wintered in so high a latitude, except at Spitzbergen which is warmed by ocean currents.

And so the first part of the winter went by, with a few short journeys by Kane, Hans, Bonsall, and Morton, for hunting and reconnaissance in the neighborhood of the brig. In the course of these trips Kane and his men were surprised to find in several places, within a few miles of Rensselaer Harbor, signs of human habitation—deserted Eskimo huts in groups of three or four. Kane thought them temporary camps of migratory hunters who had gone south to their permanent winter homes. When spring returned, he thought, they might well come back with the walrus and seal.

For a time in November Kane was shut in by his "wretched rheumatism," but after a week, in order to keep going, forced himself to brave the outer world daily. He found that he could walk twenty or even thirty miles a day without signs of cardiac disturbance. He and Hayes and the quasi naturalists of the party collected biological and geological specimens. He kept his men active by sending them on reconnaissance trips and by promoting simple sports, such as "fox chase" around the deck, or football on the ice. Indoors, card games, chess, and reading broke the monotony. One night in November Captain Kane and Surgeon Hayes read to the assembled crew passages from a recent novel, *David Copperfield.* The men got up a fancy-dress ball, and Kane started a newspaper, the *Ice-Blink,* with the motto *In tenebris servare fidem.* On December 14 the whole party celebrated Henry Grinnell's birthday. The crew had a special dinner of marled beef and a can of grog apiece; the officers sat down to a regular dinner, navy style, and drank the health of Henry and Cornelius Grinnell and the Grinnell family in general. This was the last forced show of homely festivity until the sun returned in the spring. On Christmas Day there was no holiday-making; the sole entry in Kane's journal was the solemn phrase, "The birthday of Our Lord Jesus Christ." Winter darkness and monotonous diet were beginning to daunt the most cheerful of this lonely company. Even Eskimo Hans, who well knew the harsh Greenland winter at Upernavik, moaned that "Never in my life had I seen the dark season like this, to be sure it was awful. I thought we should have no daylight any more. I was seized with fright and fell a-weeping. I never in my life saw such darkness at noontime."[17]

Dr. Kane did all he could to avert sickness by good hygiene aboard ship. He kept the men busy scrubbing and scraping the decks and bulkheads and

Winter Life on Board Ship
Woodcut from sketch by Dr. Kane, *Arctic Explorations, 1853, '54, '55*, 2:172

took special pains to keep the enclosed space well aired and dry. "Never was a vessel better ventilated and more exempt from smells," he wrote in his journal in October—no small boast, considering that he had twenty men and fifty dogs on the little vessel. Every Sunday after prayers Kane mustered the crew for a health inspection and followed it by a thorough inspection of the living quarters of officers and men. He hoped above all to keep down scurvy, that worst plague of men long at sea. He had Petersen, the former cooper, brew two barrels of beer, thought to be antiscorbutic. Late in October, when frozen fresh meat was running low and the hunters were no longer bringing much game, he began issuing the cabbage he had brought along in barrels of brine. This should have helped, though we do not know how it was preserved. If cooked before pickling, the antiscorbutic vitamin may have been leached out. At any rate, early in November, Brooks, the stalwart deck officer, was in bed with scurvy pains in his joints; by the 24th he and also McGary were showing decided signs of the disease—patchy discolorations of the skin and swollen gums. Kane dealt out raw potatoes—not much of an antiscorbutic, as we know now—and lime juice, of which he had too little. During the winter almost every one of the twenty men had scurvy in varying degree.

The dogs as well as the men finally succumbed to the darkness, cold, and half-starvation. They began in January to fall ill with peculiar symptoms of nervous derangement. Kane thought this was a canine form of scurvy, Hayes that it was caused by eating salt meat. It was probably due, in part at least, to vitamin deficiency. Some of the dogs died in a few days, others only after weeks of illness. The men took them below deck, fed, caressed, and nursed them, but in vain. Before the sun returned the nine splendid Newfoundlanders and thirty-five of the Eskimo dogs had died. Kane's entries in his journal are pathetic; after the Grinnell birthday dinner, "Turk, our best dog, died:" on January 13, "We have now no chance of a journey by dogs." Troubles multiplied. On January 27 the journal reads:

> Placed John Huzza [i.e. Blake] in solitary confinement, vacating for that purpose my own state-room. Except in complete separation from his associates, every indulgence is given to his comfort. His offense was mutinous conduct, refusing to obey orders, threatening to kill our dogs and other acts of insubordination.
>
> This was his fourth offense. Huzza is a hard worker but dangerous and turbulent man. His influence on the crew is of the worst description.

This odd form of punishment—relief from hard labor and the captain's stateroom for a cell—was enforced for thirteen days until Hussey-Blake was returned to duty.

Dr. Kane's determination kept him going through this time of darkness, even though before the daylight returned, in mid-March, the thermometer had reached 46° below zero, the frozen fresh meat was all consumed, and only one barrel of potatoes remained. The crew's spirits revived with the coming of the sun. "We talked encouragingly," Kane wrote, "of spring hopes and summer prospects, and managed somehow to force an occasion for mirth out of the very discomforts of our unyielding winter life."

# 9

# A Disaster, and New Ventures

THE CLIMAX of Dr. Kane's effort was now fast approaching—the time, long dreamed-of and planned-for, when he was to leave his winter base and set out with a few picked men into the unknown farthest north, to reach the Open Polar Sea he expected to find there, and perchance to discover some trace or even survivors of Sir John Franklin's expedition. The journey would be perilous. The shore of the basin (since named after him) in which *Advance* lay trended strongly to the east. To follow the ice belt would greatly lengthen the distance to be covered. The sledge party would therefore have to strike directly north over the rugged waste of ice that stretched beyond Kane's vision from the brig's masthead.

It was for such a journey that Dr. Kane had equipped his sledges, procured his supplies, and gathered in Newfoundland and Greenland the fifty dogs that had crowded the decks of *Advance* the summer before. But the loss of the dogs during the winter enforced a radical revision of the plan. The men would have to take their place, dragging the sledges laden with supplies and carrying a portable boat for the hoped-for traverse of open water beyond the ice. Without the dogs, travel would be slower, the work more exhausting. In any case, however, the first step was to lay down a large cache of food and stores, well beyond that left at the glacier by McGary in October. To put this final cache on the direct line of march toward the Pole, Kane planned to place it on the western shore of the basin—a shore never trodden by civilized man, distant from the eastern shore at its nearest point only about sixty miles. By taking a direct course northward from Rensselaer Bay, a depot party could reach the western shore (now called Ellesmere Island) by a jour-

Tracking along the Ice Belt
Woodcut from sketch by Dr. Kane, *Arctic Explorations, 1853, '54, '55,* 1:79

ney of perhaps seventy-five miles, and, if the shore ice there was smooth enough, could proceed as far northward as its strength and supplies permitted.

Kane was anxious to set out on this crucial stage of his plan, but the traverse of Kane Basin obviously presented terrible difficulties—great hummocks of ice interspersed with bergs, deeply drifted snow, temperatures far below zero and at times icy winds. Carl Petersen asserted later that he had warned against an enterprise so hazardous and probably impossible so early in the season, and said that Ohlsen protected himself by demanding a written order from the commander of the expedition.[1] Kane says nothing of any such objections. Be that as it may, preparations for the advance party, begun in February, were well under way during the first three weeks of March. New sledges must be built, old ones repaired, a portable boat was to be constructed, and for the travelers tents and boots were needed. Kane kept his men—all who were able to work—laboring hard at these preparations. The return of daylight, and some fresh food—rabbits and foxes brought in by Hans and Petersen—had improved the crew's health. Dr. Kane felt that he could assemble a party for the depot trip and still have enough men to keep headquarters at the brig. In spite of the discomforts of life aboard ship, preparations were completed, as Kane had hoped, by the third week of March. On Saturday the 18th he had a big Eskimo-type sledge made ready, with the small boat strapped to the top of its load of supplies. To test the runners, eight men attached themselves to the lines, but were scarcely able to move the sledge. The temperature at the time was 49° below zero. Thinking that the poor traction was due to the thin runners of the sledge cutting through the crusted snow, Kane very reluctantly ordered the boat to be left behind and one-fourth of the food taken off.

The depot party to be led by Henry Brooks[2] included Wilson, Sonntag, Ohlsen, Petersen, Baker, Schubert, and Hickey. On Sunday, March 19, the party was ready to leave. Dr. Kane gave them as a parting gift his last two bottles of port and the whole of the cake from his brother Tom's wedding that he had brought from Philadelphia. After morning prayers and the usual weekly inspection, all hands went out on the ice, the travelers donned their harnesses, tightened the draglines, gave three cheers for things in general and three for Doctor Kane, and pulled away northward over the ice. Petersen's pessimistic view of the undertaking was immediately confirmed when the men found great difficulty in dragging the still heavy sledge. His reasoning has since been supported by an expert on polar travel, A.W. Greely, who recounts the story of this party in his book, *True Tales of Arctic Heroism,*[3] with admiration of Kane's courage but disapproval of his judgment. Kane, he says, had committed two errors frequent in Arctic work—overloading and too early a start in periods of extreme cold. A sledge ordinarily slips along because hard snow or ice melts slightly under its runners, creating a film of water on which they glide. At very low temperatures, however, the ice does not melt but stays as dry as sand and creaks as the sledge is dragged over it. Kane himself saw that Brooks's men, as they started away, were making hard work of it. With serious concern for them he followed their trail that evening and found that at 8 P.M. they had encamped only five miles from the brig. Petersen told him that nothing but the cold had retarded the Eskimo sledge; no sledge of any other construction, he said, could have moved at all under existing conditions. Kane left the men resting under their buffalo robes and returned to the brig.

As commander he prided himself on his caution and care for the men, but a more experienced leader would surely at this point have postponed the trip. Instead, he met the situation with a characteristic outburst of energy and rash determination. As soon as he reached the brig, at about 10 P.M., he called together all the rest of his crew and put them furiously to work getting ready another sledge, this time one of Admiralty design, with broad runners. Working his men until one o'clock in the morning, he had its runners scraped and polished, and fitted it with new tracking-ropes and an entirely new canvas cover. On this sledge (one to which he had earlier given the name "Faith") he again loaded the two hundred pounds of pemmican and the boat that had been discarded the day before. He and four of the men hauled the sledge through the Arctic twilight which in March lasts all night at that latitude, to the camp where Brooks's men were sleeping in their tent. By stealth he took away their sledge and packed its cargo on the "Faith." This done, his four men silently hitched themselves to the tracking lines, and Kane whispered, "Now, boys, when Mr. Brooks gives his third snore, off with you."

The trial succeeded; "Faith" ran nimbly over the ice. Thereupon they wakened the sleepers with three cheers and once more bade them farewell. Thus began again, with the gaiety almost of a schoolboy lark, the perilous journey by which within a fortnight the lives of the whole party were to be placed in direst jeopardy. Kane and his midnight workers returned to the brig, taking with them the Eskimo sledge. Next day at noon McGary, mounting to the crow's nest, espied the depot party moving ahead easily about twelve miles from the brig. The thermometer had risen to about 22° below zero.

There was now more room aboard ship and an opportunity for housecleaning. To save fuel, Kane had the forward bulkhead taken down and moved the men's sleeping quarters aft, thus reducing the amount of space that had to be heated. Hans and McGary brought in a few foxes which the men skinned to make fur mittens, socks, and muffs, and then cooked them for dinner. Preparations went on for Kane's northward trip which he planned to lead as soon as the depot party returned with assurance that they had successfully deposited the final cache of supplies and the boat. Upon this time of hope and relative comfort, disaster broke like the crash of an iceberg.

At 11 P.M., Sunday, April 2, Dr. Kane and the men with him on the brig were cheerfully at work in the cabin, making moccasins, when they heard an unexpected clatter of steps on the deck above. A moment later Sonntag, Petersen, and Ohlsen came staggering down the companionway. Their faces were haggard, their limbs swollen, and they were scarcely able to speak. The story they gasped out to Kane was that Brooks's party had made its way northward with very great difficulty, dragging their overweighted sledge across rough floes and in many places through tortuous passages between sharp-edged hummocks up to fifteen feet in height. Thick fogs and fresh snow impeded the march. On two days they made no progress at all, on another only a mile and a half, and on their best day seven miles. Even though they had abandoned the boat and some of the pemmican, they had at times to divide the remaining load and carry it forward in two hitches, thus traveling over the same road three times. By morning of the 29th of March they had traveled, in all, less than forty miles. Increasing exhaustion made it certain that they could never reach the western shore of the basin to deposit their cache. Brooks in desperation ordered a return to the brig. Traveling southward over exceedingly rough ice and through deep drifts, they made seven miles and pitched their tent at half-past eight. The cold was bitter and their clothes were sifted through with fine snow. Too weary to care for themselves properly they crawled into their sleeping bags without brushing off the snow or removing their boots and socks. Next morning, March 30, the temperature was 57.5° below zero. Brooks, Wilson, Baker, and Schubert were so badly frostbitten that they could not walk. Jefferson Baker was too weak to go on and the others were utterly exhausted. Without help from the brig all eight of them faced death by freezing. Those who could still walk—Sonntag, Ohlsen, Petersen, and Hickey—all volunteered to walk to the brig, about thirty miles distant to the south. Under orders from Brooks, Hickey remained at the camp to care for the four helpless men. The other three left at 10:20 A.M. and reached the brig at 11 P.M., having walked the whole way without stopping and without food and water.

The three messengers had barely told their shattering story when Kane was in action organizing the rescue. Who should go with him? Dr. Hayes obviously must remain at the brig, ready to care for the victims of the disaster if, indeed, Kane could find them out on the snow-drifted ice. Goodfellow was still too ill with scurvy to leave the vessel; seamen Stephenson and Whipple were barely convalescent but could at least help Hayes when the sick men were brought in. Kane would lead the rescuers, whatever the risk to his own health, and would take all the rest of the men from the brig, Bonsall, McGary, Morton, Godfrey, Blake, Riley and Eskimo Hans.[4] One of the three men who had brought the call for help would have to go along as guide. Petersen and Ohlsen thought that a rescue party burdened with supplies could not possibly cover in a single march the distance they had taken thirteen hours to do traveling light. Because prompt relief was so urgently necessary Kane resolved to take the gamble by marching with practically no camping gear and the least possible supply of food. The men packed a small tent, a package of pemmican, a cookpot, and nothing more. They put Ohlsen into a sleeping bag with his legs wrapped in dogskins and eiderdown, and strapped him onto the sledge with a couple of buffalo robes under him for a cushion and the tent and bag of pemmican at his feet. The men carried only

The Rescue Party of April 1854
**Woodcut from sketch by Dr. Kane, *Arctic Explorations, 1853, '54, '55,* 1:188**

the clothes they wore. In less than three hours after the arrival of the messengers they started toward their goal, a tiny white tent in the icy wilderness somewhere to the north, more or less thirty miles away.

Ohlsen, Kane hoped, could guide them by recalling the appearance and bearings of icebergs he had seen on his way back to the brig. One such berg, of fantastic shape, well known to the men as the "pinnacly berg," could clearly be seen in the half-light, but beyond that mark Ohlsen was of no help, for he fell asleep, and when he awoke after sunrise he was mentally confused. Thus they trudged ahead all the daylight hours. As darkness came on they had still not found the camp. Arriving at a long level floe which must be somewhere in the neighborhood of the lost men, Kane ordered the men to pitch their tent, leave the sledge and its food supply with only a parcel of pemmican for each to carry, and fan out in search of footmarks. Ohlsen, though still irrational, had recovered the use of his legs. Some of the others were now as badly off as he; McGary and Bonsall, among the sturdiest, were seized with trembling fits and shortness of breath, and Kane fainted twice on the snow. About 7 P.M., when they had been out nearly eighteen hours, Eskimo Hans spied through the dusk a faint sledge track and then human footsteps. Following these the rescuers saw at last a little American flag fluttering from a hummock and below it on a tentpole barely above the snow a Masonic banner someone of Brooks's party had carried with him.

Entering the tent, Kane found the four frostbitten men alive and Irish Tom Hickey still able to care for them. There were now fourteen men at the tent. With the cooking gear of Brooks's men the newcomers melted ice to assuage their thirst. Pemmican was their only food. Kane's companions, who by this time had been on their feet twenty-one hours, desperately needed sleep, but the tent could hold at most eight. Allowing each in turn to sleep for two hours, Kane ordered the others to keep from freezing by walking outside. Finally he had the four helpless invalids baled up in blankets and furs and lashed them onto the sledge "Faith" they had used on their fruitless journey to the north. On the sledge he also put the tent, and food which might last for fifty hours. The sledgemen stood round the "Faith" while Kane said a brief prayer, and then they started for the brig.

On the way Kane had great difficulty keeping the men from lying down in their tracks. After about six hours on the march some of them began to show alarming signs of collapse, and he had to let them make camp. Leaving McGary in charge, with orders to allow the men four hours rest and sleep, Kane with one man would push on to the tent they had left in the ice, where he would melt ice and thaw out a meal of pemmican. William Godfrey volunteered to go with him—Godfrey, the insolent trouble-maker of the autumn. Now, in the face of death, and sharing with his commander the responsibility for their comrades, he rose to a great height of courage and probably kept Kane from breaking down on their lonely march. Both, said Kane, were half-stuporous and tortured by the desire to sleep. Kane tells of seeing, as they approached their temporary goal, a bear that had just knocked down the tent; Godfrey says that the bear was a product of Kane's distorted imagination.[5] Without speaking to each other they rolled up in the buffalo bags from the sledge and slept three hours. When they awoke, Kane's beard was frozen to his robe, and Godfrey had to cut him out with his jacknife.

Before the rest of the men arrived, Kane and Godfrey had some water ready and warm food in the cookpot. Refreshed by the brief stop, the united party went on toward the brig, which they reached at 1 P.M. on March 31. Bonsall had gone ahead the last few miles to alert Dr. Hayes, who sent Petersen and Whipple to meet them two miles out. Kane by this time was so far gone with fatigue and lack of sleep that the last hours of the march passed like a half-remembered dream.

Hayes was now the only officer in condition to care for his commander and the other men in various states of physical exhaustion and mental confusion. Surely no greater burden of responsibility was ever cast upon a young physician in his first year out of medical school. His official report to Dr. Kane, written four days later, describes the appalling situation with which he had, almost single-handed, to deal.

> Messrs. Brooks and Wilson, J. T. Baker, and Pierre Schubert, lay on the sledge sewed up in buffalo-robes and other furs. The remainder of the party were drawing the sledge. As they passed me, I was startled by their ghastly appearance. They gave me not even a glance of recognition, and when I hailed them they met me only with a vacant, wild stare. Their persons were covered over with frost; from their beards were suspended large lumps of ice; their tread was slow and feeble; and it was a sad sight to see what had three days previous been a party of strong and vigorous men now all bent down as with the weight of years.
>
> For sixty-six hours they had been constantly on foot and exposed in the low temperatures of from 35° to 50° below zero. They had had no rest since leaving the vessel. The loss of sleep, the constant exposure, the depressing effects of the extreme cold, and the great fatigue consequent upon their long journey, had produced alarming prostration. They were almost to a man delirious. Keeping the direction of the vessel as if by instinct, they knew of nothing that transpired. When they arrived at the ship, and when you gave the order to halt, they all dropped the lines and made for the ship's side, the same instinct directing them to their beds.
>
> There was therefore some difficulty in getting force enough to attend to the sick, and it was with a little delay that they were carried to the upper deck,

where they were properly allowed to remain some time before taking them into the warm air of the cabin.

Having placed them in their bunks, that had previously been fitted up with as much care as possible, dressed their wounds, and attended to their present wants, my attention was directed to the remainder of the party. I found they had rolled into their bunks "booted and spurred" just as they had come in from the ice, and were all now fast locked in a heavy sleep, from which it seemed impossible to awake them; and, indeed, I made no effort. With them, as with the wounded, what they most needed was rest and quiet.

Reaction soon commenced. What had before assumed only the form of the simplest mental aberration now broke out in raving delirium, and for two days the ship presented all the appearances of a mad-house. Not an individual of the party escaped, although some were much more seriously affected than others. Many of them seemed to think themselves out on the ice perishing with cold, and when they at last awoke, most of them had not the least remembrance of what had occurred during the last twenty hours of the journey. Except small doses of morphine, it seemed impolitic to do any thing for them at the first outset of their wild raving. The excessive sleepiness had completely overpowered them, and they would only partially arouse at intervals, and give vent to an imploring cry for aid or an exhortation to hurry on.

At last, after twenty-four hours, they began one by one to awake and ask for food. They were in this state for forty-eight hours; and Mr. Ohlsen, who had been eighty hours constantly exposed, and had travelled not less than one hundred and twenty miles, was unconscious of what was taking place for the greater part of two and a half days. He would ask for food frequently, eat with great voraciousness, and again fall back into a torpid sleep, seeming to recognize while awake nothing but the meal which he was eating. His brain-symptoms were accompanied by strabismus. During his sleep his mind ran continually upon the tent on the ice, and he seemed to think himself pushing forward, guiding the party to it; conscious still, seemingly, of being the only one who knew where it was.[6]

Kane, surprisingly, was the last to collapse and one of the first to recover. He too became irrational for some hours, but the peculiar form his delirium took gave Hayes an opportunity to inject a bit of comic relief into his otherwise tragical report.

After seeing that the sick were comfortably cared for, you laid down in your cot, and I began to congratulate myself that you had escaped; but after two or three hours I heard you suddenly cry out, "Halloo on deck there!" On going aft to ascertain what was wanted, I received instructions to "call all hands to lay aft and take two reefs in the stovepipe." As to all hands being now temporarily crazy I had no further doubts; for I would respectfully submit that your mind might perhaps have been at this moment a little wandering.

Schubert, Hayes reported, would have to have one of his feet amputated, Baker part of one and perhaps both. Wilson and Brooks also were badly frostbitten and might require amputation of toes. Of the depot party only Hickey remained well and sound. The rest of the ship's company were all in poor condition; every one of them showed symptoms of scurvy.

"The week that followed the disaster," wrote Kane, "left me nothing but anxieties and sorrow. Nearly all our party, the rescuers as well as the rescued, were tossing on their sick-bunks, some of them frozen, others undergoing amputations." On the morning of April 5, Jefferson Baker was found to be dying, of tetanus, the two doctors agreed. He lingered until April 8. Kane deeply mourned the loss of this young friend whom he had known longer than any other member of the crew—a man, he said, of kind heart and true principles. Baker's shipmates—those who could walk—in sad procession carried his coffin ashore to the observatory hut, the only place outside the brig that was proof against marauding bears. There they laid the coffin upon the pedestals they had built for the theodolite and transit. Captain Kane read the burial service, sprinkling a handful of snow over the coffin for dust. There was no way to bury the corpse safely in the still frozen ground. For weeks Kane, Sonntag, and the others who took daily turns reading the thermometers and magnetometer had to do their work close beside the corpse of their dead comrade. Before long Pierre Schubert lay beside Baker, dead of erysipelas following the amputation of his foot. On his deathbed, as long as he had breath to spare, he was heard singing the gay French songs of Béranger.

On the day before Baker died,[7] Kane was sitting by the sick man's bunk when he heard a startling cry from the seaman keeping watch on deck, "People halloaing ashore." Although he had known, from the visible remains of huts near the brig and from old sledge tracks, that Eskimo hunters had been in the neighborhood, perhaps even in the past year or two, what he saw when he reached the deck was a staggering surprise. "There they were," he wrote, "on all sides of the rocky harbour, dotting the snow-shores and emerging from the bleakness of the cliffs, wild and uncouth, but evidently human beings." The exuberance of this description might suggest that visitors were arriving in droves, but actually according to Kane's own journal, there were eight of them. They wore hooded fur jumpers, white bearskin trousers and fur boots. To these Eskimo visitors with almost beardless features who had never before seen white men, Kane and his bearded crew probably looked equally wild and uncouth, and even more animal-like.

Calling Petersen from his bunk to act as interpreter, Kane went out on the ice, unarmed and waving his empty hands, to meet the leader of the Eskimos. This man, nearly a head taller than Kane, powerfully built, went

Dr. Kane's Sketch of the First Visit of the Etah Eskimos

Meeting with the Eskimos
Woodcut based on Dr. Kane's sketch (preceding illustration),
*Arctic Explorations, 1853, '54, '55,* 2:202

fearlessly aboard ship. He told Petersen that his name was Metek and, to the utter astonishment of the explorers, said that he and his companions lived in a village called Etah only seventy miles, by way of the ice belt, south of the brig. *Advance* had been within a few miles of them when Kane on his way through Smith Sound in August, 1853, had made his cache at Lifeboat Cove near Littleton Island. Their hamlet was the northernmost permanent human habitation in the world. They were quite unknown to their semi-civilized kinsmen in the Danish settlements, and their language was somewhat different. Although Petersen and Hans could converse with them, they could not understand everything the men of Etah said.

While Kane and Metek were getting acquainted in the cabin, Tom Hickey extended hospitality to the rest of the visitors by taking out to them slices of bread, corned pork, and lumps of sugar, but the men declined to taste such food. They showed no fear, however, and brought up their sledges and more than fifty dogs within two hundred feet of the brig. Dr. Kane finally allowed the whole party to come aboard. Excited by the novelty of the situation, the Eskimos were boisterous and rough, exploring every part of the vessel, handling everything they saw, and trying to carry away every detachable object they touched. It was difficult to keep them out of the forecastle, where Jefferson Baker lay dying. They brought their own provisions aboard, boiled some walrus meat in a borrowed iron pot, ate the rest raw, and when their curiosity and their appetite were both satisfied, went to sleep in the hold.

Next morning Kane held a powwow with them, secured a pledge that they would return in a few days with more meat, and bought four dogs for a few needles and beads and a bundle of old barrel staves. Before letting them go he seized the opportunity to sketch their sledges, marvelously put together from small pieces of bone tied with thongs of hide, and equipped with runners of walrus-tusk ivory. He sketched too their lances, and their knives of steel, which had been traded from the Cape York Eskimos, who in turn got the metal from passing whalers. After the visitors left, Kane found that they had taken away, unauthorized, an axe, a saw, and some knives. On April 11 another small party of five old men and boys arrived. Kane gave them presents but told them that none of the Etah people would again be allowed aboard the brig unless the stolen articles were returned. In spite of this, when the five left, one of them sneaked around to Kane's India rubber boat lying on the floe and cut it to pieces to get bits of its wood frame. A few days later a youth named Myouk arrived from Etah by dog sledge. Questioned about the ruined boat, he claimed to know nothing of it. Kane gradually learned that these people of another era were by necessity communistic, freely sharing their equipment with each other; but he could not allow them to strip the brig of essential articles. He therefore had Myouk confined to the hold. The lad refused to eat, but sang, talked to himself, and wailed until late in the night. Somehow he escaped; in the morning he and his dogs were gone, and Kane was not altogether sorry.

Kane's discovery of the Smith Sound Eskimos—if indeed it can be called a discovery seeing that they presented themselves to him—was perhaps not a sensational ethnographic event. These people were not greatly different from their fellow Eskimos to the south. But Kane made them, the loneliest of human beings, known to the rest of the world by his accurate and often charming drawings and descriptions of the men, women, and children of Etah, their clothing, their sledges and weapons, their housing and habits. He created for Americans of his day their standard image of the Inuit tribesmen. Above all, his tactful dealings with these people, combining firmness with kindness, was to repay him well when he and his men would probably have perished without their aid. Moreover, the friendship he built helped to keep the way open for all his successors from Hayes in 1860 to Peary and MacMillan in the twentieth century, who traveled northward through Smith Sound and Kane Basin, along the "American route to the Pole."

By mid-April the health of the crew was improving. Sunlight and fresh food had greatly diminished the signs of scurvy. In his journal Kane entered with relief that thirteen officers and men were off the sick list. He and Hayes had now much less medical work and nursing to do. Hayes had carried a heavy burden during the critical time after the rescue of Brooks's party with all its aftermath of amputations, Brooks's delayed healing and Schubert's fatal illness. Extreme fatigue can be the only possible excuse for a strangely unprofessional act when, on April 13, Hayes wrote to Kane a letter in which he refused to carry on medical duties except at hours selected by himself. To this, Kane replied with a "kind understanding letter." Nothing more came of this aberration of the harassed young surgeon.

Before the end of April, Kane was ready to set out upon another trip to the north. His plan was to follow the ice belt to the great glacier he had named after Humboldt. From the cache left there the previous October he would pick up a supply of pemmican and make an attempt to cross the ice to the American side. "This was to be," he wrote, "the crowning expedition of the campaign, to attain the Ultima Thule of the Greenland shore, measure the waste that lay between it and the unknown West, and seek round the farthest circle of the ice for an outlet to the mysterious channels beyond." Although he still had hopes of finding traces of Sir John Franklin's expedition, the geographical object of the journey loomed larger in his mind. Across the broad basin in which his vessel lay he had seen between the distant mountain tops of the western shore a gap suggesting a deep indentation of the coast. This, for all he knew, might be a channel marking off Ellesmere Island from another land to the north which he was later to name after Henry Grinnell. Since he did not yet know whether the basin was open toward the north, an inlet on the western shore might offer a more promising route toward the Open Polar Sea. If possible he would enter it and see whither it led.

He left Ohlsen in charge of the brig, Brooks being still confined to his bed following amputation of his toes. McGary would take the leading sledge in advance with Morton, Riley, Hickey, Stephenson, and Hans; Kane himself would follow next day with a new light sledge built by Ohlsen. His companion was to be Godfrey, now the expedition's best dog driver and a

"Tennyson's Monument," North Greenland
Engraving by J. McGoffin from drawing by J. Hamilton based on sketch by
Dr. Kane, *Arctic Explorations, 1853, '54, '55*, 1:224

bold and resourceful traveler. They had seven dogs, including three survivors of the old stock and four acquired from the Eskimos. On the sledge
they had pemmican, bread and tea, a small tent, and two sleeping bags of
reindeer skins. For his geographical observations Kane had a good sextant
with an artificial horizon, and a dip-circle, and carried on his person a light
chronometer and telescope.

McGary left on April 25, Kane on the 26th. Both parties at first made
good progress. On their third day out, Kane and Godfrey caught up with the
others. Kane was enchanted by the majesty of the Greenland coast between
Rensselaer Harbor and Humboldt Glacier. The cliffs, indented by great bays,
rose to nine hundred or a thousand feet above the sea, and behind them lay
the precipitous and deeply cloven face of the stupendous ice cap that covers
the whole of northern Greenland. Approaching latitude 79°, Kane found the
red sandstone cliffs strikingly eroded by the action of frost and wind and
water, which had etched the stratified rock to give the impression of jointed
masonry, and here and there had left fantastic columns and battlemented
masses standing apart from the native rock. Kane found time to stop and
warm his hands enough to sketch two of these strange appearances. Most
astonishing of all was a slender solitary column rising gracefully to a height
of 485 feet, and as precisely finished, he wrote, as if it had been cast for the
Place Vendôme. Stirred by the grandeur of the scene, on his sketch he wrote
the name of Alfred Tennyson. This was a double compliment; Tennyson's
wife was a niece of Sir John Franklin, and Tennyson was the poet he most
admired. On the voyage Kane had read over and over again to himself and
to his men Tennyson's two volumes of 1842. Henry Brooks, that unlettered
seaman, long remembered Kane's reading of *Ulysses*, with its haunting paral-
lels to Kane's whole life and his desperate venture to the north.

> Death closes all: but something ere the end,
> Some work of noble note may yet be done,
> Not unbecoming men that strove with gods.
> . . . Come, my friends,
> 'Tis not too late to seek a newer world.
> Push off, and sitting well in order smite
> The sounding furrows; for my purpose holds
> To sail beyond the sunset, and the baths
> Of all the western stars, until I die.
> It may be that the gulfs will wash us down:
> It may be we shall touch the Happy Isles,
> And see the great Achilles whom we knew.
> Tho' much is taken, much abides; and tho'

We are not now that strength which in old days
Moved earth and heaven; that which we are, we are;
One equal temper of heroic hearts,
Made weak by time and fate, but strong in will
To strive, to seek, to find, and not to yield.

When, two years later, Kane was choosing illustrations for his book, he had his artists make from his hasty sketch the grand engraving of "Tennyson's Monument." When the reader turns a page and suddenly comes upon it, he is startled by the vision that stirred the emotions of Dr. Kane and his men when they first saw it. Tennyson hung a colored print of the engraving in one of his rooms at Farringford, and he sent Kane an autographed set of the volumes in which "Ulysses" first appeared.[8]

The party was in serious difficulties as early as May 3, when McGary's contingent had been out eight days, and Kane, with Godfrey, seven. They ran into heavy snowdrifts, and as they struggled on, the men began to give way. Several of them were again showing signs of scurvy. Three were suffering from snow blindness. Stephenson complained of pains in his chest and was quite unfit for travel. Even Hickey was barely able to help drag the sledge. To make matters worse, they found that the food caches had been ravaged by polar bears who had pushed aside the heavy rocks and broken open the iron casks of pemmican.

On May 4, Dr. Kane, while taking an observation for latitude, was seized with a sudden pain and fainted. When he regained consciousness, he went on for a while but could not keep up the pace or withstand the "otherwise comfortable temperature of 5° below zero." His left foot was frozen to the instep, and his legs began to swell. The men strapped him to the sledge and at his insistence doggedly kept on. This day Kane got his first clear view of the Humboldt Glacier from a distance of about twenty miles. Ill and cold as he was, he made a few sketches of it, but the sight called forth only his scientific interest rather than the romantic enthusiasm he had felt beside Tennyson's Monument. He did not care for his drawings. There was too much white surface, he says, and badly fading distances. Immensity alone, without picturesque detail, baffled even as skilled a draftsman as Kane.

He was to see no more new wonders on this journey, for while in view of the glacier he became half-stuporous, and the men, taking command of the situation, gave up the forward march, as much on their own account as his. Even Morton, strongest of the party, began to weaken. Kane said later that he owed his very life to five brave men, Morton, Riley, Hickey, Stephenson, and Hans, themselves scarcely able to travel. By forced marches they got him back to the brig and into Hayes's care on May 14. The young surgeon thought that Kane's collapse was due to scurvy complicated by typhoid fever —an improbable diagnosis, but Hayes like Kane before him had been a student under William Wood Gerhard, and was perhaps inclined to consider any stuporous condition a sign of the disease Gerhard had newly put in the medical literature by distinguishing it from typhus. Kane's symptoms of fever and edema were, no doubt, caused by endocarditis persisting from his many attacks of rheumatic fever and now exacerbated by fatigue and exposure.

When, a fortnight later, Dr. Kane was able to resume command and take thought for the future, he was told that Pierre Schubert had died ten days before. The rest of the crew were better, though only three were able to do full duty. Soon, he hoped, further exploration might be undertaken and continued until warm weather broke up the ice pack to the south and opened their way to sail homeward—if indeed such good fortune might be expected. In preparation for retreat, during Kane's journey and subsequent illness Ohlsen had stowed the hold with the unconsumed stores that had been kept on shore and on the ice; he removed the forward part of the temporary winter housing built over the deck, and refitted the forecastle for the men's quarters.

By May 12 the brig's sides were free from snow and her rigging was clean and dry. Snow birds and sea gulls were returning from the south. As a precaution if departure became possible, Kane sent McGary by dog sledge to Lifeboat Cove near Littleton Island, where he had cached a boat and provisions on the northward voyage in August 1853. McGary, making the round trip of about a hundred miles, by the ice belt, in four days, reported to Kane's relief that the cache was undisturbed. Encouragingly, McGary found that open water had reached almost to Littleton Island. Between the beleaguered brig at Rensselaer Harbor and navigable seas lay only thirty miles of impenetrable ice, which, Kane hoped, would break up by late summer.

Meanwhile there was work to do. Kane had come to the Arctic to answer two grand questions: what had become of Sir John Franklin's men and ships, and whether there was an Open Polar Sea. As yet he had found no clue to either mystery. He had not even reached beyond the great Humboldt glacier, nor set foot on the western shore of the broad basin in which his vessel lay. It was essential, therefore, to complete the circuit of the basin and to learn whether it was open either to the north beyond the great glacier or to the west by a channel between Ellesmere Island and the dimly-seen Grinnell Land to its north.

Kane's failure thus far to get beyond the glacier or across the basin with relatively large parties of sledgemen determined him now to carry on these remaining explorations with small parties driving dog sledges, to be sent out as rapidly as the condition of his few dogs would permit. To lead the first of these journeys, across the basin toward Cape Sabine, he chose Hayes, the only one of his officers qualified to make geodetic observations who was strong enough to travel. Kane himself and Sonntag were not yet on their feet. Hayes would be accompanied by only one man, Godfrey, driving the well-tried small sledge Ohlsen had built, with food calculated to last ten days.

The two men left Rensselaer Harbor on May 20, a day of warm sunshine, but in spite of fine weather their crossing to the west side of Kane Basin was difficult beyond expectation. The pack ice, broken up by huge icebergs drifting southward from Humboldt Glacier, was excessively rough, with deep snow-filled hollows between steep hummocks. Hayes soon developed a bad case of snow blindness. By May 26 Godfrey, physically exhausted and insanely desperate, was ready to quit. Hayes, telling of this dreadful trip a dozen years later in the second edition of his book *An Arctic Boat Journey*, revealed at long last how nearly Godfrey's panic had brought them to disaster.

> The embarrassments and the severity of the labor, added to the cold and general exposure of travelling over such a rough and broken track, are wearying and exhausting to a degree that can scarcely be realized without actual experience. Add to this the loneliness of the situation, where one is surrounded only by a wilderness of icy hummocks and spires, and it presents an aspect almost fearful, especially to uninstructed minds, where the power of careful reasoning is wanting. In the journey mentioned in the text, my companion, who had but little education, though, under ordinary conditions, a reliable man, became so impressed with the frightful appearance of our surroundings, and the hopelessness of the undertaking,—so overwhelmingly certain did it appear to him that we were running into the very jaws of death,—that his reason seemed to leave him. The dark and gloomy land which loomed ahead, the seemingly endless waste of broken ice which intervened, the heartless labor involved in the ceaseless struggle, the pains of snow blindnss, caused by the incessant glare of the sun upon the uniform white surface of the frozen sea over which the chilly winds were driving pitilessly, making it needful truly to arm the heart with strength, might well, in such a mind as his, fill the place with visions of unearthly significance. It was but natural, therefore, that, under these circumstances, he should desire to retreat from it. "Turn back, turn back," was the burden of his song morning, noon, and night, until, tears and entreaties failing him, he fell into a fit of madness, and exclaiming, "If not with you, then without you," he tried the rifle as a means to an escape. Fortunately for both of us, a short *rencontre* ended in such a manner as to somewhat restore his senses, and to enable me to proceed the next day with less embarrassment, and ultimately to accomplish my purpose.[9]

Godfrey, disarmed, gave up his revolt. The two men reached land next day, May 27. To the south of them was the large indentation of the coast which Kane had conjectured might be the mouth of a channel between Ellesmere Island and its northern neighbor Grinnell Land. Toward the north, Hayes could see the coast for thirty miles, with two prominent headlands which Kane later named after two Philadelphia naturalists, Joseph Leidy and John Frazier. In the afternoon Hayes and Godfrey pushed on along the ice foot, reaching latitude 79° 45'. There, on the rocks of Grinnell Land, Hayes planted the United States flag.

The men were now getting exhausted and so were the dogs. Food was running short and there was no game to be had. Hayes therefore turned southward, and spent the next day or two traveling along the shore ice and then over the offshore floe as far as Cape Sabine, the northernmost point charted by Inglefield in 1852. After taking observations to record the cape's position and connect it with the landmarks he had surveyed to the north, he started back across the sound. With Godfrey and the dogs he reached land safely a few miles southwest of Rensselaer Harbor and reached the brig on June 1. He was so badly afflicted by snow blindness that he could not present a written report to his commander for almost six weeks. He and Godfrey had traveled in all nearly 400 miles and had added to Kane's charts about 200 miles of new coastline with landmarks located. Hayes chose not to mention, in his official report, Godfrey's murderous rebellion. "It affords me great pleasure," he wrote, "to speak well of the services of my companion. He is an excellent driver, and understands well the management of the dogs."[10] No doubt Hayes mentioned the episode privately to Dr. Kane, who must have had it in mind months later when Godfrey's unstable conduct again threatened disaster, not merely to one officer but to the whole expedition.

Kane was disappointed that Hayes had seen no channel leading westward from the inlet near Cape Joseph Leidy, nor had he gone far enough north to see whether there was an outlet in that direction. To find whether there was any exit from the basin, Kane planned further exploration on its eastern shore, to get beyond the Humboldt Glacier and thence to follow the shore as far northward as possible. Six of the men were well enough for another hard journey. He chose Morton and Hans for the final stage. McGary, Bonsall, Hickey, and Riley would accompany Morton as far as the glacier, dragging a large sledge. At the start, Hans would remain at the brig for a few days, to hunt game, and would then follow on with the dog team and a light sledge. When he joined the others, Morton and he would continue toward the north, leaving McGary with Bonsall and the two seamen to attempt an ascent of the glacier.

The party set out on June 5, leaving Kane, as he wrote, with a parcel of sick men, "affecting to keep ship till their comrades get back." Hans left with the dog sledge on June 10. This last serious effort at exploration beyond the glacier went off successfully according to the plan. McGary's party reached the base of the glacier with no more than the usual discomforts and dangers, except on one night when a polar bear broke into the tent but was driven out and shot before it could injure any of the men. Hans caught up with the others on June 16. After a day's halt to rest the dogs, Morton and Hans went on. The others attempted to scale the face of the glacier but found it impossible and decided to give up before a fatal accident might occur. They returned to the brig on June 27, in good condition except that McGary was completely snow blind and, Kane feared, would be slow to recover. His report that the summer sun was making the ice belt unfit for sledge travel caused Kane much worry about the two men he had sent beyond the glacier. Pools of water were forming around the brig, and hunting parties were coming back wet to the skin. After almost two weeks of anxiety, however, Kane and Bonsall on the evening of July 10 heard a distant sound of dogs baying, and soon Morton and Hans came in view, staggering along beside the limping dogs, one of which, lame and exhausted, they were carrying on the sledge.

Morton's story, when he was warmed and rested enough to tell it, began with the usual difficulties, doggedly overcome, and led to a climax both

Open Water Seen by William Morton from Cape Jefferson
Engraving by R. Hinshelwood from drawing by J. Hamilton based on
Morton's description, *Arctic Explorations, 1853, '54, '55,* 1:307

sensational and tantalizing. The two men had traveled far beyond the Humboldt Glacier. They found Kane Basin narrowing to form a channel about thirty miles wide, to which Kane gave the name of his friend and supporter John Pendleton Kennedy. Following the shore of Kennedy Channel the men were stopped by a rugged cape jutting into the ice pack at latitude 81° 22'; and there, from the northernmost land ever trodden by a white man, Morton had seen open water stretching to the northern horizon. As he told Kane, *Advance* or a whole fleet like her could have sailed on calm waters, free of bergs or floes, perhaps even to the Pole, only 500 miles away. Morton tried to go farther along the shore, but could not pass the headland (Cape Constitution, as Kane named it). The ice belt was rotting in the warm weather of late spring, and the waves of the open sea had broken it away from the base of the cliff. Even on foot the two men could not work their way any farther. Morton climbed the rocks to a height of 480 feet, from which, looking northward, he could see the coast to a distance of forty miles, with high ridges succeeding one another until the view was lost in the distance. The unending shoreline was washed by shining waters without a sign of ice.

Morton brought back to Kane bits of vegetation he had collected from the rocks, and told of seeing hundreds of sea birds—gulls, kittiwakes, ducks, and sea swallows—already nesting on the cliffs, and so numerous that Hans had killed two with one bullet. Open water, disappearing ice, burgeoning life on the rocks and in the air—Was this the long-conjectured Open Polar Sea?[11] Kane's heart warmed to the thought. This would be, if true, the greatest discovery in the whole history of Arctic exploration. "It was well calculated," he wrote, "to arouse emotions of the highest order; and I do not believe there was a man among us who did not long for the means of entering upon its bright and lonely waters." In an uninhibited memorandum for his brother Tom, setting forth the achievements of his voyage, he wrote "The great North Sea, the Polynia, has been reached, and had not the dogs died and so deprived us of boats, we would have gone—not I, for it was Morton who took the Northeast journey—to God knows where." In his official report to the Secretary of the Navy he listed the discovery of an open and iceless sea, thronged with migratory birds; and on the map he had Sonntag draw for his book, he placed the bold words "Open Sea" beyond the northern exit of Kennedy Channel. In the text of his book, however, he was more cautious. He was too respectful of scientific authority to claim publicly, without fuller evidence, a discovery so momentous. Moreover, by the time he wrote the book, the great German geographer August Petermann had published from his professorial armchair at Gotha a review of Kane's official report, in which he allowed that Kane had proven beyond doubt his (Petermann's) hypothesis of a warm region around the Pole, but declared that Kane's open water could not be a part of the "great polar sea" called for by the hypothesis.[12]

Facing such a pontifical judgment, Kane in his book wrote carefully but with a touch of sarcasm, "How far it [the open water] may extend, whether it exists simply as a feature of the immediate region, or as part of a great and unexplored area connecting with the Polar basin . . . may be questions for men skilled in scientific deductions. Mine has been the humble duty of recording what we saw." Reviewing earlier observations of open waters in high latitudes, he wistfully said, "All these illusory discoveries were no doubt chronicled with perfect integrity; and it may seem to others as since I left the field it sometimes does to myself, that my own, though on a larger scale, may one day pass within the same category."

Dr. Hayes was much less cautious. He accepted the Open Polar Sea and staked his life on it in an expedition of his own, 1860–61.[13] Sonntag, who went north again with him, died in that quest. Twentieth-century explorers have amply shown that Morton's open water was a transitory phenomenon, a polynya formed by local currents of wind and water.[14]

# 10

# Secession

DURING the relatively quiet period when McGary, Bonsall, and Morton were away, and after the latter's return, Dr. Kane took advantage of the summer weather to make extensive notes on the animal and plant life of Rensselaer Harbor, much of which he later transcribed on many charming pages of his book. Deeply interested also in the Arctic ice, its formation, movements, and decay, he applied his considerable knowledge of geology and meteorology to its study and planned a treatise on glaciers and glacial geology. "If I can only get home again to report to Father and Grinnell the result of all this, my satisfaction and gratitude will surpass my hopes. . . . I may advance myself in my father's eyes." But, he had to ask himself, would the ice ever give way and let him get home? He awaited the summer with an increasing sense of helplessness and growing fears that he tried to hide from his men.

To keep up his own spirits as much as theirs, on Independence Day 1854 he dressed the brig with a full set of flags and dealt out of his scanty store a glass of spirits to each man, but they all knew that the brave show of good cheer concealed deep concern for the future. He had calculated that the ice of Smith Sound should break up by the end of August. A year before he had been able to force the brig to Rensselaer Harbor by August 28. This year, however, looked to be exceptional. There was still an impenetrable ice pack, twenty-five miles broad, between the brig and navigable water at the entrance to Smith Sound. What if it did not break up at all? He had a shipful of tired, hungry, ailing men. His fuel was exhausted; there was no lamp oil to light the cabin cheerfully in the darkness of another winter; there were no fresh provisions to ward off scurvy. Kane and Hayes as medical men doubted whether some of the crew could survive a second season in the Arctic, and Kane knew that the other officers shared the same dread and that the men were beginning to murmur.

This much he wrote in his journal on July 10 with an air of calm reflection, but in his cabin three days before he had poured his distress into a letter to his brother Thomas that might never reach home, heartbreaking in its combination of pride and almost incoherent despair. Recounting his misfortunes of the past year, he told of the death of the dogs, the disaster on the ice in March, the men's illness with scurvy; and gave a confused account of his own breakdown at the glacier.

> Your brother frozen out on the ice, 70 miles to the North. Typhus in a tent—two men down—bears eat up provisions—scurvy—came back and fainted six times—Now the other efforts. Can't detail them—work, work, work—No heart have I my brother save for Franklin—often our brig was left with but five of whom three were on their backs.

Then came a long paragraph summarizing the expedition's discoveries and achievements—"More than 600 miles of newly discovered coast—more than Penny and Austin together, and more than any navigator since Parry." And then a final sigh,

> Never dear brother can poor Elish go through all this again—Fresh trials are ahead, for the ice is unbroken around me—and I am well aged and worn. Yet this brig and my comrades must get back to tell their story and I must get them back at the risk of what remains to me. . . . Try to pull together the thread of this disjointed tangled skein.[1]

Next morning he was lucid again. With Hans and the dog team he drove south to the near edge of the Smith Sound ice pack to see for himself what prospect there was that it might yet break up. The open leads, he found, had advanced only four miles since his last report in May. All hope of release that summer was gone. When he got back to the brig late on July 10, he knew what he had to do. To get the whole party out to Upernavik by sledge and boats was quite impracticable so late in the season, and furthermore he was not yet prepared to desert the brig, which he thought would be a dereliction of duty, or to abandon his records and scientific collections. The only thinkable plan was a desperate one—to seek help from Sir Edward Belcher's base at Beechey Island, 600 miles away in Lancaster Sound, where he hoped to borrow a launch from Belcher and return in it to pick up the rest of his party with their equipment and the scientific materials. Kane would himself have to lead this dangerous journey; Sonntag was the only other man who could navigate well enough, and he was ill with a scorbutic pericardial

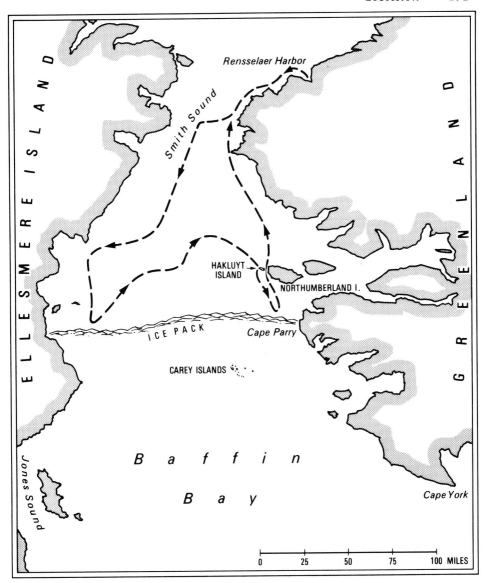

Route of Kane's Attempt to Reach Lancaster Sound by Boat, July-August 1854

effusion. On the evening of July 10 Kane wrote a letter to be left at the brig in Goodfellow's care, in case he did not return. Addressed to Mr. and Mrs. Henry Grinnell, it contained an emotional statement of his duty and his resolve to take the risk. He did not submit this plan to the judgment of his officers, for he would not lay any such heavy responsibility on them. Instead, he called them together on July 11 and told them what he was going to do. It was the most pleasant interview he had ever had with his officers. With a sense of relief, he felt, they assented to his plan, and McGary offered to accompany him. When the men were told, Morton, Riley, Hickey and Hans likewise volunteered to go. Brooks was now well enough to be left in charge of the brig.

The craft that was to carry the six men through floating ice and stormy seas was the whaleboat "Forlorn Hope," a mere cockleshell, Kane called her, 23 feet long, 6½ feet beam, and 2½ feet deep, sloop-rigged and steered by oar. Kane had her provisioned and mounted on the large sledge "Faith." On Thursday, July 14, all of the crew who were well enough started to drag the boat along the ice belt to open water, a hard journey of almost forty miles. On the 17th they launched her, and Kane's little party sailed away to the south through drift ice. At Littleton Island they had a great piece of luck: the rocky ledges were studded with nesting seabirds. The men killed two hundred of them to stock for food. From Littleton Island Kane crossed Smith Sound on a course south of west, and on the 20th he was in the open seaway of Baffin Bay and lost sight of land. The weather became so stormy that McGary, the only experienced steersman in the boat, was at his heavy oar twenty-two hours without a break. When the storm abated, they were again in pack ice, through which they alternately rowed and sailed with difficulty to the eastward again, toward Hakluyt Island near the Greenland shore, where they made camp on the night of Sunday, July 28. The rest of the journey, as far as it went, was the same story of alternately rowing and sailing through leads in the pack, which sometimes narrowed so suddenly that to avoid having the boat crushed the men had to pull her up onto the floe. She began to leak, and Kane had to keep one man bailing almost continuously. Ten miles from Cape Parry, the "Forlorn Hope" proved to be prophetically named; she was stopped by a solid pack of ice. To get a view ahead, Kane and McGary walked four miles over the drifting ice to a tall berg, which they climbed to a height of 120 feet. For thirty miles to the south Kane saw only motionless, unbroken, and impenetrable floes—and this in a region where in 1852 Inglefield and in 1853 Kane had sailed through open water with no ice in sight. There was no hope, this year, of reaching Lancaster Sound. Kane gave in to fate and worked his way back to Northumberland Island near the Greenland shore. Camping there, the men got more fresh food by killing some of the abundant auks and eider ducks, and by eating the scurvy grass that grew on the shore. On August 7 they reached the brig again.

Thus vanished another hope of escape from captivity at Rensselaer Harbor. In any case Kane's journey would probably have been useless, for Sir Edward Belcher's flotilla, from which he would have begged help, was itself in serious trouble. *Resolute* and *Intrepid,* hopelessly icebound in Melville Sound, had been abandoned on May 15, and their crews had journeyed by sledge and open boats to Beechey Island. *Assistance* and *Pioneer* were equally fast in the ice far up Wellington Channel, destined to be abandoned on August 26, and presumably Belcher's launch, which Kane had hoped to borrow, was with them there. Under these circumstances it was unlikely that Belcher's little supply ship *North Star* at Beechey Island could have given effective help.[2] Kane's effort was, however, not without some gain, for he and his boat crew were in much better health than when they left because of the generous diet of fresh birds and scurvy grass they had enjoyed for more than a fortnight. Kane's rheumatic heart had given him no trouble; "We were fat and strong," he wrote. In the long run this trip may have saved the whole party by recruiting the strength of the commander, the second officer, Morton, the two seamen, and Hans.

Until Kane returned, the men left at Rensselaer Harbor could of course not know that even if the brig were released from her imprisonment there, she would be blocked by ice in Baffin Bay. While their commander was away, their hopes were aroused by warm weather and a good breeze which promised to grow strong enough to break up the ice. The men therefore made all necessary remaining preparations for going to sea on short notice. They even brought aboard clothes that were in the wash on shore, expecting that at any hour they might be under sail to pick up Kane's boat crew on their way.

Kane himself had not quite given up hope of getting the brig out of the berth where she had lain for eleven months, and of working his way through Baffin Bay, if a fortunate gale should break up the ice within a week or two. On August 8 he got the brig afloat by sawing through a few yards of ice, and began to warp her toward a bight in the floe, where, Kane thought, the gales of late August might free her. On the 11th, with Sonntag, Petersen, Riley, and Hans, he drove to Anoatok on the Smith Sound shore to study the ice barrier once again, and found the situation worsening. New ice was in fact already forming, strong enough about the brig to bear a man's weight. That day Kane reduced the allowance of wood for cooking to six pounds per meal, one-third of a pound for each of the eighteen men, enough for coffee twice a day and soup once, besides boiling a cut of pork, the only meat now available. Next day, after inspecting the ice again, Kane wrote in his journal:

> Bad! bad! I must look another winter in the face . . . another year of disease and darkness—a year to be met without fresh food and without fuel—but I can look forward like a man, without fear but with tempered sadness, to the duties

of providing for my comrades—alas, how dependent upon my brains with their frail perishable housing. Oh body! body! damned trammeling housing investiture of blood and bones!

By this time there was no concealing from the crew his fading hopes. They too knew well enough what they had to face, and Kane, moreover, openly admitted his fear before God if not directly to his men. Each morning when they assembled for prayers he no longer asked, as in more hopeful days, "Lord, accept our gratitude and bless our undertaking," but instead, "Accept our gratitude and restore us to our homes."

In deep gloom his thoughts reverted to the graves of Franklin's men he had seen on Beechey Island in 1851. If he and his crew were fated to abandon the brig and perhaps to die in an effort to escape, he would at least leave a record for those who might come in search of him. On a conspicuous cliff looking toward the sea he had the name of the brig, ADVANCE, painted in large letters, and below it, A.D. *1853–1854.* In a niche chiseled in the rock he placed a paper enclosed in a bottle and sealed it with lead. It bore the names of all his living men and the two who had died, a record of the expedition's discoveries, Morton's report of the open sea he had found to the north, and a statement of the exact position of the "observatory" at latitude 78° 37′ 10″, longitude 70° 40′.

Kane's now unconcealed concern about the continuing blockade of Smith Sound, his altered petition to the Almighty, his redoubled efforts to save fuel, his sealing of a record into the living rock, all had their effect upon the rest of the party. They began to mutter among themselves, in furtive groupings as if something were afoot. On Monday, August 21, Kane's faithful personal aide Morton came to him with a report he had gotten from seaman Stephenson that there was an agitation to quit the ship; some of the men were about to speak to Kane, asking permission to depart, with officers to command them.

Kane's trip to the south the month before had convinced him that escape by boat was no longer possible. Nor was the brig likely to be freed that summer; but even if the coming high tides were to break up the harbor ice, it would hazardous to sail her into an ice pack in Baffin Bay that at any moment might consolidate around her. His own duty as commander was clearly to stay with the brig, as a matter both of duty and of safety; but had the men any such obligation? In the mental turmoil of this dark hour his entries in his journal were not so much those of a commander of men, but of the physician-scientist he really was.

Had I the right to make any judgment binding upon them in a case of life and death? Was I to arrogate to my own opinion such infallibility as to make it control that of others? By Morton's communication, I was made aware of men who had been official servants of the Expedition willing to leave it. There was no meeting, no disturbance, but a simple wish to exert a natural right connected with their personal safety. I differ with them as to the policy and soundness of the step and I think it a gross violation of their agreement and a violation of everything gallant and honourable. Very good! but have I the moral right to detain them? Can I look forward to the horrible contingencies of the coming long winter and see myself and the faithful surrounded by men—my equals as such—whose inclinations I had forced and whose sufferings were upon my own head?

Feeling all this I keep my own counsel and determine to inspect the ice for the last time and if the result be against the liberation of the brig to give the required permission.

On the 22d he traveled once more by sledge to study ice conditions in Smith Sound and returned at 2 A.M. on the 23d convinced that the brig could not escape. He consulted McGary as an experienced whaling man as to how the whaling captains dealt with their crews when caught by winter ice, and was told that the men were left to their own choice and the boats were put at their disposition. "All things considered," he wrote,

I have determined to call together all hands, afford them—or such as may desire it, the alternative, but with a full expression of my opinions, telling them freely why I am opposed to the step, what are its dangers, and finally insisting upon a signed paper from such as leave, placing my position in its proper light.

Meanwhile the men were talking among themselves. Petersen, as might be expected, was the chief spokesman for secession. He had a strong point when he reminded his shipmates that Dr. Kane had disregarded in August 1853 his advice to winter farther south, at a point from which *Advance* could have gotten free the next summer. Ohlsen, apparently undecided (though Kane thought him the instigator of the whole affair) acted as a sort of intermediary among the men. Dr. Hayes quietly sided with Petersen, feeling as others did that the chances of all hands' surviving would be greater if the party were divided.[3]

On Thursday, August 24, Kane assembled his officers and crew on the quarterdeck and told them why he had decided to remain at Rensselaer Harbor. Escape to open water could not succeed, he said, so late in the season, and the attempt would be exceedingly hazardous. He urgently advised the men to give up their plan, but declared that he would grant permission to any who chose to attempt it, if they agreed to go under officers chosen by themselves and would sign a paper renouncing all claims upon him and those who remained with him. He would provide those who left with boats, stores, and equipment.

Dr. Kane then called the roll, slowly and calmly, but with seething inner emotions. Those who chose to go were to say "yes," those who would stay "no." To his mounting astonishment and chagrin, eleven of the officers and men voted to go, one (McGary) postponed his decision, and only five said they would stay—Brooks, Goodfellow, Morton, Hickey, and Hans. Of these only Morton and Hickey were well enough for duty, and Hans' loyalty was uncertain. Kane had of course expected Petersen, Godfrey, and Blake to leave, and was not surprised by the decision of the crewmen who joined them, but the defection of officers and gentlemen—Hayes, Wilson, Sonntag, Bonsall—was a deep blow to his pride. In his private journal he wrote no blame of Hayes, for he realized that the seceding party might badly need medical care. About the others he was bitter.

> Sonntag's conduct seems to me indefensible, adding deceit to treachery. . . . Bonsall, whose family was mixed in with my home associations, I freely pity. For him I made an exception to my fixed intention of advising with none of the withdrawers. I took him aside . . . pointed out the grave errors of his course, the loss of respect and standing at home, etc., etc. He heard me with tears but adhered to his selfish intentions.

Later, Wilson came to him and said that he had been unhappy since he decided to leave. He had been thinking about the miserable condition of Brooks, his companion in last year's disaster on the ice, and about Kane's risking his own life to save them both. With tears he asked Kane to take him back. Kane refused to abet Wilson in what he called a double desertion, and told him to get permission from the rest of the seceders to remain with the brig. "This man," he wrote, "has gentlemanly instincts and has been reared a gentleman, but is very weak. I comforted the poor fellow as well as I could."

Between August 25, the day of the roll call, and the departure of the secession party on the 28th there was a bustle of preparations and packing. At Ohlsen's suggestion Kane assembled the seceders and advised them to choose a leader. After a brief consultation they named Ohlsen—"the best and most able for them," Kane noted, "the instigator of the whole concern, scheming and non-reliable but efficient." On the evening of the 26th, with all hands in the cabin, Kane presented a statement to be signed by the seceders, releasing him from responsibility. Petersen, not being officially a member of the crew, was not invited to sign. Ohlsen, though the elected leader, behaved like a madman, Kane wrote, refusing to sign, "although he was taking away my carpenter and most necessary man." Kane told him that. signature or no signature, he now withdrew his permission to leave—a purely psychological gesture which did not stay the unhappy man from leaving with the party, but took effect later. Sonntag demanded his pay because, he said, he might return to Germany from Upernavik. Kane paid him off and gave him a letter of recommendation to Judge Kane in Philadelphia. To Hayes he gave an introduction to the Managers of the Pennsylvania Hospital, and to the party as a whole a safe-conduct addressed to the American consul at whatever port they might reach. To all he offered his best wishes and promised a welcome if they returned.

He gave them all the supplies he could afford: two boats (one the "Forlorn Hope," the other the metal lifeboat Kane had cached in August 1853 near Littleton Island, where the seceders were now to pick it up), the use of two sledges to get the whaleboat and supplies to open water, a shotgun and a rifle, compass, sextant, chronometer and spyglass, and a fair share of such food as he had left, chiefly bread, beans, salt pork and coffee. Kane, Wilson, McGary, and Morton even shared some of their clothing with the seceders. When everything was packed and ready, First Officer Brooks ran up the expedition's flag to the brig's masthead, and all hands assembled in the cabin. Morton on Kane's order produced from some private nook a couple of bottles of champagne. From broken-handled teacups the now dissevering parties pledged each other's good health, and the seceders passed over the brig's side and departed.

Just before the secession party left the brig, Ohlsen went to Kane and offered to sign the waiver of responsibility if he were allowed to depart. Kane replied that he would consider him a deserter and would shoot him if he attempted to go. Ohlsen, crying like a woman, chose to remain. Thus the seceders began their journey without their chosen commander. When they had gone Kane, no longer able to control his wrath, poured it out in his journal.

This trial had developed the character of my company, confirmed the worthless and transformed some false gold. Bonsall, Hayes and Sonntag had never the associative gallantry and right-mindedness of Goodfellow or the whaler McGary, or the man-of-war's man Brooks. Petersen was always a cold-blooded sneak, Ohlsen double-faced and fawning and insincere. Their associates number all the crew except Morton and the Irish cabin boy Hickey. These two stand out as natural gentlemen when compared with any of the officers or men who are leaving their posts.

Sad as I feel at the dismal prospect ahead, anxious as I may be for the future of those thus severing our connection, I feel that it is a relief, a purgation, relieving me of condemned material, worthy heretofore but rotten now.

I have washed my hands of them as a man and a Christian. They go out with everything that they ask for. . . . They have left the expedition and God's blessings go with them, for they carry not the respect of good men.

When a year later Dr. Kane, with these pages before him, was writing his superb narrative, *Arctic Explorations, 1853, '54, '55,* he did not copy the bitter words he had penned in August, 1854. He laid no blame on any of the seceders, and pictured his own motives as purely humane and his own deportment as wholly calm. How could it be, incredulous readers asked, that this intense, high-tempered, iron-willed man had given in so tamely? Was not the affair really more sinister than Kane pictured it? Was he in fear of something more than discontent? Were the men, in fact, threatening a mutiny?

This suspicion has recently been explicitly stated by Villarejo, editor of Petersen's narrative of the secession;[4] but Dr. Kane's private journal, as it has been cited here, gives the answer—the usual answer to mooted problems of human conduct—his motives were mixed. He acted as he did in part from concern for his own safety and for his reputation as commander of the expedition. He did in fact dread a mutiny, not however in August, when the secession was bruited, but some time later if he compelled a discontented half or more of his crew to endure one more winter of starvation and disease. This fear he admitted clearly to himself on another page of the journal. He acted also from apprehension for the fate of the seceders in their ill-timed flight, and from sincere respect for their individual rights. He chose to take the risk of remaining with the brig, for himself and his loyal shipmates, but would not force it upon others.

Three members of the secession party subsequently published their own stories of this miserable affair—Dr. Hayes in his book of 1860,[5] Petersen in the reminiscences recently made available in English by Villarejo,[6] and William Godfrey in his *Narrative of the Last Grinnell Arctic Exploring Expedition.*[7] All three testify to Kane's fairness and generosity, and none of them hint at anything approaching a mutiny. Henry Goodfellow, who did not secede, gave similar testimony in an unpublished statement written for Kane's sister Bessie.[8] Hayes, in particular, was sensitive about the implication that he had taken part in a mutinous conspiracy. When Dr. William Elder was writing his biography of Kane, Hayes wrote to him urging him to dispel this false suspicion.[9] Dr. Kane, he said, "issued no commands and when the ship's company decided that the chances of safety were enhanced by a separation . . . he proceeded at once hastily to carry out their decision and gave them every facility."

When the seceders were out of sight from the brig, Dr. Kane wrote in his journal, slightly misquoting Charles Lamb, "They are gone, all gone, the old familiar faces." In fact he had not yet heard the last of them. Their big sled with its heavy load was so hard to drag that the men made only a few miles each day. For a week, until they reached open water and launched their boat, there was a good deal of traffic back and forth between the brig and the travelers. Kane sent Hans to bring back the big sledge, but Petersen, who had been elected leader in place of Ohlsen, kept Hans with his party until Kane sent McGary and Goodfellow to demand the sledge and Hans, under threat of force. Thus the already harassed seceders were left with only a small sledge which they had to load and unload three times on each day's journey. On September 2, fourth day of the march, Riley and Blake came back to the brig. According to Hayes, and to Petersen's diary (in a passage written by Sonntag), the two men had lost heart when the small sledge broke through thin ice and they were almost drowned; but their story to Kane was that they had been disgusted by the party's lack of discipline.[10] Blake found himself equally unhappy at the brig, where Kane gave him a cool reception, and he finally again joined the seceders. Riley, on the other hand, regained Kane's confidence. His story, confirmed by McGary, about the party's hard travel so strongly awoke Kane's sympathy that he sent Riley back with the big sledge with orders to stay with it until the voyagers reached open water. This duty Riley loyally performed. The two parties were now made up as follows: at the brig, Kane, Brooks, McGary, Wilson, Goodfellow, Morton, Ohlsen, Hickey, Riley, and Hans; heading south were Petersen, Hayes, Bonsall, Sonntag, Stephenson, Whipple, Godfrey, and Blake.

Kane's pride and determination had kept him steady during this long-drawn-out crisis but when on September 5 contact with Petersen and his party was finally cut off, and Kane was left with half his crew to face a desperate winter, the inevitable reaction broke his nerve. Writing his journal that night under the sooty, blubber-fed lamp, in a mood of mingled anger, frustration, and loneliness, his wandering, almost demented thoughts took him away from the barren scene of his torment, back to Pennsylvania's countryside and to summer days spent in boyhood among green fields and orchards beyond the Schuylkill. His present agitation called up the memory of battles he and his brothers had fought out together against the neighbors' boys. As if he were with them again, he penned a strangely childish cry for vengeance against the men who had deserted him.

> I cannot but feel that some of them will return, broken down and suffering, to seek a refuge on board. They shall find it, to the halving of our last chip—but—but—but—If I ever live to get home—home! and should meet Dr. Hayes or Mr. Bonsall, or Master Sonntag, let them look out for their skins. If I don't live to thrash them, which I'll try very hard to do (to live, I mean) why then, dear brother John, seek a solitary orchard and maul them for me. Don't honour them with a bullet and let the mauling be solitary—save to the principals, it would hurt your character to be [seen] wrestling with such low-minded sneaks.

*Advance* in Her Second Winter at Rensselaer Harbor
Woodcut from sketch by Dr. Kane, *Arctic Explorations, 1853, '54, '55,* 1:401

The next day's entry, September 6, shows him again calm and clear-headed, planning how to fit up the brig to withstand the subzero temperatures of a winter coming all too rapidly. Taking a lesson from his Eskimo neighbors he proposed to make the brig's living quarters as much like an igloo as possible. He put the men to work prying sledge-loads of moss and turf from the rocks, to be laid on the quarterdeck to make a coldproof covering. Below deck, Kane had them enclose a space eighteen feet square and line it with moss from floor to ceiling. They caulked the floor with plaster of paris and common paste, and covered it with a layer of oakum two inches thick. This well-insulated chamber was not entered directly from above, but only from 'tween decks through a narrow tunnel lined with moss, imitating the entrance of a native snow house. "We are only ten to stow away," he wrote, "and the closer the better." This shelter was already needed; on September 7, while the men were ashore gathering moss, Kane wrote, "Dreary work, cold, no fuel aboard." The temperature fell that night to 7° above zero. On the 10th he began to strip off the upper layer of deck planking (except over the "igloo") to be stacked up for firewood. For building the tunnel and stripping the deck, ship's carpenter Ohlsen was essential; it was fortunate indeed

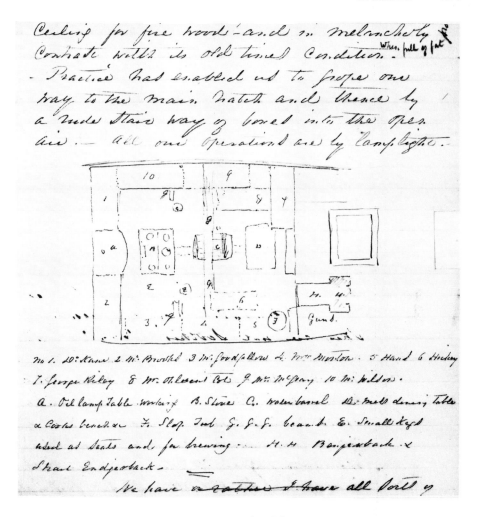

Winter Quarters in *Advance*
Sketch by Dr. Kane in his journal (Stanford University)

that Kane had been able to keep him at the brig. Ohlsen worked as ordered, but spent much of his off-time in his bunk, weeping. Kane gave him a vigorous tongue lashing, which released the taut emotions of both men and ended in a handshake.

As for food, there was still a fair supply of flour, salt pork, beans, and dried apples, but of fresh meat there were only six ducks no larger than a partridge, and three ptarmigan. Foxes were not venturing into the traps, and no hares were to be seen. Kane's Sunday meditations that week were gloomy. It was just a year since he made his decision to winter so far north, but he closed the year, he wrote, with devout if unorthodox gratitude for its blessings and faith for times to come: "The long shadows are upon us now, and work is the best expeller of these [despondent] thoughts. Trust, Elish' Kane, in that big, comprehensible non-theological God—and keep your powder dry, Elish' Kane, Keep your powder dry . . . !"

He decided to take Hans with a sledge, a kayak, and five dogs—all that were not disabled—on a hunt over the ice to shoot a seal or two, but the trip ended in an almost fatal mishap when the sledge broke through thin ice, dragging Kane and the dogs into the water. With Hans's help he saved himself and all the dogs, but got no seals and was thoroughly chilled. Back at the brig, the men, seeing him exhausted, cooked for him one of the remaining ducks. That week the thermometer fell to 4° below zero, and there was a heavy fall of snow.

On the 18th, three Eskimos appeared from Etah. Kane fed them on salt pork and let them sleep aboard ship, but in the morning they were gone with his best dog, some cooking utensils, and two buffalo robes. Although he had previously put up with the Eskimos' communistic appropriation of the expedition's equipment, he could not tolerate this last theft. He sent his two best walkers, Morton and Riley, to pursue the men forty miles to Anoatok, a hut half way to Etah, where he thought they would halt for rest. At the huts, Morton and Riley found only the boy Myouk and two women, one of them the wife of the Etah head man, Metek. The women had already cut up the robes and made them into fur jackets, which they were wearing. The two American seamen sent Myouk to Etah to tell Metek that they were arresting the women. Bundling up the stolen cookpot and pans and a good-sized cut of walrus meat, they tied the women's hands and marched them to the brig, where Kane imprisoned them in the hold for five days. Although they spent much of the time sighing, singing dolefully, and crying, they did not lose their appetites and ate the meals served to them. Metek finally arrived with another important member of the Etah tribe, bringing for ransom a sledge-load of knives, tin cups, and other articles that his people had abstracted on previous visits.

The result of Kane's vigorous action was a long powwow, with Hans as interpreter, leading up to an unwritten treaty. The Eskimos promised to steal no more, to bring fresh meat from time to time, to sell or lend dogs, and to show Kane's men where to find game. The white men promised not to harm the Etah people, to shoot game for them on joint hunting parties, to welcome them aboard ship, to give them presents of needles and thread, knives and other useful things and to trade for walrus and seal meat. Both parties pledged brotherhood and enduring friendship. When the Eskimos left, Morton and Riley went with them as ambassadors to witness the ratification of the treaty by all the inhabitants of Etah, and returned to the brig with its first fruits, a walrus flipper weighing forty pounds. The treaty was never broken.

A few days after the Eskimos' visit Henry Goodfellow gave his companions a bad fright by wandering away from the brig and getting lost. He seems to have been the youngest member of the expedition (except Hans). Kane had more than once confided to his personal journal complaints about Goodfellow's carelessness and ineptitude, alternating with praise for his loyalty to the commander, especially when he chose not to join the secession. "Faithful and gallant," Kane now wrote, "a gentleman but a conceited hobbledehoy, never able to take care of himself and now adrift among the hills." Goodfellow was away all night. Kane got out his emergency signals, burned blue lights on deck and fired Roman candles into the dark night. At 6:30 A.M. the wanderer returned.[11] A week later he committed another breach of discipline, less alarming but serious enough to be noted in the journal: "Sunday, October 8. Goodfellow stayed away from prayers."

Toward the end of September, Kane, with Morton and Hans, taking advantage of the recent treaty, joined three Eskimos on a walrus hunt near Anoatok, lasting for several days. They got into serious difficulties on the off-shore ice—a journey of much risk and exposure, Kane said—but after an unbroken walk of forty-eight miles, in twenty hours without a halt, they

Sunday Prayers
From Godfrey's *Narrative of the Last Grinnell Exploring Expedition*

Raising the Brig *Advance*
Drawing by Dr. Kane, Kane Papers, American Philosophical Society

reached the hut again. Storm-bound there for a day or two, Dr. Kane had a good opportunity to observe the hut life of the Eskimo huntsmen, which he later described in six lively pages of *Arctic Explorations*, illustrated by his sketches of their furnishings and fireplace. He even took down in musical notation a song they sang in his honor, to the words "Nalegak, Nalegak-soak—Captain, great Captain!" Living with the Eskimos was no hardship for him, for, as Hans said, he was smart enough to live as they did and to eat their food.

Descriptions of Eskimo life and ways, told with affectionate humor, enliven Kane's narrative of the fall and winter of 1854–55, otherwise a dreary tale of darkness, cold, semistarvation, and disease. By October 21, sunlight was no longer reaching the brig and the temperature had fallen to 23° below zero. Because fuel was short, the men let the cabin stove go out four hours every night, with resultant drop of the inside temperature to 45°. In the night watch, cold as the cabin was, Kane could usually write up his records and his journal. "Everything is closed tight; I muffle myself in furs, and write; or, if the cold denies me that pleasure, I read, or at least think. Thank heaven, even an Arctic temperature leaves the mind unchilled." Working at his charts, he put his drawing board on top of the still warm stove and his feet on the ashpan. He invented an ingenious rearrangement of the chimney pipe, which wrung more heat from the precious fuel. He had the men—those few who were strong enough for the heavy work—pry off and cut up for firewood the bulwarks and more of the outer decking, the bulkheads below deck, and even the lockers and shelving, until Ohlsen's survey of wood that could still be burned without making the brig unseaworthy showed that barely enough was left for one hundred days, only halfway to the time when the brig might be released from the ice.

Food like fuel was running low. The bear meat and some walrus meat that Hans had brought back from the Eskimos at Etah was gone by November 10. The daily allowance of food for the ten men was now six pounds of flour, six ounces of dried applies or dried peaches, three pints of molasses, five pints of rice, and one ounce of butter now thirty months old. A little fresh fox meat, four ounces a day, was doled out to the sickest men. Kane, although he was himself showing the first signs of scurvy, took none of the fresh meat while it lasted, but he had his own source of fresh food, private because none of the men would touch it. The brig's hold was again infested with rats, whose powers of endurance outran those of men and dogs. Consequently he caught enough rats to make soup for himself which he found palatable and nourishing. About the end of November one of the Eskimo bitches had a litter of puppies, and when she and another bitch, as hungry as the men, began to eat them, Kane killed one of them for himself, boiled and ate it. By such means he kept remarkably well, even though he was working incessantly, sharing the cooking and other chores, looking after the sick, keeping meteorological records, and taking Wilson's turn on watch—at times Goodfellow's also, for he began to think that the young man's indolence and apathy might be due to illness, perhaps tuberculosis.

For a few days in late October Kane had the men hard at work securing a proper berth for the brig. The heavy masses of ice that adhered to her in the winter created a hazard. When the tide was at its lowest ebb, and the vessel rested on the bottom, the load of ice threatened to weaken her frame. It was necessary, therefore, as Kane explains in his book, to lift her above her line of flotation and let her freeze in "on a sort of ice dock," so that the ice around and below her when it sank with the tide would rest on the bottom and cradle her. The task of lifting her required many hours of work with chain slings, cables, and capstan. While it was in progress, Kane made the lively sketch of the operation that is reproduced in this book (see page 184), one of the best of the relatively few of his original sketches remaining today.

As winter neared, the men were getting nervous and depressed. McGary in a Sunday fit of homesickness walked the deck all day without dinner or supper. Kane tried to cheer him up, but he too was feeling a heavy strain that he dared to reveal only in his journal. One Sunday after prayers he wrote down another of those self-questioning, self-justifying meditations by which he released his inner tension.

> My thoughts, my diseased craving for love and caressment, everything that unbends, I crush, strangle, before they take shape. The Father—I cease to remember his years, the Mother, I will not count her tears, weeping on her wet pillow for her firstborn and her last. Every energy of my nature—a vile nature, too—is bent to bear myself and those who lean on me out of a severe trial. If I let weakness come over me now, we—I mean all of us—are gone. But if, if the Lord does not blot me out, I will return as a man who has braved a hard temptation and abided by his task. Then those who live either with me, or after me—fearful thought!—will give me credit for something more than a blind will and a groping materialism. Oh Tom, Pat, John, Bess, oh if I could see you all of but five minutes.

In that homesick cry for love he had no word for Margaret Fox.

On the morning of December 7, Dr. Kane, lying in his bunk after an extra night watch, heard a cry from the deck, "Eskimos coming!" Five sledges there were, with teams of six dogs each. Most of the drivers were strangers to Kane and his men. They were bringing back to the brig two of the seceders, Carl Petersen and Amos Bonsall, coming in urgent distress to beg help for the men who had left the expedition ten weeks before. As Kane had pre-

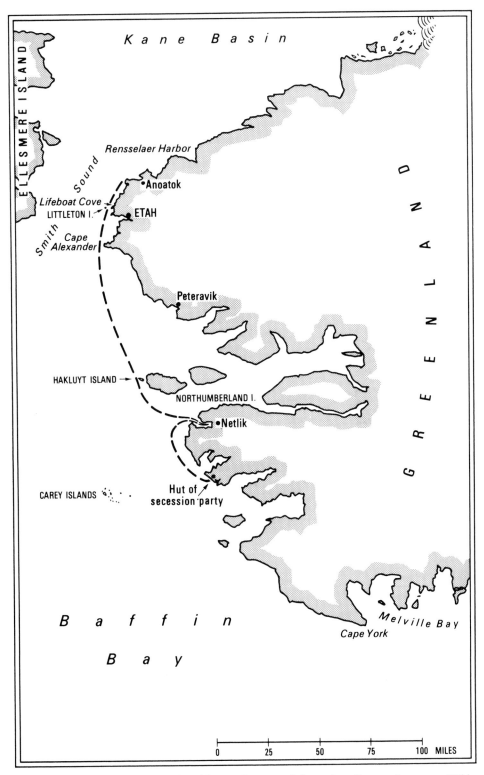

Villages of the Smith Sound Eskimos; Route of Secession Party, Autumn 1854

dicted, Petersen had utterly failed to lead his companions to safety at Upernavik. The men were stranded and living in a hut near the mouth of Wolstenholme Sound, two hundred miles south of Rensselaer Harbor, their energies exhausted, some of them ill, and their provisions nearly gone.

Kane had promised to help them if they turned back, and now he made good his pledge. By the morning after Petersen's arrival he had gotten together a hundred pounds of salt pork, freshly cleaned and boiled, some packages of meat biscuit, bread dust, and tea, to be taken by the Eskimos to the six helpless men. He did not fully trust the natives to deliver these supplies, but he had no alternative; of the brig's people, only Kane himself, McGary, and Hans were able to travel, and they could not leave the others. Bonsall, after his long journey back, was too exhausted to go, and Kane chose not to rely upon Petersen. The Eskimos departed with their load, and for four days Kane waited anxiously until on December 12 at three in the morning a new party of Eskimos from Etah and other settlements appeared bringing back the rest of the secession party.

Dr. Hayes, heavily bundled in furs, came first up the gangway, shook hands with Dr. Kane, and haltingly uttered a speech he had evidently prepared in advance. "We come here," he said, "destitute and exhausted, to claim your hospitality; we know that we have no rights to your indulgence, but we feel that with you we will find a welcome and a home."

> Poor fellows [Kane wrote], I could only grasp their hands and give them a brother's welcome. The thermometer was at minus 50°; they were covered with rime and snow, and were fainting with hunger. . . . One by one they came aboard and were housed. . . . How they relished the scanty luxuries we had to offer them! The coffee and the meat-biscuit soup, even the salt pork which our scurvy forbade the rest of us to touch—how they relished it all! For two months they had lived on frozen seal and walrus meat.

The stranger Eskimos, as Kane feared, had gone off with the supplies entrusted to them, but in the last extremity of the defeated seceders, friendly natives of Netlik—a settlement to the north of their refuge—had nobly taken over the task of getting the white men back to the brig, with the aid of other natives from the villages they passed through on the journey. Stephenson was still seriously ill with scorbutic pericarditis, and Hayes had a badly frostbitten foot. Dr. Kane gave his colleague his own berth and later amputated the gangrenous toes.

The story these men had to tell was one of false hopes and vain courage, of deprivation and misery. Six years later Dr. Hayes retold it in *An Arctic Boat Journey*—a vivid narrative to which Petersen's account, based largely on Sonntag's diary, adds useful dates and details, and William Godfrey's tale of his own woes contributes a quaint note of recrimination and self-exculpation. The journey of the eight seceders had begun well enough, though laboriously, with their dragging of the whaleboat "Forlorn Hope" over the ice belt from where Kane had left it in early August, six miles from the brig, down to open water at Eskimo Point, a haul of about thirty miles. Launching the boat on September 5, they sailed southward through alternately fair and stormy weather. While the boat was caught in a floe near Littleton Island, Bonsall, Hayes, Godfrey, and Blake walked over the ice to Lifeboat Cove, where Kane had left a cache in August 1853. They found it intact— the metal lifeboat overturned to protect a depot of food and supplies for use in case of emergency on his return. Dr. Kane had given the seceders permission to take the boat and half the supplies but had pledged the officers not to allow Godfrey and Blake to go to the cache because there was a can of spirits among the flour, pork, and rice. Why Petersen permitted the violation of this pledge has never been told, nor why Hayes and Bonsall did not stop the two seamen from getting at the liquor, as they promptly did. Blake, to the great alarm of his fellows, that night wandered off over the ice on some maudlin whim. Godfrey seems to have held his liquor better.

Kalutunah

Woodcut from sketch by Dr. Kane, *Arctic Explorations, 1853, '54, '55,* 2:140

The episode was a foretaste of various acts of insubordination by the two undisciplined seamen—Dr. Kane's "desperadoes"—during the rest of the boat journey.

The party was stormbound four days at Northumberland Island, but then got as far as Cape Parry and a little beyond. On the 18th, after a hard tussle with floe ice they made shore and found themselves near an Eskimo settlement, Netlik, from whose people—twenty-five in six families—they got fresh water and a little walrus meat.

Taking leave of Netlik they went to sea again, but were completely blocked by pack ice on September 25. With no hope of further progress they went ashore, built a crude hut in a rocky cleft, and settled down, as it seemed, for the winter. The next two months were miserable in the extreme, from cold, hunger, loneliness, and at times fear. They got a little fresh game, and the Netlik Eskimos now and then brought seal or walrus meat, but more than once their only food for days at a time was moss from the rocks. When their fuel ran out, Hayes burned three medical books he had brought along in the boat. The long dark hours passed wearily; playing cards were not usable because the players dared not remove their mittens. They had some reading matter; Bonsall, a copy of *Waverly*; Hayes, a volume of Dickens, Tennyson's *In Memoriam*, and a pocket Bible; but, Hayes said, the circumstances were too depressing for reading aloud, and the time dragged on mostly in silence.

The natives who visited them were not always in a friendly mood, and the white men suspected some of them of murderous intent. Petersen, on a visit with Godfrey to the Netlik settlement, overheard a plot to kill both of them. The Netlik head man, Kalutunah, on the whole remained friendly.

After the sun went below the horizon on October 30, despair began to weaken the men's resolve. By November 19, Blake and Godfrey were the first to talk of returning to the brig. The others were soon ready to give in, and, on November 20, Petersen, as commander of the party, decided to abandon the journey. Once back at the brig, he said, they could form a separate society independent of Dr. Kane, demanding only the hospitality due by custom to a shipwrecked crew.[12]

After hasty preparations for the trip, the party set out, dragging Stephenson, who was unable to walk, on an Eskimo sledge. After twelve miles he was too weak to go on, and the others were too tired. They returned to the hut. Hayes describes this retreat as one of almost unimaginable distress. Some of the men, unable to walk at a normal pace, fell far behind, and during the final hour the last one came to the shelter crawling on his hands and knees. Next day Petersen and Bonsall set out for the brig to get help, leaving Hayes in charge of ailing Stephenson and the four others. All their fears were wrought into Petersen's last words at departure, "If we ever reach the ship we will come back to you, or perish in the attempt, as sure as there is a God in Heaven."

At the last extremity of those who remained behind, three Eskimos from Netlik, headed by Kalutunah, came to visit the hut, bringing some meat. They flatly refused, however, to sell or hire their sledges to the white men, who began to think that the natives were simply awaiting their deaths to acquire their remaining effects. In fear, some of the men began to talk of killing the natives and escaping with their dogs and sledges. To avert so violent and dangerous an act, Hayes proposed an extraordinary ruse. He and his companions began to distribute gifts to the Eskimos—pieces of wood from the broken-up boat, a comb, pictures torn from Hayes's copy of *David Copperfield*. A meal of stewed meat followed, but while it was cooking Dr. Hayes emptied into the Eskimos' portion the contents of a vial of laudanum from his medical case. The plan succeeded; the satiated natives dropped into a light sleep, and before they awoke the white men were off with their sledges. All went well except that one team of dogs broke away and stayed by their masters. When the Eskimos awoke, they found the abandoned sledge of this team, hitched up the fugitive dogs, and caught up with Hayes's party. Daunted by his rifle, they treated the whole affair as a joke, and all hands went on to Netlik together. From then on, the returning seceders were treated kindly by the natives of the small settlements at Netlik, Peteravik, and Etah, and under the escort of Kalutunah arrived at the brig on December 7.

The day after the secession party returned, six Eskimos who had accompanied them from Netlik and Etah presented to Dr. Kane a complaint that during the journey, while resting at Kalutunah's hut, some of Hayes's men had stolen certain articles of clothing from their hosts. This was a grave charge, and the offense a dangerous one, considering that Kane had more than once punished the Eskimos for stealing the expedition's property, and considering also that the very lives of the white men depended upon good relations with the natives. After a long powwow on deck, in which Kane made every effort to appear reasonable and just, the offense was admitted. Each Eskimo was given five needles, a file, and a stick of wood. To Kalutunah and to Shanghu, another leader, Kane presented also some knives and other extra gifts. Finally he fed them a hot meal of salt pork and returned their stolen clothing. Of course, wrote Kane, after the Eskimos left, some of the brig's table knives and forks were missing, but that, he said, was merely the expression of a national trait.

# 11

# The Lowest Ebb

ALTHOUGH DR. KANE's reception of the returning
seceders was friendly, and they were grateful for it, the recent past was not to
be readily forgiven or forgotten. He treated the seceders as barely welcome
guests, having no right to resume their special duties with the expedition.
Kane himself, with Wilson and Ohlsen, kept all the watches. Coldly disregarding Sonntag's scientific qualifications, they also kept up the routine
observations of temperature, winds, and tides. With Hans's help they cooked
the meals by turns. The seceders were made to eat at a separate mess. As
for the two black sheep, Godfrey and Blake, their insubordination and
unreliability during the secession had alienated their companions as much
as their previous conduct had vexed the commander. They were left to
mess by themselves.

To the six who before the secession had been good shipmates Kane was
overtly courteous and kind, but in the midnight hours, writing in his journal, he let his feelings go.

> These wretched men have reaped the bitter fruit of want of faith. . . . God of
> Heaven! it makes my blood boil to think that men who have leaned on me,
> and like little children have been taught by me their very walk, should at the
> last in the midst of coming winter set up their puerile opinions against my
> own drearily earned judgement of the Arctic ice. Petersen, the Dane, weaned
> away from his usual caution by recollection of his home and family, never
> thought that the navigation of this great ice sea involved principles and obser-
> vations very different from the fisherman's pilotage of his little Upernavik
> home. Sonntag, a child and an abstractionist, never dreamed that meridian
> transits and lunars would not teach him to steer a bird line in a raging pack;

and here is the result—they send to me imploring succour and claiming my aid and direction as their only hope.

Whatever satisfaction Dr. Kane may have gained from saying to himself "I told them so," was overwhelmed by new troubles the seceders' return had brought upon him. The tiny moss-lined cabin he had fitted up for ten men must now shelter eighteen. The few barrels of pork, beans, biscuits, and flour he still had left must feed them all. To his list of sick and weakened men for whom he had been both doctor and nurse he now added eight half-starved men, of whom two were helpless—one of them Dr. Hayes, who might otherwise have shared this burden of medical care. Kane did not succeed in keeping to himself the strain of these days of renewed tension and redoubled labor. He was frequently out of humor, as Petersen's narrative tells us, and even the usually loyal Hans said that the doctor was often harsh to his men.[1]

Kane had been quietly angry with Godfrey and Blake ever since he was told of their raiding the whiskey in the cache in Lifeboat Cove. From what he had learned about that breach of discipline and others during the se-ceders' journey, the two tough seamen by bravado and superior physical strength had apparently behaved more or less as they pleased, and (as Kane thought) still to a certain extent dominated their comrades now that they were back in the brig. He was in no mood to tolerate further misbehavior or continued evil influence upon the other crewmen. As the situation in the brig drew nearer to a crisis, he thought much about discipline. He told himself in his journal that the character of his position required very careful management and a mixture of severity and kindness.

> The affection of the majority I endeavour to sustain by care for their wants and kindness of manner and act. The worthless and dangerous I treat with extreme caution and the extremest severity. . . . William Godfrey is a professional thief who smuggled himself into the Expedition by bribing Mr. Grinnell's wharf protégé, the old shopkeeper in the frame house. He has twice threatened me and once attempted my life on the boat going south.[2] I have criminal charges against him. John [Blake] is a spotted man; entered the brig by proxy, being concerned in the murder and mutiny on board the _____. He is a truculent, bold, and able fellow.

As commander, Kane did not delegate to his officers authority to punish a disobedient crewman. The humiliation of punishment, he said, was less when it came from his hands than from others; "I therefore always took up the offender alone face to face in the darkness and after a few words seized him and inflicted as much injury as I was able to. This way of meeting them they understood."

A week after the seceders returned, one of the officers reported insubordinate behavior by Blake and Godfrey, and later by a third man, George Whipple, the English sailor from Hull—"a poor weak unfortunate . . . completely under the influence of John." The way Dr. Kane took to punish Blake with the least humiliation was to arm himself with a heavy belaying pin, wait for the man on deck, and after a brief interview, to take up his weapon and bash Blake's skull with it. What followed had better be told in Kane's own words.

> John had a concussion of the brain from the belaying pin. I confess I tried to kill him—but Godfrey fell again after a short scuffle and was not hurt. Both of them have since behaved well. These were my only two [punishments] when George came to make the third. His nerves gave way and he fell at my feet begging mercy. He got up, after a short cuffing with my mittened hands and went below thanking me. The above reads more repulsively than [it seemed to] the subjects of my treatment. Nothing could palliate such a system but the gross worthlessness and depravity of the subjects.

The "system" worked. John Blake fortunately recovered from the scalp wound and concussion Kane had given him; Godfrey behaved himself for a while; and the little doctor, by quelling the two tough seamen, either of whom could easily have picked him up and thrown him over the brig's side, had terminated whatever influence they may have exerted on George Whipple and others of the secession party. Naturally Kane says nothing of all this in his published narrative of the expedition.

By Christmas Day a semblance, at least, of brotherhood had returned. All the officers and men, even the outcasts Godfrey and Blake, sat down to dinner together. They forgot their discomforts, Kane said, in the blessings they still could count, and they thought hopefully of the spring to come. Dr. Kane pledged himself to give them the next Christmas at their homes. He opened his last bottle of champagne, and each man raised his meager share of it in a teacup or tin cup, in a toast to "our absent friends." They even had spirit enough to joke about the food. As they passed the pork and beans that formed the main and only course, in imagination they helped themselves to turkey and roast beef, onions and cucumbers, and all the fancy dishes half-starved men might crave.

Though Dr. Kane gaily played out his role in this tragicomedy, Christmas brought him poignant memories of home as it has to countless homesick travelers, and aroused sorrowful recollections of the distress he had so often caused his parents by disregard of their solicitude for his health and safety. It brought him recollections too of his brothers and the dearly loved sister, whose Christmas cheer, he knew, must be marred by his unexplained failure to return from the north. That night in a characteristic mood of regret and self-justification, he wrote:

Christmas passed sadly for me as I thought of those who think of me. Was it only my own troubles I could bear them as I do my eiderdown coverlid; but there are those at home who think of me with fear and doubt. I can see myself, and feel sustained by the knowledge that I have fought well my battle and will alive or dead some day have their approval. To them foolhardiness, misman-agement or misfortune may explain my detention. Could they know the causes they would be comforted.

In the surge of emotions the day had roused he had a sudden overpowering feeling that he was actually seeing his home and the family gathered around the Christmas table—a vision so intimately moving that he would entrust no details to pen and paper. "I saw my home. How I saw it no journal shall ever recall."

Next morning, as so often after one of his moods of depression, he was cheerful and ready for action on behalf of his sick men. Brooks and McGary were slowly worsening, and Stephenson was very ill with a dropsical form of scurvy. "By a merciful change of conditions I am the strongest and last win-ter I was the weakest of my party, and the duty of collecting food falls on me." He must himself go to the Eskimos at Etah to get meat. Yet he was well aware that he shared the general mental deterioration that was affecting the whole party.

I don't know what is the matter with me. I can no longer give by the pen an impression of the immediate foreground, so hardworked and care [laden] that I cease to be impressed by the present in thinking of the future. Those little everyday touches which make the sketch pass by me. The same to a lesser degree pervades our company. Ohlsen has lost his memory. "Can't keep his tools." Petersen can't catch the words of our Smith Sound dialect. Wilson, Brooks, and Morton complain of enfeebled eyesight and a scant vocabulary.

All these peculiar symptoms that puzzled Dr. Kane were probably due to scurvy, although there may have been other dietary deficiencies as well. No reader of Kane's published account of the expedition, or of the private jour-nal, can fail to be impressed by the frequent mention of almost immediate improvement of physical health and morale that occurred whenever the men got a little fresh meat. "Fresh meat alone can help them," Kane wrote at a time when there was no animal food aboard the brig except the rats, which he alone would eat, and salt pork, which only made the sufferers worse. Meat must be obtained from the Eskimos even if a hundred-mile journey had to be made to get it.

On Saturday, December 30, Kane started for Anoatok with Petersen. The trip was hopeless almost from the start. The dogs, half-starved like the men, broke down; six of the team of eight were practically useless. Long before they reached the shelter of Anoatok's empty hut, Petersen, "always too cautious," wanted to return, but Kane persuaded him to walk on in the hope that a stop at Anoatok might restore the dogs. In the hut they built a fire, caulked up all openings with snow, and got the temperature up to 30° below zero. After a supper of coffee and biscuits they had a cold, uncomfortable night, and in the morning began the return to the brig, which they reached at 7 P.M., December 31.

Journal entries for the first few days of 1855 tell only of increasing illness and mental torpor. Kane found it hard to keep up his daily writing. Nevertheless, he and his officers of the watch continued without a break daily observations of the winds and the temperature of the outside air and the seawater, and of the living quarters. On January 9, the maximum outside temperature was —41.4° Fahrenheit, the minimum —69.3°, the lowest during the two winters at Rensselaer Harbor. The temperature inside the cabin averaged about 8° above zero. On Sunday, January 17, 1855, in spite of his sluggish mind Dr. Kane wrote out a long technical discussion of thermometry under Arctic conditions and the climatological significance of his observations.

During this period of extreme cold, Kane and his men were living as much like the Eskimos as possible. On January 10 they saw the sun lighting up the distant mountaintops, but, at the brig, midday darkness hung on. To light their sleeping quarters they burned in lamps of Eskimo type a mixture of pork fat and resin that filled the air with soot and grease, blackening the walls and filling the sick men's lungs with smoke. Kane's journal entry for January 10 ended: "Mr. Wilson has relapsed. I gave him a warm saleratus bath today and took his place at watch. I have now seven hours' continuous watch at one beat." Yet he could say that for the time being there was the most outspoken harmony and social comfort among the eighteen men in their 'tween-deck igloo. Even the few remaining dogs seemed to feel the need for mutual sympathy. Dr. Kane found one of them at the entrance to the men's quarters, nearly dead from cold and hunger, and took her inside to the stove. "She could not move," he said, "but completely subdued, licked my hand—the first time I had ever had such a civilized greeting from an Eskimo dog."

On January 18 Kane and Hans began a trip to Etah, hoping to get meat there, but a storm balked them at Anoatok, and Kane was so stiff and sore on his return to the brig three days later that he wrote nothing in his journal until the 30th. While he was recuperating, the "social comfort" of the party, as he called it, was sadly broken by an altercation between Henry Goodfellow and Brooks when the moody youth chose to make a butt of the older officer. "As highminded and faithful a man as I ever knew," said Kane, "his sympathy and harmlessness make it impossible for him to give offense." When poor bedridden Brooks tried to climb out of his bunk to get at his tormentor, Goodfellow threw a book at him, drawing blood from his forehead. As punishment Kane decreed that Goodfellow, no longer a gentleman passenger, was to be under ship's discipline—a nominal penalty when officers and men were alike sharing the discomforts and menial duties of the sooty cabin. "He like the rest of us is sick and wretched, but I can no longer warm to him." In fact, he said privately, he would spank Goodfellow's bottom if he again annoyed the first officer. Brooks in turn sulked for a while because Kane was so much more lenient with Goodfellow than he had been with Blake and Godfrey.

A few days later Kane wrote that the party was again united and harmonious. Indeed, on Sunday, February 4, he took a first step toward readmitting the seceders of last September–December to membership in the expedition. Faithful Tom Hickey, who had been acting for some time as cook, was suddenly too ill to work, and Kane replaced him with John Blake, "the vilest but most able man on board," not as yet restoring him to the official roll, but by private arrangement appointing him cook at thirty dollars a month. "John now has a chance and seems disposed to make the most of it." Petersen too was gradually regaining the commander's confidence. For want of anyone else, Kane was depending upon him as a hunter.

February and March 1855 passed slowly by, with a pitiful record of illness, hunger, and despair alternating with flickering hopes. Always there was the urgent need of fresh meat. Petersen and Hans occasionally shot a rabbit or a ptarmigan, and once a deer, which however putrified so quickly that the men could eat only half of it. Kane went so far in his need that he actually trusted Godfrey to try again to reach the Eskimos at Etah. Once more the attempt failed; Godfrey traveled only part way and returned saying that he was afraid of the solitude. The journal for February 22 recorded "no spirits, animal or alcoholic, wherewith to share festivity on Washington's Birthday." Kane had recurring periods of depression, revealed in troubled soliloquies in the journal, one of which hints that the romantic fervor of his last months in Philadelphia had vanished amid the arctic snows: "Yes, Elish' Kane—dream away all dreams of youth, think no longer of a married home. Bless God if you carry your gray head and wrinkles to the dear old one and then earn back old loves." That week John Blake, cook pro tem, fell ill. Godfrey, his partner in good and evil, got the job at the same pay, "not implying attachment to the roll of the Expedition," but on the 26th he fainted while on duty, and, as Kane noted, "the whole work of the household, cookery included, is done now by self and Bonsall." For three nights he kept watch from 8 P.M. to 6 A.M., and for five days never had his clothes off. Every man in the brig had signs of scurvy except Morton, who was disabled by a frozen heel, and only four could work—Kane, Bonsall, and the two hunters, Hans and Petersen. Bonsall, of the seceders, had tacitly regained Kane's confidence. "If he and I are disabled," he wrote, "what becomes of us all? God, the thought is terrible." He sent Hans to Etah on March 6. "If Hans brings meat, we can make it." Petersen was now so badly needed that Kane gave him a written offer of reengagement with the expedition on the same terms as before the secession.

The sun was now above the horizon, and inexorable needs were drawing together the two groups, the loyal and the seceders, against the day when, if they held out, Kane would lead them all on the desperate route to Baffin Bay, to Upernavik, and to their longed-for homes. Hoping for the best, he began to overhaul the official documents and scientific records of the expedition, selecting those papers most essential to preserve if he had to abandon the brig. He was already thinking much about the plan of escape by sledge, dragging the boats along the ice foot toward Cape Hatherston south of Anoatok, thence over the blockading floes of Smith Sound, and thereafter, God willing, by boat through Melville Bay and down the western coast of South Greenland. He had even begun to prepare the necessary equipment of clothing, boots, bedding, and provisions. During the tedious months of waiting he had kept the men—those who could at least sit up in their bunks—at work cutting up and stitching canvas and skins.

But Kane's overtures to the seceders had not healed all wounds. On March 5 Morton and the equally loyal Stephenson told him that certain persons on board were plotting to leave the brig with the sledge dogs and go to live with the Eskimos. Who these men were, Dr. Kane did not state in his journal. Blake and Godfrey were of course among them; since the others were never identified it is likely that one or two of the officers were involved in whatever plotting there was. Dr. Kane took this report very seriously. He kept his pistol close at hand; he had Morton watch Blake and Godfrey, and himself slept only during hours when an attempt to abscond was impracticable.

Hans returned March 10 with bad news from Etah. He had found the natives short of food and some of them on the verge of starvation. Obviously they were in no condition to help the white men of the brig. Hans had volunteered to join some of them in a hunt. With the aid of his rifle they got a walrus and a couple of seals. Some of this precious meat Hans carried back to the brig, and with him he brought the fifteen-year-old Myouk to help find game for the expedition. Thanks to the walrus meat, by the 13th all the sick men except Brooks, Wilson, and Riley were distinctly better.

On March 18, when Hans was about to leave again for Etah in search of help, Blake and Godfrey awoke Dr. Kane's suspicions by reporting sick when he could see no signs of illness. He concluded that they were planning to follow Hans and prevent him from returning with the dogs and sledge—a step that would practically cut off communication between the brig and the Eskimos and make it impossible for Kane to get his sick and crippled men away to open water when the time came to attempt an escape to the south. Nor could Petersen, the only remaining hunter, if the dogs were taken, secure meat enough to keep the party alive during the next two months. Kane therefore kept Blake and Godfrey apart by assigning them to separate tasks, and watched them as closely as possible, sleeping only in catnaps. On the morning of the 20th, Godfrey got up suspiciously early and began cooking breakfast. Dr. Kane, taking his pistol, went out through the dark, tunnel-like entrance of the living quarters and concealed himself in the 'tween-deck space just outside. He waited only a half hour before John Blake came out and went up the ladder to the deck. Ten minutes later Godfrey emerged, only to find Kane awaiting him, pistol in hand. Kane ordered him back to the cabin, sent Morton on deck to find Blake, and posted Bonsall at the inner end of the tunnel to allow no one to leave. He then explained to the rest of the men what he thought Blake and Godfrey were plotting. Godfrey confessed; then, said Kane,

> I knocked him down and mauled him until he cried for mercy. Under my mitten was a leaden fist which I had secretly manufactured and concealed for the purpose, so that I could punish him *pro re nata*. After this I read from the Logbook an affidavit signed by two witnesses that he had regularly stolen property from the brig, specifying how, when, and what articles in detail. Finally I told him that a penitentiary hung over him and that I would give him a chance to escape it by restoring him to duty and give him another trial.

Kane hoped that a beating and a threat of future imprisonment would tame the man. To confine Godfrey and his partner in treachery, Blake, as Kane had done nearly two years before on the northward voyage, was out of the question now. Godfrey declared that he would abide by Kane's orders. The impromptu court-martial was dissolved, Godfrey was turned loose, and in less than an hour he was nowhere to be found. He had made his escape and was off on foot to Etah. Kane hoped against hope that he would not have the endurance to get beyond the hut at Anoatok and would return to the brig.

On Friday, March 23, Kane out of dire necessity left with Petersen and Bonsall to make a four hours' journey to a place in the hills where reindeer had been seen. McGary was the only man left at the brig who was able to care for the sick. They got only a couple of ptarmigan which Kane gave to the sickest men. Without these occasional bits of fresh food and the coming, about this time, of direct sunshine on the brig, the party's spirits would have broken down completely. "God knows," Kane wrote, "I had laid down for myself much experimental observation and some lines of valuable exploration, but I am thankful that I am here, able to empty a slop bucket or rub a scurvied leg." The miserable, toilsome days dragged on. Bonsall and Petersen chopped wood for the stove; Kane chopped and melted ice for washing and cooking; the rest worked in their bunks or on the cabin seats, making boots and mittens and duffel bags for the coming attempt to escape. Petersen went hunting nearby and got a hare and some ptarmigan. On Tuesday, March 27, Bonsall had a scurvy blotch on his thigh, and Petersen was too tired to work. That day Dr. Kane did all the cooking and all the nursing of the sick. Fortunately on the 31st Petersen was able to hunt and brought in eight ptarmigan. Hans was still not heard from, and Kane was forced to suppose that Godfrey had gotten to Etah and persuaded or compelled Hans to give him the dogs and sledge.

On April 2, however, Bonsall, who happened to be on deck, spied a man lurking on the ice belt about a mile from the brig. It was Godfrey, and behind him were the dogs and the sledge. Bonsall, who was carrying a rifle, remained at the gangway by Kane's order while Kane advanced on foot to meet Godfrey. In a brief conversation Godfrey said that he had been far as Northumberland Island, that Hans was lying ill at Etah, and that he (Godfrey) had made up his mind to go back to Netlik and spend his life with Kalutunah and the Eskimos. For his former companions of the brig he had brought a sledge-load of meat from Etah. Kane drew his pistol and ordered Godfrey to go aboard the brig, but the man refused. Kane left him under the threat of Bonsall's gun and went aboard to get McGary to bring a set of ankle irons. Bonsall and Kane were both barely able to walk and could not have controlled Godfrey by physical force. Petersen was away hunting, and the rest were too ill to help. Kane came out from the brig just in time to see Godfrey run away, taking his chances of a shot in the back. Bonsall's rifle misfired; Kane took another rifle from the gun stand and fired at Godfrey but missed him, and the man escaped. Covered as he was by the weapons of the two officers, he made no effort to take the dog team and was last seen making his way on foot along the shore ice. To frighten Blake out of an attempt to follow Godfrey, Kane on going below announced to all hands that he would shoot down anyone caught in the act of desertion. This stand, he felt was approved by his shipmates, although they made no comments.

In his book *Arctic Explorations, 1853, '54, '55,* Kane did not conceal this episode as he had the earlier instances of trouble with Godfrey and Blake. He told it as fully in the book as he did in his private journal, omitting only a remark that—wicked as the thought might seem from a man with love in his heart for his fellow men—he could almost wish that he had killed Godfrey. What he told in his book was, however, sufficient to bring upon him a

Dr. Kane Shooting at Godfrey

From Godfrey's *Narrative of the Last Grinnell Exploring Expedition*. (Kane actually used a rifle)

charge, by an English reviewer, of cruelty to members of his crew and murderous intentions toward one of them.[3] Godfrey himself had the last word, for he too, or his ghost writer, told the story after Kane's death, in his *Narrative of the Last Grinnell Exploring Expedition*. In spite of his tone of injured innocence, his account of the affair agrees in general with Kane's. He makes the point that, having with Kane's consent left the expedition when he joined the secession party of August 1854, and never having been restored to the official roll, he was not a deserter when he absconded to Etah. By taking a sledge-load of fresh meat to the brig, he says, he had demonstrated his good intentions, and by leaving the dogs there, he had absolved himself from the charge of stealing them. Kane perhaps had anticipated both these arguments by getting loyal crew members to sign the paper accusing Godfrey of earlier thefts while he was still on the expedition's roll. He believed that Godfrey had intended to use the badly needed food in bargaining for readmittance, on favorable terms, to membership in the expedition.

The meat was indeed a godsend. "We are all well fed and merry," Kane wrote in his journal next day; and, remembering his medical school course in chemistry, went on "Flesh, flesh, flesh, Kreatin and its attendant mysteries are at work in our vitals." On April 9 his spirits were so much higher that he concluded the second section of his journal with a note of joy: "Here ends private Journal No. 2. All hands alive, and the sun within eleven days of a circumpolar track. *Jubilate!*"

The men were doing so well that Kane felt able to set out next day for Etah in search of Hans. The temperature was now comfortable, he said, only 10° below zero. Before he had gone half way, he met the Eskimo lad, who was hunting for seal, even though his recent illness had left him weak. Kane put him on the sledge and drove on to Anoatok, where they camped and Hans told his story. During his illness he had been nursed by a young daughter of Shung-hu, who had made so strong an impression upon his heart that he was forgetting the South Greenland girl at Upernavik to whom he had pledged himself before sailing away in *Advance*. Kane was happy to learn that Hans had refused Godfrey's invitation to join him in a journey to the south with the expedition's dogs and sledge. Before Hans fell ill, he and three of the Etah Eskimos had been successful in the hunt, and he had cached some of the seal meat at Littleton Island. It was a load from this cache that William Godfrey had taken to the brig.

Kane sent Hans back to Etah with instructions to open negotiations with the Eskimos for a few dogs to bolster up his own scant and weary team. Returning to Rensselaer Harbor, he found the men continuing to improve. "Thomas [Hickey] begins to relieve me in cooking, Riley to take a spell at the slops, Morton cooks breakfast, and aided by McGary and Ohlsen has finished one camp blanket. Wilson comes on slowly. Dr. Hayes begins to heal. Sonntag is less a nuisance." A couple of days later Hans came back to the brig, bringing with him the Etah head man Metek, and Metek's nephew, a fine boy of fifteen called Paulik.

About mid-April, Kane took advantage of the men's better health to go himself to Etah to continue the negotiation for dogs and, as an almost equally important objective, to recapture Godfrey. He drove with Metek, taking with him his six-shooter and a pair of ankle irons. As they drew near the village, Kane, to avoid giving his culprit a chance to get away, adopted a ruse. He disguised himself by pulling the hood of his parka over his face. With his small stature he hoped to be mistaken for Paulik, who had in fact been left at the brig. The plan succeeded. When they arrived at the huts, the whole population turned out to welcome their chief, among them Godfrey. "An instant later and I was at his ear, with a short phrase of salutation and its appropriate gesture. He yielded unconditionally at once." Godfrey, tough and reckless as he was, seems to have become deeply afraid of Kane. During the next couple of days, while the doctor was at Etah, the man was utterly docile.

He could have crushed me, but he was completely tamed and could not even meet my eye. I even went so far as to order him to clean my pistol; he received it trembling, cleaned, loaded, and returned it to me like a humble lackey. This giving him my pistol was a piece of acting on my part. I don't think Bill will attempt my life any more.

Nevertheless, on the way back to the brig, Kane kept his prisoner under observation by making him run and walk by turns, ahead of the sledge.

Before they left Etah, Kane went walrus hunting with the lad Myouk, and got a sledge-load of meat to take back with him. The Etah people would not let him have any of their dogs, and therefore he dispatched Hans to the next settlement to the south, Peteravik, to beg dogs from the ablest and most helpful of the Eskimos, Kalutunah, who was temporarily basing his hunt there. Hans carried to Kalutunah an invitation to come to the brig, and as largesse took him the precious gift of a capstan bar.

Things had gone well during Kane's absence. Petersen and Ohlsen were building sledges on which to mount the whale boats if escape to the south became inevitable. Kane wanted to make the sledges long enough to put the weight of the boat and stowage well within the length of the runners. The only available source of timber of such length was the crossbeams of *Advance*'s hull. Most of these had been burned for fuel, but Kane had saved two, and put Bonsall, Morton, and Riley at work sawing them lengthwise to make four runners—a heavy task of several days for the scurvy-weakened men. Petersen, "a first-class tinker," began to concoct portable cooking gear from empty tins and battered stovepiping. "Every detail is arranged," Kane wrote, "and if the sick go on as they have done, I do not doubt but that we can carry our boats thirty or forty miles over the ice."

On April 24, Hans returned from Peteravik with Kalutunah and a complete hunting outfit of "two noble teams of six dogs, harpoons, lances, light equipment." The party consisted of Kalutunah, Shang-hu, and a third man named Tatterat. They were bound north for a bear hunt, and Kane seized the opportunity to join them, with a fervid hope that with these well-equipped and experienced Eskimos he might achieve his aim of getting beyond the Humboldt Glacier and across the basin to its western shore.

He knew well the personal risks he was taking, weakened and weary as he was, by trying again the passage over the ice that the year before had cost the lives of two of his men, but the urge was irresistible to set foot upon the western shore and to see for himself the open water to the north, before he had to give up his exploration and the search for Sir John Franklin.

It may be [he mused in his journal] that I am reserved to take my dear friend Henry Grinnell by the hand and say "Your confidence has not been misplaced.

I have not failed you or myself." . . . It may be that I, taxed beyond corporeal existence, give way on the brink of consummating my hopes, crying "I have discovered a new land but I die."[4]

Hans, with the best rifle, was added to the party, and on the morning of the 24th they set off with a wild yell of dogs and men. The hunt began next day with a furious chase after a bear, resulting in a feast for the men and the dogs that left them all too full to move and too tired to build a snow house. They took a few hours' sleep on the open ice, the most uncomfortable, said Kane, that he could remember. This early success ruined his hopes of getting across the basin, for it convinced the Eskimos that bears were to be found on the Greenland side. No remonstrances or entreaties would induce them to abandon a promising hunt upon which they and their families depended, in order to follow the route Kane urged upon them. Giving up his hopes, he wearied of the hunt and wanted to get back to the brig to negotiate with Metek for dogs, but Kalutunah and the others kept him on the bear hunt for another day. He was repaid for his disappointment by getting a full view of the great glacier he had named for Humboldt and a chance to make a study of its glaciology that fills seven pages of his book. While his companions ate and rested, he climbed a tall iceberg and through clear air saw far to the north the peaks of that land Morton had reached, to which Kane now attached the name of George Washington.[5] He returned to the brig with Kalutunah's party, thoroughly exhausted. "Was ever so bedevilled and body-torn man, angel or devil? . . . the exposure has been ferocious . . . we have been to the great glacier and back."

Hans had asked for permission to visit Peteravik to get some walrus hide to make soles for his boots. He said he did not need the dogs; he could walk the eighty miles or more, stopping at Etah to rest. Kane reluctantly let him go, giving him commissions to execute at Etah. The boy never returned, and Kane never again heard from him directly. Almost two months later, in his last contact with the Smith Sound Eskimos, he learned that Hans had stopped at Etah, leaving the messages, and had gone on to Peteravik to visit Shang-hu, whose pretty daughter Mersuk had been his nurse when he was ill at Etah. "Hans the faithful—yet I fear the faithless—was last seen upon a native sledge, with a maiden at his side, and professedly bound for a new principality at Uwarrow Suk-suk, high up Murchison's Sound. Alas for Hans, the married man!" Dr. Kane did not live to read the next chapters of Hans's life story, in which he and Mersuk went north again with Dr. Hayes on his expedition of 1860, taking their first child with them, nor its climax in 1870 when Hans—ever faithful to Mersuk if not to his first love or to Dr. Kane, took Mersuk and the three children they had by that time, on Charles Francis Hall's vessel *Polaris* to the farthest north as yet ever reached by a ship. At Thank God Harbor, North Greenland, Mersuk gave birth to her fourth child, born nearer the Pole than any other known infant. Her story is told by General Greely in a chapter of his *True Tales of Arctic Heroism*, "The Wifely Heroism of Mersuk, the Daughter of Shang-hu."[6]

Dr. Kane mourned the loss of Hans because he had become very fond of the boy, and also because in planning the journey of escape, which he now accepted as inevitable, he looked to Hans for help in getting the party and its equipment to open water near Cape Alexander. At its start, which he scheduled for May 17, he planned to move the new long sledges, each with a whaleboat mounted upon it, along the ice belt to Anoatok. He and Hans, with the dog team and a small sledge, would carry the equipment, taking alternate trips. The four men who could not walk were to be left at the brig until the last. The hut at Anoatok would be fitted with a door and provided with bedding and cooking equipment, to serve as a way station for the sick while the slow progress of the big sledges continued. The smaller "Red Boat" was to be patched up and mounted on the rebuilt sledge "Faith" to make, in all, three boats for the long voyage down Baffin Bay that was to begin once the whole party, sick and well, could be assembled at the southern edge of the ice pack at the entrance of South Sound. Kane himself would direct and control the whole operation, shuttling back and forth with the dogs innumberable times on the eighty-mile passage along the ice belt, spending his nights either at the brig, or at Anoatok with the sick men, or with the boat party as might be necessary. Without Hans to help him, this terrific task would be lonelier, far harder, and more dangerous.

About April 27, while Kane was still away with Kalutunah, Shang-hu, and Tatterat, Brooks had sent Godfrey to Etah to get food—a trust faithfully executed. On the 30th, Godfrey returned with a heavy load of walrus meat, and in the hopeful mood that always followed a full meal of animal food Kane wrote that this critical month of April had witnessed the party's resurrection from helplessness to efficient activity, and had relieved him and two of his command (Bonsall and Petersen) from labors which must otherwise have destroyed them. Winter had passed and the spring was full upon them. His lightened cares gave way to the old urge for discovery. At 5 P.M. on May 1 he called together his officers—"by which I mean the old stock who abided by the brig"—and told them that before abandoning Rensselaer Harbor he must make one last effort to explore the western side of the basin, to look for any possible trace of Sir John Franklin's men, and for the sake of geographic science to connect Hayes's northernmost point of May 27, 1854, with a point on Kennedy Channel opposite that reached by Morton a month later, June 24. He would add the two borrowed dogs to his old team, and

Dr. Kane and His Comrades Abandoning *Advance*

"From a sketch made on the spot," presumably by Dr. Kane.

*Frank Leslie's Illustrated Weekly,* December 18, 1855

with Morton as his only companion would attempt to cross the mid-basin ice to Grinnell Land, which he had named but had never himself set foot upon. He did not ask his officers to approve this venture, but they were, he said, "with one accord impressed."

With this entry Dr. Kane's private journal ends. During the next three months he was to have neither time nor opportunity to continue it. He did not even record on what day he and Morton set out, nor just when they returned. When, the next year, he was at home writing about his last effort of exploration, to guide his memory he had only a few notes of observations by compass and sextant, made to verify his charts. The ice was as fearfully rough, its hummocks as high, as when thrice before members of the expedition had braved its terrors. "We struggled manfully," he wrote, "to force our way through—days and nights of adventurous exposure and recurring disaster—and at last found our way back to the brig, Morton broken down anew; and my own energies were just adequate to the duty of supervising our final departure." The operations of the search were closed.

On or about May 17 he began to move the large sledges, with the whaleboats cradled upon them, down from the side of the brig onto the ice belt, which had so long been their road to discovery, to the hunt, and to sustenance and was now to lead them to home and safety. The work of crossing the terraced ice belt was exhausting to the men, nearly all of them invalids, unused to open air and exercise, but they returned to the brig each night weary yet hopeful. By the 19th they had dragged the sledges three or four miles. On the morning of Sunday, May 20, 1855, all hands assembled in the now dismantled winter chamber between decks. Kane read prayers and a chapter of the Bible. He took Sir John Franklin's portrait from its frame and rolled it up in an India-rubber scroll, to be placed in one of the boats. Then he read his officers' formal reports of their final inspection and survey of the state of the expedition and of the brig, justifying and advising its abandonment. In an earnest address he told the men that the difficulties that lay before them over the five hundred miles from Rensselaer Harbor to Upernavik could be traversed with safety for all if every able man devoted himself to the protection of their sick and crippled companions, and he admonished them to place reliance upon the Power that had so often rescued them in peril. All hands without exception signed a paper in which they undertook to abide faithfully by the expedition in a spirit of union, harmony, and discipline. Dr. Kane then affixed to a stanchion near the gangway a notice to be read by whomever might come in search of them, in which he explained the abandonment of the brig and outlined his proposed journey to the south.

Those men who could walk then went on deck; the flags were hoisted and hauled down again. There was no mockery of cheers, Kane said; no final toasts were drunk. One by one the men went silently down the gangway and made their way—walking or limping—to the sledges, and the four who temporarily remained to man the brig wished them Godspeed.

# 12

# Escape

Dr. Kane had planned every detail of preparation and organization for the journey of escape. Each man had an Eskimo suit of fur—trousers, jumper, and hood. The men had made for themselves three pairs each of boots to be worn over heavy socks and fashioned of canvas faced with walrus hide, with an inner lining cut from the Brussels carpet that once covered the cabin floor of *Advance*. To prevent snow-blindness they wore slotted wooden goggles of Eskimo type. Sleeping bags of buffalo fur and eiderdown quilts were bundled for the journey in waterproof canvas. Every man had his individual numbered bag for personal effects, to be stowed in an assigned place. The provisions, which consisted only of melted fat and powdered biscuit, tea and coffee, with some bits of dried meat for the sick, were also packed in waterproof bags, shaped to fit into the sheer of the boats. These were to be carried to open water by sledge, then stowed for the voyage. The expedition's records were carefully bundled and wrapped. Cooking was to be done with the light stove that Petersen had made from old tins. Much, of course, had to be left behind, the heavier scientific instruments, heavy tools, the useless daguerreotype outfit,[1] and Kane's books. He hoped to the last to save his natural history collections and actually packed and carried them to the way station at Anoatok, but with intense regret abandoned them there.

For the sledge journey, Kane divided the party, other than himself and the four invalids, into two messes of six men each. Brooks, who was to be commander of both boats, was in immediate charge of one, and Dr. Hayes of the other. Kane would have no such lack of discipline and order as with the unsuccessful secession party of last August. On the route there was to be a regular daily schedule, beginning in the morning with prayers; every man had his fixed place at the drag-lines, and all were to take turns at cooking, the boat captains alone excused. Hayes was responsible for keeping the log, and Sonntag for recording the course and checking the position of landmarks. Temperature readings were to be recorded every three hours.

It was impossible for the six men of each crew to drag the heavy weight of their own sledge and boat. The two leaders, Brooks and Hayes, were barely able to walk, and few of the others were strong enough to do a man's full share of labor. Both crews therefore joined in hauling first one sledge, then the other, trudging three miles for each mile of distance gained. Returning each night to the brig, by May 24 they had made seven miles; but on that day the sleeping bags were brought down, and thenceforth the men slept in the boats, whose canvas housing offered little protection against the chill night air, still below zero. Kane, with his six dogs and a light sledge, had already managed to get the four invalids down to the relief hut at Anoatok and to make them as comfortable as possible in its dismal shelter. Three of them—Wilson, Goodfellow, and Whipple—were still almost helpless, but Stephenson could get about enough to keep the lamps burning, melt water, and warm up the food Kane left for them. He himself was incessantly driving back and forth between the brig, the slowly advancing boat party, and Anoatok, conveying the stores and provisions, seven hundred pounds of which had still to be forwarded to caches along the line of march. Meanwhile Ohlsen, Petersen, and Morton, between their stints with the boat crews, were patching and caulking the "Red Boat," which on May 25 they carried on the small sledge to join the two larger boats.

Some of the Etah Eskimos lent a hand to Kane in his tireless travels. On the 26th their head man, Metek, went to the brig with the doctor and Morton to bake bread from flour purposely left aboard. Later, the youth Sip-su and an old man by the name of Nessark turned up and helped with the sledge driving. By the 28th all the stores were at Anoatok or farther on at Navialik near Cape Hatherton, where Kane expected to launch his three boats on open water. On one of his seesaw trips about the first of June he was caught by a very severe storm and had to spend a night alone on the rocks. The boat parties continued their progress, a few miles each day. They passed the half-way station at Anoatok, and, again leaving the sick men behind them, went on.

The sun was getting higher, the air warmer, and the ice belt was softening. At times the men had to let the boats down onto the pack, which itself was beginning to weaken and break up. On June 5 the whaleboat "Hope," cradled on its sledge, crashed through the ice, dragging six men into the water. With great difficulty it was pulled up onto the ice again, without loss of life.

An Episode in the Escape Journey
Engraving by J. C. McRae from drawing by C. Schuessele and J. Hamilton,
*Arctic Explorations, 1853, '54, '55,* 2:237

Fearing that the route between Anoatok and the boat parties might be cut by the thaw, Kane had Goodfellow brought down to the boats, and warned Stephenson to have the others ready to leave at a moment's notice. Nessark, the old Eskimo from Etah, conveyed them next day to the boats. On the 7th, Morton, who had been sent to Etah for food, returned with several Eskimos, a few dogs, and a full supply of meat and blubber. Kane took Metek to the brig with him to get the last remnants of pork fat and on the way back to pick up Stephenson, last of the four left at the Anoatok way station.

The whole party would now have been reunited at the boat crews' camp, had not a tragic accident befallen one of the best and strongest men. As Kane and Metek, with Stephenson on the sledge, neared the boats, they were shocked to come upon Christian Ohlsen, sitting all alone and faint with pain on a rock beside the recent sledge tracks of his companions, where they had perforce left him while they went on a few miles to make a camp where he could be cared for. He told Kane that earlier in the day, while the men were dragging the boat "Hope" over broken ice, her stern dropped into the water and she was kept from swamping only by the greatest efforts of the men. Ohlsen by prodigious strength held her steady while his fellows pulled the sledge back on the ice, but under the strain he suddenly sustained a grave internal injury. Ohlsen died a few days later, on June 12, moaning to the last about his wife and child at home.[2] They buried him as best they could in a sort of trench and covered the corpse with rocks. Dr. Kane, who had depended greatly upon this skilled and intelligent man, and had long since gotten over whatever grudge he might have held from the days of the secession, deeply mourned him.

The toilsome journey to open water continued a few days more, but the trudging men were not to be without help and sympathy. When on June 16 they reached the mouth of the little bay on which, a few miles inland, lay the village of Etah, the whole of Metek's tribe, except for two women and an old blind man—twenty-two in all, men, women, children, and babes —came to meet them. This was the farewell gathering of the white men and the Eskimos, for the boats lay less than a mile from open water. There Kane's party, delayed by a rainy southwester, remained for two days, but the Eskimos stood by them and helped to carry the luggage over the last mile of rocks and ice. In sheer gratitude for their help, Kane walked up to Etah to visit the blind man left there with the two women. Returning to the shore, he called the Etah people together on the ice beach to receive his parting thanks for their generous friendship and assistance during the past few months. He gave them all parting gifts—the greatest treasure, his amputation knives from his surgical case—to Metek and Nessark; to the rest such lesser items as he could spare—needles and thread, a few pieces of clothing—and the dogs to the whole community, except the two favorite leaders of his sledge team, which he was taking in the boats.

Thus they parted with mutual gratitude and affection, the Eskimos returning to their huts, the white men to their boats with high hopes, now, of reaching their far distant homes.

Kane, in his report to the Secretary of the Navy, stated that in the thirty-one days between May 17 and June 18 the men had walked 316 miles, transporting the boats over 81 miles of the ice belt and the floes; he himself had shuttled back and forth 1,100 miles—almost incredible feats for them and for him, considering the recent illnesses and semistarvation of the men and their commander's rheumatic heart. Fortunately the four sick men had withstood the rough travel from Rensselaer Harbor to the ice front surprisingly well and were stronger than when they were taken from the brig. Even more fortunately, the start for home had brought together the whole party in mutual confidence and in loyalty to the leader whose admirable planning and personal courage had brought them over so difficult a stage of their pathway to safety. If there was as much as a moment of anger or disloyalty, it was not recorded. All we know in detail of this last stage of the expedition comes from Kane's book, *Arctic Explorations, 1853, '54, '55.* What notes he kept at this time are not now to be found; if they contained any complaints about his officers or men, no hint of them got into his book, nor have those others who mentioned the escape journey in their written recollections—Hayes,

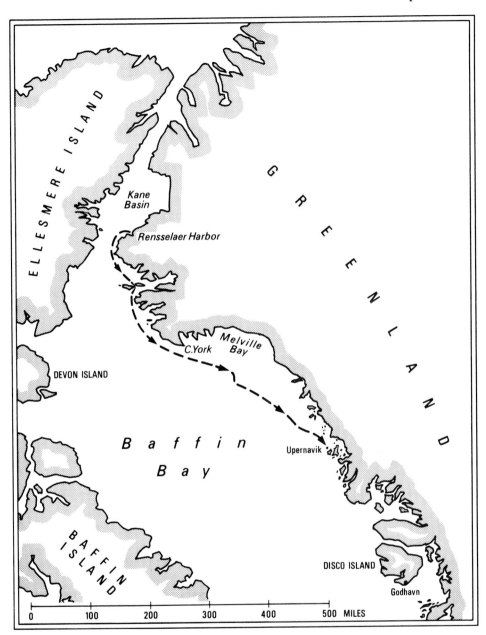

The Escape Route by Sledge and Boat, 1855

Petersen, Bonsall, Goodfellow, even Godfrey[3]—mentioned any word of discontent or serious dissension. There was, as in any group of weary, desperate men, some grumbling and some despondency, but no more than Kane could

deal with. "During our passage through the ice in open boats on that perilous journey of more than eighty days," wrote Bonsall, "by his judicious
management he not only cheered the dispirited and quieted the querulous
and discontented, but he so dispensed the provisions as to give no one the
slightest cause for complaint (a most difficult operation, as anyone who has
had to do with starving men can testify.)"

The necessity for continuous vigilance and faithful allegiance was by no
means over when the three boats sailed away from Cape Alexander. Before
them lay a voyage of about 500 miles to Upernavik, as hard and dangerous
as the passage on the ice had been, on the rough waters of Baffin Bay, much
of it through its dreaded eastern bight, Melville Bay, and this in open boats
with the scantiest of provisions.[4]

The party was not able at once to take to the boats. The rainstorm became
a gale; two nights and a day dragged by before they could embark. At 4 P.M.
Tuesday, June 19 the sea was quieter, the sky clear, and with flags flying they
set sail: Kane in "Faith" with McGary, Petersen, Hickey, Stephenson, and
Whipple; Brooks in "Hope," with Hayes, Sonntag, Morton, Goodfellow, and
Blake; Bonsall with Riley and Godfrey in the little "Red Erik." (Oddly,
Kane forgets to mention Wilson at this point.) A fresh wind at the start made
it impossible to land at Sutherland Island, where Kane had planned to stop
for supper. The men had to do their cooking in the boats. The passage
continued rough toward Hakluyt Island. "Red Erik" swamped in a choppy
sea; Riley and Godfrey swam to "Faith" and Bonsall to "Hope," and Kane
had to tow the half-sunken boat into a sheltered cleft in an old ice floe
where the tired men could sleep in the boats.

On Hakluyt Island next day they put up a tent for the sick and shot a few
birds to eat with their usual supper of tallow and bread-dust soup. On the
morning of the 22d they sailed through a snowstorm to Northumberland
Island, where there were myriads of auks, some of which they caught for
their evening meal. On the way, next morning, across Murchison Channel
to Cape Parry there was floating ice dense enough to force them to run up
to a floe, unlash the sledges from the gunwales of the boats, drag the boats
onto the ice, cradle them on the sledges and drag them on over the floe.
Landing on Cape Parry, Kane walked to nearby Netlik and sent Petersen
to Tessiusak, another nearby Eskimo settlement, to get news of Hans, but
in vain.

The voyage went on, with every day new labors and varying difficulties
with ice and rough seas. On June 25, running under sail before a fair wind
through open leads in the floe, Kane was at the steering oar of "Faith" for
sixteen hours continuously. Food was running low; the daily allowance of
broth, with tea when fresh water could be got by melting ice cut from a

small approachable berg, was not sufficient to maintain the men's energies. The frequent labor of pushing and dragging the boats through broken ice was almost too much for them. Off the cliffs near Wolstenholme Sound, in very rough water, the boats were dangerously nipped between crashing and crumbling masses of ice, but luckily were released with minor damage to the men and craft. When the gale forced them against the rocks, they pulled the three boats onto a ledge and there camped for three days. Harsh as the shelter was, it gave them rest and sleep, and the cliffs were so crowded with breeding eider ducks that the men gathered eggs by the hundred—"A merrier set of gourmands never surfeited in genial diet," Kane wrote. He named the place "Weary Men's Rest" and made a sketch of it for his book. When on July 3 the wind moderated, he launched the boats again and sailed away, fortified by a round of eggnog made from auks' eggs and the contents of his liquor flask.

The next week saw uneventful progress, mostly under sail, to the neighborhood of Cape Dudley Digges. On the 11th the boats came upon a long tongue of floating ice extending into the sea from a glacier not marked upon their charts. Kane tried to work a way through this barrier but had to give up the attempt. His men were again weakened by lack of fresh food since leaving Weary Men's Rest, and the boats had been strained by stormy seas and frequent dragging on and off the floes. "Hope" especially was greatly weakened. The men patched her leaks with wood from the runners and crossbars of a sledge. To make matters worse, there was no sign of open water ahead. Climbing an iceberg, Kane could see as far as Cape York, the northern promontory of Melville Bay. The waters of the bay were covered with dense ice; there was nothing to do but await the advance of summer. Working the boats toward shore, Kane found a strong remnant of last winter's ice belt[5] in front of a little cave in the rock, offering a safe place for his boats. Above this shelf wild cliffs rose more than eleven hundred feet. Their terraces were swarming with nesting seabirds—auks and tridactyl gulls. Just beyond the ledge was a sheltered mossy cove and, over it and beyond, a glacier seven miles wide. Amid the moss were growing the northern plants, ranunculus, saxifrage, duckweed, and scurvy grass. Here was the place for a glorious rest, Kane told his companions, never revealing except to two trusted men that before them in Melville Sound lay seemingly impassable floes. He gratefully named the place "Providence Halt." Amos Bonsall, in his brief mention of the escape journey,[6] hints that some of the men did not delight, as Kane did, in the charms of this place; anxious to get on with the homeward journey, they were impatient with the two long halts at Weary Men's Rest and Providence Halt. Undoubtedly, however, the respite from constant danger and labor came at the right time to restore their energies for the long haul across Melville Bay.

Their departure from Providence Halt on July 18 began with a near disaster. When they launched the whaleboat "Hope" from the icy shelf on which she and her consorts had been hauled up for the week past, she fell into the sludge ice below, carrying away some of her rail and bulwark, and losing overboard two precious pieces of equipment—the best shotgun and the teakettle that also served for melting ice and making coffee. Henceforth a tin can had to serve these essential needs. As for food, for the rest of the voyage, which might well take two or three weeks, they had the barest sufficiency for the sixteen men. A count taken three days later showed 50 pounds of flour and the same amount of cornmeal, 80 pounds of the Gail Borden meat biscuit that had so long been a mainstay, and 348 pounds of the bread Kane had baked on his last trip to the brig. For meat they were for the time being fairly well off; while at Providence Halt they had killed more than 250 of the little Arctic auks or "lumme." These—skinned, gutted, and dried on the rocks—would give them at least a pittance of animal food. Each bird yielded four ounces of meat, and, at the rate of one bird per day per man, they would last almost two weeks. There were also some dozens of fresh birds' eggs. The list of foodstuffs does not specifically include any edible fat, though later in his narrative Kane mentions an allowance of "tallow" to accompany the biscuits. He did have "pork slush," 112 pounds of it to be used for fuel. Possibly some of this, diverted to human consumption, was dignified by the name of tallow. Some firewood from the brig was still available and later in the boat journey the "Red Eric" was to be broken up and burned to warm the meat-biscuit broth and to brew tea and coffee.

Refreshed and strengthened by the week of rest at Providence Halt, Kane and his men found the next stage of their journey almost a holiday excursion. Rowing along or at times gliding under sail through the quiet leads where the pack-ice had drifted away from the shore, except where a protruding glacier forced them farther from land, they saw signs of spring along the cliffs, green moss and nesting auks. Kane was almost euphoric about their daily halts. "Our happy oarsmen, after a hard day's work, made easy by the promise ahead, would stretch themselves in the sunshine and dream happily away till called to the morning wash and prayers. We enjoyed it the more, for we all of us knew that it could not last."

They reached Cape York on July 21. Here the open leads along the shore, that for three days had given them a carefree route, were obliterated by a great floe extending far to the south. Whether to camp again to wait for the shore ice to open, or to dare a passage along chance leads in the seaward floe, was the difficult choice Kane had to make. Calling his officers together, he explained the situation and began preparing to reembark. The "Red Eric" was broken up to be taken along for fuel. Kane had the men build a cairn on a prominent headland, left in it a record of the party's stop, and marked it with a red shirt hung on a stick of wood.

Travel through the pack fairly matched the reputation of Melville Bay for difficulty and danger. The leads were narrow and shifting; great hummocks of ice and occasional bergs blocked the view ahead, and to make matters worse, fogs often closed in upon them. One evening Kane awoke from a weary sleep to find that the steersman of the leading boat had lost his way through the main lead they had been following. Steering a wrong course toward the shore instead of westward toward more open water, he had locked the two boats in a little channel not twenty yards wide, whose icy margins were closing in. There was nothing to do but haul the boats up on the ice, again cradle them upon the sledges,⁷ and drag them over the pack to open water. This unwelcome task took three days until they came upon an open lead and again launched the boats.

The long detour had cost them a dangerously large share of their remaining provisions. The men's strength was waning from the hard work of dragging the boats on an ever-decreasing food supply. After a careful survey of the larder, Kane had to reduce the daily ration still farther, to five ounces of bread-dust, four ounces of "tallow," and three of bird meat. One day when he ordered the men to haul "Hope" over a tongue of ice, her crew was too weak to budge her, and all the men together could barely keep her moving. While they were tugging at the draglines, the other boat, "Faith," was suddenly freed from her temporary berth by a cleft in the floe and started to drift away. Her loss would have been fatal. At that moment the wind brought a flat cake of ice to the floe on which the men stood. Kane and McGary instantly sprang upon it, succeeded in floating it to the drifting boat, and brought her safely back.

Because of this new shortage of food, Kane felt it urgently necessary to get to the more open sea, where he could travel under sail and get as quickly as possible to a shore where animal food could be found. For two days this effort failed; heavy bergs surrounded the boats, and a strong wind brought the pack upon them. When they finally reached the open bay they were in the path of the great icebergs drifting southward to the Atlantic. The boats were so battered and unseaworthy that they had to be baled constantly day and night. The men were showing serious effects of malnutrition, shortness of breath and swollen feet, insomnia and low fever. Fortunately they spied a large seal resting on a patch of ice. With intense caution, one of the boats, moved by a single scull astern, glided silently nearer and nearer to the seal. Petersen stood in the bow, ready with his rifle but tense with anxiety. Kane withheld the signal to fire until they came within easy range; Petersen pulled the trigger, and the seal fell dead on the edge of the ice pan. The men, Kane says, were almost crazy with excitement. They rowed frantically to the ice pan, hauled their prey to a safe distance from the edge and fell upon it with their knives, crying and laughing hysterically as they hacked away at the carcass. "It was not five minutes," he said, "before every man was sucking his bloody fingers and mouthing long strips of blubber." Not an ounce of the seal was lost; its intestines went into the soup kettle, the flippers were cut off and chewed, and the liver was eaten warm and raw. That night the men made a great fire with two planks of "Red Eric" and reveled in a feast of roast seal.

At this point in his narrative, Kane reveals why he had taken in the boats two Eskimo dogs, his favorites, "Toodla" and "Whitey." They were to be pets at home if all went well, but at the last resort were to be killed and eaten. As McGary had said, they were "meat on the hoof." Once, when fresh meat was lacking before the halt at Weary Men's Rest, Kane was on the point of killing the two dogs, but could not bear the sacrifice. Now they were finally safe, for the men of the expedition were not again to feel desperate hunger. These creatures that had never known a tree or a green field were spared to romp with Kane in the woods at Fern Rock. A day or two later Petersen shot another seal, and from then on there was a full supply of fresh meat.

On August 1 Kane sighted the Devil's Thumb, a landmark known to all voyagers in Melville Bay. Now in familiar waters, the boats were soon among the Duck Islands and halted south of Cape Shackleton. Weary of rough water and sea ice, Kane chose to finish the voyage, one of the most difficult and perilous ever made by man, by taking a cautious route through quiet waters among the islands rather than the more direct outside passage. There, one morning after a bivouac on the shore, Petersen came to Kane with the story that he had just seen an Eskimo paddling along in his kayak, in search of eiderdown. He recognized the man and cried "Paul Zacharias, don't you know me? I'm Carl Petersen." "No," said the Eskimo, "his wife says he's dead," and with a stolid expression of wonder he paddled away.

Two days later they were rowing in a mist among the islands, when they heard voices, voices of Danish men, coming toward them in a small shallop.

Petersen, who had been very quiet and grave, burst into an incoherent fit of crying, only relieved by broken exclamations of mingled Danish and English. "'Tis the Upernavik oil-boat! The *Fräulein Fleischer*! Carlie Mosyn, the assistant cooper, must be on his road to Kingatok for blubber! The *Mariane* [the one annual ship] has come, and Carlie Mosyn—" and here he did it all over again, gulping down his words and wringing his hands.

It was Carlie Mosyn, sure enough. The men in the battered whaleboats, begging him for news of the world, learned of the Crimean War and the siege of Sebastopol. Mosyn could say but little about America, for no whalers had called of late, but he had at least one thrilling piece of information: a fortnight ago two vessels flying the Stars and Stripes, a steamer and a bark, had passed up Baffin Bay and gone into the ice to look for Kane's party. Carlie Mosyn had one more tale to tell, one that must have been a shattering thing for Kane to hear, though in his book he tells it calmly. The pastor at Upernavik had received a German newspaper containing word that someone had found relics of Sir John Franklin's expedition in possession of Eskimos on the peninsula of Boothia—a thousand miles south of where Kane had dreamed Franklin's men might be found, living or dead—and had learned from the Eskimos that they had perished to a man in a vain effort to escape from *Erebus* and *Terror,* icebound on the coast of King William Land.[8]

After one more night's halt, Kane's party went on, and presently, on the morning of August 6, spied the sunlit peak of Sanderson's Hope that rises above the settlement of Upernavik. The village was hidden in mist, but Carl Petersen could tell where it was by the baying of the dogs and the sound of a bell that was calling the workmen to their day's employment. The steersmen of "Faith" and "Hope" headed their craft into the harbor, and amid a crowd of cheering children the travelers hauled their boats for the last time upon the rocks.

> For eighty-four days we had lived in the open air. Our habits were hard and weather-worn. We could not live within the four walls of a house without a distressing sense of suffocation. But we drank coffee that night before many a hospitable threshold, and listened again and again to the hymn of welcome, which, sung by many voices, greeted our deliverance.

The kindly people of Upernavik fitted up a loft to house Dr. Kane and his men until they could leave for home. Although the unexpected arrival of sixteen hungry and needy men must have strained their resources of food and domestic supplies, they willingly shared what they had. Captain Amundsen of the little supply ship *Mariane,* which was soon to return to Denmark, offered to take the Americans aboard and put them ashore at the Shetland Islands, whence they could obtain passage to New York by way of a Scottish or English port. Kane thought best to accept this offer. Knowing nothing about the plans of the American vessels that had gone northward in search of him, he knew all too well that if they followed his own route of two years before, they might themselves have to winter in the ice. On September 6, therefore, the men of the expedition, all but Petersen, left Upernavik in the *Mariane.* Dr. Kane's two dogs went with them. On the vessel's deck was the whaleboat "Faith"—all they had to bring back of *Advance* and her fortunes, Kane said, except the furs on their backs and the expedition's documents.

*Mariane* put in at Godhavn for a few hours on September 11, delaying her departure as long as possible in hopes of getting news of the American relief ships. Whatever anxiety Kane may have felt for the fellow countrymen who were gallantly risking their ships and their own lives to find him, would have been redoubled if he had known that his young brother, John Kintzing Kane, Jr., was aboard one of the relief vessels now in the ever-perilous waters of Baffin Bay. He would have been reassured by knowing that the squadron was commanded by a highly capable naval officer, a veteran of the Wilkes Expedition to the South Polar seas, Lieutenant Henry J. Hartstene.[9]

In the fall of 1854, Kane's family and his sponsors in official and private circles had become more and more anxious about him and the men who had gone with him into the unknown region north of Baffin Bay. Not a word had come from them since they left Upernavik on July 24, 1853; they had vanished as completely as Franklin's ships in 1845. Whalers returning from Melville Bay reported a very cold summer in 1854, with heavy ice to the north. If indeed Kane's vessel had not met with disaster, it must be locked in behind the frozen, berg-filled waters of Smith Sound, its crew in distress, perhaps starving. Henry Grinnell and Judge Kane, feeling the deepest weight of uncertainty, began to stir up talk of a relief expedition. On November 17, 1854, the judge, addressing a meeting of the American Philosophical Society in its hall in Philadelphia, got a committee appointed to prepare a memorial to Congress. Grinnell followed suit in New York and Boston. The New York Chamber of Commerce addressed an appeal to the Senate and House; similar appeals arrived from Boston and Philadelphia business organizations, and the newspapers took up the cause in vigorous editorials. From Baltimore, John Pendleton Kennedy, former Secretary of the Navy, gave his support, and at Washington the eminent scientists Joseph Henry and Alexander Dallas Bache spoke for the Smithsonian Institution and the Coast Survey.

The slow pace with which the Senate and House of Representatives acted upon these urgent appeals must have almost maddened Grinnell and Judge Kane, and everyone else who had the fate of *Advance* and her men at heart. The Pennsylvania and New York congressmen naturally took the initiative. On December 11, 1854, Representative Thomas B. Florence of Pennsylvania introduced a resolution to request the House Committee on Naval Affairs to consider sending two vessels. A member refused unanimous consent to suspend the rules so that the resolution could be debated. A week later Senator Richard Brodhead of Pennsylvania introduced a similar resolution in the Senate and by an eloquent speech got it adopted, though not without opposition. Senator Badger of North Carolina feared that Congress was committing the government to support a chain of search expeditions—Kane seeking Franklin, another party looking for Kane with equal likelihood of getting lost, and so on indefinitely. The same fear was voiced in the House. On January 15, 1855, Brodhead asked for a joint resolution of the two houses. Senator Hunter of Virginia doubted the humanity of these perilous Arctic expeditions; Senator Mallory of Florida more hopefully pointed out that Captain Inglefield's successful summer voyage of 1853 showed what a steamer could do. The joint resolution was passed and sent to the House, which assented to it and returned it to the Senate, where on February 3 Senator Joseph R. Chandler of Pennsylvania secured its adoption by a very dramatic speech. President Franklin Pierce signed it on February 5, and on March 3 both houses agreed to tack onto the pending Navy Appropriation Bill an appropriation of $150,000 for the expedition.[10] On that day the little party of icebound men at Rensselaer Harbor were at their lowest ebb, down to their last bits of fresh meat, every man tainted with scurvy, and the temperature 51° below zero.

The navy, at last free to act, went ahead rapidly to secure and equip two vessels specially purchased for the voyage, a clipper bark of 327 tons, renamed *Release,* and a propeller steamer of 558 tons, with barkentine rig, now to be called *Arctic.* Both were sent, as *Advance* and *Rescue* had been five years before, to Brooklyn Navy Yard to be strengthened and fitted out. Even before the relief expedition was assured, as early in fact as December 1854, Kane's friends of the first Grinnell Expedition were begging for a chance to lead or join the voyage. William Murdaugh, first officer of *Advance* in 1850–51, wrote from his ship at Buenos Aires offering to command the relief squadron or to accept a post under De Haven. The late second officer of *Advance,* William I. Lovell, volunteered, in a letter to Judge Kane, to be one of those "to rescue my old friend and shipmate, the Doctor." Samuel P. Griffin, commander of *Rescue* in 1850–51, wanted to command the rescue squadron. Gibson Carruthers, ship's carpenter of *Advance* in the earlier cruise, asked to be a watch officer on the new voyage.[11] In England, Lieutenant Sherard Osborn of the Royal Navy, whom Kane had met at Beechey Island in 1850, proposed to Lady Franklin that he should take out an English steamer to search for the Americans.[12]

The two men best fitted by experience to command a relief expedition were obviously De Haven, who had brought back *Advance* safely in 1851, and Griffin, his admirable colleague of *Rescue.* De Haven, weakened in health by the cruise of 1850–51, did not volunteer, and Griffin was in trouble with the navy because of some act of insubordination. In the end the Secretary of the Navy, John C. Dobbin, chose Lieutenant Hartstene, twenty-seven years in the navy, to command the squadron, with Lieutenant Charles C. Simms as acting captain of *Arctic*. Lovell was made acting master of *Release* under Hartstene. Dr. Kane's brother John, who at the age of twenty had just taken his M.D. degree at the University of Pennsylvania, volunteered and was at once accepted by the navy, given the temporary rank of assistant surgeon, and assigned to *Arctic*.[13] Another Philadelphia physician, James Laws, was also given a temporary naval appointment as surgeon on *Release*. He and John Kane were in fact very welcome in spite of their inexperience, for no regular navy surgeon had volunteered for the cruise.

The relief expedition sailed from New York on May 31, 1855, two years to the day after *Advance*. The voyage was well recorded; besides Hartstene's formal report to the Secretary of the Navy, three of his officers kept private records. The manuscript diaries of two of them, Laws and Lovell, are to be seen in the Stefansson Collection at Dartmouth College. The third diarist was Dr. John Kane, who shared his father's and his eldest brother's talent for writing clear, readable English. His lively account was published in *Putnam's Magazine* soon after the squadron returned.[14] The passage to Newfoundland was stormy; John Kane was terribly seasick, and his medical colleague Dr. Laws was so miserable that he thought he would not live through the cruise. Between Newfoundland and Greenland one night *Release*, which was towing *Arctic*, slower under sail, struck an iceberg head on and was in turn fouled by *Arctic* ramming her. In spite of the heavy shock to both vessels there was no great damage. A few days later only skilled seamanship by the "incomparable" Lovell (as Dr. Laws calls him) averted an even more dangerous collision with a berg.

The squadron made port at last at Upernavik, where Dr. Laws was asked by the governor to give medical attention to Carl Petersen's wife, who was grieving to the point of illness, sure that her husband was dead with the rest of Kane's men. Whalers returning from the north warned Hartstene that Melville Bay was practically impassable that season, but he ventured on and got through to Cape York in spite of several bad nips. Several times, Laws says, the ships' stores and the men's clothing were packed and ready on deck in case the crews had to abandon ship. At one time the ice was so thick that Hartstene felt it necessary to post himself in the crow's nest to watch for leads through the pack. Having recently sprained an ankle, he could not climb the rigging and had himself hoisted in a bosun's chair to the lookout and stayed there on watch, in freezing weather, for thirty-six hours.

Once into the North Water the two vessels had an easier time. Following Kane's course, Hartstene sailed into the entrance of Smith Sound until he was stopped by the dense pack over which Kane's men had dragged their boats only two months before. Thinking themselves beyond the northern limit of human habitation, Hartstene and some of his men, rowing along the shore on the watch for signs of Kane's party, were startled to hear human voices. For a moment they thought they had met the men they were looking for, but found they had come upon Eskimos. These strangers took Hartstene, John Kane, and other officers to their village in a beautiful sheltered valley beside an inlet several miles from the sea; it was, in fact, Etah. There John Kane was thrilled to see, in possession of the Eskimos, many articles from *Advance*—pots and pans, a knife and fork, broken oars, part of a telescope recognized as Dr. Kane's. The Americans with difficulty communicated with the men of Etah, working with an Eskimo phrase book, eked out by sign language. The bright lad Myouk, who had been much with Kane's party, knew a few words of English, and, by showing him sketches of ships and boats and figures of men, the officers learned that a great captain named "Kayen" and a company of men had abandoned their ship north of Etah and had gone south into Baffin Bay.

After thoroughly searching the shores and islands south of Cape Alexander, Hartstene thought it best to head southwest, crossing the Bay toward Lancaster Sound and Beechey Island, which Kane had said he would try to reach if in difficulty. Heavy pack ice, however, blocked the way into Lancaster Sound. Sure now that Kane's party could not have gone that way and must, as the Eskimos had said, have ventured to cross Melville Bay in their boats, Hartstene returned through the great middle ice with only one mishap—another collision with an iceberg against which *Release* was repeatedly thrown by wind and waves for several terrible hours. Heavy northerly winds drove both vessels to the south of Upernavik and forced them to make port at Godhavn.

Thus it was that on September 11, just as the Danish brig *Mariane,* with Kane's party aboard, was about to pull away from the Godhavn wharf, two vessels flying the Stars and Stripes came into the harbor. Kane's men hastily debarked and lowered the "Faith" into the water for the last time. With her little flag flying, Brooks at the tiller, and Governor Olrik of Godhavn beside Kane in the stern, "Faith's" crew lay to their oars and the rest followed in another boat. They were soon enough under the lee of *Release,* from whose battered railings the men of the rescue party looked down at them. "The men in the boats," wrote John Kane, "were long-bearded and weather-beaten; they had strange, wild costumes; there was no possibility of recognition. Dr. Kane, standing upright in the stern of the first boat, with his spy-glass slung around his neck, was the first identified; then the big frame of Mr. Brooks; in another moment all hands of them were on board of us." As the two captains greeted each other, said Dr. Kane, "the rigging was manned by our countrymen, and cheers welcomed us back to the social world of love they represented."

# 13

# The Traveler at Home, Once More

RELEASE AND ARCTIC sailed directly from Godhavn to New York and hence were unreported until they appeared off Sandy Hook on the early afternoon of Thursday, October 11, 1855. They did not lack a welcome. Proceeding up New York Bay to Quarantine, the rescue ships were recognized by vessels at anchor and under way, whose crews dipped their flags and shouted cheers across the water while the forts on shore saluted them with a roar of cannon. By the time the two vessels hove to off the Battery, the whole city knew that Kane and his men were home again. A crowd gathered at the Battery landing and newspaper men came out in force. Aboard *Release* and *Arctic* the reporters found Kane's companions all well and Kane himself fully recovered from the hardships of the expedition. The *New York Times* man noted that "The Doctor has improved in personal appearance in his absence. He brings home a bronzed face, a long and heavy black beard, a shock of hair just whitening a little—a sort of iron grey,—a stouter body and a hand with a hearty grip."

As soon as he could get away, Kane went ashore to the Astor House, where a gay evening party had hastily gathered to meet him. Friends and admirers crowded around him, and he was so beset that he could hardly make way to the door to be driven to Henry Grinnell's home at 17 Bond Street, followed by the reporters. The *Herald* said next day that Grinnell "received the Doctor with such a welcome as comes only from the depths of the heart," but the great merchant's words, however affectionate, were as homely as those of a father to a son. "I have no *Advance* with me," said Kane sadly. "Never mind," said Grinnell, "You are safe; that is all we care about. Come into the parlor and tell us the whole story."

Next morning all New York read what the doctor had told Grinnell and the reporters, and when Kane saw it spread over the whole front page of the *Times* under thirteen breathless headlines, he knew that he had won the fame he so long had craved. Under these captions there followed an interview recounting the entire course of his journey and his escape from Smith Sound: "We give it as we heard it from his lips." There were interviews also with two junior officers, one from *Release* and one from *Arctic*. William Morton got his share of glory, for Dr. Kane had made him a hero for a day by telling of his journey beyond the Humboldt Glacier and his report of seeing an Open Polar Sea. Other New York newspapers—the *Tribune*, the *Herald* and lesser sheets—also reported the expedition's return with enthusiasm rivalling that of the *Times*. By next morning, October 13, daily papers from Boston to Philadelphia and Washington and all the cities and towns to which the telegraph now reached were telling of the Arctic heroes' return. But for Kane fame could wait a while. What he longed for most was to be at Fern Rock with the family he had dreamed of in so many homesick hours, to see in his mother's eyes the light of affection and pride, and to hear "well done" from the father whose approval, often denied, was as dear to him as the nation's plaudits.

It is ironical indeed that before Doctor Kane could cross the parental threshold Judge Kane's name was also in the headlines, on October 13, to be greeted with detestation while his son was being glorified. On the 12th the judge had issued from his federal court in Philadelphia a long-awaited decision in the Passmore Williamson case refusing to quench a writ of habeas corpus; it instantly brought down upon him the abolitionists' full measure of wrath. Next day, for example, an editorial in the New York *Herald* slyly contrasted the judge's action with the noble achievements of his son:

> This new opinion makes every State a slave State, in defiance of its own constitution and laws. Judge Kane is the Columbus of the new world of slave-whips and shackles which he has just annexed, and is entitled to all the rank of a discoverer. His insulting inhuman persistence . . . is the acme of outrage and cruelty.[1]

For several days thereafter the *Herald* and other antislavery papers continued to editorialize in the same strain.

These newspaper attacks did not, of course, affect Elisha Kent Kane's desire to see his family. Far more troubling was the thought that his return to Philadelphia would fling him headlong into a personal situation that could only cause him pain and probably humiliation. He had taken it for granted that Margaret Fox was still at school with Mrs. Turner at Crookville, awaiting his coming to revive the loving hopes he had formed for their

**New-York Daily Times.**

# DR. KANE HOME AGAIN.

## The Second and Third Arctic Expeditions Safely Ended.

### Arrival of Propeller Arctic and Bark Release at New-York.

### THE ADVANCE LEFT IN THE ICE.

### NEW LANDS FOUND.

### A Bridge of Ice from Greenland to the Continent.

### AN OPEN SEA FOUND.

### NO TRACES OF SIR JOHN FRANKLIN.

### LATITUDE 82° 30′ N. REACHED.

### LIFE IN THE FROZEN REGIONS.

### ON SLEDGES FOR THIRTY DAYS.

### Detailed and Interesting Account of the two Expeditions.

### DR. KANE'S OWN ACCOUNT.

DR. KANE, the intrepid Arctic navigator, after having been given up as lost, has returned safe home, with the loss of but three men on his whole expedition. He left his brig frozen up in the Arctic Sea, on the 24th of May, 1855, went three hundred miles over the ice to the sea, and then in open boats thirteen hundred miles to Upernavik in Greenland. After waiting for

VOL. V.....NO. 1269

from the fact, that the entire circuit of Smith's has been effected, and its shores completely cha

#### THE OPEN POLAR SEA.

But the real discovery of the Expedition open *Polar Sea.* The channel leading to these was entirely free from ice, and this feature w dered more remarkable by the existence of a or solid belt of ice, extending more than o dred and twenty-five miles to the southward. sea verifies the views of Dr. KANE, as expre the Geographical Society before his departure

The lashing of the surf against this frozen b ice was, we are assured, impressive beyond a tion. Several gentlemen with whom we hav versed, speak of it with wonder and admiratio

An area of three thousand square miles wa entirely free from ice. This channel has been after Hon. JOHN P. KENNEDY, late Secretary Navy, under whose auspices the Expedition wa

The land to the north and west of this chan been charted as high as 82° 30′. *This is the land to the Pole yet discovered.* It bears the Mr. HENRY GRINNELL, the founder of the ex which bears his name.

#### THE WINTER OF 1854–'55.

The extreme severity of the previous season evident that the brig could not be liberated be Winter set in. She was fast imprisoned in th of a large field of ice. The provisions, a abundant, were not calculated to resist scur the fuel, owing to the emergencies of the p Winter, was deficient in quantity.

Under these trying circumstances DR. KANE party of volunteers, on an attempt to reach the of Lancaster Sound, in hopes of meeting the expeditions, and thus giving relief to his ass passed in an open boat over the track of B travel, riding out a heavy gale. They found a terrupted barrier of ice, extending in one grea shoe from Jones' to Murchison's Sounds, ar forced, after various escapes, to return to the b

Front Page, *New-York Daily Times,* October 12, 1855

future. Whatever the degree of his commitment to the girl, which before his departure for the Arctic had gravely disturbed his parents in spite of his efforts to hide it from them, the story would now inevitably get about. Such a denouement could only mar his return to the family. Moreover he was no longer quite sure that he wanted to marry Margaret.

As a matter of fact she was not in Crookville but in New York City. From Clinton Place, where she was staying, she had heard the guns on October 11 as the forts roared a welcome to Hartstene's squadron. While Dr. Kane was being entertained by his friends that evening, she was impatiently expecting him to ring the doorbell and fling himself into her arms. Before narrating the last months of this doomed romance, we must repeat that practically everything we know about the affair comes from Margaret's ghost-written *Love-Life of Dr. Kane,* published after his death to justify her claim that he wanted to marry her against the wishes of his parents and had in fact entered into an unconsummated common-law marriage. The story her book tells is no doubt biased, but enough gossip was spoken and printed at the time to suggest that in general it is true, though the extent to which Kane was really committed to Margaret can now never be known.

Certain it is that after a few months of docile endurance of her exile at Crookville with the kindly Mrs. Turner, Margaret became restless and willingly accepted invitations to visit friends in New York. Cornelius Grinnell, to whom Kane had entrusted the management of the money he left for Margaret's board and tuition, together with final authority to direct the program he had made for her, leniently granted her appeals for leave of absence. She stayed several times with a friend, Mrs. Ellen Cochrane Walter, a well-placed widow, friend of the Grinnells, whose home was at 60 Clinton Place (now Eighth Street).[2] Meanwhile Margaret's mother and her sister Katie were also in New York, holding séances in a house on Tenth Street, not far from Clinton Place.

Early in October 1855, Margaret left Crookville for another stay with her friend. Her story about Kane's return is that when from Mrs. Walter's house she heard the harbor guns welcoming the relief squadron on the afternoon of October 11, she became so excited that Mrs. Walter would not let her go out. The two women waited all evening for Kane to come. On the morning of the 12th they still had heard nothing from him, and finally Mrs. Walter sent a note to Cornelius Grinnell in nearby Bond Street to let him know that Margaret was in New York. That night, worn out with waiting, Margaret went to her mother's residence on Tenth Street, where late in the evening an old friend, her physician Dr. Edward Bayard, came to say that a carriage, no doubt bringing Dr. Kane, had stopped at Mrs. Walter's door on Clinton Place. Hurrying there, she was devastated to learn that the caller

My dear Mr Grinnell
             I owe to Mrs Turner
for Board and tuition Eighty
Seven Dollars
             When do you Expect to
See the Dr? I wish you would
please tell me. I have received
the Book. I am indeed very
much pleased with it. Do he
not have to meet so many dangers
face to face? Please tell me when
the Dr Expects to return —
             Very Sincerely
                  Yours
Cornelius Grinnell Esqr}  Maggie Fox
New York.
             Tuesday April 10th 1854

Margaret Fox to Cornelius Grinnell, April 10, 1854
Original in Kane Papers, American Philosophical Society

was not Kane, but Cornelius Grinnell, who had come to bring Dr. Kane's excuses; he was suffering from rheumatism; his relatives and friends were troubled about his engagement to Margaret; but he would come to her as soon as he could. Ominously, Grinnell had asked Mrs. Walter, on behalf, he said, of Dr. Kane's family, to turn over to him the letters the doctor had written to Margaret. Unless this request came from Kane himself, we must assume that one of his brothers, Thomas or Robert, had come that day from Philadelphia to begin at once the family's efforts to dissuade him from marrying Margaret.

Next morning, October 13, the story in *Love-Life* goes on, Dr. Kane, in naval uniform, came to the house on Clinton Place and asked to see Margaret. Mrs. Walter told him that the girl was completely broken down and would not see him, but under Mrs. Walter's persuasion she came downstairs. Dr. Kane, "walking the room in a fearful state of excitement," rushed to her and taking her in his arms kissed her brow again and again. But when at last he spoke to her their transports gave way to gloom, for he told her that however much he loved her, his family's opposition was so violent that any idea of marriage must be postponed indefinitely. For the present they must be to each other only as brother and sister. By this time both were in tears. Taking pen and paper he then drafted a statement for her to sign, which he said was to satisfy his mother, acknowledging that their relations were merely friendly and no engagement of marriage existed. From loving consideration for his distress and embarrassment, she said, she copied the statement in her own handwriting and signed it. He then called Mrs. Walter into the room and to her amazement showed her the paper. "Maggie, is this true?" she cried. "No, no," said the girl, "Dr. Kane knows it is not." In spite of Mrs. Walter's remonstrances he took the statement away with him. A few days later, he brought it back to Margaret and watched her tear it up.

Kane left for Philadelphia late on this day so dramatically described in the *Love-Life*. There is no record of his reunion with his family, a scene we can well believe was too intimate to be recorded. After tasting the comforts of home for a few days, he went back to New York to settle the affairs of the expedition. On other such trips during the next few weeks he always saw Margaret, maintaining for a time the farce of a brotherly relationship. On these journeys he was often accompanied by William Morton, lately of *Advance,* now again his valet and his sick-nurse in periods of illness.

At home he quickly took up the task of putting on permanent record the events and results of his expedition. Urgently wishing to prove himself a scientist above all, he had long planned to write a monograph on Arctic ice, describing and analyzing its formation, the movements of pack ice and icebergs, and the glaciers, for all of which he had made extensive notes and numerous sketches; but he never found time for such a book. His prime task now was to tell the human story of the expedition—its adventures, successes and failures, its discoveries and its tragedies, its imprisonment and escape. For a book of this kind intended for general readers he had in fact already won an eager public, by his narrative of the first Grinnell Expedition, published after he left on the second voyage. That his first book was a success, he learned from a letter his father wrote to him on May 29, 1855, for delivery by the relief expedition if it found him alive.

> Your book, Franklin's fate, and the action of Congress in consequence of your failure to return have given you quite a historical notoriety. We have letters from the best officers of the British Admiralty, altogether flattering, and much is expected from your "Narrative" of your present cruise. Be prepared therefore for a two years' writing and printing labour when you get clear of Arctic ice, beard and breeches. I am offered a large price for the right of publishing it.[3]

Judge Kane had entrusted his son's first book to Harper and Brothers of New York. They brought it out in excellent style, with handsome engravings and woodcuts based on Kane's sketches, and it was very well received at home and abroad. George Templeton Strong, the New York diarist, said, "It is far more attractive than any narrative of northern voyages and discovery that I have met. Franklin's first journey has a strong tragic interest, but this far exceeds it in clearness and picturesqueness of description and conveys a much more distinct image of the perils and marvels of the Polar ice." The London *Atheneum* reported that the book was "Profusely and admirably illustrated, one of the most interesting of the kind that we have seen, and deserves a place by the side of our own most cherished records of Arctic adventure."[4]

Harper and Brothers issued the book in March 1854, but only after grave difficulties. A first printing of several thousand volumes lay in their warehouse awaiting the publication date when the building was totally destroyed by fire, December 10, 1853. With great enterprise, the firm quickly repaired the loss of Kane's and other books, some of which had to be completely reset. Apparently *The U.S. Grinnell Expedition* had been stereotyped, and the plates, stored elsewhere, escaped the fire as did the steel engravings. Only a few woodcut blocks were lost. Another printing with new title page and front matter, a few new cuts and added lithographs, was made up for Harpers by their printer.[5]

Judge Kane must surely have approved the typography and illustrations of the book, but he was not satisfied with Harpers' handling of financial arrangements on Dr. Kane's account. Continuing his letter of May 29, 1855, he informed the absent author that

> Your book has earned for you much fame; but as yet no profit. The Harpers were burnt out at the close of 1853, and the first edition of some 4,000 or 5,000 copies totally destroyed. In their account as sent to me they charge these as part of the edition, making you lose ½, and they make you debtor besides for the cost of all the illustrations save only one half of the wood cuts. The result is that they leave you in debt on an edition of some 9,000 copies in all. It is a rascally account.[6]

Dr. Kane, therefore, with his father's advice found another publisher soon after his return from the Arctic. The *New York Evening Post* reported on November 15, 1855, that Dr. Kane had contracted with Messrs. Childs and Peterson, of Philadelphia, to bring out his account of the late expedition. Mr. James Hamilton, the artist who had designed the plates for Kane's earlier book, would prepare the illustrations.

George William Childs was only twenty-six years old when he took on Kane's book, but he had already shown great business ability and an unabashed talent for publicity. With Peterson, who attended to editorial matters while Childs did the promotion and the front office work, Childs had built up one of the largest publishing houses in the country. As soon as he had the contract he began to urge Kane not to write for geographers and other scientists, but for the general public; with the talent displayed in his first book and his now international fame, the story of his expedition could well become a best seller.[7] Kane had already shown how he could turn his earlier journals into a highly readable volume. He now had at hand practically all the material he needed for the new book; his journal of the second expedition had only to be pruned of technicalities and of his personal reveries, his worst moments of despair and of anger, and his sharp judgments of his shipmates. The manuscripts of the journal, now at the Historical Society of Pennsylvania and Stanford University, show the pencil marks by which he indicated to his copyist the parts he chose to print. Never giving in fully to Childs' demand for a popular book, he resolved to retain much of his scientific comments on Arctic geology, natural history, meteorology and glaciation, mingled with the narrative of adventure, and hoped thus to make the book interesting to readers of all ages and differing interests.

On November 15, when Kane was in New York on some business of the late expedition, a friend took him to dinner at the Century Club, then in Clinton Place, quite near the home of Mrs. Walter, Margaret Fox's friend. Among a small group at dinner that evening was William Makepeace Thackeray, nearing the end of the American tour on which he presented in many cities his famous lectures, "The Four Georges." George William Curtis, author of a popular column, "The Editor's Easy Chair" in *Harper's Monthly Magazine,* was another of the party. From him we have the tale of Kane's first and only meeting with Thackeray. After dinner, then as now always a memorable function at the Century Club, the gentlemen stayed on for a long evening chat. Kane won Thackeray's heart at once by telling him that one winter night at Rensselaer Harbor he had noticed one of his men entranced for hours over a book, and, looking over the sailor's shoulder, saw that it was *Pendennis.* Someone asked Kane to tell about the expedition, and, as Curtis said later, "The party listened like schoolboys might listen to Sinbad the Sailor. The tale was marvellous, but the Centurions believed it." Another guest said it was like listening to Marco Polo. When Kane had finished, Thackeray rose from his chair and walked to Kane's side, his bulky frame towering over the slightly built explorer, and asked the host of the evening, "Do you think the Doctor will permit me to stoop down and kiss his boots?"[8]

While in New York, Kane of course called on Margaret Fox. The brother-and-sister pretense was wearing thin, and in fact they could hardly maintain it when all the city's newspapers were either saying or denying that they were about to be married. The rumor seems to have gotten into print, unaccountably, when an upstate newspaper, the *Troy Daily Whig,* only eight days after Kane returned from the Arctic, printed the following piece of gossip.

> DR. KANE—A gentleman of this city informs us that Dr. Kane, of the Arctic Expedition, is soon to be married to Miss Margaretta Fox, the second sister of the "Fox Girls," at whose residence in Hydesville, Wayne County in this State, the spirit rappings were first manifested. Dr. Kane became acquainted with the Fox family in New York. During his absence, Miss Fox, his said-to-be affianced, has been attending a young ladies' school in Philadelphia.[9]

A week later the *New York Herald* copied this item, crediting it to the Troy *Whig;* on October 31 the *Evening Post* printed it in shorter form, crediting the *Herald,* but added that it had the best of reasons for saying "the story was without a shadow of foundation." The *Express* copied this almost literally, the next day. On November 6, the *Tribune,* Horace Greeley's paper, shook a grandfatherly finger at its gossipy contemporaries:

> We wish the several journals which have originated reports, pro and con, respecting the persons above named, would consider whether they have or have not perverted their columns to the gratification of an impertinent curiosity. What right has the public to know anything about an "engagement" or semi-engagement between these young people? If this were a monarchy, and one or both of them were of the blood royal, there would be an excuse for reports and

speculations with regard to their relations to each other; but, in the actual state of the case, such intimations as have appeared in the journals are not to be justified. Whether they have been, are, may be, are not, or will not be "engaged," can be nobody's business but their own and that of their near relatives. Then why should the press trumpet their names in connection with each other?[10]

Margaret Fox and Elisha Kent Kane were not of the blood royal, but they were both nationally famous and the papers were making the most of the rumor. The Kane family finally took steps to quench it by planting a denial in a Boston paper, which was reprinted by the *Daily Pennsylvanian* of Philadelphia:

> The foolish story of the engagement of Dr. Kane, the Arctic navigator, to one of the spirit-rapping Fox girls, is thus explained by a Philadelphia correspondent of the Boston *Traveller*:—Sometime previous to the departure of Dr. Kane on his last expedition, a subscription was started in New York by a number of liberal, kind-hearted gentlemen, for the purpose of educating one of the Fox sisters, a remarkably bright, intelligent girl, and worthy of a better employment than "spirit rapping." Dr. Kane was applied to, and feeling somewhat interested, from pure motives of humanity subscribed with a sailor's liberality. On his return, by invitation of the gentleman supervising her education, he called to witness the improvement of his protegée; and from this simple incident has arisen the engagement story.[11]

The *Pennsylvanian* went on to say that such philanthropic zeal was an honorable peculiarity of the Kane family; the judge constantly evinced it; Colonel Thomas L. Kane lived in the daily exercise of almost boundless benevolence; Robert P. Kane, Esq., followed the same pattern, and now it appeared that Dr. Elisha Kent Kane was governed by the same spirit of liberality. Persons unaware of this noble trait, said the *Pennsylvanian*, were attempting to put a different countenance upon the action of one of the gentlemen concerned.

A more sophisticated observer of the human scene put the whole affair in simpler terms which probably expressed the judgment of most outsiders who knew something about it: "I am sorry to be informed that being thoroughly in love with Miss Fox (spirit rapper) he had not the courage to marry her against the opposition of his family. The passion and the cowardice are both strange and the latter painful as diminishing one's regard for what I had thought a heroic character."[12] To others who puzzled over this inconsistency, Margaret's book of 1866 gave a belated answer. "Let those who are disposed to condemn his conduct consider the circumstances in which he was placed: his present want of pecuniary independence, his education in erroneous ideas of social elevation, and the incessant torture to which he was subjected from the urgent remonstrances of friends and the sneers of those indifferent to him."[13] As for the "strangeness" of Kane's passion, it needed no explanation for those who understood his temperament. His love for Margaret had flowered in the last late years of his romantic youth, all of a piece with his descent of Taal volcano, his swordplay at Nopaluca. To court this young communer with the spirits had been as exotic as climbing the Vocal Memnon or practicing medicine at Whampoa. It gave him another chance to disengage himself from the conventional ways of his family and at the same time was an outlet for the philanthropic spirit which was indeed an honorable peculiarity of the Kanes. It was his private version of King Cophetua and the beggar maid. In his heart he knew the idyll might not last. Once he wrote to Margaret, "Remember, then, as a sort of dream, that Doctor Kane of the Arctic Seas loved Maggie Fox, of the Spirit Rappings."[14]

But two years of responsible command since he left Margaret at Crookville had ended his belated spiritual adolescence. Worn out by his exertions and hardships in the north, with the seeds of rheumatic fever in his limbs and in the lining of his heart, he now faced the heavy labor of writing his narrative of adventure. In these next years there could be little room in his life for the half-educated girl he had left behind in 1853; and, moreover, he had now no heart for a break with his parents. Through all his wander years he had deeply loved his mother, and as he matured had come to new respect for his talented and influential father. Thus the torture to which (in Margaret's phrase) he had been subjected by his parents' opposition to his entanglement with her came not so much from their obduracy as from his own troubled, wavering spirit.

Margaret's family also were concerned about the continuing newspaper reports and word-of-mouth gossip, which they thought were compromising her reputation. According to the *Love-Life,* Kane's attentions to Margaret were not welcomed. At this time, obviously, if he had chosen he could easily have broken off the semi-clandestine engagement, but either lingering affection or a quixotic sense of duty to Margaret, or both, held him to his course. He soon managed to break the barriers of Mrs. Fox's disapproval. At Christmas time he sent Margaret and Katie a box of bonbons, and when in January 1856 he had occasion several times to go to New York he always called at Tenth Street. One winter day he took the two girls on a sleigh-ride. Several times, Margaret said, he accompanied her to vespers at St. Anne's Roman Catholic Church on Eighth Street. He had more than once advised her to become a Catholic.[15] This statement, at first surprising, is not incredible. Now that his experiment of making a cultivated lady of her had ended, and she was back with her mother, he was afraid that she would return to the spirit rappings. The Church, abhorring such errant cults as spiritualism, would shelter her from heresy and give her the strength of its abiding faith. Eighteen months after his death she was, in fact, baptized a Catholic at St. Peter's Church on Barclay Street, New York.

To Mrs. Fox, a Methodist, and to the calculating older sister Leah, Margaret's leaning toward Rome was, no doubt, an added reason for concern about Elisha Kane. At any rate there was also fresh newspaper gossip about the alleged engagement, which led Mrs. Fox, in February 1856, to forbid Kane ever again to visit Margaret or even write to her. So the affair swung back and forth until in the autumn it came to its woeful end.

Five weeks after his return from the Arctic, Dr. Kane made his only recorded address about the expedition. On November 16, 1855, he gave an informal talk before the American Philosophical Society—the small but celebrated learned society of which his father had long been an officer and to which he had himself been elected in 1852.[16] He was too busy writing his book to give any time to public lecturing. The first part of his literary task, preparation of the narrative text, went rapidly. By Christmas 1855 he was able to send Childs and Peterson about three hundred pages of his journal, marked for copying by an amanuensis but subject, he said, to interpolation and extraction. In a few days another batch followed. Evidently he had resigned himself to Childs's demand for a popular book, for he asked Mr. Peterson, who was the literary man of the firm, to make sure that he had sufficiently excised certain passages describing too intimately the domestic habits of the Eskimos. In pruning his journals, he said his aim was to make a center-table book, as fit for the eyes of children as for those of refined women.[17] Nevertheless, a few months later he told Childs, with more than a hint of sarcasm, that, in the new passages he was inserting between the excerpts from the journal, "I attempt to be more popular and gaseous—this latter inflated quality in excess. Most certainly my efforts to make this book readable will destroy its permanency and injure me. It is a sacrifice."[18] But he did not delete all the noisome sights and smells of Eskimo life, the bloodshed of a bear hunt, nor the sufferings of starving and scurvied men. Lady Franklin, when she read the book, was appalled by its realism, which she feared would hurt the cause of polar research.[19] In addition to the passages of scientific interest which Kane insisted upon retaining, he managed to get Childs to print sixty expensive pages of astronomical, geodetic, geophysical, climatological, and meteorological tables, for which he enlisted at his own expense the assistance of Charles A. Schott of the U.S. Coast Survey and of August Sonntag, and also a twenty-page technical enumeration of Arctic plants by Elias Durand, a Philadelphia botanist. Childs was getting more than he had bargained for.

Kane in his intense way devoted recklessly long and late hours to the labor of writing and of putting together the appended official reports of his expedition and that of Hartstene, with the statements of his officers and men about the various special journeys they had made from the base at Rensselaer Harbor—eighty pages to be collected and edited. He also put much effort into the illustrations that were being made from his sketches by James Hamilton and the engravers on steel and wood. His correspondence with Childs at this time, shuttling every few days between Fern Rock and the publishers' office at 124 Arch Street in downtown Philadelphia, frequently included advice and criticism for the artists and directions for the placement of the more than 300 plates, text figures, and tailpieces which add much to the charm of the book. According to Elder, Hamilton lived at Fern Rock for a month in order to render Kane's sketches, some of which were finished drawings, others mere outlines, into the beautiful watercolor and wash drawings from which the steel engravings were made. Kane had the last manuscript pages of the text ready before July 4 and the appendices by the end of August, although his work of writing had been interrupted by at least five trips to New York on the business of the late expedition and to Washington for consultations at the Coast Survey headquarters and the Smithsonian Institution. Besides all this there was proofreading to be done in the hot weather of late summer, for Childs wanted to get the book out while the public was still crying for it, and began to print it while Kane was still at work on the later chapters.

Fatigue and irritability portending the breakdown of Kane's health appear in his letters as early as May 1856. When Childs begged him for copy to keep the printers busy, Kane sharply replied

> You tell me that "unless you keep them [the printers] in copy, they will not work on the book any longer." With this, my dear Sir, I have nothing to do. As for copy, no effort of mine shall be spared, but as to your printers I pray you not to pain me by a narrative of trials, with which I certainly sympathize but am unable to remedy. . . . Truly your friend, with all apologies for a very crusty letter which nevertheless you deserve.[20]

On June 7 he wrote to Childs, "Authordom has again overdone me. I shall have to take a spell again soon;" on the 14th, "My health is nothing extraordinary under this extreme heat, but I think I have accumulated enough nerve force to carry me through to that ominous, pleasant word *Finis;*" some time in July, "With little spirit of congratulation and much weariness I send you this preface, which completes my task. . . . Now that the holy day is at hand, I am ungrateful enough to complain that it finds me without capacity to enjoy it."

But there was still work for him on the book. The following weeks were full of problems, putting the appendices in order, revising the tables, proof-reading. Late in July Kane reported to Childs that a few days before he had "jumped on the owl train, gone to New York and brought back Sonntag, who had the original records of astronomical and magnetic matter with him."[21] On this trip to New York Kane took a day or two off for a holiday on Long Island with Cornelius Grinnell, but had to admit to Childs that something was wrong. "I get weaker every day. I tried Long Island bathing with my friend Grinnell, but could not stand it."[22]

Long before the printing was done, Childs began an intense publicity program by distributing specimen pages to the newspapers. He got them to print articles about the forthcoming book, some of them in the form of a long biographical sketch of Kane by Dr. William Elder, a friend of the family and a well-known writer. He furnished the booksellers with large broadsides bearing illustrations from the book, and as soon as possible sent advance copies to scores of famous people, including Alfred Tennyson, William H. Prescott, Winfield Scott, Charles Sumner, Louis Agassiz, Nathaniel Parker Willis, William Cullen Bryant, and Washington Irving, and got testimonials from them all. He fed the newspapers with glowing advance reviews, many of them so much alike as to suggest that he or Peterson had ghosted them. Having sold almost 20,000 copies of the two-volume work before publication, he brought it out at the end of September 1866 under the title *Arctic Explorations: The Second Grinnell Expedition in Search of Sir John Franklin, 1853, '54, '55*. It was an immense success. Author and publisher had jointly accomplished one of the boldest, speediest, and most profitable feats of bookmaking in the history of American publication up to that time.

This triumph put an end to a great scheme Childs had concocted before he could be sure how salable the book was going to be—a scheme that caused its author a good deal of annoyance while he was writing it. Before Christmas, 1855, when Kane had barely begun piecing together the first excerpts from his Arctic journals, it occurred to Childs that whether or not the book was a popular success, he could cover his costs by persuading Congress to buy a large number of sets for patriotic distribution to schools, colleges, and other favored institutions in the members' constituencies. Twenty years before, the government had subsidized Charles Wilkes's *Narrative* of his expedition to the South Seas; why not another example of daring American scientific enterprise? Childs would be happy to sell for the purpose any number of sets and would give Kane a 25 percent royalty on them. Kane, unaware of how such a deal might look to inquiring legislators, at first acquiesced. He was in need of funds; he had put his own savings into the expedition, was largely dependent upon his father, and had in fact been forced to ask Childs for an advance of $600.

Childs began his campaign in the Pennsylvania Legislature in January 1856 by getting a member to introduce a resolution commending the results of the expedition to the patronage of the U.S. government. Early in March a letter signed "Potomac," urging favorable action on a joint resolution about to be submitted to Congress for the purchase of $125,000 worth of Dr. Kane's book, appeared in the Philadelphia *Public Ledger* and was copied by Washington newspapers. Childs was in Washington at this time. Kane, seeing his name used in this kind of wire pulling, wrote Childs a deeply pained letter, and on April 30 wrote again, even more strongly, saying that Richard Brodhead, Senator from Pennsylvania, had written to Judge Kane insinuating that his son was acting with Childs to push the appropriation. To Childs, Kane disclaimed any part in the affair and said he was sending his brother Robert Patterson Kane to Washington to keep his name out of it. The Committee on Library of the House of Representatives recommended the purchase, and a joint resolution reached the floor of both houses. There was a good deal of sentiment for the purchase and, on the other hand, strong opposition on the ground that it might open too wide a field of literary patronage. Its most vocal opponent, Senator Brodhead, proposed a direct congressional grant to Kane instead of the purchase of books from Childs.

Kane had frankly hoped for governmental recognition of his services as explorer, but he wanted the distinction more than money and he recoiled at the idea of direct payment. The affair dragged on for most of the year. In July, Childs, to Kane's intense annoyance, attempted again to stir up interest in Congress. "Your kindness I fully appreciate," Kane wrote to Childs,

> but depend upon it that a continuation of the question would be unpleasant to my feelings and prejudicial to my real interests. Besides I have washed my hands of all connection with the book and therefore with yourself. My expedition and its merits are neither in your hands nor my own and I beg you to leave unmolested the action of Congress, for this coupling of my name with the book will interfere with any expression of disinterested feeling on the part of the Senate and thus stand in the way of that which I value far beyond either books or money, viz., an honorary testimonial in recognition of our party.[23]

Finally, in December 1856, the joint resolution was defeated by the Senate's vote of nonconcurrence.[24] By this time Childs and Peterson were selling the book so well—65,000 copies in its first year—that neither they nor Kane needed a governmental subsidy.

The enterprising young publisher went on to other successes and a long career as a newspaper magnate; for Kane, the writing of *Arctic Explorations* was the beginning of the end. He was ill enough now to see that all his own projects for the future and those that others had made for him must be set aside while he tried to regain his health. One of these plans he could put off without great disappointment. Childs, eager as always for his financial benefit and Kane's as well, had been talking for months about a course of public lectures to begin in the fall when the book, he hoped, would have built up the public's desire to see and hear its heroic author. Dr. Kane, with his now established fame and the publicity-minded Childs as impresario, in that age of lecture-loving audiences might well have outdrawn even Dickens, Thackeray, and Emerson. Apparently Childs wanted to put Kane on his personal payroll as his star performer. Kane, before his health worsened, had been quite willing to take the rostrum again. Although he did not care to tour the country in Childs's employ, he would accept Childs's offer to serve as booking agent and adviser. In September, clinging to hope, he wrote, no doubt with Judge Kane's cautious advice, "I liked your plan and thank you for its suggestion. Any direct connection between us in the capacity of lecturer would have been distasteful to me, but your services to aid and direct the arrangements of my course I thankfully accept."[25]

By mid-July, however, he knew he could not go through with a tour; the lectures must be indefinitely postponed. Another and more attractive but equally impossible proposal stirred up Kane's longing for action that was ever in his mind and heart; to put it aside was deeply painful. Lady Franklin wanted him to lead a final search expedition to King William Land, where John Rae had in the summer of 1854 found traces of Sir John's men who had perished on that desolate shore. Rae had by no means learned enough to satisfy the persistent lady, bringing back only secondhand stories of the Eskimos about a band of white men who in 1848 abandoned their ships off King William Land and came to their deaths struggling on foot toward the Canadian mainland. That these were Franklin's men Rae proved by purchasing from the natives a score of pieces of silver tableware bearing the crests and initials of seven officers of *Erebus* and *Terror,* including Franklin himself. This was evidence enough that the expedition had come to a disastrous end, but Lady Franklin hoped that some of its people might still be living, perhaps among the Eskimos, and in any case she wanted to recover the expedition's records which might show that Sir John had actually discovered a Northwest Passage.

The Admiralty was, however, unwilling to risk any more lives or spend more money, since it seemed certain that Sir John's men were all dead. Because naval officers and men were not to be had, Lady Franklin's only hope was a private expedition, if necessary under a foreign leader. Kane's discoveries and his daring escape from the ice had already won him the admiration of British Arctic experts. In May 1856, the gold medal of the Royal Geographical Society, rarely bestowed, had been presented to him in Philadelphia by the Queen's minister to the United States, John F. Crampton, after a ceremony in London at which the American Minister, George M. Dallas, accepted it by proxy.[26] Lady Franklin had formed a high opinion of Kane from his letters, and had gained from them an impression that he would consider taking command of her little steamer *Isabel* on a voyage to King William Land.[27] She, however, wanted the cruise to go *via* Bering Strait, whereas he had serious objections to that route, and in any case the state of his health soon ended any possibility that he could go again to the Arctic. However, she still wanted his advice and the benefit of his now great prestige, in support of a new plan to which she had turned in consequence of an extraordinary event, the reappearance in Baffin Bay of H.M.S. *Resolute.* That ship, late of Sir Edward Belcher's squadron, hopelessly ice-bound two years before in Barrow Strait, had been abandoned on May 12, 1854, by Captain Henry Kellett and his crew. On September 10, 1855, *Resolute* was found, afloat and seaworthy, almost a thousand miles away in the drifting pack ice of Baffin Bay at north latitude 74° 41', by an American whaler, the *George Henry* of New London. In sixteen months the deserted ship had been carried eastward through Lancaster Sound and down Baffin Bay by the same strong current that had driven De Haven's *Advance* and *Rescue* along the same route in 1851. Captain James M. Buddington of *George Henry,* with a skeleton crew of eleven men, manned *Resolute* and navigated her with the aid only of the skipper's pocket watch, a quadrant, and a defective compass, through heavy weather and high seas, to port at New London. When the Admiralty waived all claim to the derelict vessel, Congress appropriated $40,000 for her purchase, had her refitted at the Brooklyn Navy Yard, and offered her as a gift to Queen Victoria and the people of Great Britain. On November 13, 1856, under command of Captain Henry J. Hartstene, *Resolute* sailed to Southampton, where at Lady Franklin's suggestion the sturdy ship received the unusual honor of a royal salute, and in mid-December at Cowes she was formally presented to the queen with a great flourish of Anglo-American goodwill.[28]

To Lady Franklin in London and Henry Grinnell in New York the recovery of *Resolute* seemed an act of Providence. If the Admiralty would spare no ship, here was another, already dedicated to the Franklin Search, her seaworthiness tested by storm and ice, her new sails and rigging ready for sea. Lady Franklin began to summon friendly advisers to persuade the Admiralty to send *Resolute* to King William Land. She badly needed Kane in London to support her campaign and hoped that the United States Navy would put him in command of *Resolute*'s voyage to England.

She did not know how deeply his Arctic privations and the long strain of writing through the hot summer had undermined his health, nor did he himself feel the seriousness of the increasing fatigue and depression that had led him to postpone a lecture tour. The disease that lurked in his joints and in the lining of his heart was now insidiously progressing; no excruciating joint pains this time, nor any violent thumping of the heart, but a daily low fever with loss of weight, emaciation, and bodily weakness. In spite of these signs of disease, Kane hoped that all he needed was a period of rest. Though it was obvious that he could not take command of *Resolute*, he clung to the possibility of being in England when she arrived, and of pleading with the Admiralty to send her again to the Arctic seas. The journey, he thought, would not overstrain him and would in fact fit into a plan he had made, to go abroad for rest and recuperation.

After Kane's mid-July trip to New York to fetch Sonntag and the charts, Henry Grinnell wrote to Lady Franklin, July 17, 1856:

Dr. Kane came to New York day before yesterday and returned yesterday. He passed an hour with me at my house. I never saw him look so bad; he is but a skeleton or the shadow of one; he has worked too hard. He says he must be off, and now thinks of leaving in a few days for Havre, from there to Switzerland; pass a month among the glaciers, quietly recruit his health, and then go to England. . . . He is every day attacked with the remittent fever, better known here as fever and ague.[29]

Kane himself, a few days later, wrote to Lady Franklin

It was my intention to have sought repose and health by a few weeks' sojourn in Switzerland, but I will come to England to confer with you, and return for a longer visit after I have attempted to relieve your cares. . . . My book, 900 pages of *ad capitandum* sacrifice, has left my hands. . . . I have no fault of health but a complete inability to withstand hot weather and indoor life.[30]

His decision to begin his health-seeking trip with a brief stay in England was reinforced when early in August the London mails brought him letters from General Sabine and other prominent Arctic experts urging him to go to England to help them convince the Admiralty of the value of a final expedition. He told his friend Childs that he did not see how he could hold back; Sir Roderick Murchison and Sir Francis Beaufort agreed that his acceptance was the only thing that could unite the sympathies of the government and Lady Franklin's friends.[31]

But every day his fever and headaches grew worse, and he saw that his

needed rest could not wait until he got to Europe. On August 24 he wrote
to Margaret Fox, who was in Canada with her mother visiting relatives,

> I am very sick, and go this afternoon to Brattleboro, Vermont, to which address
> send me a letter at once, saying when you will be back; what is your mother's
> health, and above all, dear Maggie, whether I can be of use to you. Say this to
> your mother; she will understand me; and be assured that I make the offer in
> the sincerity of a long-tried friendship.
>
> This may seem to you a cold letter; but remember that strange eyes may see
> it, for it may never reach you. The best answer to all your fears is to show the
> caution with which I guard you and your name. Should a passing thought of
> sorrow come to you on my account, I would never forgive myself. Except for
> words of praise, my tongue shall be as a closed book.
>
> But just to think of it! You will see me again before I cross the water, for I
> cannot leave until the tenth; and as soon as your letter reaches me, will hasten
> to New York. There I will meet you as a sister, and part from you as from one
> who has the highest possible claim to my brotherly affection and honorable
> regard.[32]

At Brattleboro there was a well known "water cure" establishment founded
by a German physician, Dr. Robert Wesselhoeft, with extensive buildings
and attractive grounds. Kane had himself been there with his sister Bessie
in the summer of 1852 for a stay that ended when he was called home by the
worsening illness of his younger brother William. His choice of this place
for a "cure" must have shocked his colleagues of the regular medical profession, for its methods were based on two heresies of the day, homeopathy
and the Priessnitz variety of hydrotherapy. The sanatorium's strict regime
for all diseases can only have harmed a man suffering from subacute endocarditis. The daily routine was to awaken the patient at four o'clock in the
morning, roll him up in heavy blankets until he was hot and clammy with
sweat, and then plunge him into cold water.[33] This treatment, Dr. Wesselhoeft claimed, had in no case proved to be injurious; but it was to say the
least uncomfortable. Dr. Kane stood it for three or four weeks and then
moved for two or three weeks more to the quiet home of a relative of the
Grinnells at Stockbridge, Massachusetts, in the Berkshire Hills.[34] At the
end of his stay in New England he told his father that after six weeks
devoted to health only, he was pretty much as he was.

It was like the Kane of younger days that he did not ask his father's advice
about going to England until he had quite made up his mind to go. From
Brattleboro he wrote to the judge on August 31,

> The "Resolute" bill has passed and she will now be formally presented to the
> British Government. This matter has been a subject of deep anxiety to Lady

Franklin and has been worked for by Mr. Grinnell and myself. An application will be made to the Admiralty to introduce a propeller and it rests with me to command her or not. Looking ahead and feeling as I now do—*this dream must be over*—my health is gone—on this head I say nothing more. You may imagine all that I feel. But Lady Franklin's means are limited and my intermediation and influence with the Admiralty could procure her from the Naval Dock Yards nearby all that she would need; my withdrawal would be on the other hand both a loss and a misfortune.

The six hundred dollars places it in my power to go to England and a voyage would perhaps be of service. On this head the Doctors say "yes." I know that I ought to take an interest in what I am about and I know all too well that I take no interest in any earthly thing; there's no health in this.

Now if you think well of this transatlantic scheme—personally I don't care the toss of a copper about it—but clearly do I think that duty requires my presence, if I owe a duty to the interests of this Arctic search, which has for six years been my one topic—If you think well of it write to old Marcy and say. . .
[The rest is an outline of facts to be given to William L. Marcy, U.S. Secretary of State, for him to use in getting the Navy Department to recommend Lady Franklin's plan to the Admiralty.][35]

Kane was booked to sail for Liverpool on October 11 aboard S.S. *Baltic* of the Collins Line. The steamship company had given him, free of charge, accommodations for himself and William Morton. On the ground of ill health he declined an invitation to a farewell dinner to be given him on the 10th by Mayor Vaux of Philadelphia and a score of leading citizens.[36] Instead, several days before departure he went to New York to stay at Mr. Grinnell's house. While there he saw Margaret several times, according to her report, and once took her and Katie to the opera at Niblo's Theatre. One afternoon he and Margaret went together (she says) to make formal calls on several friends, among them General Winfield Scott, leaving cards of adieu. These visits, if they really occurred as stated, came as near to public announcement of an engagement as anything Dr. Kane ever ventured to allow. He had an ambrotype portrait made of Margaret to take with him; he gave her a set of *Arctic Explorations* especially bound, and bought her a diamond bracelet at Tiffany's. His attitude toward her was in every way that of a prospective husband, she says, and indeed once in private he crowned her with an impromptu wreath of flowers and declared her his wife.[37]

According to Margaret's book, on one of his last evenings before sailing Dr. Kane came to the Foxes' house for supper and spent the evening with Margaret. Tired and depressed, he talked despondently of what might happen. He was ill, he might die; would Margaret come to him if he should need her? When she said she would surely do so, he proposed that they should then and there formally declare themselves husband and wife, in the presence of her mother. The scene that ensued, like everything that occurred between Kane and Margaret in this October of 1856, is related only in *The Love-Life of Dr. Kane*. There is no other record, and the four witnesses were linked to the Fox family by blood, friendship, or servitude. The story is told here, therefore, with no assurance that it is true wholly or in part, and with a reminder that Margaret's subsequent claim for a widow's dower, which depended upon the validity of this peculiar ceremony, was litigated for ten years. Mrs. Fox and Katie were called into the parlor where the two young people were sitting, with the domestic servant and an unnamed young woman who was spending the evening with the family. Dr. Kane said that he wanted them to witness a solemn declaration he was about to make. Standing beside Margaret with his left arm around her, and holding her right hand, he said "Maggie is my wife, and I am her husband. Wherever we are, she is mine, and I am hers. Do you understand and consent to this, Maggie?" Margaret answered that she did. He then explained to those present that under the law, by this ceremony they were married as legally and indissolubly as if in church. "It shall be made public in May," he told them, meaning no doubt that by that time the royalties accruing from his book would make him financially independent of his family.[38] In the *Love-Life* Margaret's editor cited in a footnote several legal opinions supporting the validity of a common-law marriage such as this, even if not consummated.

Kane and Margaret saw each other once or twice more before the *Baltic* sailed, and parted weeping, as they had done three years before on the eve of another voyage fraught with hopes and fears. At Mr. Grinnell's house on Bond Street on the morning of sailing-day, October 11, Kane signed a last will and testament in the presence of Mr. and Mrs. Grinnell and their daughter Silvia. As executors of his estate, which would consist largely of the royalties coming to him from his book, he named his brothers Thomas and Robert. He bequeathed $5,000 to Robert, to be paid out at once in the event of his death, and left the whole balance of the estate to such members of the family as Judge Kane might designate, explaining that "members of the family" meant his mother, brothers, and sister. Margaret was not mentioned, but there is no reason to doubt her statement that the special bequest to the lawyer brother Robert was intended for her under a private understanding between the brothers.[39]

She did not see Kane sail; he left her at the door of her mother's house, as he went to join a party of friends who were going to say their farewells at the ship.

# 14

# The Last Journey

IT WAS A RARE thing for Elisha Kent Kane, veteran sea-goer, to travel on a first-class passenger ship, but he appreciated the comfort of a quiet and speedy voyage across the Atlantic. Morton took excellent care of him, and whenever he felt able to go on deck there were Philadelphia friends aboard with whom to chat. For the first time in his life he was not seasick on the ocean, probably because physical weakness kept him mostly recumbent in his berth. Morton even had a glimmer of hope that he might be improving. *Baltic* docked at Liverpool on October 22, and Kane went to the Adelphi Hotel, standard resort of arriving Americans, to rest before going on to London. At the hotel he received the unusual compliment of a formal call by the mayor of Liverpool with a deputation of the city council, to welcome the heroic commander of *Advance*.[1] The state of relative comfort that he had enjoyed aboard ship came to an end a day or two after landing, when he developed a heavy cold with a bronchial cough, and he was feeling miserable when he and Morton left for London on October 25.

Where he stayed in London is not clear. Writing to Lady Franklin, who was out of town, he dated the letter from the residence of Edward (later Sir Edward) Sabine, distinguished Arctic traveler and geophysicist;[2] but whether he was Sabine's guest or lived at a hotel, Lady Franklin, after she returned to London, came to visit him daily and with her characteristic energy took charge of his affairs, or tried to. Kane was too ill to appreciate her assiduous attentions, in which she did not forget for a moment that he was there to support her campaign for another expedition. She did not understand, he thought, how ill he really was; she clung to the idea that he might yet take command of her ship. With feverish irritation he wrote to his father that he wanted to get away from London. Ever since he had landed at Liverpool, he said, he had been going downhill, and he must go to a warmer climate. He had thought of Algiers, Palermo, Madeira, and even of the West Indies, which he liked best. As for Lady Franklin,

> she offers to go to Madeira with me. She comes here daily and kisses "my pale forehead." Dear Father, the woman would use me, if she could, even now. There was a disposition which I put my foot on occasionally, to ignore my position as [not the] leader of the Expedition. . . . She wants me to go to Madeira simply because it insures my return to England when she has a scheme for me to urge her case before Prince Albert. She has been skirmishing around this for some time and I shall not be sorry when the proper moment enables me to say "As long, Lady Franklin, as I was the recognized leader of your party I would have felt it a duty to apply, etc., but my health having forced me to withdraw, any application on my part as an American would be an impertinence."[3]

However great Kane's longing for rest in a warmer climate, to leave England at this time would be a bitter disappointment. The whole Arctic corps of commanders, he told the judge, were planning a dinner in his honor; and he wistfully thought too of the charts of new shores his expedition had mapped, which he had brought with him to discuss with English geographers, and of the papers he might have read before learned societies. Perhaps, after all, if only he gained a little strength, he might go to southern France and return later to carry on his planned consultations and enjoy the friendship of the English naval officers and men of science.

He pulled himself together sufficiently to carry out part of his duty to Lady Franklin; on October 28 he was received in Whitehall by the Lords of the Admiralty.[4] The little Assistant Surgeon, U.S.N., found himself for two hours in consultation as an Arctic expert with Sir Charles Wood, G.C.B. (later Viscount Halifax), First Lord; an Admiral of the Red, an Admiral of the Blue; two high-ranking navy captains, and Captain John Washington, F.R.S., chief hydrographer. The British government expressed its feelings toward Kane by the gift of a handsome silver service of coffee pot, tea pot, sugar bowl and cream pitcher, on a tray inscribed as follows[5]:

Presented by

THE BRITISH GOVERNMENT

to

ELISHA KENT KANE M.D.

of the

UNITED STATES NAVY

AS A TOKEN OF SINCERE GRATITUDE
for his gallant and generous exertions in command of
THE AMERICAN ARCTIC EXPEDITION
dispatched to afford assistance to
SIR JOHN FRANKLIN AND THE OFFICERS AND CREWS
of Her Britannic Majesty's ships "Erebus" and "Terror"
between the years 1850 and 1855

Kane stayed in London only eight days. His friends, anxious about his increasing weakness and loss of weight, wanted to get him out of the city's smoke-laden atmosphere. Among them was a Mr. William Cross, an English broker with New York connections who owned a villa called Champion Hill at Camberwell, now a part of southeast London, but then a suburb.[6] He took Kane there on November 2 as house guest pending a medical consultation. A few days later he accompanied Kane to the consulting room of Sir Henry Holland, favorite physician of the Court and of London society. This eminent gentleman found, as he wrote to Dr. Robley Dunglison of Philadelphia, friend of Judge Kane, that Dr. Kane was suffering from rheumatic swellings of various joints, shifting from one to another; chills and fever, rapid pulse, dry cough; much reduction of flesh and strength.[7] Rather surprisingly, he did not find evidence of active endocarditis, nor indeed of any serious cardiac disorder, though the signs point clearly, in present-day terms, to bacterial endocarditis with subacute bronchitis.

After seeing Kane a second time, Sir Henry declared that he was quite unfit for travel to the south of France, and favored Kane's own plan to go to Cuba. Sir Henry was all the more willing to recommend the sea voyage because he was told that Cornelius Grinnell, who was in Paris on business for his father's firm, would accompany Kane to Havana. The prospect of Grinnell's aid in the rapidly worsening situation overcame Lady Franklin's wish to have Kane go to Madeira. She sent for Grinnell to come at once.

There was to be a stated meeting of the Royal Geographical Society on November 10, with its president, Rear Admiral Sir Frederick Beechey, in the chair, at which Kane would have had the happiness of meeting many British Arctic travelers and other geographers, but he was too ill to attend. The warm-hearted Scotsman, Sir Roderick Murchison, director of the British Geographical Survey, proposed a resolution of sympathy, saying that no person who ever came to England deserved a warmer welcome than Kane, whose efforts had called for the approbation of every man of science who had attended to the progress of his search and read the remarkable book he had recently published.[8]

Cornelius Grinnell arrived, as expected, on November 11. Alarmed by Kane's condition, he made definite arrangements for the voyage to Havana, booking passage for Kane and Morton on the steamer *Orinoco,* to sail from Southampton on November 17. Grinnell could not, after all, go with them, having left unfinished business in Paris when he hurried to London on Lady Franklin's call. She, devoted and determined woman, took Kane's illness and departure very hard. "I cannot tell you how unhappy and absorbed my aunt has been by Dr. Kane's illness," wrote her niece by marriage and secretary, Sophia Cracroft, to Henry Grinnell.

> He has been most strongly urged to prefer Madeira, but he has, after much vacillation, decided upon the West Indies, which has the perhaps overwhelming advantage of being nearer to the United States. She [Lady Franklin] suggested that she ought to accompany him and see him comfortably settled in his new abode—a step which would not only have irrevocably settled the fate of the future search, but would have seriously affected her health, by the anxiety of such a position and by the effect of the W. India climate, which is absolutely dangerous to her constitution.[9]

Before leaving, Kane asked to see Dr. Thomas Watson (later Sir Thomas), acknowledged head of the London medical profession, in consultation with Sir Henry Holland. Dr. Watson may not have told his patient all that he found; according to Kane, "He auscultated my lungs and found no vice other than the cold on the chest which so depresses me. My inability to throw it off is explained by my extensive want of power and this wretched land of fogs."[10]

Three days before sailing he wrote to his mother

> As to my disappointment, it is but one of many. My life has been marked by crises, and I trust that this, like others, will be but to establish better things . . . so avoiding the harsher regions of the Atlantic, I cross with the tropic winds and work my way homeward in sunshine. So ends my visit.[11]

Cornelius Grinnell went down to Southampton in the railway compartment with Kane and Morton, to see them off. The voyage was smooth, and again Kane was not seasick; but swelling and pain of the joints, which had recurred since his arrival in England, caused him acute suffering. *Orinoco* arrived at St. Thomas on December 2. While waiting there for a passage to Havana, Kane was the guest of a Mr. Swift. The fever continued, with profuse night sweats, but Kane was able to walk about the house and once drove out with his host. On December 20 he and Morton left St. Thomas on a vessel bound for Havana. The first morning out the sea was very rough and he was seasick, but in the afternoon he slept while Morton was busy about the cabin. Suddenly he awoke moaning and almost speechless. Morton called the ship's doctor, who gave Kane an anodyne. Twenty minutes later Morton saw that Kane's right arm and leg were paralyzed and he could not speak at all. It was an apoplectic stroke; an embolus, a fragment of tissue from a heart valve damaged by bacterial infection, had broken off into the blood stream and was carried along to block an artery of the brain. He remained conscious and was shortly able to sit up with support.

Word of Kane's illness in England had reached his family in Philadelphia by direct ship. As soon as his parents and brothers knew when he was leaving for Cuba, Tom Kane sailed from New York by the weekly steamer for Havana. He was on the dock when his brother was carried ashore, and took him to a small hotel. A local physician, Dr. Riverand, attended Kane and later called into consultation a Boston doctor, F. S. Ainsworth, who was visiting Havana. By Ainsworth's account, Kane slowly rallied, partly recovering the use of his right hand and wrist, and was even able to move his forearm, but his speech remained thick and his memory was defective. The doctors allowed him once or twice to be taken for a drive.

Judge Kane could not go to his son because his court was in session. Mrs. Kane was anxious to go but, having quite recently been exposed to a case of smallpox, delayed her departure for several days. With her other doctor son, John K. Kane, Jr., she sailed from New York January 7, 1857, and arrived at Havana on the 12th or 13th. Elisha, thus surrounded by a devoted quartet—mother, two brothers, and Morton—reverted to memories of childhood. In Elder's sentimental words, "Heroism had not hardened him; the world had not weaned him from his heart's dependency upon home affections." Two or three times a day he wanted his mother to read the Bible to him. His mind would have been at rest except for his longing to be at home, expressed with almost childish urgency, in broken speech, with dimming eyes. Physically he seemed to be getting no worse. Passage to New York was booked for early February, but departure was postponed because of unfavorable weather. On the morning of February 10 Kane suddenly suffered another stroke, more severe than that of December, for when he regained some degree of consciousness he was paraplegic—all his limbs were deprived of motion. The doctors did not vex him with drastic treatment. A few leeches and cold applications to the head were all they thought advisable. For a few days, until February 16, he lingered thus. In his last hours there were no indications of suffering, and he died apparently from simple exhaustion, so quietly that his mother, who was reading the Bible at his bedside, went on reading until the others told her that his life had ended.

Dr. Ainsworth, reporting a month later to the Boston Society for Medical Improvement, found the tenacity of life in this case quite remarkable.

A constitution broken down by chronic disease of many years' standing, a series of hardships and exposure almost unheard of, with all the depressing addition of care and responsibility—followed by an affection which for several months threatened his life; add to all these an attack of apoplexy, paralyzing entirely the right side, and in two months after a relapse affecting the whole body, and one can hardly conceive how life could have been sustained for so long a period as five days after the last shock.[12]

So much for the medical aspects of Dr. Kane's passing. In those evangelical days, religion as well as medicine had its postmortem questions to ask. Some of Kane's near relations and others who felt concern about his soul wanted assurance that he had taken the Protestant way to heaven. Rumors got about that he had died a Roman Catholic, based perhaps—who can say—on his occasional churchgoing to St. Anne's in New York with Margaret Fox, or on his Irish name, or the known Catholic element in his heritage and early education, or his death in Spanish territory. One fanatic adduced the fact that Dr. Kane had a cross painted on the cliff above the burial place of Jefferson Baker and Pierre Schubert.[13] The fact that in 1853 he had joined a Masonic lodge in New York and took a Masonic banner with him to plant in the far north below the Stars and Stripes should have been enough to prove him no Catholic, but at any rate Dr. Elder in his biography of Kane went out of his way to state that no clergyman of any denomination ever visited him in Havana, and that he never held membership in any church other than that acquired by birthright and baptism in infancy, in the Presbyterian congregation to which his parents belonged. This cautious statement hints that in adult life Dr. Kane had no church affiliation. Indeed, some of his kinfolk feared that he had strayed altogether from the Christian flock. His sister Bessie wrote to their aunt Mrs. George Gray Leiper in the first grievous days after Kane's death, "Today we received a letter from Johnny dated Havana February 19 which tells us all we most longed for yet scarcely dared to hope. . . . That our prayers were answered, and that he died a Christian, is so great a cause of rejoicing that it seems almost wrong to grieve."[14]

In fact, neither the rumors of his conversion to Rome nor his sister's evangelical assurance were quite to the point. Kane would certainly have called himself a Christian, but he had his difficulties about the Trinity and about predestination. In a reflective mood one Arctic night in December, 1854, he wrote in his journal

Now I, poor Kane, can understand "right" and—poor benighted devil—with certain reservations of an earthy nature can practise it, but then on the other hand I can't comprehend the Holy Ghost. It is the devil of a dilemma! I mean

Obsequies at Havana

From *Frank Leslie's Illustrated Newspaper,* March 21, 1857

no profanity, but a real honest expression of regret. I've nothing to do up here but "good," in fact cannot do any harm if I were to try. I pray three times a day for and with the whole squad: treat them not only as myself but a great deal better than myself, yet according to Boardman it's all of no use.[15]

If Kane had ever cared to define his religious position he would probably have considered himself an Emersonian Unitarian; but he was prayed for in Catholic churches in Philadelphia, nor did orthodox Presbyterian clergymen deny his right to heaven. One of them, standing by his coffin, declared that "The Advance is on the ice, the Eric is in ashes, the Hope is on a far-distant shore, the Faith—'the precious relic'—is in possession of his country, and Kane is in heaven. He will need the craft no more, for now he walks with the Evangelists upon the crystal and stable sea."[16]

Dr. Kane's body was taken from Havana to Philadelphia on a funeral journey the like of which Americans had never seen. A detailed account of it takes up 103 pages of William Elder's biography. It began at Havana the day after Kane's death, when the American consul called together United States citizens resident and transient in the city to share in a public demonstration of respect to their lamented fellow countryman. The consul read a letter from the Captain-General of Cuba, Don José de la Concha, offering the government barge to convey Kane's body to the ship that was to carry it to New Orleans. On February 20 the casket was borne on men's shoulders to the Plaza de Armas, followed by more than eight hundred persons, citizens of the United States and other foreign countries, together with representatives of the University of Havana, the Spanish Army Medical Corps, the Board of Health, and various civic bureaus and societies. Two military bands played dirges. At the waterfront the state barge received the casket, the Spanish flag was lowered, and under the Stars and Stripes the barge was rowed to the New Orleans packet *Cahawba*, followed in procession by the boats of the steamer and of many other ships in the harbor. Aboard *Cahawba* the Governor of Havana, Don José Ignacio de Echevarria, pronounced a brief discourse on Dr. Kane's heroic ideals, to which Consul A. K. Blythe felicitously responded.

The family party—mother and two brothers, with William Morton—traveled aboard *Cahawba* to New Orleans. On their arrival there on February 22, the mayor of the city came aboard to proffer the escort of a local military company, the Continental Guards, as the coffin was carried to the City Hall, where Kane lay in state until time for the departure of the Mississippi River steamboat, to which the remains were escorted by a large procession. The pallbearers were twelve officers of the army and the navy; they were followed by several military companies, civic officials, foreign consuls, members of the Masonic order, and a delegation of the Sons of St. George, a "large and imposing body of Englishmen."

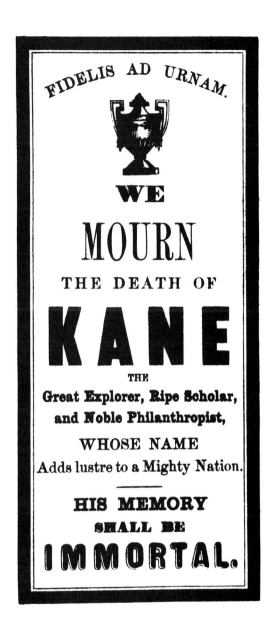

Badge Worn by Committeemen at Kane Obsequies, Cincinnati, Ohio
Kane-Childs Album, Dreer Collection, Historical Society of Pennsylvania

At every town the steamboat passed on her week-long trip up the Mississippi and Ohio Rivers to Louisville, people were standing on the levees and wharves to see her go by. Judge Kane and his son Robert left Philadelphia in time to meet the boat at Paducah and traveled with the family party to Louisville, where their arrival was announced by the tolling of bells and firing of minute guns. Here the formal ceremonies were repeated, with a procession of city officials, Masonic dignitaries, delegations of medical men and lawyers, citizens in carriages, citizens on horseback, citizens on foot; and there was a lying-in-state at Mozart Hall, with a guard of honor. From Louisville the judge and Mrs. Kane, foreseeing the strain of similar proceedings to come at Cincinnati, Columbus, and Baltimore, left for Philadelphia, where the most elaborate ceremonies of all were of course to take place. Their three sons remained with their dead brother.

Next day the steamer, ascending the Ohio River, was met halfway to Cincinnati by another boat bearing the committee for that city, each committeeman wearing a large mourner's badge of white silk, printed in black. At the landing the committee delivered the casket to twenty-four pallbearers. The procession of Cincinnati included the Governor of Ohio and his suite, federal and state judges, the mayors of Cincinnati and of Covington and Newport, Kentucky, and civic groups from "The Pioneers of Ohio" to the Butchers' Benevolent Association. Here the trip by river steamboat ended and the railway took over. The inevitable procession was short, from the steamboat wharf to the railway station. Many houses along the way were draped in black. William Morton followed the hearse alone on foot, Kane's three brothers behind him in a carriage preceding the military and civilian organizations. The casket was placed for a time upon a bier in front of the station, to be viewed by the people, and was then carried to a magnificent railway car draped in black inside and out. Now began the earliest of those strange funeral journeys by rail that have thrice torn the heartstrings of our people—Kane's in 1857, Lincoln's in 1865, and Robert Kennedy's in 1968. At Xenia the people streamed over the tracks, delaying the train's slow progress, as they did at Trenton in our time, and all through the afternoon and the night, stood silently at every stop. At Columbus the body lay in state at the state capitol, in the Senate chamber, where the public crowded in to hear a veritable flood of secular and religious declamation, solemn, high-flown, and monotonously alike from the first salutation to the last Amen. These addresses to God and man, with those spoken earlier at Louisville and later at Baltimore and Philadelphia, have been preserved in Elder's biography of Kane, a precious exhibit of mid-century Americana, the funerary oratory of a young and striving nation. At smaller cities in Ohio, West Virginia, and Maryland, where the casket was not taken off the train, the people gathered

Dr. Kane's Body Lying in State, Independence Hall, Philadelphia
From *Frank Leslie's Illustrated Weekly Newspaper*, March 28, 1857

at the railway stations amid tolling of bells, at Bellair and Benwood, Zanesville and Wheeling, Fairmount, Cumberland, at Martinsburg where the Baltimore committee boarded the train, at Harper's Ferry and at Ellicott's Mills.

At Baltimore there were bigger crowds and a grander procession than the smaller inland cities had seen, with sailors from the great harbor, soldiers from Fort McHenry, and the Marine Band from Washington. Kane's casket was carried from Camden Station to the Maryland Institute on a gun carriage drawn by four horses. Bells tolled in church steeples and fire towers from eleven o'clock in the morning until four in the afternoon. Foremost citizens of Maryland composed the committee to receive the remains, among them Johns Hopkins, Reverdy Johnson, and Kane's friend John Pendleton Kennedy, the latter of whom delivered in sadly thoughtful words the only address in the whole spate of oratory from New Orleans to Philadelphia that mourned Kane as the man he really was, not the flag-draped superhero of more flamboyant speechmakers.

The funeral cars from Baltimore arrived at Philadelphia on the afternoon of Monday, March 11, and were met by a large guard of honor including the First City Troop of Cavalry, the artillery company of Washington Grays, several hundred city police, and a dozen committees representing civic organizations, local and from other cities. As the hearse moved on with muffled drums, in a light rain, to Independence Hall, it was accompanied not by Morton alone of Kane's Arctic companions, but also by seven others, officers and seamen of *Advance*, all who could be gathered together in Philadelphia —Hayes, Bonsall, Goodfellow, Brooks, Stevenson, Hickey, and the unabashed Godfrey. They spread the lost brig's weather-worn flag over her commander's coffin and walked on beside it. At Independence Hall the attendants placed upon the coffin Kane's ceremonial sword of honor surrounded by a chain of flowers, and a splendid wreath marked only "To the Memory of Dr. Kane, from Two Ladies"—no names, no sentimental words. Those who for three days passed through the hall to pay their personal respects to the dead hero could only wonder from whom this silent tribute came.

At noon on Thursday, March 14, the coffin was carried from Independence Hall by a detachment of seamen from the Navy Yard, across Independence Square to Walnut Street, where it was placed on a funeral car twelve feet long, whose wheels were concealed by rich drapery. At its four corners were upright spears with golden heads; around these were entwined the national flags of Great Britain, Spain, Denmark, and the United States. Above the center of the car was a domed canopy of black cloth with white stripes, from which broad ribbons of white silk ran to the heads of the spears. The dome was ornamented with white stars and lined with white silk. The car was drawn by four black horses, each with a groom appropriately attired.

The procession that followed the funeral car was so great that merely to list the participating military, civic, educational, scientific and philanthropic organizations requires more than two pages of Elder's book. The cortege wound through the city streets, along Walnut Street, past the house where Kane was born, then by Seventeenth, Arch, and Seventh streets to the Second Presbyterian Church. The coffin was set upon a bier in front of the church to be viewed by the crowd while the whole procession marched past. "Few scenes," said a reporter, "have ever been presented of more solemn grandeur." When the coffin was carried into the church, those who could get inside heard a service of prayers and eulogy led by three prominent ministers. When the service was over and the crowd outside dispersed, the coffin was taken to the family vault in Laurel Hill Cemetery accompanied by the honorary pallbearers, among whom were the Governor and the Chief Justice of Pennsylvania, Henry Grinnell, a bishop, two commodores, two celebrated lawyers, and two professors of medicine.

The chairman of the committee of arrangements for the obsequies summed them up by stating[17]

The proceedings which marked the whole progress of the remains of Dr. Kane, from his death-bed to the sepulchre, were one of the most distinguished eulogies that a people has ever pronounced upon one who claimed no distinction as a leader of armies or as a director in statesmanship, and the outburst of public feeling and demonstration of general regard will be the proudest monument that can be raised to the lofty and gentle qualities, the enterprise, the philanthropy, the science, and the friendship of Elisha Kent Kane.

# 15

# Time's Appraisal

DR. KANE was mourned as "a great explorer, ripe scholar, and noble philanthropist." Great explorer he certainly was; ripe scholar he did not live to be, though he wrote with a scholar's pen. The philanthropy for which he was praised—his part in the Franklin Search—was indeed nobly intended but was unavailing because he let himself be led astray by his ambition to reach the dreamed-of Open Polar Sea. An appraisal of his career and achievements must therefore deal chiefly with the geographical discoveries of his expedition and with the remarkable literary talents that made his *Arctic Explorations, 1853, '54, '55* the best written and most readable book on that subject in the English language.

Kane's major contribution to Arctic geography was the exploration and first mapping of the important waterway that leads northward between the western shore of Greenland and the eastern shore of Ellesmere Island, from about latitude 78° 28′, the farthest point in Smith Sound reached in 1851 by Inglefield, to about 80° 58′, the most northerly point seen by William Morton and Hans Hendrik of Kane's party on June 24, 1854. The southerly part of this waterway is the broad expansion now called Kane Basin; the northerly part is the narrow reach that Kane named Kennedy Channel for his friend and patron John Pendleton Kennedy. A strong southward drift of pack ice and large bergs through this channel virtually assured Kane that it must communicate, at its unseen northern end, with the Arctic Ocean. The truth of this conjecture was proved within the next two decades by subsequent explorers—Dr. Isaac I. Hayes in 1860 and Charles Francis Hall, who in 1870 passed through Kennedy Channel into Hall Basin and on through Robson Channel to the Polar Sea.

These men completed the preliminary reconnaissance of what came to be called "the American route to the Pole." Later expeditions favored by warmer weather and more open water followed up the beginning made by Kane, Hayes, and Hall: the British captain George Nares in 1875–76, Augustus W. Greely in 1881–83, Robert E. Peary on several voyages from 1898 on, Donald B. MacMillan on numerous expeditions from 1913 to 1954.[1] On the northern tip of Ellesmere Island, Peary based his traverse of the frozen ocean toward the North Pole in 1909.

These later explorers owed a great debt to Kane not only for opening their route to discovery, but also for the legacy of trust he left with the Eskimos of Smith Sound and especially those of Etah. He did not live to make good his promise to return and help them find a better homeland farther south; but they survived in spite of their harsh environment. Peary had his wife with him through two winters among these friendly people. She bore him a daughter at Bowdoin Harbor in Inglefield Sound, to the delight of the people of Etah and neighboring villages. Later Donald MacMillan and the enigmatic Dr. Frederick Cook both wintered safely with the Smith Sound Eskimos.

Incidental to Kane's exploration of the polar route was the discovery of the great Humboldt Glacier in May 1854. As to this enormous river of ice spilling over from Greenland's ice cap and grinding its way into Kane Basin, Kane made a wrong and confusing guess. He thought that the glacier's bed marked the northern end of Greenland, separating it from the land beyond to the north, called by him Washington Land. Knowing from Morton that only the relatively narrow Kennedy Channel lay between Washington Land to the east and Grinnell Land to the west, Kane mistakenly thought that Washington Land should be grouped with Ellesmere Island and its neighbors of the Canadian Archipelago, rather than with Greenland. This concept led to his confusing statement that the Humboldt Glacier is "a mighty crystal bridge which connects the two continents of America and Greenland."[2] Later explorers made it clear that Greenland extends all the way to the Arctic Ocean as does Ellesmere Island on its side of the passage.

An important part of the expedition's exploration was the attainment and preliminary mapping by Isaac Hayes of the western shore of the basin north of Inglefield's farthest point. Kane's claim of this land for the United States, whose flag Hayes planted upon it, was invalidated when Peary found in 1898 that there is no channel separating Grinnell Land from Ellesmere Island, of which it is simply the northern part.

The first duty of an explorer of new lands or seas is to map them as accurately as possible. Kane did all he could, with the means at his command, to fulfill this obligation. In general, his surveys were sufficiently correct to require but little revision on major points by those who later repeated them. Because, however, he was charged with inaccuracy on certain details, particularly the mapping of the most northerly parts of Kane Basin and of Kennedy Channel, his methods call for a brief description. Any position on land can be determined, as at sea, by observation with a sextant and chronometer, with sufficient accuracy to facilitate navigation and small-scale mapping. The highest altitude above the horizon reached by the sun in its daily course across the sky gives the latitude, and the moment at which the sun reaches that point gives the longitude. At sea nature provides the horizon; on land the observer must use an artificial one, a small vessel containing mercury. In the first volume of Kane's *Arctic Explorations* there is a chart, and in the second volume a table, showing fifty-nine stations from the southern entrance of Smith Sound to the farthest mountain seen to the north by William Morton in June 1854. Ten of these stations were located by sextant,[3] but the accuracy of the observations was limited by various difficulties. Many of them were made in the field with a pocket sextant and a pocket chronometer instead of the more reliable instruments available on shipboard and in the little observatory hut that Kane built on a knoll at Rensselaer Harbor near his icebound brig. Outdoors in subzero weather it is not easy to handle a sextant precisely. The observer either wears clumsy mittens or risks freezing his fingers to the metallic instrument. At temperatures below −38° Fahrenheit the artificial horizon is useless because the mercury congeals. Furthermore, at very high latitudes the sun's apparent path is so much flatter than in lower latitudes that it is almost impossible to detect the exact moment at which it reaches its apogee. Finally, neither Kane nor his astronomer, Sonntag, got farther north than the southern edge of the Humboldt Glacier; the observations by sextant farther north were made by Morton, an uneducated seaman taught to "shoot the sun" by Sonntag only a few months before he stood, alone with Eskimo Hans, on the cliff at Cape Constitution at noon on June 24, 1854.

One of the charted positions, that of the observatory at Rensselaer Harbor, was determined astronomically with considerable accuracy. Sonntag had at his disposal four navy-tested chronometers, a theodolite, a transit instrument, and a small but good astronomical telescope. With the latter he observed four celestial events, namely two occultations of Saturn and one of Mars, in January, February, and March of 1854 respectively, and an eclipse of the sun on May 15, 1855. It speaks well for the scientific zeal of the expedition that half-starved men, worn down by illness and on the eve of starting on a well-nigh hopeless retreat, should have taken the time to observe the eclipse. The longitude ascertained by these astronomical observations was checked by timing several culminations of the moon. The position thus determined, 78° 37′

N, 71° W, was in fact correct within narrow limits and is accepted by twentieth-century cartographers. As a base line for triangulation Kane took the
distance between Rensselaer Harbor and Cape Inglefield to the southwest,
not actually measured but closely estimated at thirty miles. From this somewhat dubious base, by triangulation and by intersecting bearings from points
visited by sledge, he worked out the positions of numerous capes, promon-
tories, and small islands visible from Rensselaer Harbor and from the field
stations. Between these more or less exactly determined stations he located
other points relatively to them by "dead reckoning." At sea a navigator,
knowing the capacities of his vessel, the wind velocity, and currents, may
estimate his distance traveled with some accuracy; but dead reckoning on
sledge journeys over rocky shores and the rough ice belt could be hardly
more than a guess. Kane states[4] that on a trip in March 1854 a distance
measured by pacing was found correct to within one-thirtieth of the whole
distance traveled in six days.

At Cape Jefferson, to which only Morton and Hans Hendrik penetrated,
Morton made his northernmost sextant observation. Beyond that he located
two other headlands by dead reckoning—or sheer guess—Cape Constitution,
the northernmost point he actually reached, and Mount Edward Parry, seen
only in the distance. Under the circumstances he could not have been accurate. Hayes, exploring the Ellesmere Island shore across Kane Basin, worked
by equally crude methods liable to similar errors.

The first public criticism of Kane's mapping was presented at a meeting
of the Royal Geographical Society on April 12, 1858, fourteen months after
his death, by Dr. Henry Rink, Inspector in Greenland for the Danish Government.[5] Rink spoke with a good deal of authority; he had traveled exten-
sively in North Greenland, though not beyond the head of Baffin Bay, and
had written a book describing the ice cap of the island. He wrote with acer-
bity; Kane had published conclusions about glaciation which Rink claimed
as his own. He praised Kane's contributions to Arctic natural history and his
account of the Smith Sound Eskimos, but as to the geographical data and
interpretations he sharply disagreed. He disparaged the discovery of the
Humboldt Glacier, denying Kane's conclusion that it is a terminal riverlike
channel by which the Greenland ice cap discharges its burden into the sea—
a Mississippi of ice, so to speak. It is, said Rink, only one of the numerous
glaciers that spill down to the coast through the fiords of the great island. He
correctly believed that the land north of the Humboldt Glacier is part of
Greenland, not (as Kane had supposed) a separate island of the Canadian
archipelago. Above all, he did not accept Morton's calculations by sextant
and dead reckoning, believing the stated positions to be much too far north.
Rink's words were taken, by some hearers at least, to imply that Morton had

falsified his figures, presumably to make a sensational report to Dr. Kane. From this suspicion Morton was exonerated years later by General Greely, who wintered north of that region in 1881–82. Greely says that Morton's description of the landmarks is, "though simple, yet so accurate and free from exaggeration as to prove conclusively his entire honesty," even though his observations by sextant and dead reckoning were erroneous.[6]

From the reports of the London meeting at which Rink presented his critical assessment of Kane's claims to discovery, it is clear that this sharp attack embarrassed the Arctic captains and the officers of the Royal Geographical Society. Eighteen months earlier, immediately after Kane's report to Secretary Dobbin reached the English newspapers, they had soft-pedaled an officious armchair explorer, Charles R. Weld, who in a letter to the *London Times* expressed serious doubts of some of Kane's statements.[7] This was all in the family, so to speak; Weld was a relative of Sir John Franklin, whom he had helped with business arrangements for his fatal voyage, and the British geographers counted Kane as one of their own. They had awarded him their Gold Medal, and they mourned him sincerely, if less effusively than his fellow countrymen. They felt that Rink, by doubting the veracity of Morton—the man Kane most deeply trusted of all his companions—had impugned Kane himself when Kane was no longer among them to defend himself and Morton. Furthermore, Rink's disbelief that the land Morton had visited north of the Humboldt Glacier was distinct from Greenland potentially raised an issue of sovereignty between Denmark and Britain. Discussion of Rink's paper at the meeting had therefore to be very discreet, all the more because no one present, including Rink himself, had ever set foot on Greenland beyond Cape York. Sir Roderick Murchison and Rear Admiral Sir George Back spoke of Kane's noble qualities and high distinction, but finally Captain Richard Collinson (later Admiral Sir Richard), veteran of the Franklin Search and a great admirer of Kane, reported that he had carefully reviewed Morton's report to Kane as printed in *Arctic Explorations, 1853, '54, '55.* Applying his own experience of Arctic travel to Morton's dead reckoning, Collinson estimated that Kane's stated position of Cape Constitution must be about 30 to 45 miles too far north—a significant error but less serious than Rink had hinted.

At a subsequent meeting of the Royal Geographical Society, June 14, 1858, a letter was read from Alexander Dallas Bache, superintendant of the U.S. Coast Survey, stating that he had asked Charles A. Schott to replot from Kane's notes and charts the positions of Capes Madison, Jackson, and Jefferson as well as Cape Constitution and Morton's farthest northing at Cape Independence. Schott located the latter at 80° 53′ north latitude as against 81° 15′ on Kane's chart. The errors in general were of the order of 30 to

50 miles. That respecting Cape Constitution was a little larger by Kane's triangulation than by Morton's observations.[8]

In brief, Rink's criticisms were justified, if not so damaging to Kane's reputation as a geographer as Rink seems to have thought. Although Kane's charting of the more northerly landmarks was in fact not accurate, it should be added that his positions for points near Rensselaer Harbor and to the south and west of it, for example Cape Sabine and Hakluyt Island, are correct within a few miles. It is true that Humboldt Glacier is not the northern boundary of Greenland, nor is it a terminal outlet of the ice cap.

Greely sums up the matter by saying that "These blemishes on Kane's great work doubtless arose from two causes: first, his implicit confidence in the ability and accuracy of his subordinates, and second, his poetic temperament, "which transformed into beauty the common things of life and enhanced their interest by striking contrasts of high lights and deep shadows."[9]

Dr. Kane's reputation as an explorer does not rest solely, however, on such details as the exact location of his landmarks or how nearly his expedition approached the North Pole. He set a new pattern for polar exploration that lasted until our age of Arctic travel by airplane, submarine, and giant tankers. Instead of the large, heavily manned ships of the earlier Franklin Search, he depended upon a small party and a small, very strong, but readily maneuverable vessel. This latter choice was not altogether his own. Partly imposed upon the first Grinnell Expedition by the lack of government support, it was made good by Henry Grinnell when he fitted out *Advance* and *Rescue* in 1851, and by De Haven's bold and resourceful handling of the tiny brigs. Kane repeated it when in 1853 he took *Advance* farther north than any other ship had ever gone in the western hemisphere. Kane's use of such a vessel was followed successfully by Peary when he built *Roosevelt*, by MacMillan with his staunch schooner *Bowdoin*, and by Amundsen with *Gjoa*.

Kane's other contribution to the methods of Arctic travel he learned for himself, also from necessity. This was his cooperation with the Eskimos and adoption of some of their ways of life. In this also he was followed by his American successors. Had he lived to undertake another venture to the polar region, he would no doubt have utilized all he had learned at Rensselaer Harbor, coming even closer to Vilhjalmur Stefansson's program of living entirely upon Arctic game and fish.

Kane wrote both of his books against advancing illnesses. As mentioned in chapter 7, the manuscript of *The First United States Grinnell Expedition* was not quite finished when its author sailed from New York on the second voyage, May 31, 1853. He had intended to recast some of the chapters and to add one or two on collateral topics. In fact the last chapter of the book, as printed, was written by his father from notes and descriptions left behind in Philadelphia.

In style and content, *The First Grinnell Expedition* has many of the virtues that came to full flower in its successor, *Arctic Explorations, 1853, '54, '55.* A couple of excerpts from the former must serve to illustrate Kane's clear and vigorous descriptions, the humanity and the poetic feeling which lift his books far above the run of Arctic travelers' narratives.

> It fell calm, and I had an opportunity of visiting the shore. The place where we landed was in latitude 76° 04′ N., nearly. It was a little cove, bordered on one side by a glacier; on the other, watered by distillations from it, and green with luxuriant mosses. It was, indeed, a fairy little spot, brightened, perhaps, by its contrast with the icy element, on which I had been floating for a month and a half before; yet even now, as it comes back to me in beautiful companionship with many sweet places of the earth, I am sure that its charms were real.
>
> The glacier came down by a twisted circuit from a deep valley, which it nearly filled. As it approached the sea, it seemed unable to spread itself over the horse-shoe-like expansion in which we stood; but, retaining still the impress marks of its own little valley birthplace, it rose up in a huge dome-like escarpment, one side frozen to the cliffs, the other a wall beside us, and the end a rounded mass protruding into the sea.
>
> Close by the foot of its precipitous face, in a furrowed water-course, was a mountain torrent, which, emerging from the point at which the glacier met the hill, came dashing wildly over the rocks, green with the mosses and carices of Arctic vegetation; while from the dome-like summit a stream, that had tunneled its way through the ice from the valley still higher above, burst out like a fountain, and fell in a cascade of foam-whitened water into the sea. [Pages 135–36]

> The crowning feat is the every-day one of catching the seal. For this the kayack is constructed, and it is here that its wonderful adaptation of purpose is best displayed. Without describing the admirable astuteness with which he finds and approaches his prey, let us suppose the kayacker close upon a seal. The line-stand is carefully examined, the coil adjusted, the attachments to the body of the boat so fixed that the slightest strain will separate them. The bladder-float is disengaged, and the harpoon tipped with its barb, which forms the extremity of the coil.
>
> In an instant the kayacker has thrown his body back and sent his weapon home. Whirr! goes the little coil, and the float is bobbing over the water—not far, however, for the barb has entered the lungs, and the seal must rise for breath. Now the harpoon is picked up, its head remaining in the victim; and the kayack comes along. Here is required discretion as well as address. The hunter has probably but two weapons, a lance and a knife. The latter he can

not part with, and even the lance brings him to closer quarters than the safety of his craft would invite; for the contortions of a large seal thus wounded may tear it at some of the seams, and the merest crevice is certain destruction. If he has with him the light javelin which he used for spearing birds, he may be tempted to employ it now; but this, I believe, is not altogether sportsmanlike. The lance generally gives the *coup-de-grace*.

And now, from the greasy and somewhat odoriferous recesses of the kayack, you see him taking a dirty little coil of walrus hide, bearing several queer little toggles of bone. With a knowing gash of his knife, he makes a hole in the under jaw of the seal: the bone is passed through; and the seal, towed along-side, comes in to rejoice the expectant wife and children. [Pages 482–83]

The book's faults are those of youth and pride of intellect, and in many passages provincialism surprising in an author who had seen so much of the world. No doubt Judge Kane, himself a talented writer, polished up some unrevised passages as he readied the manuscript for publication. Dr. Kane, when he was writing the second book, told George W. Childs that he never sent a page to press without showing it to his father. But *The First United States Grinnell Expedition* remained the work of a young man and a Philadelphian.

This provincialism resulted from the way in which the first book was put together. Dr. Kane had promised his brother Thomas, he tells his readers, that while he was surgeon on *Advance* he would keep a journal to furnish topics for a fireside conversation when he came home again. From this private record he drew most of the material for the book. Brothers Tom, "Pat," John, and Willie and sister Bessie could appreciate better than any out-of-town reader the grandeur of an iceberg "about twice as large as Girard College," or the size of an open lead in Baffin Bay ice "as broad as the Delaware at Trenton or the Schuylkill at Philadelphia," "a lump of ice about as large as Washington Square." The cabin was smaller than their father's library. Fragments of the pack in Barrow Strait were seldom larger than the Rensselaer dining room.

Nor did Judge Kane tone down the evidences of a young savant's pride in his scientific knowledge in such a passage as the following:

The sea abounded with life. Cetochili, as well as other entomostracan forms which I had not seen before, lined, and, in fact, tinted the margins of the floe ice; and for the first time I noticed among them some of those higher orders of crustacean life, which had heretofore been only found adhering to our warping lines. Among these were asellus and idotea, and that jerking little amphipod, the gammarus. Acalephae and limacinae abounded in the quiet leads. The birds too, were back with us, the mollemoke, the Ivory gull, the Burgomaster, and the tern; and while the little Auks crowded the floes below, feeding eagerly upon the abundant harvest of the ice, the air above us was filled with swooping crowds, equally intent on their marine pasture grounds. I cannot think that the powerful mandible of the Fulmar petrels ever condescends to the surface forms of acalephae. It is true that they follow in the stormy wake of vessels, like the Mother Carey's chickens, but their food is of a higher grade. It was a curious spectacle to see them fighting for the garbage of our vessel, and gormandizing on the blubber of our game. [Page 124]

Kane's humor also is in this first book at times sophomoric, though always graphic.

[At very low temperatures] all our eatables became laughably consolidated, and after different fashions, requiring no small experience before we learned to manage the peculiarities of their changed condition. Thus, dried apples became one solid breccial mass of impacted angularities, a conglomerate of sliced chalcedony. Dried peaches the same. To get these out of the barrel, or the barrel out of them, was a matter impossible. We found, after many trials, that the shortest and best plan was to cut up both fruit and barrel by repeated blows with a heavy axe, taking the lumps below to thaw. Sauerkraut resembled mica, or rather talcose slate. A crowbar with chiseled edge extracted the laminae badly; but it was perhaps the best thing we could resort to.

Sugar formed a very funny compound. Take *q.s.* of cork raspings, and incorporate therewith another *q.s.* of liquid gutta percha or caoutchouc, and allow to harden: this extemporaneous formula will give you the brown sugar of our winter cruise. Extract with the saw; nothing but the saw will suit. Butter and lard, less changed, require a heavy cold chisel and mallet. Their fracture is conchoidal, with haematitic (iron-ore pimpled) surface. Flour undergoes little change, and molasses can at −28° be half scooped, half cut by a stiff iron ladle.

Pork and beef are rare specimens of Florentine mosaic, emulating the lost art of petrified visceral monstrosities seen at the medical schools of Bologna and Milan: crow-bar and handspike! for at −30° the axe can hardly chip it. [Page 259]

This kind of writing of course exposed its author to the charge of pedantry. James Laws, surgeon of *Release* in the rescue expedition of 1855, wrote in his diary that "Dr. Kane's book has been voted a humbug, by all the officers of the squadron. It is a vain striving after the scientific, with but little information."[10] That is much too severe; more tolerant readers will smile rather than frown at such flaws. They did not trouble an anonymous critic in the *North American Review*, who wrote:

With a quick eye for observation, a cool and ready judgement, and a devoted sympathy with the objects of the voyage, he combines the gift of agreeable narration, and has related his manifold experiences in unknown Arctic climes, in language of singular point and expressiveness.[11]

The book's charm was enhanced by plentiful illustrations, which Harper and Brothers generously entrusted to highly competent artists. All the pictures were based on Kane's sketches. Five full-page engravings, the prime embellishment of the work, combine in a masterful way the artistic talents of Kane himself, the Philadelphia painter James Hamilton, and a distinguished engraver, John Sartain.[12] Kane's sketches, said Hamilton, were often of the slightest description, but showed talent by his rendition, with a few quick strokes, of essential features of the subject and the feeling and texture of the sea, rocks, and ice.[13] Not all of Kane's drawings were slight sketches; the rendition of *Advance* in the picture "Raising the Brig" (reproduced in this volume, page 184), shows a sure and practiced hand, and some of his water colors are of professional quality and finish.

For the book, Hamilton rendered Kane's drawings in watercolors, in a free and romantic style showing the influence of J. W. M. Turner. Sartain, with sentiment rivaling Hamilton's, then engraved three of these watercolors and two other plates directly from Kane's original sketches. The three brilliant Romanicists thus produced a wonder-world of grand icebergs, of towering cliffs, and of the two tiny brigs battered by gales and almost crushed between rocks and ice. These scenes, it must be remembered, represent one of the most ruggedly icebound and mountainous regions of the far north. Together with similar views in Kane's second book, they built up in the minds of American readers a picture of the Arctic wildly different from the tundra and level floes of the north Canadian shore described, for example, by Vilhjalmur Stefansson in *The Friendly Arctic*.[14]

In addition to these five plates, 125 woodcuts are scattered through the text. Mostly small, they illustrate every conceivable feature of the first Grinnell Expedition from landscapes and seascapes to scenes of life aboard ship, hunting, and nautical equipment. Most of the cuts are unsigned, but five bear the names Lossing-Barritt. Benson J. Lossing, well-known New York engraver on wood, and his kinsman Barritt probably executed all or most of them.

Kane's two-volume report of the second Grinnell expedition, *Arctic Explorations, 1853, '54, '55*, is a greater book than its predecessor. The work of a man matured by responsibility and hardships, it is free of the provincialisms, the youthful pedantry, and the labored humor of the earlier report. Its lighter passages, no longer sophomoric, reflect a compassionate heart; its erudition, no longer burdensome, illuminates the narrative. Discriminating critics at home and abroad at once recognized its exceptional combination of literary distinction with popular appeal. George William Curtis, experienced man of letters, wrote to Kane

> You would not believe me if I should tell you how much I like it, how excellent it seems to me in every way. As a personal narrative it is unquestionably at the head of our Arctic literature, which is a literature by itself—and there is not a boy in the land to whom your name will not be as famous and dear as Robinson Crusoe. So young to be so famous, and to have deserved such fame to its utmost award,—is not that something?[15]

The author of a comprehensive review in the London *Saturday Review* devoted his comment largely to the book's literary merit.

> We cannot but feel proud that the English language should be the mother tongue of the hero of such a tale. Looked at merely from a literary point of view, the book is a very remarkable one. Dr. Kane frequently apologizes for the haste, the roughness, the compression, and the fragmentary character of many parts of his work. We do not think the apology is necessary. The general impression which the book conveys is graphic to the last degree, and its effect is greatly heightened by what Dr. Kane speaks of as defects. It consists almost entirely of extracts from a journal kept at the time, connected by narrative matter more or less compressed from it. An attentive reader can trace the feelings and prospects of the little knot of icebound prisoners, and of their gallant leader, with extraordinary clearness, for Dr. Kane is obviously a cultivated man, and by no means unaccustomed to watch the processes of his own mind. The hoping against hope, the determination to look at the bright side of things, and the effort to write himself into a cheerful frame of mind, which may be detected in the lines penned by the light of the dim perpetual lamp, in the filthy little den into which the crew was crowded—penned, too, when all but the writer had half forgotten their troubles in sleep—seems to us far better worth having than any amount of artistic composition. One of the most curious vestiges of these feelings is to be found in the enforced gaiety and levity of the writer—gaiety which cannot be mistaken for anything else than what it is— the only possible refuge from utter despondency. He laughs at scars, not because he has never felt a wound, but because he has felt so many that laughter is for the time being his only resource against weeping over them. . . .
>
> We hope, on a future occasion, to say something of the scientific results of this wonderful expedition—the most daring and the most terrible in the records of maritime adventure.[16]

The book is lavishly illustrated. It has far more steel engravings than its predecessor, twenty-one in all, including the frontispieces of the two volumes, which are portraits of Dr. Kane and Henry Grinnell engraved from daguerreotypes by the celebrated photographer Matthew B. Brady. Of the nineteen Arctic scenes, seventeen are from sketches by Dr. Kane. Two, not so designated, were probably designed by the artist from verbal descriptions aided by Kane's sketches of similar subjects. Fourteen of the nineteen plates were engraved from watercolors or wash drawings made from Kane's sketches by James Hamilton, one from a drawing by Hamilton and Christian Schuessele, and two from drawings by other artists.

Sartain, interpreter of Kane's visions of the first Grinnell expedition, had no part in illustrating *Arctic Explorations, 1853, '54, '55.* All the plates in those volumes were engraved by men of lesser talents and reputation, though the best of them, "Tennyson's Monument" in volume 1 and "Icebergs near Kosoak" in volume 2 (both of them from the burin of John McGoffin) rival Sartain's force and brilliance. Both are from drawings by Hamilton, which suggests that the neo-Gothic splendor and mystery of these two plates and those of the earlier book are ascribable to James Hamilton as much as to the engravers.

The woodcuts in *Arctic Explorations, 1853, '54, '55,* numbering almost 300 in the two volumes, were executed by the New York firm of Van Ingen-Snyder. The title pages declare them all to be from sketches by Dr. Kane. There is, however, one amusing piece of evidence that some were made from verbal descriptions. In a memorandum to one of the wood engravers, he wrote

> Mr. White will oblige me by making up at his earliest convenience, 1. a powerful team of seven Eskimaux dogs—very wolfish in character, two of them with arched (hyena) backs and all driven abreast—one driver with long whip running along side—a second figure sitting sideways on sledge. Scene: a level completely hedged in by icebergs.[17]

The picture made from these directions appears as the little vignetted cut on page 238 of volume 1, a fully plausible scene quite comparable to those that followed Kane's actual sketches. In some other cases the artists had the merest pictorial hints upon which to base their woodblocks. An example of this type of illustration appears on page 157 of the present book, picturing the first visit of the Eskimos. The method does not make for accuracy. Kane in his private journal says there were eight men in the party; the woodcut shows eleven Eskimos and has Kane carrying a gun, whereas he says that he went out on the ice unarmed to meet the newcomers. Most of the woodcuts, however, were no doubt made from Kane's more finished sketches and follow them closely.

Though *Arctic Explorations, 1853, '54, '55* is a masterpiece of travel literature and had an enormous sale, it was not the kind of book to win a broad reputation for the author as a man of letters, as did, for example, Doughty's

*Travels in Arabia Deserta* or T. E. Lawrence's *Seven Pillars of Wisdom.* It was too special, too far removed from the everyday interests of the reading public, to influence contemporary literature. The only writer of the highest class whose work reveals extensive acquaintance with Kane's books is Henry David Thoreau. On many pages of *Walden, or Life in the Woods,* Thoreau refers to Kane's narrative of life among the icebergs. But he was a special reader, as mighty a world traveler in his armchair as Kane was in action.[18]

Another writer of armchair travels, at a lower level of literary distinction, was Jules Verne, prolific pioneer of science fiction. His two books of Arctic adventure, written a decade after Kane's return from the north, are based on extensive reading of the literature of the Franklin Search and especially of Kane's books. In *Les Anglais au Pôle nord* and *Le desert de glace,* Jules Verne set the fantastic adventures of his British heroes and their American rival amid scenes obviously derived from Kane's narratives, and he adapted for his own plots several episodes of the second Grinnell Expedition. Verne's Captain Hatteras, for example, commanded a brig called not *Advance* but *Forward.* He lost his vessel near Smith Sound; some of his crew left the expedition in an ill-fated secession; he planned to escape by boat down the west coast of Greenland to Upernavik. At last, however, completely outdoing Kane, he again turned northward, reached open water beyond Cape Washington, launched a sloop somewhat improbably built from wreckage, and triumphantly sailed to the North Pole. There he found a marvel exceeding the wildest conjectures of Maury and Kane—a volcano spouting fire and smoke over the Open Polar Sea! These fictional explorers of the French novelist have occasion more than once to refer to the real Kane, whom Jules Verne evidently ranked as an outstanding discoverer.

Kane's adventures are now largely forgotten, since the days of Thoreau and Verne, and the contemporary admiration of his books has almost disappeared from the literary criticism of our time, but his life story has never quite lost its appeal to writers for children. Juvenile books and magazine articles based on his books began to appear soon after his death and are still coming out from time to time.[19] Robert E. Peary, for example, was first awakened to the lure of Arctic travel when in 1862 at the age of six he saw in a Sunday-school paper a story based on *Arctic Explorations, 1853, '54, '55,* illustrated by a picture, taken from page 133 of volume 2, of Eskimo boys playing shinny on the ice with walrus ribs for sticks. He kept the article among his childish treasures, and it is now in the National Archives with the bulk of his papers.[20] Who can say how many young Americans of later generations, like Peary, directly or indirectly acquired from Kane's books the inspiration for adventurous travel? One, at least, is the writer of this biography, whose memories of the icy scenes in *Arctic Explorations* lingered in his mind until in young manhood he responded to a call, not indeed to the farthest north, but to hospital work in Labrador.

Elisha Kent Kane has nowhere a monument in bronze or stone. In the first flush of grief and adulation after his death, a Kane Monument Association was organized, but did not survive the troublous times that soon followed. Three months after he died, John Brown of Ossawatomie began the bloody struggle for abolition of Negro slavery. Before long the stonemasons were building forts, not monuments; the foundrymen were casting not statues but cannon. Philadelphians had more urgent uses for their money than to commemorate the triumphs of peace, and when the war was over every city and town had its own heroes of the battlefield. Dr. Kane's name, however, remains on Arctic maps and charts. When *Arctic Explorations, 1853, '54, '55* was first off the press, one of its most eager readers was Peter Force of Washington, editor and historian deeply interested in Arctic geography. Unfolding the map in volume 1 he saw that Kane's name nowhere appeared among the dozens of national figures, friends of the Grinnell Expedition, and relatives after whom Kane had named various capes, bays, harbors, and islands. Noting also that the wide basin where *Advance*'s cruise came to an end bore no name at all, Peter Force took his pen, wrote the words "Kane's Sea" across the open space, and sent the map to the publisher. Taking the hint, Childs called for his engraver and had the map revised.[21] All copies of the book published after the late autumn of 1856 carry the name of Kane across that first stretch of the American route to the North Pole. On present-day maps of the Arctic regions the wording is "Kane Basin."

A modern vessel of the United States Navy now bears Kane's name to the seven seas. U.S.S. *Kane*, a recently commissioned survey ship, is equipped for the most advanced types of hydrographic exploration. Kane could have asked no more suitable honor from the Service that, through John Pendleton Kennedy and Matthew Fontaine Maury, encouraged him to carry on his own pioneering survey.

In 1861 Lady Franklin, visiting the United States at the age of sixty-three, with her characteristic energy made the then difficult journey to the Big Trees of California. The authorities honored her presence by naming one of the giant sequoias after her and another after Kane. Thus Kane acquired a living monument taller at least than most that are made with hands.[22] Today, alas—*sic transit gloria*—nobody remembers which big tree it is that was dedicated to Dr. Kane.

One of his posthumous honors reached a still higher elevation and will last longer. In 1878 the director of the astronomical observatory at Athens, Greece, J. F. J. Schmidt, on his authoritative map of the moon attached Kane's name to a crater thirty-four miles in diameter, appropriately located on the far northern part of the moon's surface. This designation has since been officially recognized by the International Astronomical Union.[23] Astronauts may some day visit Kane Crater.

Although no memorial column or pedestal bears a sculptured likeness of Dr. Kane of the Arctic Seas, and his fame as a national hero barely outlived his days on earth, he would no doubt deem it the greater honor that his name is still known to travelers and explorers in distant regions of the sea and sky.

# Epilogue

The little band of Dr. Kane's Arctic companions was soon scattered, some of them bound for new adventures, others to more prosaic careers. One of them, Isaac Hayes, was to win for himself a considerable reputation as an Arctic explorer; two of the other officers were to serve gallantly in the Civil War. Most of the seamen lived out their lives unnoted and unrecorded. We hear the last of them at Dr. Kane's funeral.

DR. ISAAC I. HAYES, fully committed to the hypothesis of an Open Polar Sea, organized an expedition of his own to Kane Basin and beyond, in 1860–61, which he described in his book, *The Open Polar Sea,* 1867. During the Civil War he was an army surgeon at Satterlee General Hospital, Philadelphia. Another expedition in 1869 contributed further to the geography of northern Greenland (*The Land of Desolation,* 1871). Settling finally in New York City, Dr. Hayes was a member of the New York State Assembly from 1876 until his death in 1881 (*DAB*).

AUGUST SONNTAG shortly after the return of the expedition joined an astronomical party going to Mexico. During his absence a Philadelphia publisher put out under his name a shoddy book, *Professor Sonntag's Thrilling Narrative of the Grinnell Expedition,* 1857, which he promptly disowned. In 1859, Sonntag was appointed vice-director of the Dudley Observatory, Albany, N.Y., but relinquished the post to join Hayes's expedition of 1860–61. In January 1861 he died following a fall into icy water near Northumberland Island (Hayes, *Open Polar Sea,* p. 231).

CARL PETERSEN, who remained in Greenland, was decorated by the King of Denmark for his services to Greenland explorations. In 1857 he joined

Captain Leopold McClintock in his notable cruise to King William Land (F.L. McClintock, *Narrative of the Fate of Sir John Franklin and His Companions*, London, 1859). Petersen's account of his travels with Penny and Kane (*Erindringer fra Polanderene*) was published in Copenhagen in 1857. (Oscar M. Villarejo, *Dr. Kane's Voyage to the Polar Lands*, Philadelphia, 1965, pp. 18, 31; I.I. Hayes, *An Arctic Boat Journey*, Philadelphia, 1860.)

HENRY GOODFELLOW was captain and later major in the 26th Pennsylvania Infantry, 1861–64. He was brevetted lieutenant colonel of volunteers for "gallant and meritorious service" at the battle of Gettysburg, and was promoted to colonel in 1865 for gallant conduct in the Wilderness and at Spotsylvania. (F.B. Heitman, ed., *Historical Register and Dictionary of the United States Army*, Washington, 1903, vol. *1*.)

JOHN WALL WILSON was in 1857 sailing master on a New York vessel. During the Civil War and afterward he served with credit in the U.S. Revenue Service. (John Wall Wilson Papers, APS.)

HENRY BROOKS died fifteen months after Dr. Kane (June 29, 1858) from the effects, it was said, of scurvy and other sufferings of the expedition. (*General Register of the U.S. Marine Corps. 1782–1882*).

AMOS BONSALL returned to farming not far from Philadelphia, in Delaware County, Pa. He outlived all his companions of 1853–55. In old age, he published his brief, time-blurred memories of the expedition, in Rudolf Kersting, *The White World*, New York, 1902.

WILLIAM GODFREY was for a time at least in Philadelphia after the expedition, working as an omnibus driver. In his self-justifying book, *Godfrey's Narrative of the Last Grinnell Expedition*, Philadelphia, 1857, he said that he could not get a better job because of Dr. Kane's unfavorable report of his conduct in *Arctic Explorations, 1853, '54, '55*. He is said to have volunteered for Hayes's expedition of 1860 but was not accepted (undocumented memorandum in Dow Papers, Stefansson Collection, Dartmouth).

JOHN BLAKE, alias William Huzza or Hussey, was at sea at the time of Dr. Kane's funeral. In 1860 he wrote to I.I. Hayes from U.S.S. *Sabine* off Greytown, Natal, volunteering for Dr. Hayes's expedition (a striking example of the lure of the Arctic!) but was not accepted. (Letter, January 14, 1860, Stewart Collection, Glassboro State College, Glassboro, N.J.)

THOMAS HICKEY was working, at the time of Dr. Kane's funeral, at Charles Smith's Foundry, Philadelphia.

WILLIAM MORTON remained in touch with the Kane family for some time after Dr. Kane's death. With the approval of Dr. Kane's executors (his brothers Thomas L. and Robert P. Kane) Morton became in 1857 part owner of a traveling exhibit called "Panorama of Dr. Kane's Arctic Voyage" in which he seems to have acted as narrator, in Arctic costume. He was allowed the use of the boat "Faith," Dr. Kane's rifle, Eskimo clothing, and one of the dogs Kane had brought home from North Greenland. (Letters in Kane Papers, APS; William Morton, *Dr. Kane's Arctic Voyage, Explanatory of a Pictorial Illustration of the Second Grinnell Expedition*, New York, 1857, pamphlet.) Morton went to the Arctic again on Charles Francis Hall's expedition of 1871 as second mate of S.S. *Polaris*. (George S. Tyson, *Arctic Experiences*, 1874, pp. 111–112.)

HANS HENDRIK led an adventurous life with the wife he found at Peteravik (see chapter 11, p. 204), as he recorded in *Memoirs of Hans, the Arctic Traveler, Serving under Kane, Hayes, Hall, and Nares, 1853–1876*, London, 1878. See also Augustus W. Greely "The Marvellous Drift of Captain Tyson" and "The Wifely Heroism of Mersuk" in *True Tales of Arctic Heorism*, New York, 1912. Edwin G. Rich in *Hans, the Eskimo*, Boston, 1934, narrates the life of Hans and Mersuk in quasi-autobiographical form, without crediting his sources (Kane, *Arctic Explorations*; Hayes, *Open Polar Sea*; G. E. Tyson, *Arctic Experiences*.)

GEORGE STEPHENSON was, at the time of Kane's funeral, storekeeper on a transatlantic passenger vessel, S.S. *Baltic* of the Collins Line. Later he was a night inspector at the U.S. Custom House, New York. He died at the age of thirty-nine. (undated, unidentified newspaper clipping in Grinnell scrapbook No. 6, American Geographical Society, New York.)

JAMES McGARY was associated with Morton's panorama in the summer of 1857; he died while it was at Boston, on or about September 2. (*Boston Journal*, September 5, 1857.)

GEORGE RILEY and GEORGE WHIPPLE, seamen, were at sea at the time of Kane's funeral. (*Philadelphia Evening Bulletin*, March 14, 1857; the article gives the employment of all members of the party as of that date.)

MARY LEIPER and HELEN PATTERSON, the two cousins who had been in love with Elisha Kent Kane (chapter 4), made happy marriages during his lifetime. Mary Leiper married in 1851 a distant cousin, John H. Thomas of Baltimore. Dr. Kane gave her a piano as a wedding present. She died in 1893. Helen Patterson married in 1856 James W. Robbins, D.D., who became headmaster of the Episcopal Academy, Philadelphia. They had four children. She lived to the age of 94. (Information from letters and memoranda in possession of Mrs. A. Waldo Jones, Vinings, Ga.; copies at APS, Philadelphia).

MARGARET FOX is said to have suffered from severe depression for months after Dr. Kane's death. She returned to her family and ultimately resumed her role as spiritualistic medium. Her book, *The Love-Life of Dr. Kane,* New York, 1866, was not widely read. Her claim for a widow's share of Kane's estate was litigated for several years with results unsatisfactory to both sides (correspondence in Kane Papers, APS). Her later career was one of gradually increasing decline accelerated by intemperance. She died in 1893. (Earl W. Fornell, *The Unhappy Medium,* Austin, Texas, 1964; Herbert G. Jackson, Jr., *The Spirit Rappers,* New York, Doubleday and Co., 1972; for a fuller but somewhat fictionalized account, see Miriam Buckner Pond, *Time Is Kind,* New York: Centennial Press, 1947.)

# Notes

## Abbreviations

APS       American Philosophical Society

*Arctic Explorations, 1853, '54, 55*    E. K. Kane, *Arctic Explorations: The Second Grinnell Expedition in Search of Sir John Franklin, 1853, '54, '55.* 2 vols. Philadelphia: Childs and Peterson, 1856. Reprinted in "Physician Travelers" series, New York, Arno Press, 1971.

*DAB*       *Dictionary of American Biography.*

*DNB*       *Dictionary of National Biography.*

EKK       Elisha Kent Kane.

Elder       William Elder, *Biography of Elisha Kent Kane.* Philadelphia: Childs and Peterson, 1858.

Godfrey, *Narrative*    *Narrative of the Last Grinnell Exploring Expedition in Search of Sir John Franklin, with a Biography of Elisha Kent Kane, from the Cradle to the Grave, by William Godfrey, one of the Survivors of the Expedition.* Philadelphia: J. T. Lloyd, 1857.

Hayes, *Arctic Boat Journey*    Isaac I. Hayes, *An Arctic Boat Journey in the Autumn of 1854.* Boston: Brown, Taggard, and Chase, 1860. Second ed., Boston: Ticknor and Fields, 1867.

HSP       Historical Society of Pennsylvania.

JKK       John K[intzing] Kane.

Journal, HSP

E. K. Kane, private journal of the second Grinnell Expedition, first part, formerly erroneously listed and cited as "Logbook" of *Advance*, MS, HSP.

Journal, Stanford

Latter part of MS private journal. Stanford University Library.

Kane-Childs Album

Album containing letters from E. K. Kane to George W. Childs, with sketches and other memorabilia. Dreer Collection, Explorers, HSP.

*Love-Life*

[Margaret Fox] *The Love-Life of Dr. Kane, Containing the Correspondence, and a History of the Acquaintance, Engagement, and Secret Marriage between Elisha K. Kane and Margaret Fox.* New York: Carleton Publisher, 1866.

Peabody Library

George Peabody Branch, Enoch Pratt Free Library, Baltimore.

Stefansson Collection, Dartmouth

Dow Papers, Stefansson Arctic Collection, Dartmouth College Library.

U.S. Grinnell Expedition

E. K. Kane, *The U.S. Grinnell Expedition in Search of Sir John Franklin, A Personal Narrative*, New York: Harper and Brothers, 1853.

Villarejo

Oscar M. Villarejo, *Dr. Kane's Voyage to the Polar Lands.* Philadelphia: University of Pennsylvania Press, 1965. (Edition, with introduction and comment, of Carl Peterson's account of the second Grinnell Expedition, from a manuscript English translation in the Stewart Collection, Glassboro [N.J.] State College Library.)

Narrative statements without citation of source are based on Elder's *Biography* or on Kane's private journal of his Arctic expedition (1853–55).

## Chapter 1

1. Sarah Kane Morris, *A Letter from Mrs. Thomas Morris to Her Nephew, the Honourable John Kintzing Kane . . . Containing Many Facts of Family History Interesting to the Descendants of John Kane and His Wife Sybil Kent*, etc. (New York, 1889); E. P. Oberholtzer, *Philadelphia: A History of the City and Its People*, 4 vols. (Philadelphia, 1906), 430–31; Elizabeth D. W. Kane, *Story of John Kane of Dutchess County, New York* (Philadelphia, 1921; John K. Kane, *Autobiography* (see note 5 below).

2. Franklin B. Dexter, *Biographical Sketches of the Graduates of Yale College, 1701–1745* (New York, 1885), pp. 384–85.

3. E. D. W. Kane (note 1 above).

4. Oberholtzer (note 1 above) 3:43.

5. For John K. Kane see *DAB*; also Oberholtzer (note 1 above); Henry Simpson, *Lives of Eminent Philadelphians* (Philadelphia, 1859). His own recollections give intimate views of state and national politics from 1825 to 1849: *Autobiography: Myself from 1795 to 1849* (privately printed, Philadelphia, 1949), with appended genealogies, family letters and other memorabilia.

6. Sully's portraits of John K. Kane and his wife are now in the possession of Mrs. Francis Trimble of Philadelphia at her country home in Chester County, Pa. They were reproduced in black and white in *Century Magazine,* n.s. 34 (1898): 489, and in the J. K. Kane, *Autobiography* (note 5 above). For technical details see Edward Biddle and Fielding Mantle, *Life and Works of Thomas Sully* (Philadelphia, privately published, 1921), pp. 194–95.

7. Fern Rock was situated in North Philadelphia, in the southeast angle between Old York Road and Chelten Avenue. The house stood about 400 feet east of the former and 300 feet south of the latter. At the beginning of the twentieth century it formed part of a suburban hotel. The area is now fully built over with more recent constructions. For Rensselaer and the building of Fern Rock, see J. K. Kane, *Autobiography*, pp. 83–84.

8. The story of Judge Kane's having committed his son to prison seems to rest upon family tradition. Thomas's contempt of court would presumably have been of the criminal variety, but no record of such a charge against him appears in the criminal dockets of U.S. District Court No. 2 (now at the U.S. National Archives). Documentation of the story by contemporary newspaper accounts, if they exist, or possibly from records of the Court of Appeals, may be left to a future biographer of Thomas Leiper Kane; Zobell (note 13 below) merely repeats the story without evidence.

9. Thomas Leiper, *DAB*.

10. For Martha Ibbetson Gray, see Elder, pp. 14–16. The original testimonial letter is owned by Edward F. Leiper, Media, Pa.

11. J. K. Kane, *Autobiography*.

12. Charles K. Shields, "The Arctic Monument named for Tennyson by Dr. Kane," *Century Magazine,* n.s., 34 (1898): 483–92.

13. For Thomas L. Kane see *DAB*; also Albert L. Zobell, *Sentinel in the East: A Biography of Thomas L. Kane* (Salt Lake City: Nicholas G. Morgan, 1965); *The Private Papers and Diary of Thomas Leiper Kane, a Friend of the Mormons*, ed. O. O. Winther (San Francisco: Gelber-Lilienthal, 1937). See also Robert D. Hoffsommer, "The Bucktails," in *Civil War Times*, Gettysburg, Pa. 4 (1966): 16–21.

14. For the younger children of J. K. Kane, see Oberholtzer (note 1, above), and J. K. Kane, *Autobiography*.

## Chapter 2

1. William Elder, *Biography of Elisha Kent Kane* (Philadelphia: Childs and Peterson, 1858).

2. Samuel M. Smucker, *The Life of Dr. Elisha Kent Kane and Other Distinguished American Explorers* (Philadelphia: G. C. Evans, 1858; 2d ed., 1860).

3. Information on Father Waldron was kindly supplied by the Very Reverend Thomas J. Walsh, Vice-Chancellor, Archdiocese of Philadelphia.

4. Personal information from the late Francis Fisher Kane, Esq., of Philadelphia.

5. Margaret Fox, *The Love-Life of Dr. Kane* (see *Love-Life* in list of abbreviations above), p. 284.

6. Titian Peale's letter to John K. Kane is in the Library of the American Philosophical Society, in whose *Proceedings* it has been printed in part, 82 (1940): 541.

7. [Sir] John Franklin, *Narrative of a Journey to the Shores of the Polar Sea, in the Years 1819–20–21–22* (London, 1823).

8. Samuel X. Radbill, ed., "The Autobiographical Ana of Robley Dunglison, M.D.," *Transactions of the American Philosophical Society*, Philadelphia, n.s. 53, part 8, (1963).

9. Elder says that Kane went to the University of Virginia in his sixteenth year; this is improbable, because the university did not ordinarily admit students less than sixteen years of age. Charles Shields, Kane's brother-in-law, says that he entered the university in his seventeenth year ("A Sketch of the Life of Elisha Kent Kane, M.D., U.S.N.," in Kane, *Arctic Explorations* [later editions] Hartford, Conn., 1868, 1881).

10. James Park McCallie, "Elisha Kent Kane," *Alumni Bulletin, University of Virginia*, 1st ser., 6 (1889): 103–6.

11. MS letters of Robert Patterson, Stefansson Collection, Dartmouth.

12. Elder's discreet words "the best of authority" (regarding Kane's neurosis) perhaps refer to Dr. Robley Dunglison, Professor of Medicine in the Jefferson Medical College, who was an intimate of the Kane family from the time of Elisha's first illness until the end of his life.

13. Robley Dunglison, in *The Medical Student, or Aids to the Study of Medicine* (Philadelphia, 1837; 2d ed. 1844), says that at the University of Pennsylvania the requirement of a two years' apprenticeship was then "rarely attended to."

14. Some of Kane's clinical memoranda are in the Gratz Collection, HSP, and in Yale University Library.

15. MS memorandum in Stefansson Collection, Dartmouth.

16. Elder, pp. 40–41.

17. George W. Corner, "Hero with a Damaged Heart: The Clinical History of Elisha Kent Kane, M.D.," in *Medicine, Science, and Culture: Historical Essays in Honor of Owsei Temkin* (Baltimore: Johns Hopkins Press, 1968), pp. 249–63.

18. Jacques-Louis Nauche, article in *Receuil des Transactions de la Société de Médecine Pratique*, 1831. The history of kiesteine has been well summarized by Mark Marshall, "The Kyesteine Pellicle; an Early Biological Test for Pregnancy," *Bulletin of the History of Medicine* 22 (1948): 178:95.

19. Radbill (chap. 2, note 8 above).

20. Elisha Kent Kane, "Experiments on Kiesteine with Remarks on its Application to the Diagnosis of Pregnancy," *American Journal of Medical Sciences*, n.s., 4 (1842): 13–37.

## Chapter 3

1. Letter, Abel P. Upshur, Secretary of the Navy, to EKK, March 1, 1842, Navy Records, U.S. National Archives.

2. The portraits (for one, see p. 69) were reproduced in an article by Dr. Kane's broth-

er-in-law, Rev. Charles W. Shields, "The Arctic Monument Named for Tennyson by Dr. Kane," *Century Magazine* (n.s. 34): 483–92, 1898.

3. Letter, EKK to Secretary Upshur, January 30, 1843, Navy Records, U.S. National Archives.

4. Letter, JKK to A. Thomas Smith, Acting Secretary of the Navy, May 28, 1843, Navy Records, U.S. National Archives.

5. Letter, Secretary Upshur to EKK, July 21, 1843, Navy Records, U.S. National Archives.

6. Much of Elder's account of Dr. Kane's travels and adventures before 1847 is taken literally from a statement prepared in August 1857, seven months after the doctor's death, by JKK, partly from memory, partly from letters which he was then putting at Elder's disposal. JKK to William Elder, August 19, 1857, Kane Papers, APS.

7. Mary W. Williams, *Dom Pedro, the Magnanimous Emperor* (Chapel Hill, N.C.: University of North Carolina Press, 1937).

8. Events on *Brandywine's* voyage are cited here from her logbook, in the Navy Records, U.S. National Archives, to whose staff the author is much indebted. The volume of the logbook for the first part of the trip (to Rio) is missing, but the American Philosophical Society has a version of the entire logbook kept as an exercise by Midshipman William Weaver (Kane Papers).

9. Claude M. Fuess, *The Life of Caleb Cushing*, 2 vols. (New York: Harcourt, Brown, 1923).

10. Mary T. Leiper to EKK, May 23, 1843. EKK Papers, APS. Later letters are in the same collection.

11. Henry Simpson, ed., *The Lives of Eminent Philadelphians, Now Deceased, Collected from Original and Authentic Sources* (Philadelphia: Brotherhead, 1859), "Elisha Kent Kane" (anonymous), pp. 618–20. Simpson in his preface lists Thomas L. Kane among those who assisted him. "Sombava" may be an error for Sumatra.

12. The EKK Papers at APS contain, in a parcel of miscellaneous notes on travel, an incomplete account of the visit to Taal in Kane's hand, and also the note he penciled on the rim of the volcano.

13. The EKK Papers contain a description of one of these diplomatic ceremonials.

14. Copies of *The Friend of China and Hongkong Gazette* are among the EKK Papers, APS.

15. Peter Parker, "Thirteenth Annual Report of the Ophthalmic Hospital at Canton, including the period from the 1st January, 1844, to the 1st July, 1845," *Chinese Repository* (Canton, 1845): 449–64. A visitor to the hospital about eight months later found the patient in excellent health (George B. Stevens, *The Life, Letters, and Journals of the Rev. and Hon. Peter Parker, M.D.*, [Boston: Boston and Chicago Congregational Sunday School and Publishing Society, 1896], p. 247). I am indebted to Prof. Edward V. Gulick of Wellesley College for apprising me of this operation.

16. EKK Papers, APS, Whampoa Medical Affairs, fragment of diary or letter.

17. EKK Papers, APS, Whampoa Medical Affairs, agreement with G. C. Lunn.

18. EKK, The *United States Grinnell Expedition in Search of Sir John Franklin, A Personal Narrative,* (New York: Harper, 1854), p. 474.

19. EKK Papers, APS, Miscellaneous Notes.

20. As to the route from India to Egypt, if Kane accompanied Tagore he would have sailed in S.S. *Bentinck* of the P. & O. Line, which left on March 8, 1845 (Kossory Chaud

Mittra, *Memoir of Dwarkanath Tagore* [Calcutta, 1870]), and followed the newly established steamer route via Madras, Ceylon, and Aden to Suez. Travelers bound for Europe crossed the Isthmus by rail to Alexandria, where another P. & O. ship awaited them (Halford L. Hoskins, *British Routes to India* [New York: Longmans Green, 1928]). Kane's name, however, does not appear in the passenger list of *Bentinck* in the *Bengal Hurkarii*, Calcutta, March 8, 1845. Since his memorandum now in the library of the APS (see note 19) places him in Madras on March 2, it is probable that he never reached Calcutta, but met Tagore at Madras and boarded *Bentinck* there for Suez. Elder has a different story. He says that Kane traversed Persia and Syria. Kane, moreover, told William Parker Snow (note 24, this chapter) six years later that he had once been in Syria. This part of the problem, however, is easily solved; Kane's memorandum of his journey includes an entry "May 30, Syria." He evidently stopped at a Syrian port on the later traverse of his journey from Egypt to Greece. Another entry in the memorandum "Apr. 3, Suez" supports the idea that he traveled by the P. & O. steamer from India to Egypt.

I owe the reference to Mittra's biography of Tagore and a transcript of *Bentinck's* passenger list to Professor Blair B. Kling of the University of Illinois.

21. This Nile trip is one of the few episodes of his travels in the East for which we have his own account. A memorandum book in the EKK Papers, APS, Notebook No. 7, covers the entire trip. Elder cannot have seen it, for in the sequence and itinerary of the journey it does not agree with his account.

22. Elder, p. 80.

23. Cf. [Karl] Richard Lepsius, *Letters from Egypt, Ethiopia, and the Peninsula of Sinai*, trans. Leonora and Joanna B. Horner (London: H. G. Bohn, 1853).

24. Elder, taking literally a remark Kane made some years later that he "had eaten locusts in Sennaar," implies (p. 83) that Kane reached a point well up the Blue Nile. So long a trip upriver could of course not have been accomplished in the time Kane spent in Egypt. In view of his general truthfulness, this mention of Sennaar poses a problem. We must assume that the remark was more poetic than factual.

25. Washington Irving to EKK, February 8, 1845 (address missing), EKK Papers, APS.

26. William Parker Snow, *Journal of the Prince Albert in Search of Sir J. Franklin* (London: Longmans Green, 1851). For Snow's other travels, see the sketch of his life in *DNB*.

## Chapter 4

1. Elder's statement, in his biography, that Kane hated the cruel discipline of the navy was no doubt intended to counteract an accusation, resented by Kane's family and friends, that Kane himself visited severe and unusual punishment upon two of his Arctic crew in 1853–55; see chapter 8.

2. Copies of letters, JKK to George Bancroft, Secretary of the Navy, in Stefansson Collection, Dartmouth.

3. EKK to Helen Patterson, May 7, 1846, EKK Papers, APS.

4. The strong opposition of the Leipers to cousin marriage was made known to the author by a member of the family, Mrs. A. Waldo Jones, Vinings, Georgia.

5. J[ohn] T[aylor], Jr., to EKK, "Hazlewood," February 4, 1846; C. C. Van Wyck to EKK, May 27, 1846, EKK Papers, APS.

6. Logbook of U.S.S. *United States*, Navy Records, U.S. National Archives.

7. George Clymer, "Notices of the African Station," *American Journal of the Medical Sciences*, n.s. 33 (1859): 366–89.

8. Radbill, (see chapter 2, note 8, above), p. 184.

9. EKK to Jane Leiper Kane, July 13, 1846, EKK Papers, APS.

10. See chapter 1, p. 13 and note 8.

11. For de Sousa, see Gilberto Freyre, *Problemas brasilieros de Antropologia*, 3d ed. (Rio de Janeiro: José Olympio, 1962).

12. EKK, Notebook 5, EKK Papers, APS.

13. Richard Francis Burton, *A Mission to Gelele, King of Dahome*, 2 vols. (London, 1864).

14. TLK to EKK, November 12, 1846. EKK Papers, APS.

15. Letter, G. A. Prentiss to EKK, January 5, 1846, EKK Papers, APS. Prentiss, born at Keene, N.H., in 1809, had an uneventful career in the navy. He retired with the rank of commander in 1864 for medical reasons; was commissioned commodore on the retired list in 1867 and died in 1868. Information from F. Kent Loomis, Captain, USN (ret.), Asst. Director of Naval History, Navy Department, Washington, D.C.

16. Thomas Dillard, quoted by Elder, pp. 106–7.

17. Alexander Bryson, *Report on the Climate and Principal Diseases of the African Station* (London: Clowes, 1847). This report gives a horrifying account of the ravages of tropical fevers in the British ships on the West Coast patrol.

18. Henry A. Ford, *Observations on the Fevers of the West Coast of Africa* (New York: Jenkins, 1856).

19. EKK to JKK, April 6, 1847, EKK Papers, APS. The "magnetic telegraph," first put into practical use in 1844 between Washington and Baltimore, had been extended to Philadelphia only a year or two before the date of this letter.

20. Letter, C. C. Van Wyck to EKK, August 27, 1847, EKK Papers, APS.

21. James K. Polk, *The Diary of James K. Polk During his Presidency, 1845 to 1849*, 4 vols. (Chicago: McClurg, 1910).

22. Charles W. Eliot, *Winfield Scott, The Soldier and the Man* (New York: Macmillan, 1919).

23. EKK to Jane Leiper Kane from Cincinnati, Ohio, dated October (error for November) 11, 1847; EKK to JKK from Louisville, Ky., November 12, 1847. EKK Papers, APS.

24. Stefansson Collection, Dartmouth.

25. For Dominguez see Justin W. Smith, *The War with Mexico*, 2 vols. (New York: Macmillan, 1919), 2: 306, n. 19, and Brackett (note 26 below).

26. Albert G. Brackett, *General Lane's Brigade in Central Mexico* (Cincinnati: H. W. Derby and Co., 1854).

27. *The Pennsylvanian*, Philadelphia, March 24, 1848.

28. For the American doctors' diagnoses, see a letter in the *Philadelphia Inquirer*, March 25, 1848, written (as shown by internal evidence) by the surgeon in charge of the U.S. Army General Hospital at Puebla, presumably Lieutenant A. B. Campbell; see also another letter cited by Elder, pp. 125–26.

29. W. W. H. Davis, "Three Pennsylvanians, Biographical Sketches of . . . General Robert Patterson, James Madison Porter, and Elisha Kent Kane," MS, incomplete, not dated, Bucks County Historical Society, Doylestown, Pa.

30. Winfield Scott, *Memoirs of Lieutenant-General Scott, LL.D.*, 2 vols. (New York: Sheldon, 1864), 2: 567.

31. Elder, p. 137.

32. See notes 27 and 28, this chapter.

33. The sword presented to Kane in February 1849 is now at Kane Manor inn, Kane, Pennsylvania.

34. Kane's report to the Secretary of War was printed by Elder, pp. 122–24. The relevant portion follows:

> Philadelphia, July 21, 1848
>
> Sir:—I left Perote fortress on the 3d of January, 1848, under orders to report to General Scott at the city of Mexico. My escort consisted of a party of lancers, Mexicans in the pay of the United States, commanded by Colonel Domingues.
>
> On the 6th of January, at a place intermediate to Ojo de Agua and Nopaluca, some twenty-five miles from Puebla, we encountered a body of Mexicans escorting Generals Gaona and Torrejon and other officers. After a short action, we succeeded in routing them, taking forty-four prisoners. Circumstances having made the two generals prisoners, they claimed my special protection against Domingues's band, who sought to kill them after the surrender; and in the effort to shield them against a charging party, headed by Lieutenant Rocher, I received a severe wound from a lance in the region of the bladder, my horse having immediately before been struck down by a lance under the shoulder from the same party.
>
> I succeeded in raising him up and keeping him till we reached Nopaluca, when he sank from exhaustion. I was transferred to another animal, but, finding myself unable to ride, was placed in a Mexican car with the rest of the wounded.

35. The letter of Judge and Mrs. Kane to General Gaona is copied from a MS draft initialed JKK, JLK, accompanied by a Spanish version dated "4 de Marzo," 1848, Stefansson Collection, Dartmouth.

36. James K. Polk (see note 21, this chapter), p. 259.

37. *Supply* was a vessel of 547 tons (George F. Emmons, *The Navy of the United States from the Commencement, 1775–1853* [Washington: Gideon and Company, 1853]).

38. EKK to Jane Leiper Kane, February 2, 1849, Stefansson Collection, Dartmouth; EKK to JKK, September 6, 1850, Kane Papers, APS, typescript copy, provenance not stated.

39. EKK to JKK, March 8, 1849. Transcript in EKK Papers, APS.

40. Elder, pp. 139–40.

41. Logbook of U.S.S. *Supply*, Navy Records, U.S. National Archives.

42. EKK to Jane Leiper Kane, Charleston, S.C., January 16, 1850. EKK Papers, APS.

43. Elder, pp. 141–42.

## Chapter 5

1. A definitive account of Franklin's expedition of 1845 is that of Richard J. Cyriax, *Franklin's Last Arctic Expedition* (London: Methuen, 1939).

2. *Erebus* was a vessel of 370 gross tons; *Terror*, of 340 tons. Their ominous names were given them before they were used in polar exploration, both having been built as bomb vessels. Evidently English naval explorers were not superstitious about ships' names; nevertheless these two vessels came to their end in a place of darkness and terror.

3. Lady Franklin's letter of April 4, 1849, and Secretary Clayton's reply are printed in

full in Joseph P. Comegys, "Memoir of John M. Clayton," *Papers of the Historical Society of Delaware*, Wilmington, 4 (1882): 178–87.

4. Silas M. Burrows of New York, later of San Francisco and Hong Kong, was something of an eccentric with, it seems, an obsessive interest in assisting shipwrecked mariners. (See his queer little book, *America and Japan, Russia and the Republic of New Granada*, n.d., ca. 1866. Copy at N.Y. Public Library is titled *Russia and America*. Claiming acquaintance with Lady Franklin, he asserted that it was he who appealed to Henry Grinnell on her behalf and acted for him in purchasing *Advance* and *Rescue* (letters, Burrows to John M. Clayton, June 22, 1849, and to Edwin J. De Haven, May 20, 1850, New York Historical Society, Misc. MSS, De Haven). Burrows's name is in fact mentioned in a couple of letters that passed between Lady Franklin and Grinnell.

5. *Messages and Papers of the Presidents*, Washington, D.C., Government Printing Office, 5 (1849–1861):25–26.

6. A printed copy of Grinnell's petition to Congress is at the New-York Historical Society, Misc. MSS, De Haven.

7. Letter, Henry Grinnell to Lady Franklin, printed without date in W. F. Rawnsley, *The Life, Diaries and Correspondence of Lady Jane Franklin, 1792–1875* (London: Erskine McDonald, 1923).

8. For the proceedings in Congress see *Congressional Globe*, n.s. 21 (1850), part 1, pp. 664, 684, 842, 884–91.

9. Correspondence at the New-York Historical Society, Misc. MSS, De Haven.

10. The instructions of Secretary of the Navy William Ballard Preston to Lieutenant E. J. De Haven are printed in EKK, *U.S. Grinnell Expedition*. De Haven's own copy is at the New-York Historical Society, Misc. MSS, De Haven.

11. John Kirtland Wright, *Human Nature in Geography* (Cambridge, Mass.: Harvard University Press, 1966), chapter 6, "The Open Polar Sea."

12. Matthew F. Maury, *The Physical Geography of the Sea*, 1st ed. (New York: Harper and Brothers, 1855), chapter 8, "The Open Polar Sea."

13. For the route in 1850 of the journey from Mobile to New York, see Seymour Dunbar, *A History of Travel in America*, 4 vols. (Indianapolis: Bobbs-Merrill, 1915), 3: 1122–23.

14. JKK, *Autobiography*, p. 85. This letter must have been written about May 18, 1850; the date appended by the editor presumably pertains to the letter referred to in note 15 below.

15. Jane Leiper Kane to Elizabeth Kane on or about May 21, 1850 (JKK, *Autobiography* [chap. 1, note 5, above], p. 86). It is an odd coincidence that someone in the Patterson household, a servant no doubt, bore the name of Disco, a Greenland port that Elisha was soon to visit, and the Kane family coachman was called Godfrey, a name later to have sinister significance for Dr. Kane (letter in possession of Mrs. A. Waldo Jones, Vinings, Georgia, printed in JKK *Autobiography*, p. 86).

16. Albert L. Zobell, *Sentinel in the East, a Biography of Thomas L. Kane* (Salt Lake City, 1965), pp. 52–53. Zobell says the garment was a buffalo robe.

## Chapter 6

1. Elder, pp. 150–51.

2. Robert P. Carter, Diary, Stefansson Collection, Dartmouth.

3. Letter, EKK to Thomas Harris, typescript copy, Stefansson Collection, Dartmouth.

4. William Parker Snow, *Voyage of the Prince Albert in Search of Sir John Franklin* (London, 1851).

5. Vilhjalmur Stefansson, *The Friendly Arctic* (New York: Macmillan, 1921).

6. *Proceedings*, APS, 5 (1848–55): 159–62.

7. Elder, pp. 151–52.

8. Kane did not, of course, mention this presumptuous advice in *U.S. Grinnell Expedition*, but told his mother in a letter of August 21, 1850 (probably posted via *Prince Albert* from Lancaster Sound). Stefansson Collection, Dartmouth.

9. Kaare Rodahl, "Toxicity of Polar Bear Liver," *Nature* 164 (1949): 530–31. In 1855 Kane and several of his men on the Second Grinnell Expedition were made ill by eating the livers of polar bears taken farther north, in Kane Basin (*Arctic Explorations, 1853, '54, '55*, 1: 392–93).

10. The manuscript of a statement by Captain Horatio Ommanney, commanding *Resolute*, to De Haven and Penny, dated September 11, 1850, outlining plans for continuing the search from the region of Griffith's Island, is at the New-York Historical Society, Misc. MSS, De Haven.

11. The original draft of Griffin's report to De Haven, dated September 13, 1850, on the inadvisability of continuing the cruise, and an account of *Rescue*'s difficulties in the ice pack on September 11, are also among the De Haven papers (see note 10, this chapter).

12. Peter Force, *Remarks on the English Maps of Arctic Discoveries in 1850 and 1851, Made at the Ordinary Meeting of the National Institute in May, 1852*, pamphlet (Washington, 1852), pp. 23 ff. See also *North American Review* 78 (1853): 254–60.

13. Joseph-René Bellot, *Journal d'un voyage aux mers polaires* (Paris, 1854).


## Chapter 7

1. De Haven's report to William A. Graham, Secretary of the Navy, was printed in Kane's book, *U.S. Grinnell Expedition* (see chapter 3, note 18, above), appendix B, pp. 494–508.

2. MS diary of Joseph Henry, at the Smithsonian Institution, Washington, D.C., entry of Thursday, January 1, 1852. The author is indebted to Mr. S. Dillon Ripley, Secretary of the Smithsonian, and Mr. Samuel T. Suratt, Archivist, for calling attention to Joseph Henry's comments.

3. George Gray Leiper to Martha Leiper, transcript of letter, January 29, 1852, Stefansson Collection, Dartmouth; location of original not stated.

4. The quotation is from a memorandum in Kane's hand, EKK Papers, APS.

5. *National Intelligencer*, Washington, D.C., issues of December 29 and 31, 1851, and January 3, 1852.

6. *Evening Bulletin*, Philadelphia, January 21, 1852; *The Sun*, Baltimore, January 30, 1852.

7. *Proceedings of the American Philosophical Society* 5 (1854): 266–67.

8. EKK to Henry Grinnell, May 7, 1852, EKK Papers, APS.

9. *Proceedings of the American Philosophical Society* 5 (1854): 284.

10. Friedrich P. Wrangel, "On the best means of reaching the Pole," *Journal of the Royal Geographical Society* (London) 18 (1848): 19–23.

11. Sir John Barrow, "Note on the Paper of Admiral the Baron von Wrangel on the best means of reaching the Pole," ibid., pp. 24–25.

12. Charles H. Bohner, *John Pendleton Kennedy: Gentleman from Baltimore* (Baltimore: Johns Hopkins Press, 1961).

13. EKK to J. P. Kennedy, November 14, 1848; John Pendleton Kennedy Collection, George Peabody Branch, Enoch Pratt Free Library, Baltimore.

14. MS journal, John P. Kennedy, vol. 7, entry of December 5, 1852. Kennedy Collection, Peabody Library.

15. Edward A. Inglefield, "Report on the return of the *Isabel* from the Arctic regions," *Journal of the Royal Geographical Society* (London) 23 (1853): 136–45; *A Summer Search for Sir John Franklin, with a Peek into the Polar Basin* (London, 1853).

16. Adolphus W. Greely, *Handbook of Polar Discoveries*, 3d ed., revised and enlarged (Boston: Little Brown and Company, 1907).

17. *Bulletin of the American Geographical and Statistical Society* 1 (1853): 84.

18. EKK, (chapter 3, note 18, above), *U.S. Grinnell Expedition*, appendix F, pp. 543–52.

19. The most recent biographies of Margaret Fox are those of Earl W. Fornell, *The Unhappy Medium: Spiritualism and the Life of Margaret Fox* (Austin: University of Texas Press, 1964), and Herbert G. Jackson, Jr., *The Spirit Rappers*, New York, Doubleday and Co., 1972.)

20. Fornell (note 19 above), pp. 25–26.

21. Horace Greeley, *Recollections of a Busy Life* (New York: J. B. Ford Co., 1868); Glyndon B. Van Deusen, *Horace Greeley: Nineteenth Century Crusader* (Philadelphia: University of Pennsylvania Press, 1953).

22. N. P. Willis in the *Home Journal*, New York, cited by Fred Lewis Pattee in *The Feminine Fifties* (New York: D. Appleton-Century, 1940), p. 241.

23. *Love-Life*, p. 24. Miriam Buckner Pond, in *Time Is Kind: The Story of the Unfortunate Fox Family* (New York: Centennial Press, 1947), states (p. 219) that Margaret Fox was assisted in writing the *Love-Life* by Joseph La Fumée of the *Brooklyn Eagle*.

24. *Love-Life*, p. 33.

25. Ibid., facsimile letter, following p. x.

26. The anonymous editor of *Love-Life* claimed that Margaret Fox was barely thirteen years old in the autumn of 1852; but Franklin W. Clark, in "The Rochester Spirit Rappers" (unpublished master's thesis, University of Rochester, 1933, originally entitled "The origins of spiritualism in America," typewritten MS at the New York Public Library) cites a deposition of Margaret's mother in 1848 stating that she was then fifteen years old. If born in 1833, she was nineteen in 1852 when she first met Kane. The article on Kane in *DAB*, by Margaret Elder Dow, gives Margaret's birthdate as October 7, 1833.

27. *Love-Life*, pp. 36, 37.

28. Sophia Cracroft to her mother, December 7, 1852. Franklin Papers, Scott Polar Research Institute, Cambridge, England.

29. Frances Leigh Williams, *Matthew Fontaine Maury: Scientist of the Sea* (New Brunswick, N.J.: Rutgers University Press, 1963), chapter 9, note 35, p. 540.

30. *Love-Life*, pp. 51–52. Undated, unaddressed draft in EKK Papers, APS. See also Henry Grinnell to EKK, February 1, 1852, EKK Papers, APS.

31. *Love-Life*, pp. 65–66.

32. EKK to John Pendleton Kennedy, February 22, 1853, Kennedy Collection, Peabody Library.

33. EKK Papers, APS.

34. EKK to Edwin J. De Haven, December 30, 1852. New-York Historical Society, Misc. MSS, De Haven.

35. Henry Brooks to EKK, January 27, 1852, EKK Papers, APS.

36. EKK to George W. Justice, Esq., March 27, 1853; also list of contributions, APS Archives. Sonntag's name is variously spelled with one or two *n*'s; he himself spelled it with two (letter to EKK, May 13, 1853, EKK Papers, APS).

37. Correspondence between EKK and Matthew F. Maury, November 1852 to January 1853, U.S. National Archives, Record Group no. 37.

38. S. F. Baird to George P. Marsh, March 8, 1853, in W. H. Dall, *Spencer Fullerton Baird: A Biography* (Philadelphia and London: Lippincott, 1915).

39. For the history and characterization of Kane's first book, see chapter 15, pp. 263–67.

40. EKK to John Pendleton Kennedy, Kennedy Papers, Peabody Library.

41. Margaret Fox to EKK, undated letter, EKK Papers, APS.

42. EKK to Margaret Fox, March 19, 1853, EKK Papers, APS. The Reverend Francis L. Hawks, D.D., learned and influential Protestant Episcopal clergyman, was a founding member and for some years president of the American Geographical Society.

43. Mrs. Fox to EKK, March 1853, EKK Papers, APS.

44. Mrs. Fox to EKK, March or April 1853, EKK Papers, APS.

45. F. L. Hawks to the Reverend Dr. Croswell, March 22, 1853, EKK Papers, APS.

46. *Love-Life*, pp. 129–30.

47. Elizabeth Lieper to EKK, undated letter, EKK Papers, APS.

48. The author is indebted to "Answers and Queries" of the Philadelphia *Evening Bulletin* and to Mr. Bert Anderson, Director, Chester County Historical Society, for helping to locate the long-forgotten village of Crookville.

49. C. Grinnell to Margaret Fox, printed in *Love-Life*, p. 155.

50. Elder, p. 189.


## Chapter 8

1. "Letter from Henry Goodfellow," Elder, pp. 276–77.

2. Letter, John Wall Wilson to I. I. Hayes, January 26, 1860, John Wall Wilson Papers, APS. "In his book he is a mean, contemptible man, says not a word about me [with regard to the depot party of March 1854, see chapter 9, note 2, below] but gives the entire credit to others. Now there is a day of retribution coming. The [un]fair side of that expedition shall yet be shown up and humbuggery of that sly Fox shall be exposed." In fairness to Wilson it should be said that he served with credit as an officer in the U.S. Revenue Ser-

vice in the Civil War and later (memorandum on his record in the John Wall Wilson Papers, APS).

3. Dr. Kane is referring to the family burial vault in Laurel Hill Cemetery, Philadelphia, which is in the Egyptian style that flourished in the 1830s.

4. Letter, EKK to Elizabeth L. Kane, June 5, 1853. Typewritten copy, EKK Papers, APS, location of original not shown.

5. EKK to S. F. Baird, ca. May 12, 1853, Baird Papers, Smithsonian Institution, Washington, D.C.

6. EKK to Cornelius Grinnell, dated "House of Governor of Upernavik, July 20th, 1853," Historical Society of Pennsylvania, JKK Papers, Box D-4 (fair copy not in EKK's hand.)

7. Henry Goodfellow, "The facts relating to the separation of the ship's company of the brig *'Advance'* in the fall of 1854, written out by Henry Goodfellow at the Command of Miss Bessie Kane." Typescript copies, EKK Papers, APS, and Stefansson Collection, Dartmouth.

8. Godfrey, *Narrative* (see list of abbreviations above).

9. EKK, Address to American Geographical Society, Dec. 14, 1852 (see chapter 7, note 17, above).

10. Hayes, *Arctic Boat Journey*, 1st ed. (see list of abbreviations above), pp. 203–4.

11. EKK to Cornelius Grinnell, see note 6 above.

12. Villarejo (see list of abbreviations above), p. 60.

13. Villarejo, pp. 61–62.

14. Villarejo, p. 63.

15. In the text of *Arctic Explorations, 1853, '54, '55*, Dr. Kane erroneously calls this headland "Cape Francis Hawks," but the running head reads "Cape John W. Francis," and the latter name appears on the chart accompanying the book. By this title Kane honored a well-known New York physician (1789–1861) active in the city's social and literary life. Another headland on the western shore of Kane Basin, and farther to the north, he later named after the Reverend Francis L. Hawks, a cofounder and sometime president of the American Geographical Society, the same Dr. Hawks who had suggested a school and boarding home for Margaret Fox (chapter 7, p. 123 and note 42, above) .

16. Dr. Hayes, when he was again at Rensselaer Bay in 1861, found no trace of *Advance*, which had evidently been carried away and broken up by the ice. Isaac I. Hayes, *The Open Polar Sea* (New York: Hurd and Houghton, 1867), p. 288.

17. Hans Christian Hendrik, *Memoirs of Hans, the Arctic Traveller Serving under Kane, Hayes, Hall, and Nares, 1853–1876. Translated from the Eskimo Language by Henry Rink*, ed. George Stephens (London, 1878).

## Chapter 9

1. Villarejo, p. 78.

2. In a bitter letter of 1860 to I. I. Hayes, cited in chapter 8, note 2, John Wall Wilson said that Kane appointed him, not Brooks, to lead the depot party of March 1854, and added that to prove this he still had several written orders from Kane to him as leader. Kane, he implied, was deliberately misleading when he stated in *Arctic Explorations*,

*1853, '54, '55* that Brooks was in charge of the party. Sonntag, however, in his report to Kane on the journey (*Arctic Explorations* 2: 348–52) written on April 4, 1854, said that Brooks gave the command to return to the brig; and Dr. Hayes, in his *Arctic Boat Journey,* p. 16, mentions "Brooks and his party."

3. Augustus W. Greely, *True Tales of Arctic Heroism in the New World* (New York: Scribner, 1912), p. 96.

4. Kane says (*Arctic Explorations, 1853, '54, '55* 1: 189) that he had nine men with him, but a check of names mentioned by Kane and Hayes in their accounts of this rescue gives only the seven mentioned here, plus Ohlsen. A picture of the rescue party in *Arctic Explorations* 1:188, presumably from a sketch by Dr. Kane, shows seven men drawing the sledge with apparently one (Ohlsen) lying on it. This is correct if we suppose that Kane does not appear because he was making the sketch. A corresponding discrepancy occurs in 1:192, where Kane says there were fifteen men in the whole party (Brooks's party and the rescuers), whereas the true number was fourteen.

5. Godfrey, *Narrative.*

6. I. I. Hayes, "Report of Surgeon upon Condition of Rescue-Party, March, 1854," in *Arctic Explorations, 1853, '54, '55* 2: 354–56.

7. There is a discrepancy as to the day of Baker's death between the Kane journal, which is followed here, and his account in *Arctic Explorations* 1:200, which has Baker dead in his bunk when the Eskimos appeared.

8. Charles W. Shields, "The Arctic Monument Named for Tennyson by Dr. Kane," *Century* magazine, n.s., 34 (1898): 483–92.

9. Hayes, *Arctic Boat Journey,* 2d ed., p. 379, note 7.

10. I. I. Hayes, "Report of a sledge journey to the northwest coasts of Smith's Strait by Dr. I. I. Hayes and William Godfrey," in *Arctic Explorations* 2: 365–73.

11. "Mr. Morton's report of journey to north and east during the months of June and July, 1854," in *Arctic Explorations* 2: 373–80.

12. August Petermann, "Dr. Kane's Expedition nach dem Nordpol, Mai 1843 bis Oktober 1855," *Petermann's Mittheilungen 1* (1855: 291–302).

13. I. I. Hayes, *The Open Polar Sea* (New York: Hurd, 1867).

14. A. Kolchak, "The Arctic pack and the polynias," in *Problems of Polar Research,* ed. W. L. G. Georg (New York: American Geographic Society, 1928), pp. 140–41.

## Chapter 10

1. EKK to Thomas L. Kane, July 7, 1854, HSP, Kane Family Papers.

2. George F. McDougal, *The Eventful Voyage of H. M. Discovery Ship "Resolute" in Search of Sir John Franklin* (London: Longman, 1857).

3. The idea that a separation would enhance the chance of survival of both parties is explicitly stated in Hayes's letter to William Elder, December 5, 1857 (see note 9 below).

4. Villarejo bases his argument for the existence of an at least latent mutiny on the supposition that part of the "logbook" of *Advance* was suppressed by someone, probably William Elder, to conceal the facts. Actually the so-called *"Log Book of Dr. Kane"* in the Dreer Collection, HSP, is not the ship's log, but the first part of Dr. Kane's personal journal, the second part of which is at Stanford University, California. No part of this journal was removed or destroyed. The real ship's log is apparently not now extant.

5. See list of abbreviations above.

6. Ibid.

7. Ibid.

8. The original draft of Goodfellow's statement, "The facts relating to the separation of the ship's company of the brig Advance in the fall of 1854, written out by Henry Goodfellow, by command of Miss Bessie Kane," was in 1957 in possession of Mrs. E. Paul DuPont at Montchanin, Delaware. Typescript copies are at the National Geographical Society, Washington, D.C., No. 330, Greeley Manuscript Collection; Stefansson Collection, Dartmouth College; and EKK Papers, Library, APS, Philadelphia.

9. Isaac Israel Hayes to William Elder, December 5, 1857, Glassboro State College, Glassboro, New Jersey.

10. Villarejo, p. 92.

11. It is tempting to suppose that Goodfellow was suffering with "Eskimo hysteria" (pibloktok), an anomalous mental disorder now thought by some medical writers to be caused by lack of sufficient calcium in the diet. Anthony C. F. Wallace and Robert E. Ackerman, "An interdisciplinary approach to mental disorder among the polar Eskimos of Northwest Greenland," *Anthropologia* 2 (1960): 1–12.

12. Sonntag, in Villarejo, p. 142.

## Chapter 11

1. Villarejo, p. 148; *Memoirs of Hans Hendrik, The Arctic Traveller* (London, 1878), p. 32. Whatever adjective Hans used in his native Eskimo tongue, when translated first into Danish and thence into English, it came out "haughty"; but "harsh" is no doubt what he meant.

2. This statement about an attempt by Godfrey on Kane's life "on the boat going South" is inexplicable unless something of the sort happened while the members of the crew were helping to get the "Forlorn Hope" to open water for Kane's trip toward Beechey Island in August 1854.

3. Anonymous article in *North British Review* 26 (1857): 407–42. "The attempt to take the life of William Godfrey, which no law, human or divine, can justify, was, fortunately for Dr. Kane, overruled. When an officer of a former Arctic expedition [Sir John Franklin's, 1819–22] shot a ferocious Indian of his party, the world viewed it as an act of stern necessity and personal safety, but Godfrey was neither a madman nor an enemy."

4. The quotation is from Tennyson, "The Palace of Art:"

> As in strange lands a traveller walking slow
> In doubt and great perplexity,
> A little before the moon-rise hears the low
> Moan of an unknown sea,
>
> And knows not if it be thunder, or a sound
> Of rocks thrown down, or one deep cry
> Of great wild beasts, then thinketh, "I have found
> A new land, but I die."

5. Kane's "Washington Land" is part of North Greenland, not (as he supposed) a separate island.

6. Augustus W. Greeley, *True Tales of Arctic Heroism* (New York: Scribner, 1912), pp. 367–85. Hans's own account of his marriage to Mersuk, as told in his *Memoirs*, is puzzlingly

different from Kane's and Greeley's and somewhat less romantic, but even if the earlier part of Hans and Mersuk's saga is in doubt, their experiences with the Hayes and Hall expeditions are fully authenticated.

## Chapter 12

1. Amos Bonsall, talking with a newspaper man at the time of Kane's funeral (unidentified clipping, Kane Miscellany scrapbook, Stefansson Collection, Dartmouth) said that he had expected that daguerreotyping Arctic scenery would be his main duty, but the instruments did not work.

2. Ohlsen's symptoms mentioned by Dr. Kane in his journal were slight pains in the back and "paralysis of the bladder." The injury was probably collapse of a lumbar vertebra, weakened by loss of calcium due to malnutrition, with resultant crushing of the spinal cord. Such an injury is not usually so quickly fatal, but in the acute stage of "spinal shock" the patient is unduly sensitive to cold and liable to intestinal distention. Either of these conditions may under the harsh circumstances have caused Ohlsen's death in four days.

3. Hayes, *Arctic Boat Journey;* Petersen in Villarejo; Bonsall, letter to Dr. Elder in the latter's biography of Kane; Goodfellow in his statement for Bessie Kane (see chapter 10, note 8, above); Godfrey in his *Narrative.*

4. The distance from Cape Alexander to Upernavik is about 500 miles by the course Kane took. Adding the sledge journey, the total escape route was roughly 580 miles. In a letter to John Pendleton Kennedy, written aboard *Release* just before entering New York Harbor (October 11, 1855, Kennedy Collection, Peabody Institute Library, Baltimore) Kane spoke of "open air travel by boats and sledges of thirteen hundred miles." He repeated this figure to an interviewer for the *New York Daily Times,* October 12, 1855, and Elder repeated it in his biography of Dr. Kane. The only way by which Kane could have arrived at this total was to include his own extra trips when relaying the sick men and supplies over the ice; the rest of the party, tripling their journey when hauling the sledges one at a time, may have traveled in all about 740 miles on foot and by boat.

5. In *Arctic Explorations, 1853, '54, '55* 2:269 Kane says the ice belt at Providence Halt was no more than five feet wide. No doubt this is a printer's error, for the boats, six feet wide, could hardly have been berthed on a five-foot ledge. The illustration, 2:270, made from one of Kane's sketches, shows a ledge twenty-five or thirty feet wide.

6. Bonsall letter, see note 3, this chapter.

7. In *Arctic Explorations* 2:267, Kane says that after leaving Weary Man's Rest he had two of his three sledges cut up to provide wood for repair of the boat "Hope," reserving the third sledge as "essential to our ice-crossings"; but on p. 281 he says that in order to escape from the narrowing lead "we must harness our sledges again . . . one sledge had already been used for firewood."

8. These first evidences of the fate of Franklin and his men were found by Dr. John Rae, a Scottish surgeon in the service of the Hudson's Bay Company.

9. Hartstene's name is variously spelled in letters, books, and newspapers of the period (Hartstein, Hartsteen, etc.). The form used here is that with which he signed his letters to the navy while commanding the Kane Relief Expedition (information from Capt. F. Kent Loomis, U.S.N. [ret.], Assistant Director of Naval History, Navy Department, Washington, D.C.). It is also the form used by Kane.

10. For the proceedings in Congress, see *Congressional Globe*, Washington, Reports of the 33d and 34th Congresses, 1854, 1855.

11. Letters of the volunteers, originals or transcripts, Stefansson Collection, as follows: Griffin, February and March 1855; Murdaugh, February 1, 1855; Lovell, February 3, 1855; Carruthers, February 18, 1855.

12. Sherard Osborn to Lady Franklin, February 10, 1855, transcript in Stefansson Collection.

13. JKK, Jr., to J. C. Dobbin, Secretary of the Navy, March 2, 1855, transcript in Stefansson Collection.

14. JKK, Jr., "The Kane Relief Expedition," *Putnam's Monthly Magazine of American Literature, Science, and Art* 7 (1856): 451–63.

## Chapter 13

1. *New York Herald*, October 13, 1855.

2. Mrs. Walter was a sister of John Cochrane, at the time Surveyor of the Port of New York, later a U.S. Senator.

3. JKK to EKK, May 29, 1855, Kane Papers, HSP.

4. George Templeton Strong, *Diary*, 4 vols. (New York: Macmillan) 2:165, under date of April 1, 1854; *Atheneum*, London, December 3, 1853, pp. 1583–84.

5. Joseph H. Harper, *The House of Harper* (New York: Harper and Brothers, 1911), pp. 92–98. Before the fire a few copies were sent to Judge Kane for private distribution, one of which he gave to the American Philosophical Society. Another is at the Library Company of Philadelphia, whose librarian, the learned bibliographer Edwin Wolf, 2d, kindly advised the author in comparing these surviving volumes with the printing that reached the general public.

6. See note 3, this chapter. In May, 1856, Dr. Kane settled his account with Harpers by purchasing the copyright of *The First United States Grinnell Expedition* for $1,200. Dreer Collection, Explorers, HSP.

7. George W. Childs, *Recollections* (Philadelphia: Lippincott, 1891), pp. 13–14. Kane's letters to Childs cited in this chapter are preserved in an album presented by Childs to Ferdinand Dreer, a Philadelphia collector of manuscripts, Dreer Collection, Explorers, HSP.

8. James G. Wilson, *Thackeray in the United States* (New York: Dodd, Mead, 1904), pp. 66–67; Joseph H. Harper (see note 5, this chapter), pp. 125–26. Wilson ascribes the story to George William Curtis, but it does not appear in contemporary issues of the "Editor's Easy Chair," *Harper's Monthly Magazine*.

9. *Troy Daily Whig* (N.Y.), October 19, 1855; *New York Herald*, October 26; *New York Evening Post*, October 31; *New York Express*, November 1.

10. *New York Tribune*, November 6, 1855.

11. *Daily Pennsylvanian* (Philadelphia), November 10, 1855.

12. E. Peshine Smith to Henry C. Carey, Albany, N.Y., April 25, 1857, Edward Carey Gardiner Collection, HSP.

13. *Love-Life*, p. 215.

14. Ibid., p. 49.

15. Ibid., pp. 284–85.

16. *Proceedings of the American Philosophical Society* 6 (1859): 154.

17. Kane-Childs Album (see list of abbreviations above), item 15.

18. Ibid., item 17.

19. Sophia Cracroft to Henry Grinnell, November 14, 1856, H. J. Rawnsley, *Life, Diaries, and Correspondence of Lady Franklin* (London, 1923), p. 226 .

20. Kane-Childs Album, item 17.

21. Ibid., item 32.

22. Ibid., item 38.

23. Ibid.

24. *Congressional Globe*, March 13, August 11, 1856; *Washington Intelligencer,* April 19; *New York Times*, December 18; George William Curtis, in *Harper's Monthly Magazine* 14 (1857): 562.

25. EKK to Childs, September 23, 1856, Josiah Trent Collection, Duke University Library.

26. *Journal of the Royal Geographic Society* 26 (1856): clxvi–clxvii.

27. Lady Franklin, Domestic Journal, June 6 and 8, 1856, pp. 92, 94, Scott Institute for Polar Research, Cambridge, England.

28. George F. McDougall, *The Eventful Voyage of H. M. Discovery Ship "Resolute" to the Arctic Regions* (London: Longmans, 1857), pp. 452–78.

29. Rawnsley (see note 19, this chapter), p. 218.

30. Rawnsley, p. 219.

31. Kane-Childs Album, item 41.

32. *Love-Life*, pp. 257–58.

33. Mary R. Cabot, "The Weselhoeft Water-cure," in *Annals of Brattleboro* (Brattleboro, Vermont: Hildreth and Company, 1922), pp. 563–74.

34. EKK to JKK, September 6, 1856, EKK Papers, APS.

35. EKK to JKK, August 31, 1856, EKK Papers, APS.

36. *Philadelphia American and Gazette*, October 10, 1856.

37. *Love-Life*, pp. 263, 272.

38. Ibid., pp. 269–72.

39. The will of Elisha Kent Kane is filed in the Office of the Registrar of Wills, Philadelphia (City Hall Annex), 1857, book 38, no. 207, p. 160.

## Chapter 14

1. EKK to Mrs. John K. Kane, October 23, 1856, EKK Papers, APS.

2. EKK to Lady Franklin, undated, ca. October 26, 1857, Scott Polar Research Institute.

3. EKK to JKK, late October 1856, EKK Papers, APS.

4. *Illustrated London News*, November 1, 1856.

5. The silver service presented to Dr. Kane by the British Government is now owned by

Mr. E. Kent Kane of Kushequa, near Kane, Pennsylvania, who kindly supplied the inscription.

6. William Cross's wife was related to Kane's sister-in-law, Mrs. Thomas L. Kane. The Crosses were the parents of John Walter Cross, who married Marian Evans ("George Eliot") after the death of George Henry Lewes. Charles W. Shields, "The Arctic Monument named for Tennyson by Dr. Kane," *Century Magazine* N.S. 34 (1898): 483–92.

7. Radbill (see chapter 2, note 8, above), p. 176.

8. *Proceedings of the Royal Geographical Society*, November 10, 1856, 1 (1855–57): 82.

9. Sophia Cracroft to Henry Grinnell, November 14, 1856, Scott Polar Research Institute.

10. EKK to S. Weir Mitchell, in Elder, p. 235.

11. EKK to Mrs. John K. Kane, November 14, 1856, EKK Papers, APS.

12. F. S. Ainsworth, "The Sickness and Death of Dr. Kane," *Boston Medical and Surgical Journal* 51 (1857): 129–31.

13. Cited in a letter to the *New York Times* dated September 25, 1856; undated clipping, Grinnell Scrapbook No. 6, American Geographical Society.

14. Elizabeth Kane to Mrs. George C. Leiper, February 26, 1857, collection of Mr. Lee G. Martin, New York, N.Y.

15. Journal (Stanford) for December 5, 1854, p. 198. Henry Augustus Boardman, a well-known minister and author, was pastor of the Tenth Presbyterian Church, Philadelphia.

16. Rev. J. M. Steele, "Prayer Offered While the Remains of Dr. Kane lay in the Senate Chamber at Columbus, Ohio," Elder, p. 328.

17. Elder, pp. 385–86.

## Chapter 15

1. George Nares, *Narrative of a Voyage to the Polar Sea during 1875–76* . . . , 2 vols. (London: S. Low, Marston, Searle, & Rivington, 1878); Augustus W. Greeley, *A Handbook of Polar Discoveries,* 3d ed. (Boston: Little, Brown, 1906), pp. 200–207; John Edward Weems, *Peary, the Explorer and the Man* (Boston: Houghton, Mifflin, 1967); Everett S. Allen, *Arctic Odyssey, Life of Rear Admiral Donald B. Macmillan* (New York: Dodd, Mead, 1962).

2. *Arctic Explorations, 1853, '54, '55* 1: 225.

3. Ibid., 2: 400–404.

4. Ibid., p. 404.

5. Henry Rink, "On the Supposed Discovery of the North Coast of Greenland and an Open Polar Sea; the Great Humboldt Glacier; and Other Matters Relating to the Formation of Ice in Greenland, as Described in 'Arctic Explorations in the Years 1853, '54, '55, by Elisha Kent Kane, U.S.N., Philadelphia, 1856," *Proceedings of the Royal Geographical Society,* 1858, 2: 195–201.

6. Augustus W. Greely, *Explorers and Travellers* (New York, Scribner, 1894), p. 264.

7. *Times,* London, October 28, 1855.

8. *Proceedings of the Royal Geographical Society,* 1858, 2: 359, 360.

9. Greely, *Explorers and Travellers* (see note 6, this chapter), p. 263.

10. James Laws, MS journal, Stefansson Collection, Dartmouth, p. 40.

11. *North American Review* 78 (January 1854): 672–81.

12. For James Hamilton, John Sartain, and Benson J. Lossing, see *DAB*.

13. Elder, p. 221.

14. Vilhjalmur Stefansson, *The Friendly Arctic* (New York: Macmillan, 1921).

15. George W. Curtis to EKK, October 5, 1856, EKK Papers, APS.

16. *Saturday Review*, London, November 22, 1856, no. 2, pp. 660–62.

17. New York Public Library, MS Collection, EKK folder.

18. John Aldrich Christie, *Thoreau as World Traveler* (New York: Columbia University Press/American Geographic Society, 1965).

19. The most recent such book is that of Adrian Stoutenberg, *Elisha Kent Kane, Arctic Challenger* (Philadelphia: Macrae Smith, 1963). Jeannette Mirsky's *Elisha Kent Kane and the Seafaring Frontier* (Boston: Little, Brown, 1954), is for adult readers. There is also a novel, based on Elder's *Biography* and Margaret Fox's *Love-Life*: Jay and Audrey Walz, *The Undiscovered Country* (New York: Duell, Sloan and Pearce, 1958).

20. Weems (see note 1 above), p. 9.

21. Elder, pp. 229–30.

22. Frances J. Woodward, *Portrait of Jane: A Life of Lady Franklin* (London: Hodder and Stoughton, 1951), p. 319.

23. J. F. J. Schmidt, *Charte der Gebirge des Mondes* . . . (Berlin: D. Reimer, 1878); Mary A. Blagg and K. Müller, *Named Lunar Formations* . . . , 2 vols. (London: P. Lund, Humphries, Ltd., 1935).

# Index